Human Resource Management

IN AUSTRALIA

Ashly Pinnington and George Lafferty

OXFORD
UNIVERSITY PRESS

OXFORD
UNIVERSITY PRESS

253 Normanby Road, South Melbourne, Victoria 3205, Australia

Oxford University Press is a department of the University of Oxford.
It furthers the University's objective of excellence in research, scholarship,
and education by publishing worldwide in

Oxford New York

Auckland Bangkok Buenos Aires Cape Town Chennai
Dar es Salaam Delhi Hong Kong Istanbul Karachi Kolkata
Kuala Lumpur Madrid Melbourne Mexico City Mumbai Nairobi
São Paulo Shanghai Taipei Tokyo Toronto

OXFORD is a trade mark of Oxford University Press
in the UK and in certain other countries

Copyright © Ashly Pinnington and George Lafferty 2003

First published 2003
This book is copyright. Apart from any fair dealing for the purposes
of private study, research, criticism or review as permitted under the
Copyright Act, no part may be reproduced, stored in a retrieval system,
or transmitted, in any form or by any means, electronic, mechanical,
photocopying, recording or otherwise without prior written permission.
Enquiries to be made to Oxford University Press.

Copying for educational purposes

Where copies of part or the whole of the book are made under Part VB
of the Copyright Act, the law requires that prescribed procedures be
followed. For information, contact the Copyright Agency Limited.

National Library of Australia
Cataloguing-in-Publication data:

    Pinnington, Ashly.
    Human resource management in Australia.

    Bibliography,
    Includes index.
    For undergraduate business students and MBA students.
    ISBN 0 19 551477 7.

    1. Personnel management—Australia. 2. Industrial
    relations—Australia. I. Lafferty, George. II. Title.

    658.300994

Edited by Tim Fullerton
Text designed by Patrick Cannon
Cover designed by Racheal Stines
Typeset by Kerry Cooke
Printed through Bookpac Production Services, Singapore

Contents

Figures and Tables — iv
Preface — vi
Acknowledgments — viii

Part 1 Definitions — 1
1 What is HRM? — 3

Part 2 Context — 27
2 The Environment of HRM — 29
3 Australian Industrial Relations — 49
4 Labour Law — 71

Part 3 Managing Human Resources — 91
5 Employee Resourcing and Careers — 93
6 Motivating Employees — 120
7 Financial Rewards and Performance Management — 141
8 Learning and Development — 171
9 Managing Change — 207

Part 4 Future Developments — 231
10 Conclusion — 233

Glossary — 243
Notes — 261
Bibliography — 288
Index — 312

Figures and Tables

Figure 1.1 Human resource system	7
Figure 1.2 A map of the HRM territory	8
Figure 1.3 Strategic management and environmental pressures	11
Figure 1.4 The human resource cycle	12
Figure 1.5 The Schuler et al. model, objectives and purposes of HRM	14
Figure 1.6 A model for investigating human resource strategies: the European environment	21
Figure 5.1 Human resource flow	95
Figure 6.1 Maslow's hierarchy of needs	122
Figure 6.2 Porter and Lawler's model of Vroom's expectancy theory	128
Figure 6.3 Hackman and Oldham's job characteristics	131
Figure 7.1 The reward system	143
Figure 7.2 A typical graded pay structure	145
Figure 7.3 A broad-banded structure	146
Figure 7.4 A competence and performance-related pay curve	147
Figure 7.5 A pay spine	148
Figure 7.6 Four components of performance management	159
Figure 7.7 The manager's role in performance management	161
Figure 7.8 Linking measurements to strategy	164
Figure 7.9 HRM and performance	165
Figure 8.1 Human resources and national competitiveness	174
Figure 8.2 From systematic training to the learning company	180
Figure 8.3 Kolb's experiential learning cycle	183
Figure 8.4 Honey and Mumford's four learning styles	185
Figure 8.5 Dixon's and Kolb's learning cycles	186
Figure 9.1 Force field analysis	215
Figure 9.2 The change process	215
Figure 9.3 Reger et al., on reframing the organisation	217

Figure 9.4	The transition curve	219
Figure 9.5	Nadler and Tushman's four types of organisational change	220
Figure 9.6	Patrick Dawson, Organisational Change: A Processual Approach	228
Figure 9.7	The eight-stage process of creating major change	229
Table 1.1	Guest's model of HRM	9
Table 1.2	Storey's twenty-five-item checklist	17
Table 2.1	The stock of foreign direct investment	31
Table 2.2	Characteristics of the world's 100 largest TNCs (1999)	31
Table 2.3	Civilian population aged 15 and over, labour force status, annual average	34
Table 2.4	Civilian labour force, by birthplace, annual average, 1999–2000	35
Table 3.1	Trade union members, total numbers	57
Table 3.2	Trade union members, percentage of total employees	57
Table 4.1	Significant dates in Australian Industrial Relations and Labour Law	87
Table 5.1	Old deal	98
Table 5.2	New deal	99
Table 7.1	Reward trends	144
Table 7.2	Purcell's types of performance-pay system	156

Preface

The aim of this book is to introduce human resource management (HRM) in a way that is both challenging and rewarding. As a textbook it presents ideas that have both academic and practical relevance, and it has been designed to stimulate critical discussion and learning. We explore the issues surrounding the way people are managed in organisations from both an HRM perspective and an industrial relations (IR) perspective. Frequent reference is also made to differences in the implementation of HRM between countries. The different perspectives of HRM and IR are presented without trying to force them into an identical view of the world. The authors have a strong interest in human resources and the workplace, but rather than write on the subject through one authoritative voice, we present the debate on HRM from two perspectives.

This book offers a comprehensive introduction to key concepts and practices in HRM. We have written with the assumption that the textbook will be used for learning through both individual study and discussion. It is intended for undergraduate students interested in how people are managed at work and is suitable for postgraduates who are relatively new to the subject, particularly MBA students seeking an introduction to core or specialist modules in HRM. *Human Resource Management in Australia* presents the fundamental concepts and issues of what is a comparatively young subject. Through reading it, you will come to understand more about how employees have been managed in the past and how they are managed now, and you will be encouraged to investigate ways that people may be better managed in the future.

The book is divided into four parts. Part 1, comprising chapter 1, explores definitions of HRM by introducing and reviewing competing HRM models. Part 2, the next three chapters, considers the wider environment within which HRM functions: chapter 2 assesses the environment's influence on strategy, chapter 3 discusses the distinctive characteristics of Australian industrial relations and the strong influence of processes of internationalisation, and chapter 4 examines the specific influence of the Australian legal regulation of employment on HRM.

Part 3, made up of the next five chapters, concentrates on the policy and practice of managing human resources in work organisations. Chapter 5 on employee resourcing and careers covers issues concerning how employees are moved into, through, and out of organisations and examines how changes in resourcing have influenced careers. Chapter 6 on motivating employees examines old and new theories of how people are motivated at work. Chapter 7 on rewards and performance management concentrates on the 'extrinsic' factors of motivation and discusses new approaches to rewarding employees. Chapter 8 on learning and development overviews training and development in organisations, including health and safety at work, and discusses innovative approaches to learning. Chapter 9 deals specifically with concepts of organisational change and advice on management practice in implementing change. Finally, Part 4, containing chapter 10, reviews some of the book's primary themes and considers the future of HRM.

The book's ten chapters are well suited for use in one-semester modules comprising ten or more lecture sessions, and with this in mind the book has deliberately been kept concise. It provides the main points for an introduction to the subject, promoting active learning and discussion without being overly detailed. The dialogue between HRM and industrial relations perspectives across the chapters is lively and we hope that you will enjoy it, share our enthusiasm for the issues presented, and benefit by learning from a study and debate on human resource management. Many of the theoretical developments in HRM and major research studies have their origins in the USA or Europe. The book's focus, however, is on Australia and therefore it concentrates on HRM theory, research, and practice that is either of international relevance or is particularly significant to Australian workplaces.

Finally, a brief note is required to explain the way the book is structured. Each chapter contains an introduction and a summary to help you maintain your orientation and review main points; suggestions for further reading for those who wish to know more about some of the main topics covered; study questions designed to let you engage with the material and absorb it more thoroughly by relating the concepts to the real world and to your own experiences. Case studies are provided at the end of each chapter. Those in chapters 2–9 are based on real organisations and experiences; those in chapters 5–9 were reported to the authors by general managers, human resource managers, and other employees in the organisations concerned. For reasons of confidentiality, pseudonyms have been used for the names of organisations and some of the case details have been altered.

Acknowledgments

Our thanks to Tony Edwards and Gail Prosser for their contribution to an earlier book on HRM published in 2000 by Oxford University Press. Grateful acknowledgment to undergraduate and postgraduate students of Harvard University, London Business School, University of Warwick, University of Queensland, University of Exeter, Coventry University, Henley Management College, and ICPE University of Ljubljana for feedback on draft chapters and case studies.

PART I
Definitions

CHAPTER 1

What is HRM?

CHAPTER CONTENTS

Introduction

1 North American and British models of HRM
Soft HRM
   The Harvard model, Beer et al. (USA)
   Guest (UK)
Hard HRM
   The Michigan model, Fombrun et al. (USA)
Soft and hard HRM
   The Schuler et al. model – objectives and purposes of HRM (USA)

2 Industrial relations perspectives on HRM
Kochan's framework for labour relations (USA)
Storey on HRM v. personnel management (UK)

3 The influence of Japanese management practices
Oliver and Wilkinson

4 The European environment of HRM
Brewster and Bournois

Summary
   Study questions
   Further reading

Introduction

Human Resource Management (HRM) is a new way of thinking about how people should be managed as employees in the workplace. In much the same way as there are different roads to success, HRM is not one theory but an evolving set of competing theories. As a tradition of thought on managing people, HRM is most commonly traced back to seminal works written by American academics during the early 1980s. These American and American-inspired theories, or models, of HRM are sometimes subdivided under two schools of thought, 'hard' HRM and 'soft' HRM. Both of these schools will be discussed in this chapter. In essence, hard HRM focuses on managing and controlling employees so as to achieve the organisation's strategic goals, whereas soft HRM gives more recognition to the needs of employees and the importance of their commitment to the organisation.

In the employment relationship, employees contract their labour in exchange for various types of rewards from employers. Whether they are working full time or part time, employees seek to obtain from the employer what they consider to be equitable terms and conditions of employment. At the minimum, most employees expect to be managed and treated fairly. Indeed, as levels of education become higher, a greater proportion of the population worldwide expects more than this: people seek a range of intrinsic rewards such as job satisfaction, a degree of challenge, a sense of career progression, and satisfying relationships with co-workers. HRM has been proposed both as a way to meet these expectations and as a more effective way of managing employees, although there is considerable disagreement as to how far HRM can be implemented.

Advocates of HRM have presented it as having a role to play in both the private and public sectors. In the private sector, if the employer fails to manage the human resource well enough to compete successfully in the market place, then ultimately the business will fail. The company may decline slowly where competition is weak or it may rapidly become bankrupt where competition is strong. The public sector, likewise, has an interest in effective management of employees, and the standards and quality of public sector services are highly dependent on employees' motivation, skills, and service orientation. HRM, therefore, is about effective management of the employment relationship and applies to management activity in all organisational settings, even unpaid and voluntary work.

This chapter provides an overview of several different theories and approaches to HRM; subsequent chapters explore the application of HRM principles and practices in organisations today. The theories covered in the following sections come from some of the best-known North American and British writers on HRM and include the 'soft' and 'hard' distinction, industrial relations perspectives, and a European model of HRM. The influence of Japanese management practices on HRM is also introduced. This is because the Japanese methods have been so strongly influential in prompting executives and academics to reflect on how businesses are run by comparing how human resources are managed in the East with how they are managed in the West.

Australia has its own distinctive tradition of employment regulation, which has evolved since the nineteenth century. However, the introduction of HRM in Australia occurred several years after much HRM theory had already been developed. Therefore, the reader should not be surprised that, given the origins of most HRM theory and practice, unavoidably, much of this chapter will refer to developments in the USA and the UK. Indeed, throughout this book we shall be reflecting on the relevance of HRM theory and practice emanating from other countries, with a particular focus on its application to Australian organisations.

1 North American and British models of HRM

Soft HRM

The Harvard model, Beer et al. (USA)
HRM was launched as a course in 1981 at Harvard Business School. It was the first new course in Harvard's core curriculum to be introduced in nearly twenty years. It was established because there was widespread feeling among Harvard's faculty that new developments in the fields of organisational behaviour, organisation development, personnel administration, and labour relations were best represented in a new course. In 1985, Richard Walton published an article in the *Harvard Business Review* called 'From Control to Commitment in the Workplace', which popularised soft HRM as a distinctive approach to managing human resources. His argument was that effective HRM depends not on strategies for controlling employees but on strategies for winning employees' commitment. The Harvard model, first put forward in 1984 by Michael Beer et al. in the book *Managing Human Assets*, takes a soft HRM perspective similar to that of Walton and was devised primarily to inform general managers of improved ways of managing people. The model recommends that general managers must hold greater responsibility for HRM. How to get general managers more involved in HRM has been a major preoccupation for organisations in the 1980s and 1990s and so we now consider Beer's model in more detail rather than Walton's, which concentrates on the mutual concerns of employers and employees.

The Harvard model proposes that many of the diverse personnel and labour relations activities can be dealt with under four human resource (HR) categories: employee influence, human resource flow, reward systems, and work systems.[1] These are general responsibilities that managers must attend to regardless of whether the organisation is unionised or not, whatever management style is applied, and whether it is a growing or declining business.

Employee influence is the question of how much responsibility, authority, and power is voluntarily delegated by management and to whom. One of the critical questions here is: if management share their influence, to what extent does this create compatibility (the word used by the authors of the Harvard model is 'congruence') of interests between management and groups of employees? The assumption the authors make is that any influence employees have should be compatible with management's purpose and priorities. *Human resource flow* concerns managing the flow of people into, through, and out of the organisation. This means making decisions on recruitment and selection, promotion, termination of employment, and related issues of job security, career development, advancement, and fair treatment. Managers and personnel specialists, according to the Harvard model, must work together to ensure that the organisation has an appropriate flow of people to meet its strategic requirements.

Reward systems regulate how employees are extrinsically and intrinsically rewarded for their work. Extrinsic rewards are tangible pay and benefits: pay, overtime pay, bonuses, profit sharing, pensions, holiday entitlement, health insurance, and other benefits, such as flexible working hours. Intrinsic rewards are intangible benefits and are said to strongly influence employees' motivation, job satisfaction, and organisational commitment. Intrinsic rewards are rewards from the work itself, such as sense of purpose, achievement, challenge, involvement, self-confidence, self-esteem, and satisfaction. The Harvard model recommends that employees should be highly involved in the design of an organisation's reward systems but observes that final decisions, besides meeting employees' needs, must be consistent with the overall business strategy, management philosophy, and other HRM policies. *Work systems* are the ways in which people, information, activities, and technology are arranged, at all levels of the organisation, so that work can be performed efficiently and effectively.

Policies in these four areas must be designed and applied in a coherent manner because, as Beer and his co-authors argue, HRM is considerably less likely to be effective where policies are disjointed, made up of odd combinations of past practices, and are *ad hoc* responses to outside pressures. The four policy areas must satisfy the many stakeholders of the enterprise—for example, shareholders, employees, customers, suppliers, communities, trade unions, trade associations, and government. Employees are major stakeholders of the enterprise and it is the responsibility of managers to establish systems that promote employee influence. Some people would say that managers do not consider enough how to facilitate employee influence; indeed, Beer et al. claim that, of the four areas discussed, employee influence is the central feature of an HR system, as illustrated in the triangle in figure 1.1.

A further recommendation of the Harvard model is that, when making HRM policy decisions, managers should consider the 'four Cs': commitment, competence, congruence (compatibility), and cost-effectiveness. That is, managers should ask to what extent the policies they implement will: enhance the *commitment* of people to their work and the organisation; attract, retain, and develop people with the needed *competence*; sustain *congruence* (compatibility) between management and employees; and be *cost-effective* in terms of wages, employee turnover, and risk of employee dissatisfaction.

The authors' conceptual overview of HRM is represented diagrammatically as a 'map of the HRM territory' (see figure 1.2). They propose that HRM is closely

```
                    Work system
                        △
                       ╱│╲
                      ╱ │ ╲
                     ╱  ↑  ╲
                    ╱       ╲
                   ╱ Employee ╲
                  ╱  influence ╲
                 ╱ ↙         ↘ ╲
                ╱_____╲
Human resource                    Rewards
    flow
```

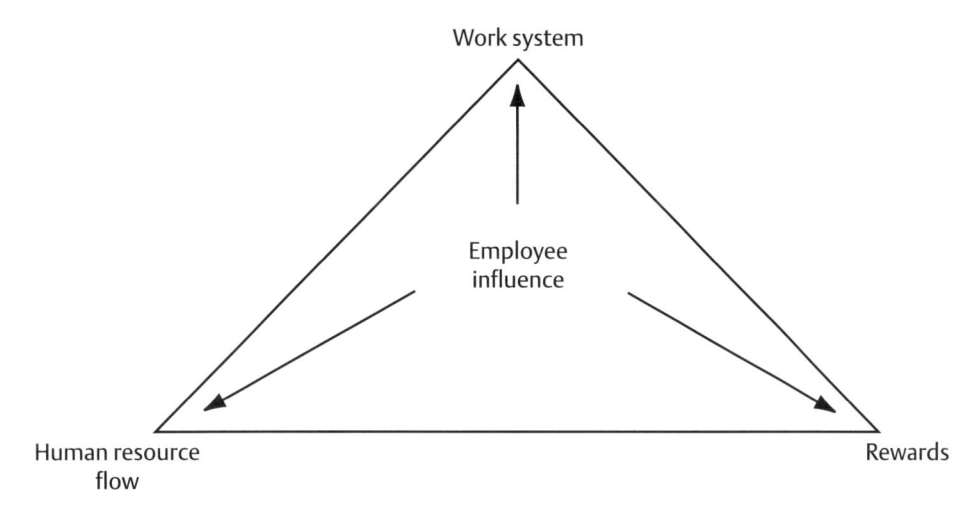

Figure 1.1 Human resource system

Source: Beer, M., Spector, B., Lawrence, P. R., Quinn Mills, D., and Walton, R. E., *Managing Human Assets*. Reprinted with permission of Free Press, a division of Simon & Schuster Inc. Copyright © 1984 by Free Press.

connected with both the external environment and the internal organisation. Their model of the territory of HRM shows that stakeholder interests and 'situational factors' (the factors that make up the context in which a business must operate) are interlinked with HRM policy choices, which in turn lead to HR outcomes. These outcomes have long-term consequences that have a feedback effect on stakeholder interests and 'situational factors', and so on. The main stakeholder interests are: shareholders, management, employee groups, government, the community, and unions. The situational factors are: workforce characteristics, business strategy and conditions, management philosophy, labour markets, unions, task technology, and laws and societal values. The long-term consequences of HR outcomes are considered under three main headings: individual well-being, organisational effectiveness, and societal well-being.

The Harvard model is soft HRM because it concentrates attention on outcomes for people, especially their well-being and organisational commitment. It does not rank business performance or one of the stakeholder interests—for example, shareholders—as being inherently superior to other legitimate interests, such as the community or unions. Organisational effectiveness is represented in the Harvard model as a critical long-term consequence of HR outcomes, but alongside the equally important consequences of individual and societal well-being. An organisation putting this model into practice would therefore aim to ensure that its employees were involved in their work and able to participate in decision making. HRM policies would be developed and implemented to meet employees' needs for influence, but within the limitation of having to be consistent with the overall business strategy and management philosophy.

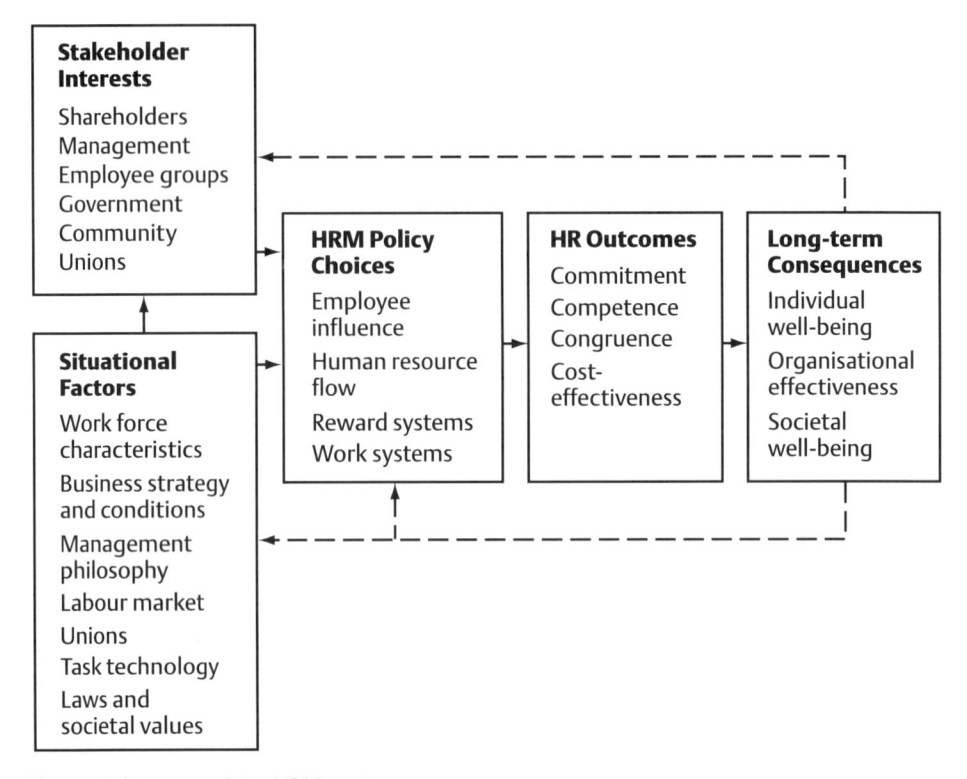

Figure 1.2 A map of the HRM territory

Stakeholder Interests
- Shareholders
- Management
- Employee groups
- Government
- Community
- Unions

Situational Factors
- Work force characteristics
- Business strategy and conditions
- Management philosophy
- Labour market
- Unions
- Task technology
- Laws and societal values

HRM Policy Choices
- Employee influence
- Human resource flow
- Reward systems
- Work systems

HR Outcomes
- Commitment
- Competence
- Congruence
- Cost-effectiveness

Long-term Consequences
- Individual well-being
- Organisational effectiveness
- Societal well-being

Source: Beer, M., Spector, B., Lawrence, P. R., Quinn Mills, D., and Walton, R. E., *Managing Human Assets*. Reprinted with permission of Free Press, a division of Simon & Schuster Inc. Copyright © 1984 by Free Press.

Guest (UK)

A second soft HRM model was proposed by David Guest in 1987.[2] Guest argued that HRM in the UK should be based on designing policies and practices to achieve four main outcomes: strategic integration (planning/implementation), high employee commitment to the organisation, high workforce flexibility and adaptability, and a high-quality workforce. Strategic integration means ensuring that the organisation's business plans are implemented through appropriately designed HR policies and practices. Companies have been criticised for treating HRM and strategy separately, therefore failing to combine HRM with the business strategy.

Guest proposed that these four HRM outcomes will lead to the desirable organisational outcomes of high job performance, stronger problem solving, greater change consistent with strategic goals, and improved cost-effectiveness, while also reducing employee turnover, absences, and grievances. However, he warned that these outcomes will be achieved only if an organisation has a coherent strategy of HRM policies fully integrated into the business strategy and supported by all levels of line management.

Guest's model is similar to the Harvard model but has seven HR policy categories instead of four (see table 1.1). Four of Guest's categories are broadly the same as Beer's Harvard categories. Where Beer refers to *human resource flow*, Guest refers to *manpower flow* and *recruitment, selection, and socialisation*; both models have *reward systems* as a category; and what Beer calls *work systems*, Guest calls *organisational and job design*. Guest's three other categories are: policy formulation and management of change; employee appraisal, training, and development; and communication systems.

Table 1.1 Guest's model of HRM

Policies	Human resource outcomes	Organisational outcomes
Organisational and job design		High job performance
Policy formulation and implementation/management of change	Strategic planning/ implementation	High problem-solving
Recruitment, selection, and socialisation	Commitment	Successful change
Appraisal, training, and development	Flexibility/adaptability	Low turnover
Manpower flows—through, up, and out of the organisation		Low absence
Reward systems	Quality	Low grievance level
Communication systems		High cost-effectiveness, i.e. full utilisation of human resources

Source: Guest, D. E., 'Human Resource Management and Industrial Relations', *Journal of Management Studies* (1987), 24, 5, September, pp. 503–21, table 11, p. 516.

Policy formulation and management of change means establishing HR policy to explicitly identify the nature of the change required in a business and manage the process of change. *Employee appraisal, training, and development* involves both informally and formally evaluating employee performance and the need for training and development. Once these have been evaluated, policies must be in place to ensure that timely and appropriate training and employee development occur. *Communication systems* are the various processes and media that the organisation uses to encourage two-way flows of information between management and employees. Typically, these systems use bottom-up and top-down methods: a bottom-up method might be, for example, an employee suggestion scheme, and a top-down method might be a quarterly newsletter on the business performance of the organisation.

Guest's model has been criticised for presenting an ideal and for assuming unrealistic conditions for practising HRM.[3] Guest himself reported ten years later, in 1997, that while considerably more research data on HRM in organisations had been gathered, the link between the adoption of HRM policies and high performance remains somewhat elusive. He described progress in the UK towards HRM as being somewhat slow and 'crab-like'. British trade unions, he wrote, have started to become more positive about HRM and will work more openly and productively with management; however, many senior managers still retain a short-term perspective on their businesses. The result is that many HR initiatives appear to employees to be management fads rather than a genuine long-term commitment to the organisation and its people.

Guest's model constitutes soft HRM for the same reasons that the Harvard model does: both give strong recognition to the needs of employees (for example, motivation and development) in the running of the organisation. Also, both are committed to employees' needs as long as the measures taken to meet those needs remain consistent with the strategy of the organisation and management aims. Guest claims his model is more straightforward than the Harvard model, which maps the territory of HRM, because he simply argues that improved implementation of just seven HR policies will result in better HR outcomes.

Hard HRM

The Michigan model, Fombrun et al. (USA)

In the same year (1984) that Beer et al. published *Managing Human Assets*, Fombrun, Tichy, and Devanna published *Strategic Human Resource Management*.[4] This book proposed a different model of HRM, frequently referred to as the Michigan School because one of its main proponents was an academic from the University of Michigan's Graduate School of Business Administration,[5] although the ideas were generated in partnership with researchers from two other well-known American universities, Wharton and Columbia. The British academic John Storey describes this model as 'hard' HRM because it emphasises treating employees as a means to achieving the organisation's strategy, as a resource that is used in a calculative and purely rational manner. Hard HRM focuses more than soft HRM does on using people as resources and as a means towards the competitive success of the organisation.[6]

It is easy to be overly simplistic when evaluating Fombrun, Tichy, and Devanna's approach to HRM. On the one hand, there are those who dismiss it as being inhuman; on the other, there are those who proclaim it to be just common sense and the only route to business success. Arguably, the strength *and* the major limitation of their approach is that it focuses on the organisation and how it can best rationally respond to its external environment. Focusing on the level of the organisation has the advantage of drawing attention to aspects partly under the control of management, such as formal strategy, structure, and preferred culture. On the other hand, attending to the organisational level may lead managers to assume that, through organisational strategy, structure, and HR systems, they have more power than they really have to change individuals and influence the external environment.

Hard HRM assumes that increasing productivity will continue to be management's principal reason for improving HRM; while this is a major factor in many private and public sector organisations, it clearly is not the only one. Fombrun et al. argue that conditions of the external environment—for example, heightened competition and market uncertainty—necessitate 'strategic' HRM, that is, HRM designed to achieve the strategies, or goals, of the organisation.

The authors proposed a framework for strategic HRM that assumes that the needs of the firm are paramount.[7] They said organisations exist to accomplish a mission or achieve objectives and that strategic management involves consideration of three interconnected issues. First, the mission and strategy must be considered because these are an organisation's reason for being. Second, the organisation's structure, personnel requirements, and tasks must be formally laid out, including systems of accounting and communications. Third, HR systems need to be established and maintained because, as the authors state, 'people are recruited and developed to do jobs defined by the organization's formal structure: their performance must be monitored and rewards allocated to maintain productivity'.[8]

The Michigan model observes that different business strategies and related organisation structures can lead to contrasting styles of HRM in activities such as selection, appraisal, rewards, and development.[9] For example, a single-product company with a traditional functional structure (that is, structured according to the various functions of the business—finance, accounting, marketing, sales, production and operations, personnel etc.) will select its people on the basis of their

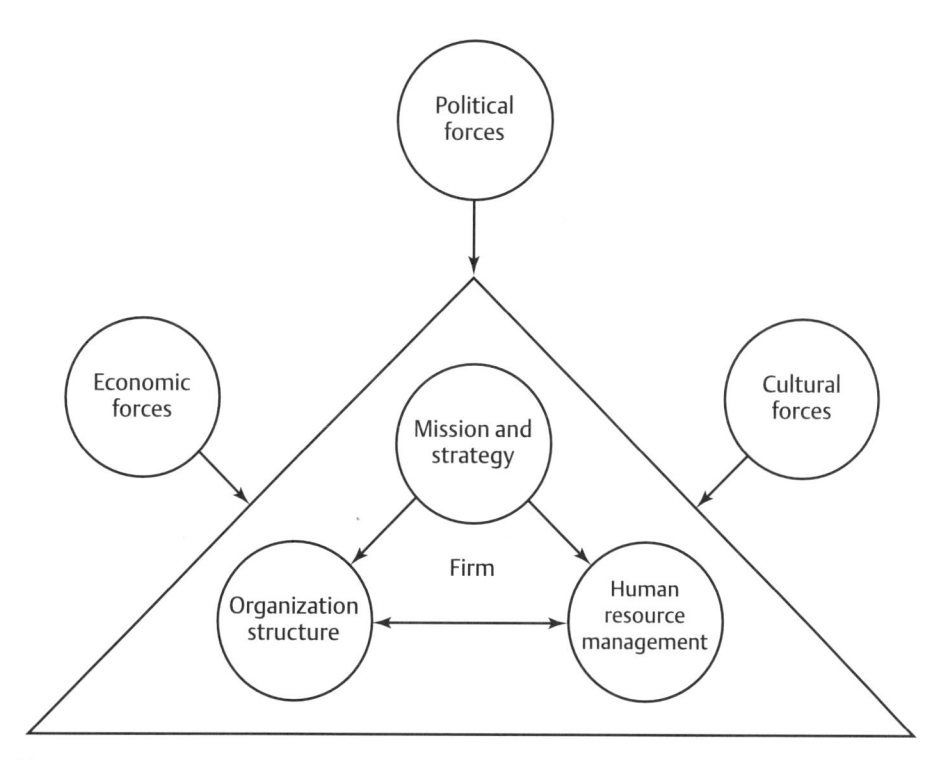

Figure 1.3 Strategic management and environmental pressures

Source: Fombrun, C. J., Tichy, N. M., and Devanna, M. A., *Strategic Human Resource Management*, figure 3.1, p. 35. Reprinted by permission of John Wiley & Sons, Inc. Copyright © 1984 John Wiley & Sons.

expertise in the specific functions. Appraisal of employee performance will be largely informal and administered via personal contact; the reward system will vary unsystematically across the functions and employee development will be limited primarily to the functional area in which the employee works. On the other hand, a company with a multi-divisional structure and a strategy for product diversification may have a very different system of HRM. Selection would be systematic and would relate to both functional experience and general management ability. The appraisal system would be formal and impersonal based on quantitative criteria such as productivity and return on investment, and on qualitative, subjective judgments about individual performance. The reward system would systematically reward contribution to the diversification strategy, and bonuses would likely be paid according to achievement of profitability targets. Employee development would be more complex and systematic than it would be in a company with a single-product strategy. In the multi-divisional company, employees are accustomed to being periodically transferred to different functions and areas of business. Individual development would be cross-divisional, cross-subsidiary, and corporate.

The Michigan model represents the external and internal factors of HRM as a triangle (see figure 1.3). Once management have decided how the mission and business

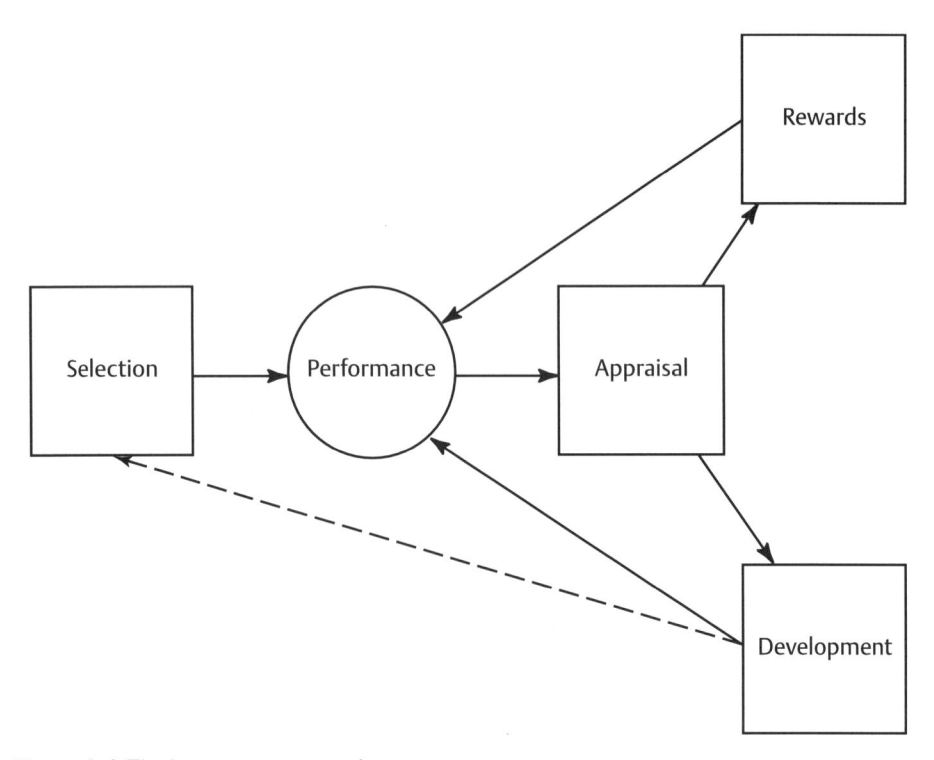

Figure 1.4 The human resource cycle

Source: Fombrun, C. J., Tichy, N. M., and Devanna, M. A., *Strategic Human Resource Management*, figure 3.2, p. 41. Reprinted by permission of John Wiley & Sons, Inc. Copyright © 1984 John Wiley & Sons.

strategy, organisation structure, and HRM are to be organised and integrated—and assuming it is an appropriate response to political, economic, and cultural forces—then they can begin to design the human resource system in more detail.

Finally, the Michigan model argues that within HRM there is a human resource cycle affecting individual and organisational performance (see figure 1.4). It describes the four functions of this cycle as follows:

> Performance is a function of all the human resource components: *selecting* people who are best able to perform the jobs defined by the structure, *appraising* their performance to facilitate the equitable distribution of rewards, motivating employees by linking *rewards* to high levels of performance, and *developing* employees to enhance their current performance at work as well as to prepare them to perform in positions they may hold in the future.[10]

The Michigan model is hard HRM because it is based on strategic control, organisational structure, and systems for managing people. It acknowledges the central importance of motivating and rewarding people, but concentrates most on managing human assets to achieve strategic goals. Subsequent empirical research has not produced evidence of organisations systematically and consistently practising hard HRM, although a longitudinal study (by Tryss et al. 1997) of large organisations (including Citibank, Hewlett Packard, and Glaxo Wellcome) found that employees were managed by tight strategic direction towards organisational goals. A company practising hard HRM would have a style of management that treats employees in a calculated way, primarily as means to achieving business goals. Its top management would aim to manage the organisation rationally and achieve a 'fit' between the organisation's strategy, structure, and HRM systems.

Soft and hard HRM

The Schuler et al. model—objectives and purposes of HRM (USA)

Most models of HRM have both soft and hard characteristics within their structure and contents. It therefore makes sense to interpret these models to the extent that they promote aspects of soft and hard HRM. Schuler et al. (1995) published a model[11] emphasising HRM's contribution to the bottom line of the firm, which can be interpreted as consistent with hard HRM insofar as it focuses on the needs of the organisation. However, in other significant respects, the model has a soft HRM focus characterised by its emphasis on employee development and supportiveness towards management–union relationships. The purposes of HRM given in the model, furthermore, are consistent with soft HRM and with the human relations tradition of promoting productivity alongside quality of work-life and legal compliance (figure 1.5).

It can be argued that Schuler et al. focus more specifically on the internal organisation and attend in less depth to its external environment, in contrast to the Harvard

14 | DEFINITIONS

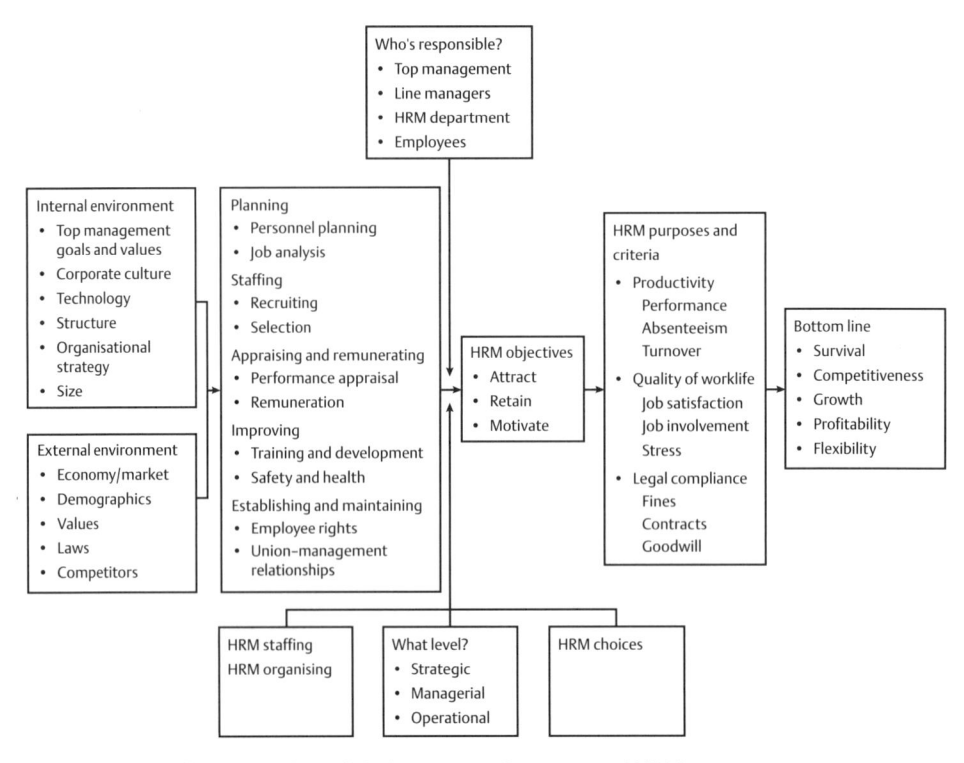

Figure 1.5 The Schuler et al. model, objectives and purposes of HRM

Source: Schuler, R. S., *Managing Human Resources*, 5th edn (Minneapolis, St Paul: West Publishing Company, 1995); A later version of this model appeared in R. Kramar, P. McGraw and R. S. Schuler, *Human Resource Management in Australia*, 3rd edn (Melbourne: Addison Wesley Longman, 1997), as figure 1.1, p. 9. It cites source: Schuler et al. (1995), 'Objectives and purposes of HRM functions and activities', p. 19.

model's pluralist emphasis on multiple stakeholder interests and situational factors. In the same vein, the Schuler et al. model portrays HRM as having three organisational objectives, namely, to attract, retain, and motivate people, which all influence the bottom line. By contrast, the Harvard model mentions HRM outcomes and their influence in terms of their long-term consequences for organisational effectiveness, and individual and societal well-being.

The Schuler et al. model portrays the three HRM objectives of attracting, retaining, and motivating employees as being served through five HRM functions: planning, staffing, appraising and remunerating, improving, and establishing and maintaining rights and relationships. These functions draw attention to functionalist approaches rather than to the HRM policy choices of the Harvard model with its soft HRM commitment to employee influence. There again, practical benefits of the Schuler et al. model are its explicit representation of HR activities (personnel planning, job analysis, recruiting, selection, performance appraisal, remuneration, training and development, safety and health, employee rights, and union–management relationships) and its questioning on the topics of who is responsible for these activities (top management? line management? HRM department? employee?) and at what levels in the organisation (strategic? managerial? operational?). Key criteria are mentioned in the model for measuring the level of HRM achievement according to its main purposes. The Schuler et al. model is helpful then for understanding ways HRM can gain greater recognition and respect in the organisation, and seeks to show the processes by which it contributes to the bottom line and strategic goals.

2 Industrial relations perspectives on HRM

Turning away from the theories of HRM that are classed as soft and hard, we now look at industrial relations (IR) approaches to HRM, which focus on trade unions and collective interests. This pluralist and collectivist viewpoint is explored in chapters 2, 3, and 4. Pluralist perspectives see organisations as being composed of coalitions of interest groups that possess potential for conflict. A collectivist perspective is characterised by an emphasis on the needs of the group—the opposite of individualism. In this section we look at an influential framework for analysing industrial relations that promotes partnership between unions, employers, and government, and at a checklist, written by Storey, for investigating points of difference between HRM and traditional personnel management.

Kochan's framework for labour relations (USA)

One of the most common criticisms of hard HRM is that it focuses exclusively on the organisation and its needs while ignoring the wider environment in which all organisations operate. Hard HRM is also criticised for having a managerialist orientation and for assuming a 'unitarist' perspective—this means that employees' needs and interests are ultimately subservient to the needs of the organisation as dictated by management. Thomas Kochan is known for being critical of unitarist approaches to HRM. He proposed a framework for analysing industrial relations that addresses the need for transformation of the employment relationship at the level of society rather than at the level of the organisation.

Kochan, Katz, and McKersie proposed in their 1994 book, *The Transformation of American Industrial Relations*, that the future of American industrial relations will be decided by the strategic choices of business, labour, and government.[12] Kochan et al. acknowledged the diversity of American IR practices but concluded that four broad patterns, or 'scenarios', of evolution are nevertheless observable.

Scenario 1 proposes a 'continuation of current trends', characterised by the continuing decline of private sector unionisation; stabilised and comparatively high public-sector unionisation; increased technological change and contracting out of services previously provided in-house (often known as 'outsourcing') as management aim to reduce the influence and scope of unions; and generally reduced innovation in HRM practices. Scenario 1 envisages a widening gap between those companies that are pursuing a highly skilled workforce, teamwork, and other human resource innovations on the one hand, and companies that are downsizing, cost cutting, and generally taking a reactive stance to employee relations on the other. A variant of this is Scenario 2, 'labour law reform', in which all of the conditions of Scenario 1 apply but at a slower rate of change. Political leaders will encourage reforms to reduce the influence of union labour in the belief that they are responsible for many of the problems in the management–union relationship.

Scenario 3, 'diffusion of labour-management innovations', argues that if reforms are combined with broader innovation in bargaining relationships between management and unions, particularly in companies that are partially unionised, then management commitment to HRM issues may be strengthened. Scenario 4, 'new organising strategies', predicts fundamental change in IR, with a transformation of the relationship between business, labour, and government, brought about by new approaches to HRM developing in the growing occupations and industries. The authors warn, though, that this scenario is the least likely to occur (although it is probably the most interesting one to contemplate).

All four future scenarios assume that IR outcomes are determined by a continuously evolving pattern of environmental pressures and organisational responses. The progress of IR unfurls over time as a result of choices made by labour, management, and government. Kochan et al. believed that the general trend in IR towards a weaker role for unions as portrayed in their four scenarios reflects the 'deep-seated resistance toward unions that historically has been embedded in the belief system of US managers'.[13]

Kochan's framework was based on analysing trends in labour relations in the USA and the scenarios extrapolate from them the different possible future outcomes for US business and society. It assumes that there is greater potential for innovation in HRM in the twenty-first century than there was in the twentieth century, although the transformation of labour relations is not something that has happened yet, either in the USA or Australia. We now consider a checklist for analysing HRM and IR that was specifically developed to identify the extent of change from traditional personnel management and IR towards HRM.

Storey on HRM versus personnel management (UK)

John Storey proposed that HRM can be understood in four different ways. First, it can be viewed as another term for personnel management, as simply breathing new life into old ideas and ways of working by changing the jargon. Second, it can signal a more integrated use of personnel-management policies and practices. Storey cited the Michigan model of strategic HRM as an example of this second view, commenting that performance in that model is affected by a cycle of HR interventions that are sequential managerial tasks; therefore, it is arguably a more integrated use of personnel management. A third use of the term 'HRM', Storey said, is to signal a more business-oriented and business-integrated approach to

Table 1.2 Storey's twenty-five-item checklist

Dimension	Personnel and IR	HRM
Beliefs and assumptions		
1 Contract	Careful delineation of written contracts	Aim to go 'beyond contract'
2 Rules	Importance of devising clear rules/mutuality	'Can do' outlook: impatience with 'rules'
3 Guide to management action	Procedures/consistency control	'Business need'/flexibility/ commitment
4 Behaviour referent	Norms/custom and practice	Values/mission
5 Managerial task *vis-à-vis* labour	Monitoring	Nurturing
6 Nature of relations	Pluralist	Unitarist
7 Conflict	Institutionalised	De-emphasised
8 Standardisation	High (e.g. 'parity' an issue) as relevant)	Low (e.g. 'parity' not seen
Strategic aspects		
9 Key relations	Labour–management	Business–customer
10 Initiatives	Piecemeal	Integrated
11 Corporate plan	Marginal to	Central to
12 Speed of decisions	Slow	Fast
Line management		
13 Management role	Transactional	Transformational leadership
14 Key managers	Personnel/IR specialists	General/business/ line managers
15 Prized management skills	Negotiation	Facilitation
Key levers		
16 Focus of attention for interventions	Personnel procedures	Wide-ranging cultural, structural and personnel strategies
17 Selection	Separate, marginal task	Integrated, key task
18 Pay	Job evaluation: multiple, fixed grades	Performance-related: few if any grades
19 Conditions	Separately negotiated	Harmonisation
20 Labour–management	Collective bargaining contracts	Towards individual contracts
21 Thrust of relations with stewards	Regularised through facilities and training	Marginalised (with exception of some bargaining-for-change models)
22 Communication	Restricted flow/indirect	Increased flow/direct
23 Job design	Division of labour	Teamwork
24 Conflict handling	Reach temporary truces	Manage climate and culture
25 Training and development	Controlled access to courses	Learning companies

Source: Storey, J., *Human Resource Management: A Critical Text* (London: Routledge, 1995), table 1.1, p. 10. An earlier version of this checklist appeared in Storey, J., *Developments in the Management of Human Resources* (London: Blackwell, 1992), figure 2.2, as 'Twenty-seven points of difference', p. 35.

the management of labour. The 'levers' of HRM (selection, rewards, etc.) are pulled in integration with one another so that the system is in line with the business strategy. Storey noted the Beer/Harvard model as being exemplary of this approach but criticised it for being too general in contrast to a fourth position, that of Richard Walton, which argues that HRM is a unique and distinct approach to employee commitment via policies of mutuality (as in mutual goals, influence, respect, rewards, and responsibility).[14]

Storey quoted work by Karen Legge that underlines three important differences between HRM and personnel management.[15] HRM more strongly emphasises development of the management team, strategic integration of business management and people management, and the management of organisational culture. Storey took this further in his 'twenty-five-item checklist' (see table 1.2). This table of differences is frequently quoted in textbooks and HRM teaching, but it must be remembered that the points are meant to highlight an idealised view of the range of opinion Storey encountered in his research interviews with managers. He conducted case research on fifteen British organisations from the public sector, the automotive, electrical and mechanical, and process industries and found that HRM was being applied piecemeal by managers rather than adopted as a coherent approach.[16] His points of difference provide a stereotypical but helpful means for describing different perspectives on HRM and personnel management/IR.

Storey's 'ideal description' of personnel management/IR is a clear picture of traditional personnel management supportive of the coexistence of management and unions. Here personnel management operates under collective bargaining arrangements in which unions have sufficient power to oblige management to negotiate and work with them. Each of the twenty-five points marks a contrast between personnel management and HRM. For example, point 6, 'the nature of relations', under the 'beliefs and assumptions' dimension, asserts that HRM admits only one legitimate interest to which all should adhere (a 'unitarist' orientation), while personnel management assumes there to be many legitimate interests in the organisation (a 'pluralist' orientation).

The twenty-five points can be used as a framework to assess an organisation's approach to human resource management. To date, however, most British companies have tended to concentrate on one or two areas of HR policy and practice, such as teamwork and employee involvement, rather than integrating a range of initiatives.[17] A similar pattern has occurred in Australia: HRM initiatives have not been especially integrated with organisations' strategy and systems.

3 The influence of Japanese management practices

We now turn to Japanese management practices and examine their influence as an alternative approach to HRM. It has been said that HR initiatives are integrated to a greater extent, both with each other and with the business strategy, in Japanese-managed organisations than they are in organisations from many other countries.

Oliver and Wilkinson

Oliver and Wilkinson offer an interpretation of HRM in the UK, chiefly relating to the manufacturing industries, based on what they call 'the Japanisation of British industry'.[18] By 'Japanisation' they mean two things: one, an evolving process during the 1980s and 1990s of emulation of Japanese manufacturing methods; and two, increasing Japanese direct investment in Western economies.

Oliver and Wilkinson concluded from their research that Japanese production methods are based on the successful management of high-dependency relationships.[19] In Japan, the economy is organised in a different manner to that in the West. Japanese managers are accustomed to high-dependency relationships and to working within a group of organisations that have long-term business relationships. This sense of mutual dependency is reflected in Japan at the level of government, where top business leaders are willing to seek consensus on how competitive business strategies should serve the national interest, and at the level of the organisation, where relationships between company unions and management are less adversarial.

In contrast, UK businesses have tended to act independently and in competition with one another, as they have in Australia. Oliver and Wilkinson observed that the stumbling block to long-term change in people management and manufacturing methods lies in the difficulty many managers have both culturally and practically in coping with greater dependency between organisations, unions, suppliers, and government.[20] The traditional approach to employment by government in the UK has been to minimise regulation of employers' interests and influence the employment relationship only so far as it concerns basic rights and legal codes of practice. Australia has been more regulated than this, through the role of its industrial awards, setting minimum pay and conditions within industries and occupations. Longer-term supplier partnerships and supplier reduction programs are comparatively new phenomena in the UK, as they are in Australia. Historically, the customary way of managing suppliers has been to keep them at arm's length and to bargain on price, which in Oliver and Wilkinson's terms constitutes a 'low-dependency relationship'.[21]

The Japanese economy grew very suddenly from 2 per cent of the world's GDP in 1967 to 10 per cent in 1987, prompting many countries to examine the causes of Japan's success. Comparative studies of Japanese corporations and corporations in other countries revealed remarkable differences in productivity and quality[22] and distinct methods of manufacturing and people management. Oliver and Wilkinson argue that developed Western countries can successfully adopt Japanese production methods, but only where an organisation is able to control and work within a wider, supportive environment.

Japanisation is not simply a matter of implementing total quality control and just-in-time (JIT) production processes. It entails the adoption of particular work practices and personnel and industrial relations systems as well, and the whole package of change is most likely to succeed where the organisation has some degree of control over its external environment. Oliver and Wilkinson noted some similarities in practice between the USA and Japan towards unions, one example being the tendency of Japanese start-up companies in the UK to adopt a strategy of union avoidance. In general, however, Japanese greenfield sites established in Australia have not pursued union avoidance, and Japanese companies have tended to work with one or more unions. Some US companies have more vigorously pursued anti-union tactics in Australia, for example, major retailer Toys 'R' Us sought to exclude unions from its megastores.[23]

British attitudes towards Japanese management practices vary from being very supportive and seeing them as the solution to British industry's problems[24] to seeing them as entailing work intensification, heightened control, and greater profits exclusively for the suppliers of capital.[25] In Australia, concerns with work intensification have not focused specifically on Japanese management methods, and Japan has been a major trading partner for a much longer period of time than in Britain. Whatever one's viewpoint, there is little doubt that HR practices associated with Japanese management methods, such as thorough selection procedures, single-status conditions for all employees in the workplace (sometimes symbolised by a common work uniform), systematic performance appraisal, and innovations in pay and rewards, have been influential across Europe, to which the last section of this chapter will now turn. It will briefly describe the characteristics of an emerging European model and discuss its relevance for Australia.

4 The European environment of HRM

Recently, interest has grown in the possibility of there being a model of HRM that is distinctly European. The model of the European environment of HRM, first produced in 1991 by Chris Brewster and François Bournois, emphasises the cultural, legal, and market contexts of human resource strategy and practice.[26] Brewster says that he prefers Thomas Kochan's framework of IR (discussed above), which, he contends, is a more comprehensive view of the range of social factors influencing HRM than other models, such as soft and hard HRM. He also proposes that the model of the European environment of HRM is partly a response to dissatisfaction with American HRM.[27] The anti-unionism of the American approach to HRM has been more consistent in US national culture than in some countries within Europe, which have shown greater willingness, during some periods of their history, to work within a social partnership.

Brewster and Bournois (1991)

In the Brewster and Bournois model, HR strategy is only partly subservient to corporate strategy because HRM is influenced by behaviour and performance from both inside and outside the organisation. The organisation and its human resource strategies and practices interact with the environment and, at the same time, are part of it.

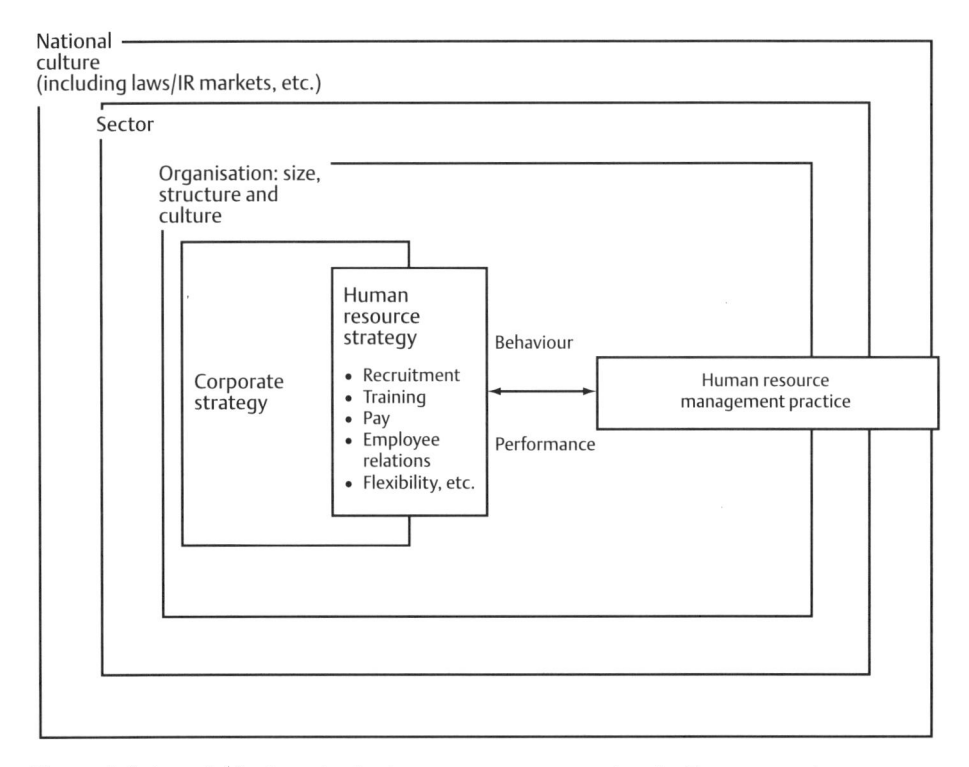

Figure 1.6 A model for investigating human resource strategies: the European environment

Source: Brewster, C. and Hegewisch, A., *Policy and Practice in European Human Resource Management* (London: Routledge, 1994), figure 1.1, p. 6. Adapted from C. Brewster and F. Bournois, 'A European Perspective on Human Resource Management', *Personnel Review* (1991), 20, 6, pp. 4–13.

The model shows that HRM policy and practice are not exclusively an organisation's choice but are also influenced by the wider environment, particularly the national culture and the industry sector the organisation operates in (see figure 1.6).

In 1995 Brewster reported the results of a survey[28] covering fourteen European countries in which three regional clusters corresponding to level of socioeconomic development were found: a Latin cluster (Spain, Italy, France), a Central European cluster (Central European countries plus the UK and Ireland), and a Nordic cluster (Norway, Sweden, Denmark). Brewster considered that the survey shows Latin countries to be at the lowest stage of socioeconomic development, the UK and Ireland next, then continental Central European countries, and finally Nordic countries at the top of the development scale.[29] The Latin culture, at the lowest stage of development, according to Brewster, is characterised by an oral culture and political structures that create docile attitudes towards authority, whereas the culture of the highest stage—that of the Nordic countries—displays a widespread collective orientation to management, extensive consultation between employers and workers, documented strategies, and (perhaps this conclusion is to be expected from an HRM researcher) substantial and authoritative HRM departments.

Despite the tendency of the national cultures to cluster into three regional groups, Brewster found some trends common across most European countries. Pay determination, according to the evidence of the survey, is becoming increasingly decentralised, and flexible pay systems are becoming more common. Flexible working practices are increasing in European countries (for example, atypical working; annualised hours; and temporary, casual, and fixed-term contracts). There is, unfortunately, also continuity in lack of equal opportunities insofar as, at senior management level, women and ethnic minorities are still under-represented. However, other opportunities vary much more by country. For example, in Greece and Spain, where women constitute a third of the workforce, there is very limited childcare provision, but in Sweden and France the provision is more extensive. Training investment is on the increase overall in the whole of Europe, particularly for managerial and professional staff, but the level of government intervention varies greatly by country.[30] The role of the HR function was also found to vary according to country, HR enjoying the greatest representation at board level in Spain and France, where 70–80 per cent of organisations have an HR director (thus contradicting, on this point, Brewster's ranking of the Latin cluster as the least developed), and somewhat less in the UK, where fewer than 50 per cent of organisations have an HR director.

European employment differs from employment in other parts of the world in that it is comparatively more unionised, and unions play a wider role in society and the workplace in European countries than they do in many other countries. Therefore, given Australia's industrial relations history (see chapter 3) it is more relevant and applicable to Australia than to some other countries in the Asia–Pacific Region. Brewster attributes some of the resilience of unions in Europe to their official recognition, as social partners, within the European Union. So, what is the model of the European environment of HRM? Essentially, it has similarities with Kochan's framework in that both accommodate partnership between unions, employers, and government. The European model assumes that national culture shapes HRM practices and that the cultures of countries within Europe are, despite their differences, more positive overall towards social partnership than is US culture. In summary, however, the European environment of HRM does not indicate a distinctive move away from personnel management; rather, what's happening in Europe is a complex mix of continuation of traditional personnel management and change towards HRM. The next three chapters will review in more detail the extent to which, in Australia, there has been continuity with personnel management and, contrastingly, the degree to which there has been change, especially in more recent years, towards HRM. The European model of HRM offers countries in Europe opportunities to benchmark their HRM/IR policies and practices against other members, and to monitor outcomes of government and employer initiatives in a variety of national cultures. At present, Australia does not have any obvious group of countries with which to compare itself, although there are some candidates in North America, Western Europe, and Asia. Exactly which countries are chosen as a basis for comparison presents a significant challenge for Australian organisations seeking to emulate good practice and to innovate in HRM.

Summary

The theories and frameworks outlined in this chapter suggest changes that have implications for the regulation of the employment relationship in Australia. The models of soft and hard HRM propose that there are better ways of managing human resources than those that have been applied in the past. These models are a mixture of the old and the new and cover many of the areas of traditional personnel management—for example, recruitment and selection, appraisal, rewards, and training and development. Hard and soft HRM share a concern for matching the organisation's strategic needs. In sum, the hard face of HRM emphasises the 'quantitative, calculative, and business strategic aspects of managing the headcount resource in as "rational" a way as for any other economic factor', while the soft face emphasises 'communication, motivation and leadership'.[31]

Guest's model of soft HRM emphasises the new by predicting the HRM factors that lead to desirable outcomes for people and organisations. These models of hard and soft HRM provide different perspectives, but all are unitarist; that is, they assume that management represents the main legitimate interest in a business, and that employees' interests are largely aligned with those of managers. The Schuler et al. model, for example, draws attention to how the objectives and purposes of HRM can contribute to the bottom line of the organisation.

Japanese management practices also are unitarist but operate by expecting a more stable and interdependent relationship among large global Japanese corporations, and between these corporations and their networks of long-term suppliers. The environmental factors an organisation must deal with strongly influence policy and practice, particularly the national government and, in the case of Japanese companies, the special characteristics of the organisation of Japanese industry. Oliver and Wilkinson assert that the Japanese approach can be adopted in other countries if the organisation can sustain sufficient control over its environment. Despite there being distinctive differences between Japan and many other countries, Japanese management approaches have played an important role in the development of HRM theory and practice.

Brewster and Bournois's model assumes the organisation and its HRM are strongly constrained by wider social forces, particularly national characteristics. Their model of the European environment of HRM draws attention to the significant role played by national culture in shaping HRM. It accords a positive role to social partnership between unions, employers, and government. Kochan's framework shares a similar emphasis on the significance of national characteristics and acknowledges the importance of partnership with unions. However, it is not as optimistic as the Brewster model, perceiving there to be less likelihood of progress in social partnership because of US employers' traditional suspicion of unions. The Kochan IR framework nevertheless differs from the other models of HRM by arguing that a stronger partnership should exist between unions, employers, and government. Kochan's framework does not advocate HRM from a unitarist viewpoint but assumes a pluralist perspective that acknowledges a long-term role for unions working in partnership with employers and government as the most effective means of reconciling their differences. This has considerable relevance for the Australian situation, which has been characterised for over a century by the central role of unions in the negotiation of wages and conditions. Also, unions at certain times, particularly during the Accord (1983–96), have been strongly involved with government and business in tripartite policy formation and implementation. Currently, the majority of enterprise bargaining negotiations are conducted between employers and unions, with the involvement of industrial relations tribunals. The idea of partnership that recognises conflicting interests therefore has been, and continues to be, part of Australian HRM and industrial relations practices.

We should make a brief diversion here to mention that this chapter has not reviewed radical theories of HRM[32] and IR, with the result that all of the models covered are normative, meaning that they don't fundamentally question the values of the society in which they exist.[33] Watson's radical definition of personnel management serves as an excellent illustration of a radical theory:

> Personnel management is concerned with assisting those who run work organisations to meet their purposes through the obtaining of the work efforts of human beings, the exploitation of those efforts and the dispensing with those efforts when they are no longer required. Concern may be shown with human welfare, justice or satisfaction but only insofar as this is necessary for controlling interests to be met and, then, always at least cost.[34]

HRM has also been strongly criticised by some academics for being a vacuous rhetoric, the ambiguity of which hides a harsher market reality of employees' labour becoming increasingly a commodity.[35] Karen Legge has proposed that HRM as a philosophy is essentially a hyping of the theory and practice of personnel management and that it has the purpose of obscuring the realities of change. A radical perspective argues that heightened competition, recession, and socio-politico-economic changes associated with pursuit of the 'enterprise culture' have presented employers and managers with constraints and with opportunities (as will be discussed in the next three chapters). Legge claims that their response has been largely pragmatic and, further, some managers, HR practitioners, and academics have sought to justify these changes to the employment relationship under the banner of progressive HRM.[36]

Returning now to sum up the models of HRM outlined in this chapter: all of them recommend change in the way that human resources are managed, although they differ in their estimates of its likelihood. Most see change as desirable but as very difficult to obtain on a large scale. Guest's model of soft HRM prescribed how management and employees should organise their work and behave in their jobs in order to achieve high organisational performance, but ten years after creating the model, he could not provide substantial evidence of its working in reality, although he remains highly committed to the possibility of a link between investment in HRM and company profitability.[37] Storey's model focuses on change by revealing differences of approach between HRM and traditional personnel management. Storey presents HRM as having the potential eventually to supersede personnel management, although he expresses strong doubt about the empirical evidence for extensive change having occurred in the UK during the 1980s. The Michigan model of strategic HRM is arguably the closest to traditional personnel management in non-union settings. It is consistent with Kochan's criticism of US employers by not being supportive of partnership with unions or tolerant of pluralist employee interests.

Three common elements of all of these models are unitarism, the need for management to adopt a strategic approach, and ensuring that organisations achieve new social goals. To a greater or lesser extent, all make the assumption that management's interests are the most legitimate ones in the running of the business. All advise that HRM ultimately must fit the competitive environment, and a prerequisite of this is that organisations be less ad hoc in their management decision making and more strategic. Finally, all predict that HRM innovations will be in the long-term social interest of employees, employers, and the nation. These three elements of HRM—the unitarist, the strategic, and the social—will be referred to throughout the remainder of this book.

The next part of the book, chapters 2, 3, and 4, analyses in detail the environment in which Australian organisations are operating today. The environmental factors highlighted must be considered by any organisation planning to adopt an HRM approach.

Study questions

1. Identify the strengths and weaknesses of soft and hard HRM. Then, hold a debate on the claim: 'Soft HRM is all heart with no head'.
2. Analyse Kochan's framework and explain how it differs from soft and hard HRM models.
3. Clarify with others each of Storey's twenty-five points of difference between HRM and personnel management/industrial relations.
4. Assess the adequacy of Brewster and Bournois's model in explaining HRM in Australia.
5. Select a case study of an organisation and assess its HRM policy and practice using two models of your choice.

Further reading

Beer, M., Spector, B., Lawrence, P. R., Quinn Mills, D., and Walton, R. E., *Managing Human Assets: The Ground Breaking Harvard Business School Program* (New York: Free Press, 1984).

Bratton, J. and Gold, J., *Human Resource Management: Theory and Practice*, 2nd edn (London: Macmillan, 1999), chapter 1, pp. 3–36.

Keenoy, T., 'HRM: Rhetoric, Reality and Contradiction', *International Journal of Human Resource Management* (1990), 1, 3, pp. 363–84.

Kochan, T. A. and Osterman, P., *The Mutual Gains Enterprise: Forging a Winning Partnership among Labor, Management and Government* (Boston: Harvard Business School Press, 1994).

PART 2
Context

CHAPTER 2

The Environment of HRM

CHAPTER CONTENTS

Introduction

1 Internationalisation and HRM
   Internationalisation
   Internationalisation and flexible labour markets
   Full employment and unemployment
   Labour force participation

2 The pursuit of competitiveness and HRM
   The implementation of HRM in Australian organisations
   Research and development, training, and the 'clever country' agenda
   HRM and the public sector

Summary
   Case study—Employment flexibility in an international hotel
   Study questions
   Further reading

Introduction

In chapter 1, we saw how HRM gained influence during the 1980s and 1990s. This growth coincided with profound changes in the social, political, and economic environment within which organisations operate. One consequence of these changes has been the intensification of competitive pressures: organisations are increasingly competing on an international basis rather than a local, state or national basis. Many of the recent initiatives by local, state and national governments have sought to promote greater competition, and in this changing context, HRM has appeared attractive to managers because it promises to provide an effective response to these competitive pressures.

The dynamics of the employer–employee relationship may be transformed by apparently external social, political, and economic factors, which need to be taken into account in order to understand that relationship more effectively. This chapter provides an overview of these factors, which constitute the environment within which HRM operates. First, it discusses the process of internationalisation, concentrating on its impact upon the labour market, management, and work practices in Australia. Second, it assesses the implementation of HRM in Australia and related issues such as research and development (R&D), training, and the role of the public sector.

I Internationalisation and HRM

Internationalisation

The economic internationalisation of recent decades has several sources. Three major developments have been the reduced barriers to trade, the rapid growth of several Asian economies, and the increasing importance of transnational companies (TNCs).[1] First, international trade of goods and services takes place more intensively and in a wider range of industries than before. A major reason for this has been the reduction or abolition of import quotas and tariffs produced through the successive rounds of the General Agreement on Tariffs and Trade (GATT) since the 1980s. International trade has been freed up by agreements within several regions of the world, although often to the disadvantage of competitors external to the trading arrangements. These developments have included the Single European Market (SEM), the North American Free Trade Agreement (NAFTA), and looser arrangements such as the Asia Pacific Economic Cooperation (APEC) grouping of twenty-one nations in the Asia–Pacific Region, including Australia. Further, there have been bilateral agreements such as Australia's Closer Economic Relationship (CER) with New Zealand. Technological advances have accelerated the growth of international trade, particularly in the service sector, largely because they have reduced the need for the provider of services to be located geographically close to the purchaser. For example, the growth of telework (conducted via computer and telecommunications technologies) has meant that certain forms of work can be done at any time during the 24-hour day and in any location.

Second, whereas for much of the period following the end of World War II in 1945 the dominant manufacturing nations were in Western Europe and North America, the subsequent rise of Japan to economic superpower status and the rapid growth of several Asian economies (such as Singapore and Korea) has intensified global competition. The 'Asian crisis' of 1997–98 stalled this growth somewhat, but there have since been signs of economic resurgence in several countries in the region.

Third, TNCs, which are defined as companies operating in more than one country, have increased their share of output, employment, and investment in almost all economies (see tables 2.1 and 2.2). Developments in international transport and communications have enabled TNCs to redistribute their production across borders and exert considerable control from their headquarters. For example, many TNCs have created cadres of global managers, who travel regularly across sites in different countries, forging closer relations between different parts of the transnational

Table 2.1 The stock of foreign direct investment (US$ billion)

Year	1982	1990	2000
Total	568	1717	5976

Source: United Nations, *World Investment Report 2001* (New York: UN, 2001), p. 10. Statistics used with the permission of the United Nations Conference on Trade and Development, Geneva.

Table 2.2 Characteristics of the world's 100 largest TNCs, 1999 ($US billion, number of employees and percentage)

Variable	1999	1998	Change 1999 compared to 1998 (per cent)
Assets			
Foreign	2124	1922	10.5
Total	5092	4610	10.5
Sales			
Foreign	2213	2063	3.0
Total	4318	4099	5.3
Employment			
Foreign	6 050 283	6 547 719	−7.6
Total	13 279 327	12 741 173	4.2
Average index of transnationality[2]	52.6	53.9	−1.3

Source: United Nations, *World Investment Report 2001* (New York: UN, 2001), p. 94. Statistics used with the permission of the United Nations Conference on Trade and Development, Geneva.

organisation. This has meant that a proportion of management personnel has become increasingly international and that, HRM approaches have had more avenues for international application.

Internationalisation and flexible labour markets

The internationalisation of Australia's economy attained political prominence with the election of the Hawke Labor government in March 1983. This newly elected government's floating of the Australian dollar removed all direct governmental controls on the value of Australia's currency, although the Reserve Bank still retains the power to influence the Australian dollar's value—for example, through official interest rate adjustments or through buying and selling the currency on foreign exchange markets. The process of deregulation, whereby government withdraws from the regulation of private business activities, has spread over the past two decades to many industries in Australia such as banking, telecommunications, and air transportation, permitting the entry of foreign competitors.

The pursuit of internationalisation of business has accompanied substantial changes in management and work practices intended to maximise productivity and profits, while reducing costs. During the 1970s and 1980s pressure grew in Australia and other developed economies for substantial deregulation of labour markets and industrial relations. The political momentum for these changes in Australia emerged from the 'New Right', which grew in strength during the 1970s, to include much of the Liberal Party and several key employer associations and to eventually exert considerable influence on the ALP. 'New Right' commentators argued that Australian labour markets were insufficiently flexible to respond to rapid fluctuations in market conditions. This inflexibility was attributed mainly to excessive union strength and an industrial relations system that they felt was too centralised and overly regulated. The industrial relations system, they claimed, prevented employers from having sufficient freedom to control the number of people they employed, the work they did, and the terms and conditions under which they worked—that is, managerial prerogative had been constrained unduly by 'third parties' (particularly trade unions). The result was that firms were often forced to pay wages above their free market level, retaining people they did not need but were unable to lay off. In the long term, they claimed, this reduced the domestic and international competitiveness of firms and raised unemployment. A range of 'economic rationalist' policies promoting decentralisation, deregulation, and privatisation were advocated to address this supposed inflexibility.

Structural economic changes, both internationally and within Australia, increased general acceptance of the 'New Right' argument, as the balance of power shifted away from labour towards capital, particularly transnational capital. Internationalisation has involved relocation of manufacturing activities from the developed economies to newly industrialising countries, especially those in Asia. It has sometimes led to a shortage of productive investment capital in domestic markets, as profits are sought by investors through investment in deregulated, international financial markets during what some refer to as an era of 'casino capitalism'. As international investment capital has been attracted to cheaper, more 'flexible' labour, the trend has been towards more competitive labour markets characterised by preference for higher levels of casual, part-time, and short-term employment, combined with persistently high levels of unemployment.[3]

Full employment and unemployment

During the extended period of economic growth from the end of World War II until the early 1970s, there was virtually full employment in Australia, as unemployment remained below 3 per cent of the workforce. Unemployment began to rise gradually during the mid-1970s, following the collapse of the system of international financial regulation established at Bretton Woods in 1944, and rose more sharply during the early 1980s. Since then it has fluctuated, but has never been reduced to the levels of the 1950s and 1960s, despite the commitment to full employment still contained in the Reserve Bank of Australia's official charter.[4] Unemployment in Australia reached a high of 11 per cent in mid-1992, and it remained close to this figure until July 1995, when it dropped to 8.3 per cent. The figure subsequently declined quite steadily until 2000, although there was an increase in the wake of global economic downturn, to 6.8 per cent in September 2001 (see table 2.3).[5]

There are also several areas of proportionally higher unemployment than the national average—for example, in many outer suburbs of major cities and various rural areas. Some non-English-speaking migrant groups also have significantly higher unemployment rates than the average. Much higher unemployment rates are found among young people (particularly those aged 15–19) and unemployment rates are chronically high among Aboriginal and Torres Strait Islander people—22.7 per cent at the 1996 census, although this was down considerably from the figure of 30.8 per cent recorded in the 1991 census.[6] A significant number of long-term unemployed people have been unemployed for a year or longer. Around a third of unemployed men and a quarter of unemployed women may be classified as being 'long-term' unemployed. There is also a sizeable amount of hidden unemployment, which includes people who have either given up the search for paid work or would be in employment, if they could find it. They are not recorded in official unemployment figures. Nor is *under*employment, which includes people in part-time or casual work who would prefer to work more hours. To give an idea of the scale of this problem, of the 2 580 600 part-time workers in August 2001, 677 000 stated a preference for working longer hours than they were at the time.[7]

During the period of near full employment, often described as the era of 'Fordism',[8] most jobs were full-time, permanent, and occupied by men. They were mainly in industries such as manufacturing, mining, and utilities (for example, electricity generation), with relatively high levels of union membership, and

Table 2.3 Civilian population aged 15 years and over, labour force status, annual average

	Unit	1994–95	1995–96	1996–97	1997–98	1998–99	1999–2000
MALES							
Employed	'000	4628.8	4718.3	4757.0	4818.9	4914.2	5023.3
Unemployed							
–Looking for full-time work	'000	414.4	400.0	400.9	386.0	357.5	312.5
–Looking for part-time work	'000	51.1	53.4	58.5	59.4	58.6	62.9
–Total unemployed	'000	465.5	453.4	459.4	445.5	416.1	375.4
Labour force	'000	5094.3	5171.7	5216.4	5264.3	5330.3	5398.6
Not in the labour force	'000	1810.2	1833.2	1892.0	1949.9	1993.4	2042.5
Civilian population	'000	6904.6	7004.9	7108.4	7214.3	7323.7	7441.1
Unemployment rate	%	9.1	8.8	8.8	8.5	7.8	7.0
Participation rate	%	73.8	73.8	73.4	73.0	72.8	72.6
FEMALES							
Employed	'000	3463.8	3582.9	3623.7	3677.5	3766.5	3893.3
Unemployed							
–Looking for full-time work	'000	224.7	210.7	223.8	215.2	194.9	179.0
–Looking for part-time work	'000	103.5	100.3	109.3	103.6	107.3	107.0
–Total unemployed	'000	328.2	310.9	333.0	318.8	302.1	286.0
Labour force	'000	3791.9	3893.9	3956.7	3996.3	4068.7	4179.3
Not in the labour force	'000	3335.1	3343.8	3390.3	3454.2	3486.6	3486.5
Civilian population	'000	7127.1	7237.7	7347.0	7450.5	7555.3	7605.8
Unemployment rate	%	8.7	8.0	8.4	8.0	7.4	6.8
Participation rate	%	53.2	53.8	53.9	53.6	53.9	54.5
PERSONS							
Employed	'000	8092.6	8301.2	8380.6	8496.4	8680.8	8916.6
Unemployed							
–Looking for full-time work	'000	639.1	610.7	624.7	601.2	552.4	491.5
–Looking for part-time work	'000	154.6	153.6	167.7	163.0	165.9	169.8
–Total unemployed	'000	793.7	764.3	792.4	764.2	718.2	661.4
Labour force	'000	8886.3	9065.5	9173.1	9260.6	9399.0	9577.9
Not in the labour force	'000	5145.4	5177.1	5282.3	5404.2	5480.0	5529.0
Civilian population	'000	14 031.6	14 242.6	14 455.3	14 664.8	14 879.0	15 106.9
Unemployment rate	%	8.9	8.4	8.6	8.3	7.6	6.9
Participation rate	%	63.3	63.7	63.5	63.1	63.2	63.4

Source: Australian Bureau of Statistics, *Labour Force Australia*, cat. no. 6203.0 (Canberra: ABS, 2001).
ABS data used with permission from the Australian Bureau of Statistics. www.abs.gov.au

whereby the male-headed 'nuclear family' sustained a strong gender-based division of labour as the norm. The end of the era of near full employment marked a relative decline in the extent of 'standard' permanent, full-time (predominantly male) employment—the 'primary' labour market. Concurrently, there has been considerable growth in 'irregular' (also known as 'non-standard' or 'contingent') employment. This rapid increase in temporary, part-time or casual, and predominantly female, jobs (the 'secondary' labour market) has ushered in what some have defined as a 'post-Fordist' era of more flexible employment and work organisation, with such working arrangements as homeworking and job-sharing.[9] The extent and character of this shift have varied significantly across the nations belonging to the Organisation for Economic Cooperation and Development (OECD).

This trend has brought new problems and challenges for workplace regulation and policy, and for trade unions. The growth of part-time and casual work, as well as the emergence of more flexible forms of work, such as job-sharing, may be conceptualised in terms of a broad shift away from Fordist forms of work and social organisation. Other associated societal changes influencing labour markets have been: an increasing diversity of family forms other than the nuclear family, including single-parent families, single-person households, couples without children, and same-sex couples; deferred entry by many young people into the workforce, which

Table 2.4 Civilian labour force, by birthplace, annual average, 1999–2000

	Employed Full-time workers '000	Employed Total '000	Unemployed Looking for full-time work '000	Unemployed Total '000	Total labour force '000	Unemployment rate %	Participation rate (a) %
Born in Australia	4900.3	6720.0	357.6	487.5	7207.4	6.8	67.0
Born outside Australia							
– Main English-speaking countries	733.6	948.2	45.9	59.1	1007.3	5.9	64.6
– Other countries	952.5	1248.4	88.0	114.8	1363.1	8.4	54.0
– Oceania	223.4	283.2	17.9	23.0	306.2	7.5	74.0
– Europe and the former USSR	856.6	1121.2	57.9	72.8	1194.0	6.1	53.3
– The Middle East and North Africa	68.5	90.2	10.5	13.2	103.4	12.8	49.8
– South-east Asia	204.4	263.5	23.4	30.1	293.5	10.2	61.2
– North-east Asia	105.1	142.8	6.4	9.6	152.4	6.3	54.8
– Northern America	38.4	49.4	2.2	3.0	52.4	5.8	72.7
– Other	189.7	246.3	15.6	22.1	268.5	8.2	68.3
– Total born outside Australia	1686.1	2196.6	133.9	173.9	2370.5	7.3	58.1
Total	6586.4	8916.6	491.5	661.4	9577.9	6.9	64.6

(a) Participation rate calculated using population estimates that exclude those in institutions.

Source: Australian Bureau of Statistics, *Labour Force Australia*, cat. no. 6203.0 (Canberra: ABS, 2001). ABS data used with permission from the Australian Bureau of Statistics. www.abs.gov.au

has become much more commonplace since the emergence of 'mass' higher education; and a polarisation between high 'work intensity' households, with two or more wage-earners, and low 'work intensity' households, with no wage earner.[10]

Labour force participation

A rapid increase in labour force participation during the 1980s, mainly attributable to more women entering the formal labour force, was followed by a slower rate of growth during the 1990s. In August 2001, the overall labour force participation rate was 63.9 per cent, which comprised 72.4 per cent of men and 55.5 per cent of women classified as working age (15–64 years old).[11]

The main area of employment growth has been in casual employment. Casual employees are defined by their lack of access to holiday pay, sick pay, and other entitlements of more 'regular' work, and they can also be dismissed or can leave on very short notice (such as one day). Their conditions of employment differ from those of part-time employees, who have access to the same employment entitlements as full-time employees on a pro rata basis (for example, 60 per cent holiday pay if they are employed on 60 per cent of full-time hours) and have greater security of employment. Casual employees are customarily paid a loading in compensation for lack of access to these benefits. Most casual employment is both insecure and peripheral, although there are many 'permanent casuals' in the workforce—people who have been employed on a casual basis over several years.

Part-time work (including job-sharing) has been widely perceived as a means of achieving greater flexibility for employees, mostly women, in combining work and family commitments. However, in recent years, the conditions of part-time work have become less regulated, so that part-time employees can be required to work a more varied number of hours over a longer period. Many employers have concluded that through these flexible working arrangements part-time workers can be as productive and cost effective as casual employees, while delivering considerably lower labour turnover and greater organisational commitment. Also, unions have often responded favourably because they have seen part-time work as offering their members greater job security and career prospects than casual work.

Casual work is most prevalent in workplaces with high levels of seasonal or daily fluctuations in demand, such as hotels or department stores. Non-standard work, therefore, is often used to achieve numerical flexibility in the workforce, but is also associated with low levels of job security, limited (if any) career prospects, and little access to training and education. Yet, although 'non-standard' work is often characterised by inferior working conditions, it may also afford employees considerable flexibility, which is not usually associated with full-time work. For example, students may prefer casual employment during vacations. So, although casual employees offer employers greater numerical flexibility, turnover is much higher among casual workers, and they are likely to have less commitment to the organisation than permanent and part-time workers. Similarly, casual forms of employment pose problems for unions, and union membership among them is typically low.

In Australia, casual employment rose by 70 per cent during the period 1988–98, accounting for an increase from 17 per cent to 27 per cent of the total workforce. This growth was particularly strong among men, increasing by 115 per cent (from 415 700 to 894 100), and the numbers of non-casual male employees actually declined by 2 per cent (from 3 127 800 to 3 064 100). The highest proportions of casual employees were in the youngest age group, 15–24 years (45 per cent) and in the oldest age group, 55 years and over (28 per cent). Casual workers are concentrated in the lowest-skilled, lowest-paid occupations, and in certain industry sectors: accommodation, cafés, and restaurants (58 per cent); agriculture, forestry, and fishing (56 per cent); retailing (46 per cent); cultural and recreational services (42 per cent); construction (34 per cent); and property and business services (31 per cent). Some sectors continue to have low proportions of casual employees: electricity, gas, and water supply (5 per cent); finance and insurance (9 per cent); government administration and defence (9 per cent); and mining (11 per cent).[12]

Higher unemployment rates and the growth of insecure, peripheral employment significantly strengthen the hand of employers in dealing with their workforces, because the large pool of prospective labour available to employers usually makes employees wary of taking any action that may antagonise management. Thus employers can initiate organisational changes and assert managerial prerogative, including HRM strategies, more readily. In the following sections, we investigate the extent that HRM has been adopted in Australian organisations, including initiatives by government and developments in the public sector designed to stimulate innovation and increase the competitiveness of the workforce.

2 The pursuit of competitiveness and HRM

The implementation of HRM in Australian organisations

Changes in the wider national and international context, therefore, appear not only to have made HRM an attractive response to greater competitive pressures but also to have made it easier to implement. What evidence, then, is there that Australian organisations have moved towards strategic implementation of HRM? Three observations should be made before addressing this question. First, all of the HRM models discussed in chapter 1 emphasise the importance of managing the workforce in a 'strategic' way, insisting that policies and practices concerning the management of people should be consistent with the long-term business strategy of the organisation. Second, all the models are fundamentally unitarist in that they stress common interests between managers and employees and have little to say about tensions and conflicts between these groups. Third, HRM's advocates envisage benefits for employees as well as for management wherever HRM is adopted. In particular, some advocates have stressed the advantages in terms of improved job security and working relationships, greater involvement in decision making, rewards based on performance, and better training.

Signs of HRM's apparent influence abound, particularly in terms of the widespread use of HRM rhetoric. It is now commonplace to hear managers of large corporations talking about the need to manage their labour in a more strategic way; many routinely refer to people as 'the organisation's most important asset', and therefore, the main avenue for achieving a competitive edge. Their espoused views are often unitarist, including talk of the need to develop a sense of shared goals and greater trust between management and employees.[13] Managers often stress the benefits to employees of the HRM-style initiatives that they are adopting. For example, it is claimed that practices such as teamworking empower people to make decisions without having to refer upwards to their manager and that the commitment to training allows employees to ensure that their skills are maximised, while performance-related pay provides rewards for people according to their performance. However, the evidence for such empowerment is hard to find on a large scale, and as yet the implementation of HRM does not appear to have led to any significant devolution of power in Australia. Indeed, some research from both Australia and overseas points in the opposite direction, towards concentration of power in managerial hands.[14]

While the role and contribution of HRM during all of these organisational and societal changes may be difficult to assess, it is somewhat easier to identify the extent that management and work practices thought to be associated with strategic approaches to HRM have been introduced. In this regard, the most recent Australian Workplace Industrial Relations Survey is a valuable resource. The survey found that, during the period 1990–95, there had been a notable increase (34 per cent to 46 per cent) in the overall proportion of workplaces with a specialist employee relations manager (which also included managers designated as human resources, industrial relations, or personnel managers). Since specialist employee relations managers were more likely to be present in large workplaces than in small workplaces, this meant that more than two-thirds of employees worked in an organisation with a specialist employee relations manager (up from 60 per cent to 69 per cent). The proportion of the largest organisations (500 or more employees) with a specialist employee relations manager increased from 87 per cent to 94 per cent in the private sector and from 92 per cent to 97 per cent in the public sector.[15]

Yet the presence of an HRM function and designated HR responsibilities need not indicate the integration of HRM in overall business strategies. In this respect, the overall AWIRS findings suggest that the importance of HRM within organisations had not increased uniformly and there were many organisations in which the employee relations area played little part in strategic decision-making processes. Notably, in those workplaces with a specialist employee relations manager, there had been no change between 1990 and 1995 in the number of workplaces where the employee relations area was consulted during the implementation of changes to the organisation of work (32 per cent). There was also virtually no change in the proportion of workplaces where the employee relations area was consulted prior to a decision being made (50 per cent in 1990 and 51 per cent in 1995).[16]

In terms of an overall strategic approach to performance management the evidence was, however, more positive, with 67 per cent of workplaces in the 1995 survey benchmarking their performance against other workplaces. The incidence of benchmarking was notably more than twice as high in those organisations with majority foreign ownership as that in organisations with majority Australian ownership. The most common benchmarking categories were, in order: customer service or satisfaction, quality procedures, operating processes, relative cost position, labour productivity, occupational health and safety, and technology.[17] The overall picture is one of a quite selective, uneven implementation of policies and practices associated with HRM. Further evidence suggests that employers, when given a relatively free rein (without the intervention of 'third parties', particularly trade unions), are pursuing the 'hard' dimensions of HRM.[18] These stress cost-efficiency, numerical flexibility, and managerial prerogative, at the expense of the 'soft' HRM emphasis on commitment, motivation, and training in order to achieve a highly committed and adaptable workforce.

The limited implementation of strategic approaches to HRM is not a purely Australian phenomenon and is revealed in research on other countries such as the UK. It may be attributed in considerable part to the pluralist character of most organisations, particularly larger, more complex organisations. Different organisational interest groups (including different branches of management) may have divergent aims and priorities, which can result in strategy emerging as a result of incremental readjustments arrived at through political interactions and compromises between different organisational actors.[19] The general social, political, and economic context further limits the extent to which strategic approaches to HRM may be implemented. These include, for example, levels of national R&D, and the skill levels of the Australian labour force. One question that has to be asked here in terms of the country's comparative performance is: Are they adequate in meeting the needs of a contemporary developed economy operating in an international business environment?

Research and development, training, and the 'clever country' agenda

Much of Australia's national policy direction since the 1980s has sought to ensure that the levels of national R&D are adequate—under the general banner of achieving a 'clever' rather than 'lucky' country, an agenda launched by then Prime Minister, Bob Hawke. In relation to other developed economies, Australia has suffered from relatively low levels of investment in R&D. While overall expenditure on R&D in Australia (1.9 per cent of Gross Domestic Product [GDP] in 1999) ranks in the mid-range of the 29 nations in the Organisation For Economic Cooperation and Development (OECD), business expenditure lags, at the seventh lowest, and was declining during the latter half of the 1990s. Business has looked to educational institutions, particularly universities, to provide the R&D that they have been reluctant to develop themselves. There has been an emphasis on partnerships between universities and business to accelerate the national R&D effort, resulting in some success. The Howard government explicitly acknowledged the limitations of Australia's R&D performance with the release of its 'Innovation Statement' in

January 2001, which foreshadowed a significant increase in R&D expenditure. Critics (including the ALP and the Australian Democrats), however, have suggested that this only partially compensates for the Howard government's previously inadequate commitment to R&D since its election in 1996.[20]

Among the most important HRM issues on the 'clever country' agenda was training and skills development, as well as proposals for creating national training policies and standards, which were designed to achieve a highly trained, more flexible workforce with skills that were portable from one workplace to another. The traditional apprenticeship system was seen as inefficient and inadequate in serving the needs of an internationally competitive economy, particularly as it was focused on older parts of the economy in manufacturing, mining, utilities, and heavy industries. Therefore, it was not geared to the expanding new technology and service sectors nor to a labour market characterised by increasing participation by women. Being focused on traditionally male areas of employment, it perpetuated considerable gender inequities in the provision of training. Apprenticeships were relatively rare in the service sector, the main source of women's employment, with hairdressing being the most significant area of apprenticeships for women. Also, many of the tasks performed by women were not classified as skills-based, but as 'natural' for women—for example, work performed by housekeepers in hotels. These informal and gendered skills consequently have been inadequately recognised and have gone relatively unrewarded.

From the late 1980s, the National Training Reform Agenda (subsequently the National Strategy for Vocational Education and Training) was designed to expand access to training for women and minority groups, as well as provide several pathways for young people to make the transition from school to work. It introduced the concept of 'lifelong learning' (as distinct from apprenticeships, usually completed during the teenage years) in recognition that the era of a 'job for life' had passed, and that people should be able to retrain and develop new careers according to life-stage considerations. The purpose of the National Training Reform Agenda was the establishment of a comprehensive national system of accessible, portable, and flexible skills and credentials.

Through the Vocational Education and Training system, Commonwealth and state governments committed themselves to the development of a national training system. This was intended to provide workers with credentials and skills that would be recognised nationally, unlike much 'in-house' or 'on-the-job' training. A system of training boards and authorities was established to oversee the development of a national scheme for training and qualifications, headed by the Australian National Training Authority. Rather than the time-based apprenticeship scheme, competency-based training was introduced, to be administered by industry training assistance boards. Training was provided in modules, whereby participants had to demonstrate their competence in particular settings and tasks, before moving on to acquire and then demonstrate competence in others. The Australian Traineeship Scheme was designed to expand the provision of qualifications and training to areas not covered by the traditional apprenticeship scheme.[21] An associated initiative was the Training Guarantee Levy, which required all organisations with a payroll of over $200 000 to commit at least 2 per cent of that sum to training, or pay a levy equivalent to the shortfall, but was abandoned in 1994, due to a lack of any substantial and demonstrable impact on training quality and quantity.

The concurrent processes of decentralisation, deregulation, and privatisation have made the achievement of a coherent, national approach to training more difficult.[22] Further, the transition away from nationally coordinated training policies under the Howard government has been paralleled in the area of labour market programs by its dismantling of the Commonwealth Employment Service (CES), which was replaced by the Job Network, a variety of private, public, and community agencies. The fundamental premise underlying this transition has been that competing private sector providers can provide a more efficient service than a single public provider. The coalition government implemented a 'mutual obligation' approach to welfare and the labour market, designed to achieve change in job seekers' attitudes to their social responsibilities. The main expression of this approach was the 'Work for the Dole' scheme, which sought to tighten access to welfare payments by unemployed people.[23] Introduced as a pilot program in 1997, 'Work for the Dole' targets people aged 18–24 years who have been unemployed for six months or more, and people aged 25–34 years who have been unemployed for twelve months or more and are receiving full payment of benefits. Participants in the scheme either volunteer for employment or are compelled to work in return for payment of benefits. 'Work for the Dole' is not specifically a training scheme, but training can be part of its programs.[24]

Under the Howard government, training has been turned over to some extent to the private sector. While the bulk of training continues to be provided by public sector agencies—most importantly TAFE (technical and further education)—private companies have competed more directly with public sector institutions for the provision of training. Australia's training system, therefore, has become increasingly market-based in recent years. The government's Modern Apprenticeship and Traineeship System (MAATS), in particular, has given responsibility for training to a variety of more market-based providers, often at the enterprise level. This process has been in contrast to the approaches adopted in several European countries (for example, France and Germany), which combine strong legislative support for training with close involvement of trade unions. In a market-based system of training, however, the temptation exists for individual employers to poach trained workers from other firms rather than carry out training themselves. Hence, the danger of poaching acts as a disincentive to employers to invest in long-term training. Some industries also have chronically high levels of labour turnover, which mean large losses in training investment, particularly if the employees leave the industry entirely, as occurs in industries such as hospitality.

The deficiencies of the market-based system stem not only from the inadequacy of the supply of skills but also from the weakness of the demand for skills. Many organisations are pressured into pursuing cost-based competitive strategies, keeping tight control over labour costs and offering jobs that are mainly routine and low-skill in nature. In these organisations, the demand for skilled labour is likely to be weak, and provision of training as part of a strategic approach to the management of labour becomes unlikely. None of this should be surprising, as firms, after all, are primarily in competition with one another to maximise profits and are less intent on achieving national goals, such as a better trained, more skilled workforce.

To what extent, then, has the introduction of HRM-style practices and greater employment flexibility brought employees enhanced access to training during the last decade? The picture is somewhat patchy at best. There has been a decline in training expenditure and hours of formal training per employee, and concerns have been raised about the quality of training supplied by many private training providers. Access to training also remains inequitable. Training opportunities in Australia remain considerably less accessible for casual workers (who are still predominantly women) than for full-time members of the workforce. Training provisions remain limited for service sector occupations (such as clerical or sales work) and for casual employees,[25] areas in which high numbers of women are employed, indicating continued inequity in training provision. The training and development benefits that can be derived from HRM are unlikely to extend beyond 'core' employees because organisations are failing to invest in the long-term future of the growing number of 'peripheral' employees.

An obstacle to the improvement in skill levels of the national labour force is the erosion of the role of the Australian public sector in training provision. Due to downsizing, outsourcing, and general cost-cutting, the public sector's historical role as a provider of training has been whittled away. Whereas the public sector had previously provided considerably more training than the private sector, expenditure and hours of training per employee declined in the public sector, while in the private sector they remained during the 1990s at their previous low levels.[26] The next section looks in more detail at the ways in which public sector management and work practices have changed to meet the demands of internationalisation, competitiveness, and accountability.

HRM and the public sector

While internationalisation has increased competitive pressures on many private sector firms, public sector organisations have also experienced pressures no less intense, although different in character. The privatisation of public sector organisations was a further key component of the Commonwealth Labor government's (1983–96) program to achieve a more internationalised, competitive economy and to reduce levels of government expenditure. Privatisation includes the total or partial selling-off of public assets to private interests or contracting out work previously done by the public sector to private firms. In Australia, by the beginning of 2002, it has included partial privatisation of Telstra, the complete privatisation of Qantas and the Commonwealth Bank, as well as outsourcing (contracting out) of public sector work to private sector agencies. HRM's impact has been particularly significant in Australian public sector organisations, as they have been restructured along lines more akin to those prevailing in large private sector companies. This process of 'corporatisation' has often involved financial stringency policies followed by programs of HRM innovation. Across the industrialised world, governments have introduced programs to achieve greater efficiencies in public sector organisation, as they have sought to reduce government expenditure. A further critical element in this process of corporatisation has been the introduction of management techniques (under a variety of names) derived largely from the private sector. Australia has been no exception to this trend, and its governments have sought to apply such management methods to the public sector derived from the private sector. This new wave of managerialism was designed to reassert managerial prerogative, with the aims of streamlining the public sector and making it more accountable. The diverse areas of public sector employment, such as public services, education, social welfare, health, policing, and emergency services have experienced the impact of 'new managerialism' and radical public sector change. The main outcomes have been privatisation in a number of areas of the public sector, organisation downsizing, and outsourcing of non-core services.[27]

In Australia, as in most other industrialised countries, the role of the state (that is, the intersecting array of governmental, legislative, and administrative agencies at local, state and federal levels) is always controversial. The state, through its provision of electricity, water, roads, public transport, communication, education, and entertainment, is present in most things we do. Few people would deny that the state has a role in any modern, complex society. It is a major source of employment and income for many people, and performs a variety of crucial social and economic activities.

Traditionally, the political right has stressed the oppressive potential of the state, particularly in relation to individual liberties, whereas the political left has tended to promote state intervention and public ownership as indispensable in the fight against poverty, unemployment, and homelessness, and in providing greater equality of access to education, and health and public services. The political picture in Australia, though, is further complicated by the presence of an influential rural population whose main political expression (the National, formerly Country, Party) has had a long allegiance to significant state intervention—for example, to provide services (such as telephone) to country areas at reasonable rates. In recent years, many National Party representatives and supporters have opposed the federal government's plans to privatise Telstra. Many have even defected to the One Nation party and its offshoots.

Until the 1970s, most industrialised countries expanded the size of the public sector. While GDP was increasing, public expenditure also grew, as did its share of GDP. It included a commitment to full employment, increasing public control of economic resources, and enhanced opportunities for social services such as education and health. This period was characterised by a degree of compromise (albeit often uneasy) between capital and organised labour, and a commitment by mainstream political parties to the broad goals of nation-building and full employment.

It was within this context that demands for privatisation came to political prominence. The principal argument mounted against public ownership was that in a world in which resources are always limited, a competitive private sector is the best way to utilise them, in order to maximise economic growth. Through the operation of supply and demand, businesses will exist only where there is sufficient demand for the goods and services they supply, and inefficient businesses will cease to exist. It was argued that private sector organisations seek to maximise output while minimising costs, but public sector organisations are by contrast inherently inefficient and wasteful of resources. By implication, then, public sector managers are characterised as more concerned with maximising their budgets to serve the public sector's inherent bureaucracy, whereas private sector managers stimulate dynamism, entrepreneurship, and investment in new technologies.

On the other hand, people who argue in favour of public ownership point to the instability of markets, capitalism's inherent tendency towards crisis (for example, cyclical economic booms and recessions), and the need for overall planning if economic resources are to be used effectively. The operation of supply and demand ('user pays'), they claim, exacerbates social and economic problems, such as increasing inequality, and consequently power becomes concentrated in the hands of a small number of major corporations. The public sector, however, is formally under the control of a government answerable to the electorate, which can mandate the pursuit of collective goals. For example, during the period following World War II, business relied heavily on the public sector to secure stable, long-term economic infrastructure such as roads and power supplies. Through policies such as cross-subsidisation the public sector can ensure equitable access to services across different regions or channel its funds into areas or industries that are seen as economically important. It can increase investment during economic downturn and provide services in areas that the private sector is unable to provide, or does so inequitably or less efficiently.

The Australian public sector has undergone a dramatic decline in total employment such that between February 1991 and February 1998, the number of public sector employees in Australia dropped from 1 721 500 to 1 456 600. Over the same period, private sector numbers grew from 4 667 200 to 5 343 700. There has also been a de facto privatisation of many public sector agencies, at local, state and federal levels, as they have sought to compete with the private sector and operate more according to a private sector model (for example, government-owned business enterprises) or as public sector organisations (for example, Telstra) that have been partially privatised. The decline has been most marked in the Commonwealth government, where employees declined from 410 800 to 266 500 over the seven-year period. The decline was less dramatic in state governments (down from 1 149 900 to 1 047 900) and at local government level (down from 160 800 to 142 300).[28] It should be noted that the reduction of Commonwealth government employment has continued under both the Labor and coalition governments, through implementation of downsizing and outsourcing policies.

Much HRM literature, especially of the harder variants, is keen to convince senior managers that it can contribute to the 'bottom line' through willingness to make 'tough' decisions. The phenomena of outsourcing and downsizing constitute typical examples of such preparedness when used primarily as methods for reducing costs and enabling organisations to concentrate on their core businesses—especially those in which they anticipate or seek a competitive advantage.[29] Outsourcing refers specifically to the contracting out of activities previously conducted within the organisation. Activities contracted out are usually those identified as peripheral, rather than part of the core business. Therefore, as has been mentioned earlier in the chapter, outsourcing is usually associated with significant downsizing (or 'right-sizing' as it is sometimes euphemistically termed), involving reduction of employee numbers to the minimum required for the most efficient operation of core business functions.[30] Through outsourcing, which may include the HRM department/team, organisations can increase their numerical flexibility: contract employees can be engaged at short notice, and such responsibilities as training and leave entitlements are deflected onto the labour hire company. Reducing the permanent labour force can also reduce union power and entrench managerial prerogative.[31]

In the public sector, pressures to outsource have been intensified by funding cutbacks and requirements for public sector organisations to act more like private sector organisations. The introduction of compulsory competitive tendering (CCT) and national competition policy ushered in an era of public sector contracting out to private sector companies. Through measures such as CCT, public sector organisations are redefined as purchasers, as well as providers, of services, one aim being to reduce the overall size of the public sector. The impact of organisational restructuring and greater emphasis on numerical flexibility have generally not delivered benefits for employees or created a more equitable relationship. Organisational downsizing affects the psychological contract between employee and employer by substantially altering expectations, with the general result that many of the retained employees experience a lack of career development and feel a greater amount of job insecurity.[32]

A distinction should also be made between short-term and long-term considerations. Research on downsizing and outsourcing has frequently found them stressful and damaging to organisational morale, and their associated cost-savings may be short-term only. The use of staff supplied by labour hire agencies also poses new problems for management, particularly if they are working side-by-side with permanent workers, but under different pay and conditions. Agency workers are unlikely to have the same commitment to the organisation as in-house workers—and there may be other problems, such as loss of 'organisational memory', issues with data security, inadequate training or lack of knowledge of the specific industry (for example, clerical workers employed in various industries such as building or education).[33] This decline in public sector employment and changed terms and conditions of work have had important ramifications, since the public sector has historically been viewed as the 'model' employer in Australia, with a responsibility to provide high-quality training and education, better wages and conditions than the private sector, and to be at the forefront of equity initiatives.

Summary

This chapter reviewed how the multifaceted process of internationalisation has intensified competitive pressures, making HRM strategies attractive to many employers. It further examined some major characteristics of Australia's social, political, and economic environment, within which HRM operates. Changes in the labour market, especially higher levels of unemployment and insecure employment, have given managers considerable potential to implement HRM strategies, although the evidence suggests uneven implementation of such strategies and a focus on 'hard' HRM goals. The chapter went on to examine the role of the 'clever country' agenda, particularly as it has affected the key HRM issue of training and skills development. It indicated how attempts to achieve coherent national training and skills have been undermined by the concurrent processes of decentralisation, deregulation, and major cutbacks to Australia's public sector, particularly downsizing and outsourcing. In the following chapter, we look at a closely related and highly controversial area of change in Australian management and work practices—industrial relations, an area that to a considerable extent has set the parameters within which HRM operates in Australia.

BOX 2.1

Case study—Employment flexibility in an international hotel

You are the human resources manager of the Luxor Grand Hotel, an international-standard establishment on the Gold Coast with 620 rooms, catering for almost equal numbers of overseas and domestic tourists. The largest group of overseas tourists is from Japan, with Japanese visitors accounting for about half of all overseas visitors to the hotel. Occupancy rates in the hotel vary widely according to the day of the week and the time of the year. In 'high season' periods such as December and January, occupancy rates are over 90 per cent. However, during some 'low season' periods, occupancy rates can be as low as 30 per cent on weekdays, although on weekends they usually increase to more than 60 per cent.

The hotel has a quite small number (125) of 'core' employees, with its permanent, mostly full-time staff concentrated in areas such as reception and food preparation. Since it opened in 1991, the hotel has relied mainly on a 'periphery' of casual employees to accommodate seasonal and daily fluctuations. The number of casual employees in any week during a year can range from as low as 100 to as many as 450. These casual employees are predominantly in their twenties, many of them either students or people on working holidays.

A recent audit of labour turnover in the hotel has indicated that the average length of employment among casual employees is only eight months, whereas for permanent full-time and part-time staff the figure is greater than four years, with 33 of these staff having been with the hotel since it began operations. Therefore, the high turnover among casual employees represents a considerable loss in terms of on-costs, training expenditure, and organisational commitment.

A group of five casual employees, all women cleaners in the 30–45 age group who are long-term residents of the local area, have approached you with a request to shift from casual to permanent part-time status. Their main interest in shifting to part-time work is to achieve greater job security, better access to formal training (which has so far been limited to irregular on-the-job training), and the possibility of structured career paths, while meeting family and other commitments.

At present, there are only 23 permanent part-time staff, but the prevailing enterprise agreement permits them to work as little as 48 hours or as much as 128 hours in any four-week cycle. You feel that a shift towards employment of permanent part-time, rather than casual workers, would provide a more reliable workforce, drawn predominantly from the local residential population, with greater commitment to the organisation and more knowledge of the Gold Coast area. There would also be considerable cost-savings through reduced labour turnover, and organisational planning should be more predictable: unlike permanent employees, casual workers cannot be required to work on particular days or at particular times. You are particularly interested in the provision of more formal training, especially with respect to Japanese language and culture.

However, senior hotel management has in the past taken the view that casual employees are easier to hire and fire and are less likely to join unions—in short, managerial prerogative can be exercised more readily with casual employees.

Case study activities
1. How would you convince senior management of the advantages of shifting towards the replacement of casual employees by permanent part-time employees?
2. How would the hotel's planning, particularly its rostering system, have to be changed to maximise the potential benefits of this shift?
3. What would be the main training priorities for different groups of employees within the hotel—for example, in reception, food and beverage preparation or cleaning?
4. Which do you see as the best forms of training provision for these different groups of employees (for example, on-the-job training or formal structured training by an external provider)?
5. Role-play the meeting between senior management and the human resources manager.

Study questions

1. In what ways has economic activity become more internationalised and how has this affected HRM practices in Australian firms?
2. You are a manager in a public sector organisation that is about to become privatised. How would you prepare for changes to the organisation of work in your organisation?
3. What advantages and disadvantages are associated with a market-based approach to training provision?
4. Describe how employment in Australia has become more 'flexible' over the past two decades.
5. What do you see as the most important benefits in adopting a strategic HRM approach, and the most significant impediments to strategic HRM?

Further reading

Australian Centre for Industrial Relations Research and Training (ACIRRT), *Australia at Work: Just Managing?* (Sydney: Prentice-Hall, 1999).
Dow, G. and Parker, R. (eds), *Business, Work and Community: Into the New Millenium* (Melbourne: Oxford University Press, 2001).
Frankel, B., *When the Boat Comes In: Transforming Australia in the Age of Globalisation* (Sydney: Pluto Press, 2001).
Hoogvelt, A., *Globalization and the Postcolonial World: The New Political Economy of Development* (Baltimore: Johns Hopkins University Press, 1997).

CHAPTER 3

Australian Industrial Relations

CHAPTER CONTENTS

Introduction

1 Industrial relations in Australia: the historical context

2 The Accord and the changing role of unions

3 Industrial relations in Australia: the present situation

Summary
    Case study—Unionisation in the retail industry
    Study questions
    Further reading

Introduction

'Industrial relations' refers to a network of relationships, institutions, and processes, and involves employers, employees, trade unions, employer associations, governments, and judicial institutions. In international terms, Australia's industrial relations system has been distinctive for the prominence historically given to centralised regulation of pay and conditions and the important role occupied by trade unions as the bargaining representative of employees. Industrial relations is far-reaching in its operations and in its impact, extending from the workplace level to regional, state, federal, and international levels.

Unions are a perennial topic of political debate. They act to various degrees as a restraint on management and restrict managerial prerogative—the capacity of employers to hire, fire, and control employees as they see fit. Many employers and their management are, however, prepared to have an ongoing relationship with the relevant unions, and to support union membership among their employees (for example, through automatic salary deduction of union dues). There are numerous industrial relations and human resource management areas where unions have the capacity to make a worthwhile contribution to the running of organisations. Unions can assist the management of organisations through their knowledge of workers' concerns and issues, and through their ability to organise internal labour markets and work practices. It is usually easier to negotiate, for example, agreements and introduce new work practices with a single organisation than repeat the process with each individual employee. Trade unions can also be very effective in implementing such policies as occupational health and safety (OHS), training and development, equal employment opportunity (EEO), staff development and appraisal, grievance procedures, or the introduction of major organisational change. Potential problems and strategies can be identified early on through union involvement, and communication and consultation with the workforce can be enhanced.

Yet, while many employers are ready to work with unions, others are demonstrably anti-union, largely because unions place additional limits on the freedom and authority of management. Unionised employees generally achieve higher wages and better conditions than non-unionised employees.[1] Unions have historically been seen by anti-union employers as an intrusive element in the workplace, interfering with the business of management.

I Industrial relations in Australia: the historical context

Industrial relations are based on the recognition that conflict of interest is an integral feature of the relationship between managers and employees—conflicting interests should be identified and addressed through appropriate mechanisms. Australia's system of industrial relations has a history dating back before Federation in 1901. The pre-Federation colonies already had conciliation and arbitration courts established to reduce industrial conflict, and all states except Victoria retain their own systems today, each with its own characteristics. The set of arbitration and conciliation institutions at Commonwealth and state levels has provided a legal framework within which employers and unions can negotiate, while industrial courts possess the power to reach judgments on pay and conditions that are legally binding on employers, employees, unions, and employer associations.

The industrial relations system has been based historically on a variety of industrial awards, which stipulate the wages and conditions (including such items as sick leave, long service leave, and the pay rates for different levels) that apply to employees within a specific industry. Over-award payments—as the name suggests, pay rates higher than those stipulated in the award—traditionally were reached through direct negotiation between employers and unions, with no involvement by industrial tribunals.

The process of establishing or varying an award consists of the union serving a log of claims on one or more employers—the log covers all employees, employers, and employer associations to be covered by the award. The serving of the log and its total or partial rejection by the employer creates an industrial dispute, which may be either active or only on paper. At this point, the relevant industrial tribunal must assess whether it can legally intervene, in order to set in motion the process of conciliation and arbitration whereby advice is given and a decision arrived at through mediation by a third party. The aim of the industrial tribunal is to achieve a settlement between employers and unions, leading to a new award and normally conducted through a combination of negotiation, conciliation, and arbitration.

The Commonwealth Court of Conciliation and Arbitration was established in 1904 to deal with issues relevant to more than one state. It was given the duty to resolve industrial disputes through the setting of legal wage rates and working conditions for different industries and jobs. The Commonwealth system's authority is drawn from section 51 of the Constitution, whereby the Federal Parliament is entitled to pass legislation 'for the prevention and settlement of industrial disputes extending beyond the limit of any one State'. The state systems, though, are based on specific pieces of legislation passed by their respective parliaments.

The Commonwealth system's mandate also required the court to make judgments on a broad range of social and economic issues, most importantly the extent to which fluctuations in market demand and the profitability of individual firms should be permitted to govern wages and working conditions. The most significant expression of this role has been the concept of a 'living wage', given its first legal foundation by Justice Higgins (second president of the Commonwealth Conciliation and Arbitration Court). In his 'Harvester Judgment' of 1907 (so called after the machinery made by the agricultural implement manufacturer in the legal case, H. V. McKay), he maintained that a company's 'capacity to pay' did not provide an adequate basis for setting wages. According to Higgins, enterprises unable to pay workers a living wage should be abandoned.

Justice Higgins saw individual bargaining between employer and employee as inherently unequal, and the purpose of the conciliation and arbitration system was to provide, in conjunction with union participation, greater balance to the employer–employee relationship. Unions were recognised until recent years as the sole legal bargaining agent for workers in particular industries or sectors, but it was seen as appropriate to extend award rates and conditions to workers who were themselves non-unionised. Therefore, non-unionists have received the same improvements in their pay and conditions as have unionists, thereby gaining from the industrial relations role of unions (some call this the 'free-rider' effect). More significantly, the system has protected workers whose employment status places them in the weakest bargaining positions. This includes people who have less marketable skills, who are employed in part-time or casual work, and who are in organisations or industries with low rates of union membership.

The Harvester judgment set not only a basic wage, but also a secondary wage, awarded according to skills and qualifications. This secondary wage included a work value component and a comparative component, to ensure that comparable work in different industries was paid at roughly equivalent rates, according to the principle of comparative wage justice (CWJ). For Higgins, wages should depend not on an individual employer's capacity to pay, but on the capacity of the entire industry and the national economy to pay, and he further stipulated that there must be a basic minimum beneath which wages should not be allowed to fall. This approach to industrial relations is based upon the principle that the worker's needs should take precedence over labour market supply and demand. Yet the implementation of this principle also meant that wages should not rise just because a company had become more profitable. Legislative intervention, therefore, installed limits to both the minimum and the maximum wage levels, reducing market-based fluctuations. Higgins set in place a two-tier model of wage fixation: wages should comprise the 'basic' wage plus a 'secondary' component, recognising skills and qualifications. Only the latter, the secondary wage, was intended to be the focus of bargaining.

Legal precedents and judgments such as Harvester and the conciliation and arbitration system itself have been a focus of intense debate throughout much of Australia's history. The system's opponents have come from both the right and the left of the political spectrum. Right-wing critics have generally attacked what they perceive as the system's rigidity and the undue legitimacy given to unions. They argue that it constitutes an illegitimate interference with market mechanisms and leads to 'excessive' wage rises. People on the left have also criticised the arbitration and conciliation system, albeit for different reasons than the right. They have often said that it 'integrates' workers, against their own long-term interest, because it effectively defuses the basic conflict between capital and labour, which they see as being at the heart of industrial capitalism. Both of these arguments share an ideological rejection of the 'corporatist' aspects of the conciliation and arbitration system, through which the representative institutions of labour, capital, and government are organised and judgments on wages and conditions are made centrally. There again, political supporters of the conciliation and arbitration system have argued for its capacity to limit industrial disputes. They draw attention to its fairness and effectiveness in achieving either negotiated outcomes or reasonable decisions that have the significant merit of being in keeping with national policy goals, such as the control of inflation.

The tension between two conflicting principles—employee needs and employer capacity to pay—has characterised the industrial relations history of wage fixation. For example, during the Great Depression, the 1931 basic wage decision reduced the basic wage by 10 per cent and the cut was not restored until 1934. Tribunal decisions have always had to take account of the national and international economic environment, and the impact of wage decisions on such areas as employment and unemployment, productivity, and international competitiveness. Governments have frequently been critical of the industrial relations process, since they are also major employers in addition to being accountable for the socio-economic impact of collective decisions on wages and conditions. On numerous occasions, the industrial courts have found themselves coming into conflict with governments. This has been acrimonious at times—the Bruce–Paige Nationalist government, in 1929, went so far as to seek the abolition of the entire system: an attempt that eventually led to a split in the government and contributed to its subsequent electoral defeat.

Australia's industrial relations system, then, has had as its primary goal the minimisation of industrial conflict. Industrial conflicts usually have multiple causes, ranging from cyclical variations in the international economy down to interpersonal disputes. The absence of conflict need not, however, indicate the absence of serious grievances in the employment relationship. In organisations and societies, open conflict only occurs from time to time and its visible signs are less apparent whenever people, feeling powerless to change anything, retreat into apathy or begrudging acquiescence. Overt conflict can take various forms, such as work-ins by employees, or lock-outs by employers. Strikes, though, are the most common and highly publicised form of industrial conflict.

Strikes are usually organised by unions, although 'wildcat' strikes are conducted without official union endorsement. They can be indefinite (some have lasted for years) or for a fixed period, for example, a 24-hour stoppage. Strikes may not affect an entire enterprise at one time: 'rolling' strikes may occur in one part of an organisation one day, and in another the next. Unions usually will conduct pickets in support of their strike action, to discourage other employees from crossing picket lines. While strikes typically generate a great deal of media publicity and are presented as an indication of 'union power', in terms of days lost at work, they are invariably less significant than losses due to other causes, such as workplace-related accidents and sickness. It is not necessarily the case that strikes are a demonstration of union power; indeed, they may indicate a relative lack of power, whereby the union has been unable to achieve its goals through less dramatic means, such as negotiation or consultation. Industrial action is usually action of a last resort, and rarely taken without consideration of its potentially adverse consequences.

Trade unions are more than simply industrial bargaining agents; they have also been politically active. Unions in Australia vary widely in their histories, traditions, political affiliations, organisational structures, memberships, and industrial strategies. There are four main types of union: industry unions, which are active only in a specific industry and cover the great majority of workers in that industry;

craft unions, based on the apprenticeship system and governing entry to the craft and to union membership (for example, carpenters); occupational unions, drawing their membership from a particular occupation (for example, clerks); and general unions, where the membership comes from a variety of industries and occupations. Some writers would also include a fifth type, 'house' (company or enterprise) unions. These unions are often established by employers to prevent the growth of more genuine union membership and are frequently referred to as 'boss's unions'.

Unions are usually led by a president and a secretary, with the latter in most cases wielding the greatest power. Often presidents are not full-time union officials, whereas secretaries invariably are. The peak union body in Australia, the Australian Council of Trade Unions (ACTU), was formed in 1927. It is based in state branches usually known as trades and labour councils. The ACTU Congress is the main policy-making forum of the Australian union movement and meets every two years. Responsibility for administering policies lies with the ACTU executive, headed by a president and a secretary. Not all Australian unions are affiliated with the ACTU. Likewise, although there have always been close links between the union movement and the Australian Labor Party (ALP), not all unions are affiliated with the ALP. The relationship between the 'political' and 'industrial' wings of the labour movement has often been strained, but has always been an important influence upon industrial relations activities and outcomes. In the next section, we examine how this relationship has shaped much of the contemporary industrial relations environment.

2 The Accord and the changing role of unions

As we saw in chapter 2, conservative and social democratic governments in the English-speaking nations have implemented economic rationalist policy programs, including privatisation, as well as the deregulation and decentralisation of industrial relations. In Australia, this process has occurred at a relatively moderate pace, in comparison to New Zealand, for example, where a process of wholesale privatisation, deregulation, and decentralisation was introduced. The relatively gradual nature of change in Australia may be attributed largely to two factors.

First, Australia's political system has acted, to a considerable extent, as a brake on rapid legislative change. Unlike New Zealand, Australia has a federal political structure, consisting of Commonwealth, state and local governments, with a Westminster-style parliamentary system. The Commonwealth and state parliaments (with the exception of Queensland) are bicameral (they have two houses): at the Commonwealth level these are the House of Representatives and the Senate. The Australian Capital Territory and the Northern Territory also have their own governments, but with lesser powers than the states. The Constitution established a division of powers between the Commonwealth and the states, but their respective powers have evolved over the years. In comparison to the USA, Australia's political and industrial relations processes are characterised by relatively 'strong' federalism, and in most disputes between the Commonwealth and the states, including industrial relations, it is the central authority of the Commonwealth that has been dominant.

Second, the Accord between the ACTU and the Labor government from 1983 to 1996 meant that the union movement had a considerable say in governmental decision making, particularly with respect to labour market policies. Consequently, Australia developed during this period a more measured process of decentralisation and deregulation than did other English-speaking nations. Industrial relations, pay, and working conditions in Australia during the lengthy period of ALP federal government were dominated by the Accord.

The government consistently sought to stand on the achievements of the Accord, which they claimed had provided economic progress and industrial stability in difficult times. These achievements included: an increase in jobs growth; protection for low-wage earners; a rise in the 'social wage' (that is, the social goods and services accessible to all citizens, such as health services); important tax reforms; and the introduction of employer-funded superannuation to employees who had never been covered by superannuation schemes. The language of the Accord, which went through several, decreasingly ambitious versions, promoted the idea of national responsibility over sectional demands (especially those of employers and employees) and promoted coherent policy formation instead of leaving issues to be resolved by the arbitrariness of the market.

The original Accord agreement, established in February 1983, was made possible only through a significant change in the political and industrial positions adopted by the ACTU. Much of the union movement at that time had come to acknowledge that unions generally had a poor public image and that they were often the first political and media scapegoats for industrial and economic problems. They recognised that many workers were unconvinced of the real value of union membership and sought to arrest the decline in the proportion of Australian workers who were union members (union density).

Several factors have been identified as contributing to declining union density. Employment has become characterised by increasing proportions of part-time and casual workers, and society is more influenced by individualist values than the collective identity forged through unionism. The decline in male employment and increase in female jobs combined with reductions in full-time employment have also coincided with declining union membership. Notably, growth of the service sector has not compensated for the erosion of numbers of employees in the traditionally strong union areas of mining and manufacturing. Alongside these structural changes in employment, decline in union membership has been exacerbated by extensive outsourcing, downsizing, and privatisation.[2]

The ACTU also was aware that there had been significant growth in support for 'New Right' anti-union policies in the Liberal and National parties, which were supported by the explicitly anti-union practices of some employers. Consequently, the ACTU and several key unions sought to forge a new role for the union movement, whereby unions were to be concerned with broader issues than simply the pursuit of better wages and conditions for their members. This meant a movement into the arena of public policy formation, in which the ACTU sought to contribute to a wide range of issues, including employment, wages, industry, training, and education policies.

The Accord was based on an explicit commitment by the ACTU to subordinate short-term objectives (most significantly, higher wages and better conditions of work) to the goal of long-term, national economic competitiveness. Two fundamental assumptions underpinned this approach: first, that the most important of all political issues is management and control of the economy; second, that the single most important economic relation in any modern capitalist society is between labour and capital. It was agreed that in order to achieve international competitiveness, sustained growth and long-term socioeconomic goals such as full employment, the key actors—government, business, and unions—would have to work together more cooperatively.

The overall impetus of the Accord, therefore, was a move by the Australian trade union movement into the political arena by pursuing a broadly *corporatist* framework and approach. Policy decisions were to be made through tripartite debate and consultation between government, business, and union bodies. The theoretical and strategic inspiration behind this shift was that of 'political unionism' largely derived from the 'Swedish model' of social democratic reform, as propounded in the joint ACTU–Trade Development Commission publication, *Australia Reconstructed*.[3] Political unionism is intended to increase participation of the labour movement in economic and industrial policy formation and its implementation is seen as leading to an overall democratisation of the economy. Improvements in wages and conditions were presented as being dependent on achieving continuous increases in national industrial competitiveness. Hence, it was agreed that unions and governments should be committed to this new corporatist responsibility as an overarching goal, while recognising that there would always be conflicting interests among the key actors. For 'political' or 'strategic' unionism, as opposed to a more directly confrontational form of unionism, 'responsibility' in the name of national goals became the priority, as voiced in a speech in 1989 to business leaders by the then ACTU secretary, Bill Kelty:

> Now unions can make change. They must make change ultimately on the basis of what is good for this nation. Unions are democratic, in my judgment, vehicles of change. But as an exercise in authority and an exercise in responsibility, their ultimate survival depends upon their capacity to take into account the national interest. You cannot have the best of both worlds. You cannot pretend to be large and important, having widespread authority and commitment, and then on the other hand, only exercise authority and responsibility on a short-term, ad hoc, self-interested basis for a small group of people.[4]

This 'political' or 'strategic' unionism emerged as an attempt to find a 'third way' between the traditional political alternatives of liberal capitalism and state socialism. As one of many initiatives that have gone under the 'third way' title, it is worthwhile considering further its heritage.[5] In Sweden, long periods of social democratic government in alliance with the trade union movement produced, at least up until the 1990s, high standards of living, low inflation and virtually full employment, even in periods of low economic growth.

These outcomes were achieved through labour market programs and industry policies designed to maintain full employment and developed through negotiations involving mainly unions and employer groups. The main objective was a decommodification of the economy through the assertion of social democratic principles countering those of the market. Social goods and services that were formerly bought and sold as commodities were to be progressively transformed into citizenship rights. Thus, the 'social wage' was expanded and public need, rather than private capital accumulation, progressively became the dominant form of allocation. A related aspect of this 'third way' in its application to Australian industrial relations strategy was the ACTU's process of union amalgamations initiated in the late 1980s, with the goal of achieving a much smaller number of larger, better resourced, more efficient unions. This strategy has been successful insofar as the top twenty unions now account for around 85 per cent of all union members.[6] The union movement, however, was less successful in arresting the decline in union density. The overall number and proportion of Australian employees who reported being trade union members in their main job declined during the 1980s, and continued to fall during the subsequent decade, from 35 per cent in August 1992 to 24.7 per cent in August 2000, as indicated in tables 3.1 and 3.2.[7]

Table 3.1 Trade union members, total numbers ('000)

	1994	1996	1998	2000
Male	1375.8	1307.5	1188.9	1095.0
Female	907.5	886.8	848.5	806.7
Total	2283.4	2194.3	2037.5	1901.8

Yearly figures for August

Source: ABS, *Employee Earnings, Benefits and Trade Union Membership, Australia*, cat. no. 6310.0 (August 2000), p. 35. ABS data used with permission from the Australian Bureau of Statistics. www.abs.gov.au

Table 3.2 Trade union members, percentage of total employees

	1994	1996	1998	2000
Male	37.9	33.5	30.0	26.3
Female	31.3	28.1	25.8	22.8
Overall	35.0	31.1	28.1	24.7

Yearly figures for August

Source: ABS, *Employee Earnings, Benefits and Trade Union Membership, Australia*, cat. no. 6310.0 (August 2000), p. 35. ABS data used with permission from the Australian Bureau of Statistics. www.abs.gov.au

The original Accord agreement was a very ambitious document. With respect to wages, prices, and incomes, its main principles were that:

- Policies should aim to ensure that living standards of wage and salary earners and non-income-earning sectors of the population requiring protection are maintained and over time increased with improvements in national productivity.
- Government policy should be applied to prices and all income groups, rather than, as has often been the case, to wages alone.
- The policies should be designed to bring about an equitable and clearly discernible redistribution of income.
- There must be continuous consultation and cooperation between the parties involved.
- Government policy at all levels should be accommodating and supportive.

Prices and incomes policies were a critical aspect of the Accord's overall strategy. Whereas in an ideal free market, wages theoretically should fall with a rise in unemployment, and prices theoretically should fall with a decline in demand, this rarely occurs. For example, companies with a market monopoly can simply absorb wage rises by increasing prices. Similarly, strong unions can maintain the level of their members' wages even though market demand for their labour may have slackened. A basic premise of the original Accord, therefore, was that prices and incomes policies were required to combat the inadequacies of market mechanisms.

However, the Commonwealth government lacked the constitutional power to control prices and non-wage incomes. A referendum introduced by the Hawke government to extend the Commonwealth's powers in this area was unsuccessful, and the Accord had no impact on people whose incomes were not governed by the industrial relations system. For example, the salaries of corporate executives continued to increase at around twice the rate of the average wage—a phenomenon that has become widespread across the developed economies, particularly in the USA.[8] One of the greater ironies of the past two decades is that increasing competition has appeared to demand the lowest labour costs but the highest management costs, substantially increasing the gap between highest and the lowest paid.

Wage increases fell behind the rate of inflation during the period in which the ALP was in government, as it negotiated from 1986 onwards the 'discounting' of wage increases to less than full indexation in keeping with growth in the consumer price index (CPI). Productivity was introduced as a major item for justifying wage increases. Non-wage increases were primarily provided through superannuation contributions by employers. 'Wage–tax trade-offs' were agreed and a two-tiered system of wage bargaining reintroduced. Real wages declined in value and profits grew considerably in relation to wages. The government's main argument, though, was that average family incomes had grown with the expansion of the labour force, in particular the increasing participation of women.

The failure of the Accord to produce much more than restraint on wages meant that wage and salary earners bore the bulk of the sacrifices demanded in the name of serving the national interest. While the Accord gave the trade union movement, through the ACTU, some say on key issues of economic policy, it did not mean that the objectives of 'political unionism' were achieved to any significant degree. In contrast to the situation that had prevailed in Sweden until the early 1990s, the ACTU was very much the junior partner in the agreement with the Labor government, which concentrated on 'efficient economic management' and retaining power over decision-making processes and policies. The Accord's main objectives were diluted over time, with subsequent versions of the agreement. Nonetheless, there were some achievements in terms of increasing the 'social wage'—that is, a process of decommodification, whereby access to social goods and services became more firmly a citizenship right. For example, the establishment of Medicare increased publicly funded access to health, although in another area, higher education, the introduction of the Higher Education Contribution Scheme, fee-paying courses, and private universities was a move towards more market-based access and allocation. The process of union involvement was also significant, particularly in that it led to the creation of tripartite (government–unions–business) institutions of decision making on economic and industry policy, such as industry councils.[9]

With the election in March 1996 of the Liberal–National coalition government led by John Howard, the Accord was effectively relegated to the status of a historical document, with debate continuing as to its effectiveness in achieving economic internationalisation, industrial stability, and steady growth. The Howard government sought to establish a more market-based system involving less government intervention, a greatly reduced role for trade unions, and decentralisation and deregulation of industrial relations. The *Workplace Relations Act 1996* was the first major legislative outcome of the Howard government's agenda.

3 Industrial relations in Australia: the present situation

The Workplace Relations Act had a lengthy gestation period, dominated largely by the rise of 'New Right' policies and the demands of many employers for greater flexibility and reassertion of the managerial prerogative. Numerous employers, business associations, and the Liberal Party saw New Zealand's *Employment Contracts Act 1991* as the kind of legislation that should be introduced. Commentators and interest groups from many perspectives viewed the arrangement in New Zealand as an example of what may eventuate in Australia, including individual employment contracts and a diminished role for trade unions.

New Zealand's Employment Contracts Act had swept away an industrial relations system that shared strong historical affinities with the system in Australia. In fact, the early development of Australian industrial relations had been strongly influenced by New Zealand's approach. The Act precipitated a significant decline in union membership and collective bargaining in New Zealand, as the incidence of individual contracts and hybrid collective/individual contracts grew. The impact of New Zealand's Employment Contracts Act has been particularly severe on the most vulnerable workers.[10]

At the state level, Liberal-led governments in Victoria (1992) and Western Australia (1993) introduced industrial relations changes that permitted individual agreements.[11] Mining industry employers were at the forefront of attempts to de-unionise their workforces through the use of individual agreements. For example, in 1993 the multinational mining corporation CRA introduced a tactic that it had previously implemented in its New Zealand operations, signing up the majority of its employees on individual contracts, including agreements for short-term wage increases conditional on employees forfeiting their rights to union representation. The ACTU mounted a campaign that eventually led to the Australian Industrial Relations Commission (AIRC) declaring CRA's action contrary to Australian law. Despite this declaration, the tactic of signing up employees on individual contracts, conditional on forfeiting union representation, has subsequently become commonplace in the mining industry. The legality of a similar tactic employed by BHP in Western Australia was upheld by the Federal Court in January 2001.

Under the leadership of John Hewson, the Liberal–National coalition launched its radical *Jobsback!* platform before the 1993 federal election. This was a set of proposals closely resembling New Zealand's Employment Contracts Act, calling for the virtual abolition of awards and a rapid introduction of individual agreements. However, the Labor Party, led by Paul Keating, won a surprise victory, and on re-election implemented the *Industrial Relations Reform Act 1993*. Mindful of the need to retain ACTU support and the complexities of Australia's combination of state and federal industrial relations jurisdictions, the Keating government adopted a more measured approach to industrial relations reform. Under the structural efficiency principle and the process of award restructuring during the second half of the 1980s, awards had already been simplified and the enterprise flexibility agreements (EFAs) introduced by the Labor government in 1993 permitted non-union agreements. The new Act reduced the role of the AIRC and encouraged enterprise bargaining. Decentralisation and deregulation of Australian industrial relations, therefore, were initiated under the Accord.

The coalition revised its industrial relations platform for the 1996 federal election. Awards and the AIRC would be retained, albeit with reduced authority, and the application of a 'no disadvantage' test would ostensibly ensure that no worker would be disadvantaged in agreements with respect to the relevant industrial award.[12] Following its election victory in March 1996, the coalition introduced its Workplace Relations and Other Legislation Amendment Bill to Parliament. Although the Bill easily passed through the House of Representatives, where the government enjoyed a large majority, it was only able to pass through the Senate with the support of the Australian Democrats, following negotiations between Workplace Relations Minister, Peter Reith, and then Democrats' leader, Cheryl Kernot. The negotiations led to certain changes being made. These included the removal of a provision to give state industrial awards precedence over federal awards, the addition of some allowable matters, and the abandonment of a clause encouraging 'competitive unionism', which would have increased competition between unions for members.

The *Workplace Relations Act 1996* constituted the single most important impetus for the implementation of unitarist HRM in Australian organisations, considerably increasing the opportunities for employers to achieve non-unionised workforces and to reassert managerial prerogative. The Act's main rationale was that direct negotiations between employers and employees would lead to more effective working relationships. Encouraging greater labour market flexibility was seen as a stepping-stone to the generation of greater productivity, efficiency, and international competitiveness. Decentralised bargaining, according to the government, would enable employers and employees to make decisions on pay, conditions, and working relationships more immediately suited to their individual workplaces, without any need for union involvement.

The 1996 Act effectively reduced the federal award system to a 'safety net' for Australia's lowest paid workers. The *Industrial Relations Reform Act 1993* had already relaxed the AIRC's power to regulate certified agreements, and the Workplace Relations Act loosened it further. Although the AIRC retained a regulatory role, its powers to make and vary awards were confined to twenty 'allowable matters'. The Workplace Relations Act created greater opportunities for non-union agreements (known as the 'valid majority' provision), industrial action was less protected than previously, and it removed entitlements on minimum wages and family leave provided by the 1993 Act. The AIRC still retained the power to hand down increases in the 'safety net' minimum wage. In national wage cases, the ACTU puts forward an ambit claim, employer associations and the government propose what they consider to be a reasonable increase (if any), and the Commission (AIRC) issues a judgment. Although in the past two decades the AIRC has formally rejected the principle of comparative wage justice (CWJ), it has nonetheless accepted the concept of minimum award wage rates adjustment, as proposed by the ACTU, giving CWJ continuing application.[13]

Increases in the minimum wage are particularly important to employees in low-wage industries, such as hospitality and agriculture.[14] Many of these employees are part of the 'working poor'. Since awards have been reduced to a 'safety net', workers reliant only on award wages—just under 25 per cent of all workers in 2000—have fallen behind those who have achieved pay increases through bargaining agreements (approximately $200 per week less on average). In 2000, female workers (31 per cent) were almost twice as likely as male workers (17 per cent) to occupy the award-dependent category, and considerably more part-time (41 per cent) than full-time (15 per cent) workers were award-dependent.[15]

The Act's main innovation was the introduction of Australian Workplace Agreements (AWAs), contracts that override federal awards and can be negotiated by employers with a group of employees or a single employee. In all states except Victoria, only those employers that are constitutional corporations can register AWAs. However, in Victoria, all employers can enter into AWAs, since that state ceded its industrial relations powers to the federal government. As of 12 March 1997, employers and employees could nominate in writing a bargaining agent to act on their behalf, and the other party must recognise that agent.

The Act established a new agency, the Office of the Employment Advocate (OEA), to oversee and ratify AWAs. The agreements must satisfy a 'no disadvantage' test and include statutory anti-discrimination and dispute-resolution clauses. If these are absent, they are routinely inserted by the OEA. The employee must receive a copy of the AWA before signing it (five days for new employees, fourteen days for existing employees), the employer must explain to the employee, between receipt and signature, the effect of the AWA, and the employee must genuinely consent to the AWA. Then, an AWA on the same terms must be offered to 'comparable employees', unless a failure to do so was not unfair or unreasonable.[16]

The OEA is obliged to reject the AWA if it fails to meet these criteria. However, if the OEA has concerns about the 'no disadvantage' test, but these are resolved by a written undertaking from the employer or action by the parties, it must pass the AWA. The 'no disadvantage' test is also 'global', rather than line-by-line. Therefore, while an AWA may disadvantage an employee in relation to the relevant award on one point (for example, pay rates), this may be 'compensated' for in another area (for example, hours flexibility).[17] If the OEA has unresolved concerns about an AWA, it must be referred to the AIRC, whereupon either party may withdraw it. The AIRC, if satisfied that the AWA passes the 'no disadvantage' test, must then approve it. If any concerns are resolved by an employer's written undertaking or other action, then again the commission is obliged to approve the AWA. An AWA may even be passed if it fails this test so long as the AIRC decides it is not contrary to the 'public interest'. A possible situation for approval would be where an employer is introducing an AWA as part of a cost-cutting strategy to deal with a short-term business crisis.

AWAs pose certain problems from the perspective of a strategic approach to HRM. Genuine individual bargaining can be very time consuming, and there is considerable evidence that the transaction costs of individual negotiations are too high to be viable for most employers.[18] Further, individual bargaining fosters an individualist philosophy, which may be incompatible with collective endeavours, including several strategies advocated by strategic approaches to HRM, for example, team-based work.[19] Due to the provision that similar terms and conditions must be offered to employees in similar positions, there is, though, limited potential for major differences to emerge between individual employees.[20]

Enterprise bargaining agreements or certified agreements (CAs) continued in the Workplace Relations Act, in revised form, under five main categories:

1. CAs with one or more unions at a workplace.
2. CAs with a 'valid majority' of employees at a workplace (a non-union agreement, similar to the EFAs of the previous Act).
3. CAs at new ('greenfield') sites where business has not yet begun, with one or more trade unions possessing rights to represent future employees.
4. Employer–union CAs to settle an industrial dispute or prevent a possible industrial dispute arising.
5. CAs covering more than one employer—these must satisfy special conditions.[21]

The 1998 waterfront dispute provided the first major test of strength between, on one hand, the government and anti-union employers, and on the other, the union movement. The direct participants in the dispute were, on the one side, the Maritime Union of Australia (MUA), aided by the ACTU and (less vigorously) the ALP, and, on the other, Patrick Stevedores, with the support of the Howard government and the National Farmers Federation. The waterfront, in Australia as in other countries, has always been a key arena of industrial conflict. In Australia, Patrick's and P&O Ports Australia hold a virtual duopoly, with over 90 per cent of the market. The dispute was part of the government's broad agenda to replace awards and union agreements with individual contracts, and was integral to its campaign to accelerate waterfront 'reform' by attacking one of the country's most militant unions.

The government and Patrick's acted together to devise a plan to dismiss the entire workforce and replace it, through a complex corporate restructuring, with non-unionised workers, whereby an ostensibly 'new' company would hire the non-union workforce, to be trained in Dubai. All employees were transferred to four labour-hire companies, and their services could be terminated without notice on the pretext of an interference or delay in the provision of those services. The company locked out its former MUA employees, precipitating a month-long confrontation that was eventually settled through the courts. The Federal Court and the High Court both found that the company had breached the Workplace Relations Act and had conspired unlawfully to replace their workforce with non-union labour. The outcome was that the original employees returned to their jobs and an enterprise agreement was negotiated, in which agreement was reached on a considerable number of redundancies. The MUA ironically benefited from the guarantees on freedom of association provided in the Workplace Relations Act, despite its generally anti-union character. While the Act guarantees the rights of individuals not to belong to a union, it also strengthens their rights to belong to the union of their choice.[22]

The Workplace Relations Act constituted only the 'first wave' of the coalition government's industrial relations agenda.[23] However, as the coalition was returned to office in 1998 with a considerably reduced majority in the House of Representatives and still no majority in the Senate, and is unlikely to have one in the foreseeable future, the unleashing of the 'second wave' was made more difficult. Indeed, when Peter Reith was replaced as Workplace Relations Minister by Tony Abbott in late 2000, Reith expressed frustration with the impediments he had faced in trying to implement industrial relations change. It is clear that with the decentralisation of industrial relations, negotiation processes and skills have become increasingly important, especially at the level of the enterprise. In the case study for this chapter, we discuss negotiation strategies relevant to managers, union representatives, and employees who have had to become more involved in negotiations on such issues as pay, working conditions, job design, recruitment, organisational change, and various conflicts.

The practical test of the Workplace Relations Act's more radical innovations, particularly AWAs, will be found in how frequently they are used and the outcomes they produce. There is evidence that many employers (including major employer organisations) have not been particularly enthusiastic about them, and the outcomes they have achieved have generally been less beneficial for employees than have either awards or enterprise agreements. In practice, the emphasis in AWAs has been on 'hard' rather than 'soft' HRM outcomes. In particular, they have been characterised by an increase in both the span and in the number of hours that employees have to work.[24] Many employees have had limited ability to balance work, family, and other areas of their lives due to working longer hours.[25] This is in contrast to the situation in some European countries, most notably France, where legislation was passed in 1998 and 2000 establishing the official 35-hour week, with any extra hours to be included as overtime.[26] This issue is likely to be of growing importance in coming years, as indicated by the ACTU's reasonable hours campaign. This led to the Australian Industrial Relations Commission commencing a test case in November 2001, to decide on whether or not there should be an award benchmark to limit the number of hours employees should reasonably be expected to work.

The impetus of recent industrial relations reforms in Australia has been towards a system that is both less centralised and less regulated. The relationship between employers and employees has changed from industrial legislation and protection towards a situation in which employers and employees, either collectively or individually, negotiate agreements more directly.[27] The re-election of the Howard coalition government for a third term in November 2001 means that the pressures for further decentralisation and deregulation will continue, although the government still lacks a Senate majority.

Summary

In this chapter, we discussed the history of industrial relations in Australia. We looked at the distinctive characteristics of Australian industrial relations, including the role of trade unions, the set of conciliation and arbitration institutions at Commonwealth and state levels, and the system of industrial awards. We saw how certain debates have characterised Australia's industrial relations history, particularly the extent to which fluctuations in demand and the profitability of individual firms should be allowed to determine wages and conditions, or should be governed by socially agreed expectations of a 'living wage'.

As we went on to examine Australian industrial relations over the past two decades, we noticed the strong influence of the processes of internationalisation considered in chapter 2, particularly in relation to demands for greater productivity and more flexible work practices. We outlined how these objectives were sought during the period of the ALP–ACTU Accord, as industrial relations moved away from centralised wage fixation to a more decentralised, deregulated environment. The trade union movement played a significant part in this process, as it sought to respond, through 'political' or 'strategic' unionism, to the problems of declining density and 'New Right' anti-union policies. The chapter then illustrated how, with the election of the Howard coalition government in 1996, a more rapid process of decentralisation and deregulation was foreshadowed, although the coalition's industrial relations changes have been considerably less dramatic than the government had originally planned. We assessed the impact of the *Workplace Relations Act 1996*, with a particular focus on its most significant innovation, Australian Workplace Agreements, and the major industrial dispute between Patrick Stevedores and the Maritime Union of Australia. This dispute was finally settled in the Federal Court. In the following chapter, we look specifically at the area of Australian labour law and how it regulates relationships in the workplace.

BOX 3.1

Case study—Unionisation in the retail industry

Background
Employees join unions for a variety of reasons. These may include the legal protection or the various services that unions offer, the role that unions play in negotiating improved pay and working conditions, and a commitment to collective solidarity with other employees. The level of union membership within specific workplaces can fluctuate considerably over time, according to a variety of factors, such as the effectiveness of union representation, the composition and concerns of the workforce, and the strategies adopted by management.

Digby's is a large suburban retail store, with a high profile in the local area. Until the mid-1990s, the level of union membership was quite high, more than 55 per cent in 1994. At that time, the workforce consisted mostly of full-time employees. However, since a deregulation of retail trading hours, allowing the store to open during evenings and on Sundays, a larger proportion of the workforce has comprised part-time staff (mainly women with young children) and casual staff (mainly school and university students). Each of these groups works predominantly on evenings and at weekends. At present, there are 90 full-time employees, of whom 42 are union members, 65 part-timers, of whom 22 are union members, and 51 casual staff, only five of whom are union members.

Role play

Roles
1 You are Lisa Donataccio, the store's union delegate. On the suggestion of the union's central office, you have commenced a membership drive. Your recruitment activities are conducted in your own free time, although you have the support of a full-time union official who visits for approximately one hour each fortnight. How would you find out what are the main concerns of the employees? What arguments would you use to encourage union members to remain members and become more active, and to encourage non-members to join? Given that you have limited time and resources, should you concentrate your efforts on a specific section of the workforce—on full time, part-time or casual staff?

2 You are Jane Pearson, a part-time employee (averaging 20 hours per week) in the same store. Your take-home weekly pay is $245 on average, and your partner, who also works part-time, has a take-home pay of around $350 per week. You are a non-union member, having let your membership lapse two

years ago—largely because, with two children under five to support, you find it difficult to justify paying the annual union dues of $270. You are approached by the store's union delegate, who asks you how the union might encourage you to rejoin. What concerns would be most important to you in reaching a decision on whether or not to rejoin?

3   *You are Wayne Sharp, the store's HR manager, a position you have held since 1999. Your predecessor, Dave Smith, the store's personnel manager for the previous two decades, had a 'live and let live' policy towards the union and consulted quite regularly on employment issues. However, you feel that a stronger union presence is unnecessary if appropriate HRM strategies are adopted. The store's senior management is also reluctant to see a stronger union presence. You have been informed by an employee that the union is conducting a membership drive. Although you have a good personal relationship with Lisa Donataccio, you are apprehensive about increased union membership. How would you respond? What tactics and arguments would you use to discourage increased union membership among the different sections of the workforce (full-time, part-time and casual)?*

Negotiation exercise 1 (see Brief notes on negotiation skills, pp. 67–69)
Role-play a meeting between Lisa Donataccio and Jane Pearson in which Lisa seeks to persuade Jane to rejoin.

Negotiation exercise 2
Two weeks later, a meeting has been arranged between Lisa Donataccio and Wayne Sharp to discuss the union's membership drive and the response of management. The membership drive has met with some success and appears to be gathering momentum, particularly among casual staff, 27 of whom are now union members, while a further three full-time and five part-time staff have joined. Lisa Donataccio has raised the issue that the union should be more directly involved in the store's strategic decision-making, and that she should be entitled to seven hours' paid time-off per week, with office space, to work on union business.

Wayne Sharp is concerned that the union is seeking an excessive role in company affairs, using its increased numbers as a bargaining tool, and that conceding to Lisa Donataccio's demands would indicate weakness on the store's part and possibly lead to further demands.

In pairs, you should seek to negotiate, in the respective roles of Lisa Donataccio and Wayne Sharp, on the union's future role within the store. Negotiation will require you to decide whether you adopt an aggressive or cooperative approach, and determine which issues are most crucial to you. The purpose of the meeting from Wayne Sharp's perspective is to reach agreement on the future role of the union and the entitlements that the store is prepared to extend to the union and to Ms Donataccio. If the negotiations break down, both parties should have alternative plans available.

Brief notes on negotiation skills

Negotiation provides a framework within which parties bargain to reach resolution of disputes.[28] There are two main approaches to bargaining. First, there is distributive bargaining ('win/lose') and second, there is integrative bargaining ('win/win'). A third approach is sometimes mentioned, called the 'accommodative' approach. However, in practice this means little more than one party capitulating by accommodating to the demands of the other party, and so it is not explored further here.

In the distributive approach to bargaining, which is very much the traditional image of industrial negotiation, the goals of one party are usually in direct conflict with those of the other. Resources are fixed (for example, in a dispute over wage levels), and each party attempts to maximise its share of resources at the expense of the other. For each party, information is critical and they may use misinformation to undermine the position of the other. This means that the distributive approach carries significant dangers—for example, it is often inappropriate to the maintenance of long-term working relationships. There are some key concepts in the distributive approach to bargaining, which can be summarised as follows:

- The *target point* (TP) is your optimal goal, where you would like the bargaining process to lead (for example, in a wage claim, a pay increase of 10 per cent). In the first round of distributive bargaining, sellers have reason to offer a price higher than their TP whereas buyers will tend to make offers lower than their TP. This can allow considerable room for concessions.
- The *resistance point* (RP) is your bottom line, which you are not prepared to go below (for example, a pay increase of only 3 per cent).
- The *asking price* (the seller's initial demand—for example, the initial union demand in a pay negotiation).
- The *initial offer* (the buyer's initial offer—for example, the initial management offer in a pay negotiation).
- The distance between the respective RPs (bottom lines) of buyer and seller is referred to as the *bargaining range* (BR)—the settlement range or zone of potential agreement.
- The *best alternative to a negotiated agreement* (known as 'BATNA') is your alternative plan, allowing you to walk away should negotiations break down. Also, there will often be games of bluff and double-bluff, for example, making a show of walking away in the hope that the other party will concede.
- The *settlement point* is one that both parties are prepared to accept, perhaps reluctantly.
- The *bargaining mix* is the combination of items and issues that are up for negotiation. When the buyer's RP is *above* that of the seller's, then there exists a *positive bargaining range* (PBR). On the other hand, when the buyer's RP is *below* that of the seller's, then there is a *negative bargaining range* (NBR). Clearly, progress is more likely if the bargaining range is positive, and arguably, part of the distributive bargaining process is for the parties to attempt to create a positive bargaining range.

During a negotiation, one common distributive bargaining strategy is to push for a settlement below the other party's RP and pressure the other party to change its RP. If an NBR exists, then the strategy will involve encouraging the other party to modify its RP or, if you feel there is no alternative, changing your RP in order to create a PBR. Basic tactics include selective disclosure or concealing of information and misinformation, and fostering in the mind of the other party the belief that the settlement you want is the best that can be achieved. To pursue such tactics successfully, you will need to possess some knowledge about the value the other party attaches to particular outcomes and the cost of delays or termination. Further tactics include getting to know the other party's BATNA and assessing its feasibility while concealing the value you attach to particular outcomes and the costs of delays or termination to your party. Time also is a critical factor in negotiation and therefore can be used tactically. The closer to a deadline or settlement, the more intense negotiations become, and parties can manipulate the actual costs of delaying or aborting negotiations through such methods as disruptive action or rescheduling meetings.

Important negotiation decisions have to be made throughout the bargaining process. Should you make large or modest initial claims? While the former leave considerable scope open for negotiation, they can lead to instant breakdown. What type of concessions should you make and how large should they be? Concessions encourage further bargaining, and too dogmatic a stance may be counter-productive. Care needs to be taken to avoid conceding too much and to ensure that corresponding concessions of comparable value are made by the other party. The closer a party is to their RP, then the less room they have for making concessions.

The second main approach to negotiation—integrative bargaining—is very different from the distributive approach. In integrative bargaining, the goals of the parties are not seen as mutually exclusive, and one party's gain is not necessarily the other party's loss. It is possible, through appropriate bargaining strategies and positions, for both sides to meet their main objectives. Parties need to be disposed to finding *mutually acceptable* solutions, requiring:

- Common interests and goals.
- Recognition of the validity of the other's role and positions using cooperative rather than competitive tactics.
- A commitment to working together.
- A high level of trust.
- Clear and accurate communication.
- Evaluation of outcomes according to how well they meet common interests and goals.

Unlike the distributive approach, the integrative approach is more suited to the encouragement of a long-term working relationship. There are certain key steps in the integrative bargaining process: identifying and defining the problems; developing a common understanding of these; seeking to identify mutual interests and goals; generating alternative solutions to problems; and developing a solution

from these alternatives. There should be a mutually acceptable definition of each problem, which is kept as simple and depersonalised as possible. The different interests should be identified:
- Substantive interests (such as the size of a pay claim).
- Process interests (how the negotiation is to occur).
- Relationship interests (how best to maintain the long-term relationship between the negotiating parties).

In evaluating alternatives, parties should seek to narrow the range of solution options, establish criteria for the evaluation of solutions before discussing them, and then evaluate possible solutions on the basis of their mutual acceptability. Subgroups can be used to investigate and report back on complex problems, in order to simplify the bargaining process. The process can also be simplified by the use of 'log rolling'—bringing together a number of small problems into a single package, to be negotiated as one. The focus throughout the integrative process should be on the generation of alternative solutions, information exchange, and a focus on common interests rather than on the respective parties' positions. In the integrative process, nothing is final until everything is finalised. Therefore, parties should be prepared to be flexible in order to reach a final agreement.

In any set of negotiations, parties must consider their overall approach in terms of distributive and integrative bargaining. For example, it could be that negotiations over pay will require a distributive approach whereas negotiations over working arrangements may be more suited to an integrative approach. The parties engaged in negotiation only have so much power to control the final outcome; often other external factors such as dramatic economic changes will influence the process. In summary, the practice of negotiation is an art developed through experience.

Study questions

1. What have been the most distinctive features historically of Australia's industrial relations system?
2. What are the main roles performed by trade unions? How effectively do you feel Australian unions perform these roles?
3. The ALP–ACTU Accord had several main goals. What were these and to what extent were they achieved? What were the main impediments to their achievement?
4. What challenges does the *Workplace Relations Act 1996* present for a strategic approach to HRM?
5. a You are the human resource manager in a mining company currently covered by a union-negotiated enterprise agreement. What arguments would you use to convince employees to move to Australian Workplace Agreements?
   b You are a union delegate in the same company. What arguments would you use to convince employees that they would be better off remaining under a union-negotiated enterprise agreement?

Further reading

Bamber, G. J. and Lansbury, R. (eds), *International and Comparative Industrial Relations: A Study of Industrialised Market Economies* (St Leonards, NSW: Allen & Unwin, 1998).

Deery, S., Plowman, D., Walsh, J., and Brown, M., *Industrial Relations: A Contemporary Analysis* (Roseville, NSW: Irwin/McGraw-Hill, 2001).

Morris, R., Mortimer, D., and Leece, P. (eds), *Workplace Reform and Enterprise Bargaining*, 2nd edn (Sydney: Harcourt Brace, 1999).

Peetz, D., *Unions in a Contrary World: The Future of the Australian Trade Union Movement* (Cambridge and Melbourne: Cambridge University Press, 1998).

CHAPTER 4

Labour Law

CHAPTER CONTENTS

Introduction

1 The role of unions

2 Conciliation and arbitration

3 The system in practice
   The impact of the *Workplace Relations Act 1996*
   The growing complexities of labour law
   Anti-discrimination and equity legislation

Summary
   Case study—Corporate failure and its consequences for employees
   Study questions
   Further reading

Introduction

The complex, inherently political issues given expression through industrial relations occur within a legal framework that is also complex and political. This chapter discusses Australian labour law (sometimes also referred to as employment law), including the system of conciliation and arbitration, the role of unions and the regulation of pay, working conditions and entitlements, and then goes on to address issues of employment equity. Labour law provides a framework of obligations, rights, and entitlements within which the relationship between employers and employees takes place. It simplifies the labour process in that these rules have been developed over time to deal with a variety of contingencies. Yet infringements of labour law are not policed with the same apparent diligence as breaches of criminal law, nor does labour law receive a comparable degree of media attention, except in the case of dramatic industrial disputes.

The role of labour law is itself highly political, with two main perspectives that often emerge in debates on employment issues. On one hand, there are those who identify the legal system as necessary to provide protection to workers, who are relatively powerless in relation to employers. From this perspective, labour law should ensure that workers can achieve a reasonable standard of living, through support for strong regulation, unions, and collective bargaining. On the other hand, there are those who argue that labour law should have a minimal role in regulating pay and conditions. From this second perspective, the best outcomes are achieved if workers negotiate individually with employers, without the intervention of 'third parties', the most important of which are unions.[1]

HRM in its unitarist variants, which emphasise common interests between employer and employee, can be seen as committed to this second view of the employment relationship—that is, if appropriate HRM techniques are implemented, there should be no need for third parties. Contract law is seen as sufficient to govern the employment relationship, and no further legal intervention should be required. Pluralist variants of HRM would be more inclined to recognise the necessity of the regulation provided by employment law, while more radical commentators would see unions not as 'third parties' but as crucial participants in the employment relationship. The power differential between employers and employees is usually so great that the employment relationship can rarely be understood as simply between individuals.[2]

I The role of unions

To a considerable extent, Australian labour law is a legacy of its colonial past. It origins can be traced back to various master–servant laws enacted in the UK over several centuries, broadly designed to enforce labour discipline. However, in the years leading up to Federation (1901) and subsequently, Australia moved away from its British origins, developing a considerably more centralised approach to the setting of pay, conditions, and general employment standards. The central role that Australia's labour law accorded to trade unions was particularly distinctive.

Unions also have a long history, with their antecedents in organisations such as craft guilds and friendly societies, again mainly British and dating back several centuries. Yet unionism as a broad social and political force—the labour movement—only gained pace during the nineteenth century in the wake of the Industrial Revolution and the rise of the factory system. Originally, the legal system was used, as in other countries, primarily to suppress unions. However, the resilience of Australian unionism eventually forced governments and many employers to recognise that unions were a permanent feature of the industrial landscape.

The foundations for many of Australia's most enduring institutions, including the industrial relations system and labour law, were laid during the latter years of the nineteenth century, preceding Federation. Experiments in compulsory conciliation and arbitration had occurred earlier in Europe and North America,[3] but it was only in New Zealand and the Australian colonies that extensive legislative frameworks were established.

The series of occasionally violent industrial disputes that occurred during the severe depression of the 1890s, extending beyond one colony for the first time, provided a catalyst for the development of a national system for settling industrial disputes. A further key event was the union-led establishment of the Australian Labor Party in 1891, which gave unions a strong political presence and enhanced bargaining power. The unions had recognised that they required a separate party of labour if the power of business and landowning interests was to be contested successfully, and if the rights of labour were to be acknowledged.

Australian labour law came to be premised on the recognition that the possibility of conflict was inherent in the employment relationship, and that conflict should be managed within an appropriate set of institutions—those of conciliation and arbitration. Fundamental to this recognition was the acknowledgment that workers had a right to organise and bargain collectively. Unionism was subsequently accommodated and even encouraged within Australian labour law, as unions were recognised in the industrial relations system as workers' sole legitimate bargaining agents.

Encouragement for union membership has varied historically. Until the 1990s, many organisations had formal or informal 'closed shop' arrangements, whereby employees were required to join a specific union once they were employed (a 'post-entry' closed shop) or whereby only union members would be sought for employment (a 'pre-entry' closed shop). Such agreements were usually not written into awards, however. 'Preference clauses', whereby union members would be given preference in employment, were also commonplace, but the Workplace Relations Act's freedom of association provisions sought to make compulsory unionisation impossible, although agreements may still encourage union membership, while not conferring preference for union members.

In recent years, then, the industrial role of unions has become less secure, with the shift towards enterprise and individual bargaining, both of which can be conducted without union involvement. The process of industrial relations decentralisation and deregulation has also meant that pay, conditions, and entitlements are less circumscribed by legal prescriptions. The reduced role of the conciliation and arbitration system, as industrial awards have been reduced to 'safety net' provisions, has also meant that unions have had to change significantly, especially in becoming more active at the enterprise level.

2 Conciliation and arbitration

The *Conciliation and Arbitration Act 1904* provided the framework for a national conciliation and arbitration system, drawing its authority from section 51(35) of the Constitution, which permits the Commonwealth government to pass legislation 'for the prevention and settlement of industrial disputes extending beyond any one State'. The states also retained their own systems of conciliation and arbitration, a source of ongoing tensions.

The authority of Commonwealth labour law, as in all other legal areas, is constrained by the Constitution. Commonwealth industrial tribunals can only intervene in cases where there is a dispute that is both 'industrial' and 'interstate', and there are considerable overlaps and duplication with the authority of state jurisdictions. According to section 109 of the Constitution, Commonwealth law shall prevail to the extent of any inconsistency between Commonwealth and state systems. This has meant that federal awards and agreements normally assume precedence over state awards. The states, though, are usually sensitive to any apparent encroachment of the Commonwealth on their jurisdictions, and Commonwealth–state disputes are commonplace in employment matters—although the Victorian government of Jeff Kennett handed over most of its industrial relations powers to the Commonwealth in 1996, following enactment of the Workplace Relations Act. Workers can have varying pay, conditions, and entitlements under the two systems, while unions, employers, and employer associations often have a presence under both state and federal jurisdictions.[4]

All Commonwealth legislation must be founded on one or more 'heads of power', the specific constitutional provisions detailing the extent of the Commonwealth's authority. The head of power under which the Commonwealth normally exercises its authority in industrial relations matters is the conciliation and arbitration power. Conciliation refers broadly to the process of bringing parties in dispute together, in order that they can settle it. Arbitration refers to the formal judicial process, whereby a third party, an industrial tribunal, reaches a decision on the dispute.

The process leads to the establishment of industrial awards, which stipulate minimum wages and conditions for specific industries and occupations. Industrial awards are not laws, but they have legal standing as expressions of labour law. Awards provide minimum standards, which respondent parties are legally obliged to observe unless they have been replaced by another form of legally binding agreement—for example, in contemporary workplaces, an Australian Workplace

Agreement (AWA). Historically, these minimum standards have been supplemented in many workplaces by 'above award' pay and conditions.

The Commonwealth's conciliation and arbitration powers were intentionally restricted by the Constitution's architects. The conciliation and arbitration head of power does not permit 'common rule' awards, where everyone working in the designated industry or occupation is covered by the relevant award. Only those parties identified as parties to a dispute or respondents to a log of claims can be covered. In contrast, state industrial tribunals do possess the authority to make common rule awards, as their powers are not drawn from the Constitution but from specific Acts of the respective state parliaments. The federal industrial relations system has had to rely on the process of 'roping in' employees. This usually means that unions must seek to name as many employers as possible in an industry, plus any relevant employer associations, as respondents to their log of claims, which can be a time-consuming, costly exercise.

Powers other than the conciliation and arbitration power have been used in various contexts to regulate employment issues. For example, the corporations power has been used to some degree since 1971, when the High Court ruled that it could be used by the Commonwealth to legislate on industrial issues.[5] In 1999, the then Workplace Relations Minister, Peter Reith, proposed the complete abandonment of the conciliation and arbitration power as the basis for industrial relations legislation, advocating its replacement by the corporations power.[6] The use of the corporations power, it was claimed, would enable the 'harmonisation' of Commonwealth and state legislation, and bring a significant number of employees not presently covered by awards under award coverage. The *Industrial Relations Reform Act 1993* and then the *Workplace Relations and Other Legislation Amendment Act 1996* both had provisions for enterprise agreements between constitutional corporations and their employees, as well as agreements under the conciliation and arbitration power. The corporations head of power has been used principally to legislate against secondary boycotts (where unions that are not direct parties to a dispute conduct industrial action in support of their fellow unionists and workers who are direct parties). Corporations, though, do not include all employers. Organisations must be incorporated and engaged in trading or financial activities as a significant component of their business.

Other heads of power have been used with respect to employment. These include the public service power, which enables the Commonwealth to regulate conditions for its own employees; the incidental power, which is used in relation to registration of employer associations and unions; the territories power, which permits common regulation across the territories; the trade and commerce power, which has been used occasionally in the maritime and airline industries; and the defence power, which was used during World War II to regulate working conditions.

Peter Reith was only one in a series of ministers who have struggled to promote 'harmonisation' of the state and federal systems of industrial relations and labour law. There have been several earlier attempts to achieve harmonisation through an extension of the Commonwealth conciliation and arbitration power—all unsuccessful. The most extensive inquiry into the federal system in recent decades, the

Hancock Committee (the Committee of Review into Australian Industrial Relations Law and Systems), conducted between 1983 and 1985, identified significant benefits in having a single national system under one authority. However, it acknowledged that there were too many political and legislative obstacles to such a system in the foreseeable future. The problem of overlapping jurisdictions seems likely to persist, so long as the states remain in existence.

3 The system in practice

Today, the Australian Industrial Relations Commission (AIRC) conducts the arbitral functions of the conciliation and arbitration system. It is headed by a president, assisted by two vice-presidents and numerous senior deputy presidents, deputy presidents and commissioners. These are formed into different panels, each of which has responsibility for dealing with disputes in a particular group of industries. An Organisations Panel, with one vice-president and at least one other presidentially ranked member, deals with matters such as union rules and amalgamations. Whereas most commission matters are dealt with by individual commission members, the Full Bench (which must include a minimum of three members, at least two of whom must be at presidential level) deals with certain other matters (including appeals under section 45 and matters referred by the president under section 107).[7]

The operation of the conciliation and arbitration system requires the legal existence of a dispute in the first instance. In practice, a dispute need not require overt conflict. Frequently, it means that the parties create a 'paper dispute' to generate judicial intervention. A dispute requires that one party (usually a union) serves a log of claims containing certain demands on another (usually an employer), and that the second party rejects all or part of this log. Each party makes certain demands and puts forwards evidence and argument to support its case in hearings of the industrial court, arbitrated by at least one commissioner. Each is legally bound by the industrial award arising from the process of conciliation and arbitration.

The concept of *ambit* is a sometimes confusing but necessary aspect of the legal process. Its rationale arose mainly from a 1910 High Court decision that the process of arbitration had to remain within the confines (that is, the respective claims) made by the parties to the dispute. Any subsequent variation of the particular award can only occur within those confines. Therefore, if a union tables an original log of claims that demands a pay rate of $750, no subsequent variation of the award can be higher than $750. Hence, a claim for $770 would require an entirely new process, with a new log of claims. Ambit claims provide a method for dealing with this problem. Unions and employers make very ambitious claims, so that any future claims can be met without the need to go through a new dispute. To those unfamiliar with the process, this can cause frustration and concern. For example, employees can be concerned that their union is making unattainable and unreasonable demands, when the union is merely playing according to the rules of the game—designed to reduce the level of actual disputation.

Negotiations can often break down, though, and lead to more overt conflict, such as strikes and 'working to rule' by employees, or lock-outs and hiring non-union labour by employers. The *Industrial Relations Reform Act 1993* gave employees and unions a limited degree of protection from legal action if they took industrial action, but only within periods in which agreements are being negotiated. This protection reduces the possibilities of employers taking punitive action (for example, dismissal) against individual employees who have participated in industrial action. The entitlement to protected industrial action was retained in reduced form in the *Workplace Relations Act 1996*.

Disputes directly between employers, on one hand, and, on the other, employees and unions are not the only ones that can occur in labour law. Occasionally, industrial tribunals may be required to make judgments on issues between different employers or different unions. For example, a company may feel that a competitor is underpaying its workforce, in order to achieve a cost advantage. The first company may seek action from the relevant tribunal to ensure that the second pays according to the legal rates. Problems of coverage can occur occasionally between unions, where different unions may have the right (specified in awards or agreements) to recruit the same groups of employees in an industry or enterprise. The problem of 'bodysnatching' (whereby unions sign up members of other unions) has been reduced somewhat by the creation of large, mainly industry-based unions through the process of union amalgamations overseen by the ACTU since the late 1980s. Yet disputes over coverage can still become heated, especially when fuelled by political or ideological differences, as can factional disputes within unions.

Responsibility for implementing the judicial functions of employment law (that is, deciding on the legality of work-related actions by employers, employees, or unions) has changed over the years. Since the *Workplace Relations Act 1996*, this responsibility has been charged to the Federal Court of Australia, which took over from the Industrial Relations Court of Australia (created only in 1994). The Federal Court's most industrially significant action since then has been its 1998 decision that the actions of Patrick Stevedores in dismissing its unionised workforce, precipitating the waterfront dispute, were illegal.

Even though employees may be legally entitled to particular pay and conditions, this does not mean they are receiving them. For example, some employers may be slow to pass on wage increases. A system of regulation also requires mechanisms to ensure compliance. In the federal jurisdiction, this is the province of two main institutions: the Industrial Registry and the Industrial Inspectorate. The Industrial Registry's primary responsibilities are to maintain a register of unions, employer associations, and businesses; publish and hold copies of awards and agreements; and provide administrative assistance to the commission. The inspectorate's role is to ensure that labour law is respected in practice, and its inspectors have the authority to ensure that organisations comply with employment standards, awards, and agreements.

Yet in practice the inspectorate has limited resources, which can mean that many areas of the workplace may be contravening the relevant Act, award, and agreements, particularly where there is no union presence to ensure observance of legal obligations. Employers may even be unaware (or claim to be unaware) that their workplace is covered by an award, and may assume that they have far greater managerial prerogative than they can exercise legally. Employees in some small businesses are particularly vulnerable, since these are less likely to have a union presence, they rarely attract the scrutiny of inspectors and, unlike large organisations, they have a low public profile. However, ignorance of labour law, as in any other area of law, does not constitute an adequate defence for employers.

These difficulties are often compounded because many workplace agreements are informal—that is, they are part of a written or unwritten agreement between management and employees that has been negotiated outside any formal bargaining process. Also, as employment agreements and contracts have become increasingly flexible in recent years, various non-wage entitlements have been included in salary packages, usually designed to minimise tax liabilities and thereby give employees more 'cash in hand'. These can include such items as superannuation contributions and vehicles, once reserved for executives but now extended to many employees.

National wage case decisions historically provided a mechanism for regulating pay rates nationally, leading to decisions on wages (either percentage and/or monetary increases) that flow on to employees in all industries. National wage case hearings begin when the ACTU (the applicant) makes an application to the AIRC for a wage increase. The usual respondent is the relevant employer association, which today is the Australian Chamber of Commerce and Industry (ACCI). The AIRC also takes representations from other interested parties, most importantly the Commonwealth government, but also state governments. Hearings, which can last for weeks or even months, take account of the different arguments on the size of wage increases and the conditions that have to be met for employees to receive that wage increase. Since 1993, though, with the introduction of enterprise bargaining amendments to the *Industrial Relations Act 1988*, and especially since the *Workplace Relations Act 1996*, national wage cases have become de facto minimum wage cases.

The stated intention of enterprise bargaining was that the great majority of workers would achieve wage rises through enterprise-level negotiation. Yet there is a substantial minority of workers who have been unable to achieve agreements and who do not receive 'over-award' payments—somewhere around 20 per cent, according to most estimates. The WRA stipulates that the AIRC has to ensure that awards provide 'safety net' increases for those workers who have not achieved a wage increase through enterprise bargaining. This is done through safety net reviews initiated usually by the ACTU making a case for a wage increase due to changes in social and economic conditions.

The impact of the *Workplace Relations Act 1996*

As we saw in the previous chapter, the *Workplace Relations Act 1996* (WRA) was ultimately less 'radical' than the Liberal Party had originally intended. On one hand, arbitration is identified in the WRA as 'a last resort' (section 89), and balance of industrial power has been shifted clearly towards employers. Yet the system of awards remains, albeit in reduced form, while unions are still important players in the system.

The Act stripped back awards to twenty 'allowable award matters', plus other matters necessary to the award's effective operation. In a significant extension of managerial prerogative, employers were also granted the authority to assert conditions unilaterally on certain matters, if agreement could not be reached with unions or employees. It allowed employers to reach certified agreements with a 'valid majority' of employees, without any trade union involvement. In practice, this provision has enabled employers to sidestep negotiations with the relevant unions by conducting non-union ballots. Even if this tactic proves unsuccessful, the employer can return to negotiating with the union or unions. The WRA reinstated provisions against secondary boycotts, legal recognition of the right not to belong to a union (but also contained the right to freedom of association), and reduced certain rights of trade union officials (for example, to enter workplaces). It also became possible for enterprise agreements reached under state law to override federal awards.

Under the WRA, unfair dismissal laws (designed to prevent wrongful dismissal of an employee by an employer) have also been weakened in relation to the *Industrial Relations Reform Act 1993*, to limit the numbers and outcomes of claims under the federal jurisdiction. Under the WRA, unfair dismissal cannot be said to have occurred unless an employer has acted with demonstrable intent to terminate an individual's employment. Allowing a contract to lapse, for example, cannot be defined as dismissal under the Act. As a definitive understanding of 'fairness' is elusive, outcomes in unfair dismissal cases can vary considerably.[8]

The termination of employment has always been one of the most contested areas of labour law, bringing managerial prerogative into conflict with the employee's right to reasonable security of employment. Reasons for termination can be individual (such as a specific employee's unsuitability for the position), strategic (such as organisational restructuring), or terminal (the collapse of the organisation itself): several dramatic corporate collapses, including HIH, One.Tel, and Ansett, have occurred recently, leaving thousands of workers jobless.[9]

Today, restructuring and the future of jobs usually figure prominently in enterprise bargaining processes, and the identification of positions and people to be made redundant is a frequent focus of industrial dispute. Employers are expected to consult with employees and unions, to take all reasonable efforts to prevent redundancies, and also to ensure that the selection of employees to be made redundant (as distinct from those who retain their jobs) is consultative, transparent, fair, and procedurally correct. In practice, though, such processes frequently lead to bitterness and demoralisation, among those who leave and among the 'survivors'.

The WRA, particularly its provision for Australian Workplace Agreements, has also had a significant impact on employee entitlements. All full-time and part-time employees are due certain entitlements, including:

- *Annual leave.* Legislation in all states and territories (except Tasmania) provides for four weeks' paid recreation leave, plus a 17.5 per cent holiday leave loading.

The Commonwealth and Tasmania lack specific legislation on annual leave, but in practice include this arrangement in their awards and agreements.
- *Long service leave.* Entitlements vary, but awards and agreements typically contain an entitlement to at least three months' leave after ten to fifteen years.
- *Sick leave.* The standard entitlement is 40 hours in the first year of employment and 64 in subsequent years.
- *Maternity leave and parental leave.* Commonwealth legislation entitles parents to a total of 52 weeks unpaid leave, which may be shared between partners. Apart from the week immediately following the birth, they cannot take parental leave at the same time. This entitlement supplements those in other federal, state or territory legislation and awards, which employees should access before accessing the Commonwealth entitlement. Paid maternity leave is still limited to a minority of workplaces, although because these are usually large organisations, often public sector, a higher proportion of employees has paid maternity leave entitlements (close to half of the female workforce). An enterprise agreement struck at the Australian Catholic University in August 2001 may prove to be a landmark in parental leave, since it provided those women staff covered by the agreement with access to up to 52 weeks' maternity leave, fourteen of which are at full pay and the remainder at 70 per cent pay.
- *Carers' leave.* As a result of a 1994 AIRC test case, carers' leave (usually to take care of a sick family member) was introduced into many awards and agreements.
- *Staff development, training, and educational leave.* These entitlements vary considerably according to industry, occupation, and enterprise, but they include such entitlements as study leave or paid attendance at training courses.
- *Cultural leave.* This was introduced to cater for the cultural obligations of different sections of the workforce (for example, leave for religious commitments).
- *Other forms of leave such as jury duty, training, and Army Reserve service.* These provisions vary according to the award or agreement.
- *Superannuation.* Since 1986, a growing proportion of Australian employees (and now a considerable majority) has been covered by compulsory superannuation schemes, which include employee contributions and employer contributions (usually around twice those of the employee). The superannuation system has been attached to various tax incentives to encourage employees to remain in the system for as long as possible, in order to achieve reasonable retirement incomes.

However, under the WRA, it has become possible to 'cash in' or 'trade off' some of them, particularly through the implementation of Australian Workplace Agreements. AWAs represent the legal incarnation of the belief that employer–employee relationships should exclude all 'third parties', since they operate to the exclusion of the relevant award. The Office of the Employment Advocate (OEA) has encouraged organisations to introduce AWAs as part of their overall HRM strategies, to look at the prevailing award and identify 'restrictive' provisions that can be eliminated through the introduction of an AWA.[10] Yet, while an AWA supplants the federal or state award that previously covered an employee, it can also include provisions from the relevant award or be read in conjunction with it. Where there is an inconsistency between the agreement and the award, the AWA prevails.

Only two provisions are compulsory in AWAs: anti-discrimination and dispute resolution. If an agreement fails to include these provisions, they are inserted by the OEA. The pay and conditions stipulated in the AWA continue to apply even after its expiry, until such time as a new agreement is made. Most AWAs place a strong emphasis on employees having to work over a large spread of hours. Usually, they also collapse penalty rates, allowances, and leave loadings into a single hourly pay rate. Leave entitlements can even be 'cashed out' if they are not taken. The AWA can replace entire entitlements specified in state laws—for example, maternity leave or long service leave. In terms of training and development, AWAs have stressed mandatory training—training to be conducted on the employer's instruction, rather than any sense of training and education linked to national social or economic objectives, or the individual employee's career or other aspirations.[11]

The growing complexities of labour law

Over the past decade, therefore, the regulation of employees' pay, conditions, and entitlements has become considerably more complicated than it had previously been, while the workforce has also become more diverse. Much of this greater variation in working arrangements has been precipitated by the impact of intensified internationalisation, as discussed in chapter 2, and accompanying demands for greater flexibility in workplace organisation. Yet the spread of international corporate activity has not been accompanied by a comparable internationalisation of labour standards, which have had at best a sporadic impact on Australian labour law. Although the International Labour Organisation (ILO) was established in 1919 with a brief to ensure adequate working standards across all nations, its powers and funding have been very limited. The ILO, through its meetings of government officials, unions and employer associations from member countries, passes recommendations and conventions that set international standards on conditions of employment. However, member countries need not ratify these nationally, and numerous countries have ratified conventions formally, while ignoring them in practice. Australia, a founder member of the ILO, does not have a particularly impressive record in ratifying ILO conventions, falling behind several European countries, although it is considerably ahead of the USA. Although the Howard government has curtailed its commitment to the ILO,[12] the country does retain relatively high labour standards in international terms.

The employment relationship is further complicated by the presence of different types of employee status (full-time, part-time, casual, permanent, short-term) as well as various workers (such as outworkers or contract workers) whose status as employees may be uncertain. There is also a large (and growing) number of people who perform voluntary work, particularly in the welfare sector, as well as people who work informally for family or friends' businesses (formerly known as 'unpaid family helpers', but now officially described as 'contributing family workers').

The growth of 'alternative' working arrangements poses further problems for labour law. These arrangements take various forms, including outwork, homeworking, and telework, which make it difficult to ensure that employees outside a central workplace receive the same entitlements and conditions (for example, a safe working environment) that apply in a central organisation. Regulation of conditions in a variety of home or mobile workplaces is considerably more complex and time-consuming than regulation of conditions in a single workplace.

The increasing usage of contract labour across numerous industries is another phenomenon that has raised new workplace issues. In many workplaces, contract workers (often recruited through labour-hire agencies) can be working side-by-side with employees, yet under quite different conditions.[13] Problems of inequity and even flagrant illegality can be particularly severe in areas of the informal workforce. For instance, many textiles and clothing outworkers (often recent, non-English-speaking migrants, engaged as subcontractors) work at home or in illegal sweatshops with pay and conditions well below legal industry standards.[14]

Contractors and subcontractors do not have the same rights and entitlements as employees, and some employers may seek to avoid employee rights and entitlements through defining their workers as contractors or 'self-employed'. These workers can be particularly vulnerable to under-pay and poor working conditions. The industrial courts, though, have the authority to investigate 'independent contractor' arrangements to assess if these are, substantively, disguised employer–employee relationships. An 'independent contractor' who is treated to all intents and purposes as an employee can be redefined by the industrial courts as an employee.

Casual employees represent a similarly, although much larger, 'grey' area for labour law. Awards and agreements can contain very different definitions of the 'casual' category—and these definitions are often tautologous, such as the description of a casual employee, found in many awards and agreements, as someone who is 'engaged and paid on a casual basis'. Since there is no coherent definition of casual employees, their status as employees is often unclear. Although many of them are employed on a long-term basis, casual workers have had little or no access to the benefits attached to full-time and part-time employment (such as holiday pay, sick pay, or maternity leave). Some headway has been made in this respect in recent years. For example, in May 2001, the AIRC granted access to twelve months' unpaid parental leave to casual employees who had been with one employer for at least twelve months. In a rare instance of bipartisanship, the ACTU application was also supported by the ACCI.

Much of the rhetoric of the past decade has suggested that 'reform' is required to 'simplify' the labyrinthine Australian industrial relations system. However, the eventual outcome has been that, in addition to the original system of awards, we now have three other types of formal working arrangement—union enterprise agreements, non-union enterprise agreements, and individual agreements—in addition to the coexistence of federal and state systems. This plethora of collective and individual agreements can mean widely varying pay and conditions within the same occupation or industry. Also, the great majority of enterprise agreements, being less comprehensive documents than the relevant award, have to be read in conjunction with the award. On issues where the agreement is silent, award conditions assume precedence. The introduction of Australian Workplace Agreements has added a further degree of complexity to employee pay, conditions, and entitlements. Overall, this has meant that managers, unions, and employees have had to develop an increased awareness of the various aspects of labour law.

Anti-discrimination and equity legislation

The increased complexity of labour law has been compounded by the growth of casual and other forms of 'peripheral' or insecure, usually low-paid, employment. Positions in this 'secondary' labour market are disproportionately occupied by women, people from non-English-speaking backgrounds, and Aboriginal and Torres Strait Islander people. For example, the principle of comparative wage justice (CWJ) was traditionally confined in the industrial relations system to white, male, full-time workers. There is little doubt that Aboriginal and Torres Strait Islander people have suffered the most extreme disadvantage in Australian society, with the highest unemployment, and the poorest health, education, and housing. Until the 1960s, just as Australia's indigenous people were denied citizenship, they were also denied the same wages as other workers. Only with the 1966 Cattle Industry (Northern Territory) Award, after a lengthy campaign by Aboriginal workers, was there a recognition in labour law that Aboriginal males should be entitled to wages equal to other males.

People from different minority backgrounds, gay and lesbian people, and people with disabilities have also experienced various forms of discrimination and inequity in employment, both direct and indirect. Historically, therefore, the disadvantage suffered by many sections of the community generally has also been very evident in the workplace. Various forms of anti-discrimination and equity legislation in federal and state jurisdictions have been introduced to address these problems.

Anti-discrimination legislation has become an important part of Australia's labour law over recent decades. The Australian Industrial Relations Commission and the Office of the Employment Advocate are required to ensure that awards and agreements do not include either directly or indirectly discriminatory provisions (for example, a discouragement of part-time employment may be seen as discriminatory against people, mainly women, with children). There are various acts at state and federal level designed to eliminate direct and indirect discrimination on a variety of grounds—including gender, race, disability, ethnic background, sexual preference, and pregnancy. Among the most significant pieces of legislative reform have been the *Racial Discrimination Act 1975*, the *Sex Discrimination Act 1984*, and the *Disability Discrimination Act 1992*. There have also been various acts passed in state and territory jurisdictions designed (with varying degrees of conviction) to address the issue of discrimination.

Labour markets, therefore, are segmented, according to various factors, such as gender, race, and ethnicity. Just as women tend to be over-represented in the lower paid sections of the workforce, so too do certain migrant groups. Migrants from English-speaking countries and northern Europe are generally higher paid and higher skilled, whereas those from elsewhere generally fare less well on the labour market. The main objective of equal employment opportunity (EEO) and affirmative action legislation has been the erosion of the *dual labour market*, whereby there are identifiably 'men's' and 'women's' jobs, with the former providing considerably better pay, conditions, and security than the latter. Such legislation, in essence, seeks to equalise the gender distribution of positions within the labour market. Its governing principles are those of employment equity and the elimination of barriers to more equitable employment outcomes.

Generally speaking, women earn less and have less promising career paths than men. Employers have traditionally chosen men rather than women to occupy positions requiring long-term commitment—the argument used to justify this practice is that labour turnover among women is supposedly higher, since domestic considerations (real or hypothesised) are assumed to take priority. Overall, women in Australia occupy the most poorly paid occupations (often in casual, temporary, or part-time work). In August 2000, average full-time adult male ordinary time earnings were $844.20 per week, while average full-time adult female ordinary time earnings were $710.90 (84.2 per cent of male ordinary time earnings). Average full-time adult male total earnings (that is, including overtime) were $896.40, while average full-time total adult female earnings were $728.80 (81.3 per cent of male total earnings). Further, males receive nearly three times as much overtime pay as females[15]. Many women also fall into the category of the 'hidden unemployed'—those who want employment but who are not included in official statistics, usually because their partners are employed or they are receiving social welfare benefits.

In Australia, the subordinate position of women in the labour market was enshrined for many decades in legislation. Justice Higgins's 'Harvester' judgment (1907) and the 'living wage' concept installed the male-headed nuclear family (nominally, with three children) as the legal norm. The male wage was deemed as that sufficient to support a family in 'frugal comfort', and women's wages were to be set, for most of the following century, at only a proportion of men's wages. Higgins' 1912 Female Basic Wage case judgment fixed the 'single unit' female wage at 60 per cent of the male 'family unit' wage. Women's wage rates were therefore based on the situation of a single woman without children: the nuclear family with a male breadwinner was set officially as the wages standard, and women, particularly sole mothers, were left in an economically parlous position.

The discrepancy between women's and men's wages fluctuated in subsequent decades, usually according to the availability of male labour. For example, during World War II, the Women's Employment Board set women's wages at 90 per cent of those for men in the same ('men's') jobs. Many of these 'men's jobs' had been occupied by women. The discrepancy in pay levels was sometimes explained in terms of economic efficiency: ostensibly, the assumption was that female workers had higher turnover and absenteeism rates and were of lower physical strength than males. However, with the postwar return of male workers, much lower rates of pay for women were reinstated, officially set in 1950 at only 75 per cent of male wage rates.

Just as explanations for women's subordinate position in the labour market may vary, so have legislative proposals to address this situation. With the growth of feminist activity in Australia from the 1960s, government responses to structural inequalities in the general workforce took a number of forms designed to break down labour market segmentation and give women access to senior and management positions. Eventually, as a result of extensive political campaigns, the principle of 'equal pay for equal work' was endorsed in the Equal Pay Case of June 1969. Award rates were no longer to include differential rates for men and women. However, due to the continuing demarcation between predominantly male and predominantly female occupations and industries, this decision ameliorated the situations of relatively few women. With the Equal Pay Case and the equal payment principle of 1972, the principle of 'equal pay for work of equal value' was given institutional expression. Employers were compelled to pay minimum wage rates according to the nature of the work performed, rather than who was performing that work. In 1974, the National Wage Case extended the minimum wage to all adult workers, and Australia ratified the ILO's Convention 100 whereby 'each member [country] shall … promote and ensure the application to all workers of the principle of equal remuneration for men and women workers for work of equal value'.

The increase in women's participation in paid work over recent decades has been assisted by a number of legislative changes at the federal level, such as maternity leave provisions, the Women's Budget Programme (1984) and, most importantly, the *Affirmative Action (Equal Employment Opportunity for Women) Act 1986*. Most state governments have initiated similar changes in line with state responsibilities, although specific arrangements vary from state to state. However, despite legislation and policies formally designed to break down labour market segmentation and to give women and other disadvantaged groups improved access to senior and management positions, Australian women have not achieved equality of opportunity in employment.

The process of decentralisation and deregulation, combined with the growth of insecure employment, has undermined to some extent the gains made in terms of equal pay and equity. Women workers tend to be concentrated in lower paid areas with the lowest union membership—areas that achieve the poorest outcomes in a decentralised, deregulated environment, and that are least likely to receive pay increases through enterprise bargaining.[16] Also, Commonwealth equity legislation has been weakened in recent years. The *Equal Opportunity for Women in the Workplace Act 1999* (EOWWA) arose from a committee established in December 1997 by the federal government to assess the effectiveness of the Affirmative Action Act. Its report, 'Unfinished Business: Equity for Women in Australian Workplaces', was presented to the government in July 1998. The Bill taken to Parliament by the government rejected or diluted several regulatory recommendations (such as workplace visits by the agency, or the retention of existing sanctions, contract compliance and naming) but accepted those that reduced the requirements placed on business. The reporting requirements placed on organisations and the possible penalties for non-compliance by the *Affirmative Action (Equal Employment Opportunity for Women) Act 1986* were not especially onerous. Naming a non-complying organisation was the most drastic punishment available. Yet the EOWWA diluted even these requirements. Like the WRA, the EOWWA was designed to provide employers with greater flexibility in meeting any obligations and to reduce the role of unions in workplace relations.

Like its predecessor, the Act places no requirements on employers with fewer than 100 employees. A 'relevant employer' in the Act refers to: (a) a higher education institution that is an employer; or (b) a natural person, or a body or association (whether incorporated or not), being the employer of 100 or more employees in Australia (Commonwealth, state and territory departments and agencies are not included, having their own legislation). An employer may be given a waiver from the reporting requirements of the Act if it has submitted reports successfully for at least three years and if it can satisfy the Equal Opportunity for Women in the Workplace Agency, formerly the Affirmative Action Agency, that it has taken all 'reasonably practicable measures to address the issues relating to employment matters that affect equal opportunity for women in the employer's workplace'.[17]

In response to employer complaints of excessive reporting requirements, paperwork, and compliance costs, the new Act introduced several changes. Reports are only required on a biennial, rather than annual, basis, are less prescriptive than previously, and the reporting requirement may even be waived, if employers have demonstrated compliance previously. The term 'affirmative action' was also dropped from the Act, and from the titles of the agency and its director, ostensibly to avoid confusion with the US affirmative action approach, with its quota systems. The government has also stressed that, while all employers should pursue EEO objectives, small business is not required to take any specific action. Organisations that need to submit an EEO report have two options: a simplified pro-forma document and a more 'flexible' report, broadly identifying EEO issues, priority EEO areas, an action plan, and EEO measures and outcomes sought. The rationale is 'outcome' rather than 'process' oriented. It is nonetheless a weakening of previous legislation that was not particularly strong.

Summary

In this chapter, we provided an overview of Australian labour law, highlighting the intensely political nature of its development. We examined the historical development of the conciliation and arbitration system, including the role that trade unions have played, the constitutional framework within which labour law operates, particularly the limitations of the conciliation and arbitration 'head of power', and the simultaneous operation of federal and state systems. We went on to look at the practical operation of the system, as a medium for the settlement of industrial disputes and the regulation of employment conditions.

The chapter then showed how labour law has become more complex in recent years, through the introduction of different types of employment agreement and the growth of different types of employment status. The increasing incidence of 'alternative' working agreements has considerable implications for employment equity, the topic on which the chapter then focused, with a particular emphasis on Equal Employment Opportunity.

Table 4.1 Significant Dates in Australian Industrial Relations and Labour Law

1901	Establishment of Australian Commonwealth: Constitution section 51 provides federal government with capacity to prevent disputes. Legislation made by States in this area is subordinate to the Commonwealth's, in cases where there is a conflict between the two jurisdictions.
1904	Conciliation and Arbitration Act passed. Establishment of Commonwealth Court of Conciliation and Arbitration (CCCA).
1907	Harvester Judgment, by Justice H.B. Higgins, Second President of CCCA. Establishes principle of 'basic wage': 'normal needs of the average employee, regarded as a human being in a civilised community'.
1909	Insufficient 'capacity to pay' by employers rejected by Higgins as a sufficient justification for wage reductions.
1920	Multi-member CCCA benches. High Court rules that CCCA has the authority to make awards which cover State workers.
1922	Following findings by Basic Wage Royal Commission that the 'basic wage' was lower than the actual cost of living; automatic quarterly cost of living adjustments are introduced.
1926	Establishment of 44-hour 'normal' working week.
1927	Australian Council of Trade Unions (ACTU) formed.
1931	10% reduction in federal basic wage (not followed by all States).
1934	Reduction in basic wage rescinded.
1943	The Institute of Personnel Management of Australia (IPMA) is established. Later to become Australian Human Resources Institute (AHRI).
1947	Establishment of 40-hour 'normal' working week. In the post-WW2 period, the concept of a 'basic wage' plus a 'secondary wage' (skills component) is established.
1956	High Court stipulates separation of arbitral from judicial powers.
1956	CCCA redesignated Australian Court of Conciliation and Arbitration. Separate Industrial Court established.
1961	National Employers' Association, first peak employers' body, formed.
1977	Confederation of Australian Industry (CAI) formed. Federal Court of Australia begins operation, assuming some of the industrial relations responsibilities previously exercised by the High Court.
1983	ALP-ACTU Accord. Election of ALP Federal Government.
1984–8	Structural Efficiency Principle. Implementation of award restructuring, multiskilling, broadbanding.
1987	Australia Reconstructed: formal ACTU model for strategic unionism. Union amalgamations to form many fewer, but much larger unions.
1991	National Wage Case endorsement of Enterprise Bargaining Principle.
1992	Formation of Australian Chamber of Commerce and Industry, from amalgamation of Confederation of Australian Industry and the Australian Chamber of Commerce.
1993	Establishment of Industrial Relations Court of Australia, subsequently dismantled in 1997, most of its responsibilities being delegated to the Federal Court.
1996	Election of the Howard Liberal-National Coalition Government, committed to a drastic reduction of the role of industrial awards. Workplace Relations Act. Australian Workplace Agreements (AWAs): can be made between an employer and a single employee or between an employer and a group of employees.
1997	Waterfront dispute between Maritime Union of Australia and Patrick Stevedores. April National Wage Case Decision affirms concept of minimum wage.
1998	Re-election of Howard Government, but it fails to implement its 'second wave' of industrial relations reform.

cont.

Table 4.1 Significant Dates in Australian Industrial Relations and Labour Law (cont.)

2001	November: Howard Government re-elected for a third term. Following an ACTU campaign, a test case begins in the Australian Industrial Relations Commission to decide if there should be an award benchmark to limit the number of hours worked by employees.
2002	Living Wage Case, May: Australian Industrial Relations Commission grants an $18 per week increase, raising the federal minimum wage to $431.40 per week. Growing debate on whether the Commonwealth Government should introduce a national system of paid maternity leave, in line with International Labour Organisation Resolution 183.

BOX 4.1

Case study—Corporate failure and its consequences for employees

This case study addresses a highly publicised occurrence of corporate failure in Australia and considers its social and legal implications. The discount mobile phone service company One.Tel prospered from investor enthusiasm for new technology companies and more specifically the dotcom boom. It grew rapidly during the late 1990s, but fell into serious financial difficulty and was put into voluntary administration in May 2001. Consequently, all of the employees lost their jobs.

One.Tel was established as a very ambitious venture under its joint chief executives Jodee Rich and Bradley Keeling. The company also attracted substantial investments from Rupert Murdoch's News Corporation and from Kerry Packer's Publishing and Broadcasting Ltd. Two of the magnates' children, Lachlan Murdoch and Jamie Packer, took on the roles of managing the News Corp and PBL investments in One.Tel. The company was listed amid considerable publicity on the Australian Stock Exchange in November 1997, with a market value of A$210 million.

Riding the dotcom boom, it fulfilled its initial promise for shareholders, with its market value soaring to nearly A$3 billion by December 1999, when its share price reached A$2.48. Both News Corp and PBL increased their investments as One.Tel grew, to 25 per cent and 17.4 per cent respectively. However, as the market collapsed, so One.Tel's fortunes plummeted. The seriousness of the company's difficulties became evident in September 2000, with the announcement of a loss of A$291 million during the financial year ending June 2000. During that same financial year, A$6.9 million had been paid in performance-related bonuses to joint chief executives Rich and Keeling.

The company's decline was so rapid that by May 2001 it was placed into voluntary administration, with approximately 1400 employees losing their jobs. They were mostly young and had been contracted under Australian Workplace Agreements. The average annual wage was around A$28 000 and they were not covered by an industrial award. It appeared initially that these employees would lose all their unpaid wages and entitlements. However, the Community Public Sector Union (CPSU) stepped in to represent the employees and the situation received intense media coverage. The plight of One.Tel's redundant staff was contrasted with the financial windfalls received by the two chief executives. Mr Rich's actions were subjected to particular scrutiny. Immediately prior to the company's demise, he had transferred many of his personal assets, including a Sydney Harbour house valued at about A$8 million, to his wife. Transferring these assets meant that they could not be used to pay creditors, shareholders, or employees if he was found legally liable for a proportion of the One.Tel debts.

The CPSU mounted a strong public campaign and instigated action through the AIRC to win for One.Tel's former employees their full entitlements. However, under Australian corporations law, the creditors must decide on the advice of the official administrator whether to hand the company back to the directors, accept a deed of arrangement, or liquidate the company. Only if the company is liquidated are the employees able to gain their full entitlements. The administrator's report recommended the winding-up of the company, a decision that One.Tel's creditors accepted. One.Tel's former employees, therefore, received their unpaid wages, leave and superannuation entitlements, and up to eight weeks' redundancy pay. Stephen Jones, a CPSU spokesperson, stated after the decision: 'This is good news for One.Tel workers. They should be congratulated on the stand they took. Their fight was right and they won.'

This case has highlighted the complexities of the Australian legal environment within which employment relations occur. There are often areas of overlap and potential contradiction of interpretation, for example, between corporations law and labour law. It was only after the requirements of corporations law were met that One.Tel employees could gain access to their outstanding pay and entitlements. The following exercises encourage you to address the social and legal issues.

Case study activities

1. In groups, discuss what you believe should be the duties and responsibilities of directors and senior managers to their employees. How far should labour law be used to ensure that these responsibilities are met?
2. 'People are our greatest asset.' In groups discuss the significance of this statement in the light of One.Tel. How might labour law help to ensure that employees are in practice the organisation's most valuable resource?
3. Australian Workplace Agreements (AWAs) replace industrial awards. The rationale behind them is that, without the 'third party' intervention of unions and industrial courts, employers and employees are able to achieve their common goals and aspirations more effectively. In the light of the One.Tel example and others with which you are familiar, discuss your views on the practical consequences of AWAs.
4. Section 44(1) of the Workplace Relations Act authorises the minister to intervene on a matter before a Full Bench of the AIRC to act in the public interest. Debate the statement that: 'The Commonwealth government has a responsibility to act to maintain the survival of companies and to protect employee job security, wages, and entitlements.'

Study questions

1. What are the two main perspectives on the role of labour law, as discussed in this chapter? Which perspective do you find more convincing? Why?
2. The Constitution sets limits on the Commonwealth conciliation and arbitration power. What practical problems do these limits cause? How might these problems be addressed?
3. What is ambit? Why can it be confusing? What advantages does it offer?
4. To what extent do you consider that Australia has a responsibility to ratify and observe International Labour Organisation conventions?
5. What do you see as the main benefits and difficulties associated with the greater 'flexibility' given to employers under the *Equal Opportunity for Women in the Workplace Act 1999*?

Further reading

Creighton, B. and Stewart, A., *Labour Law: an Introduction*, 3rd edn (Sydney: Federation Press, 2000).

Deery, S. and Mitchell, R. (eds), *Employment Relations, Individualism and Union Exclusion* (Sydney: Federation Press, 2000).

Wheelwright, K., *Labour Law* (Sydney: Butterworths, 1999)

Wooden, M., *The Transformation of Australian Industrial Relations* (Sydney: Federation Press, 2000).

PART 3
Managing Human Resources

CHAPTER 5

Employee Resourcing and Careers

CHAPTER CONTENTS

Introduction

1 Three perspectives on human resource flow policies
The individual perspective—careers
The organisational perspective—four cultures
The societal perspective—national culture

2 Managing human resource flow
Managing inflow
Managing outflow

3 Human resource planning

Summary
Case study—Adoption of competences in an Australian city council
Study questions
Further reading

Introduction

Having assessed the extent of the take-up of human resource management (HRM) in the wider Australian environment, we now turn in these next five chapters to examining more closely the HRM approach itself, beginning with employee resourcing and careers.

Employee resourcing, as an HR policy, aims to supply an organisation with the right quality and number of people to achieve its strategy. Resourcing affects the performance of the organisation and has significant social consequences for the individual and society. Employee resourcing influences employees' skill development, their commitment to the organisation, and their careers, and it has potential for positive and negative consequences on individuals' well-being. From the perspective of HRM, management should plan employee resourcing of the organisation carefully because human resource planning is one way of integrating human resources with the requirements of the organisation's strategy, although the evidence is that few organisations consistently use HR planning in practice.[1] Most models of HRM advocate improved policy and practice in employee resourcing; for example, Beer et al. proposed that general managers should become more proactive in employee resourcing by managing the 'flow' of human resources into, through, and out of the organisation.[2] They advised that organisations should develop human resource flow policies, observing that many exhibit human resource flow patterns but that managers do not plan employee resourcing, thus failing to integrate it with business strategy.

This chapter looks at employee resourcing from three perspectives—individual, organisational, and societal—and especially considers how resourcing policies and practices influence people's careers. The three stages of HR flow—inflow, internal flow, and outflow—are also covered. The second of these, internal flow, which consists of actions that affect employees' work roles, promotion, career satisfaction, and development, is considered as part of the discussion on the individual perspective in section 1. Inflow and outflow are considered on their own in section 2 on managing human resource flow. The chapter concludes with a brief look at some of the tools and techniques of HR planning, previously known as manpower or personnel planning.

1 Three perspectives on human resource flow policies

Managing human resource flow strategically means determining a flow pattern that takes into account likely effects on employee commitment to the organisation, the ability of the organisation to adapt to changing circumstances, and the culture of the organisation. Flow patterns have a profound impact on employees' security and careers, although the effect on employee commitment will be considered a higher priority from the soft HRM perspective (in which employee well-being is an important end in itself) than it is from the hard HRM perspective.[3] The pattern of human resource flow creates, sustains, or erodes the level of competence of the organisation over time. More broadly, flow patterns influence the well-being of local communities and society by creating employment or resulting in unemployment.

EMPLOYEE RESOURCING AND CAREERS | 95

Looked at another way, human resource flow is a result of the management of flow policies, systems, and practices that, taken together, ought to be a viable strategic response to three areas: employees' individual needs (personal objectives and career plans), organisational requirements (business objectives, HR plans), and social institutions (government policy, legislation, educational institutions, unions). Beer et al. represent human resource flow diagrammatically as shown in figure 5.1.

Organisational requirements
Business objectives and plans
Human resource flow plans

Individual needs
Personal objectives and life/career plans
Individual career development plans

Flow, policies, systems and practices

Inflow
Recruitment
Assessment and selection
Orientation and socialisation

Internal flow
Evaluation of performance and potential
Career development
Internal placement, promotion, and demotion
Education and training

Outflow
Termination, outplacement, and retirement

Social institutions
Government legislation
Government regulatory agencies
Educational institutions
Unions
Societal values
Public policy

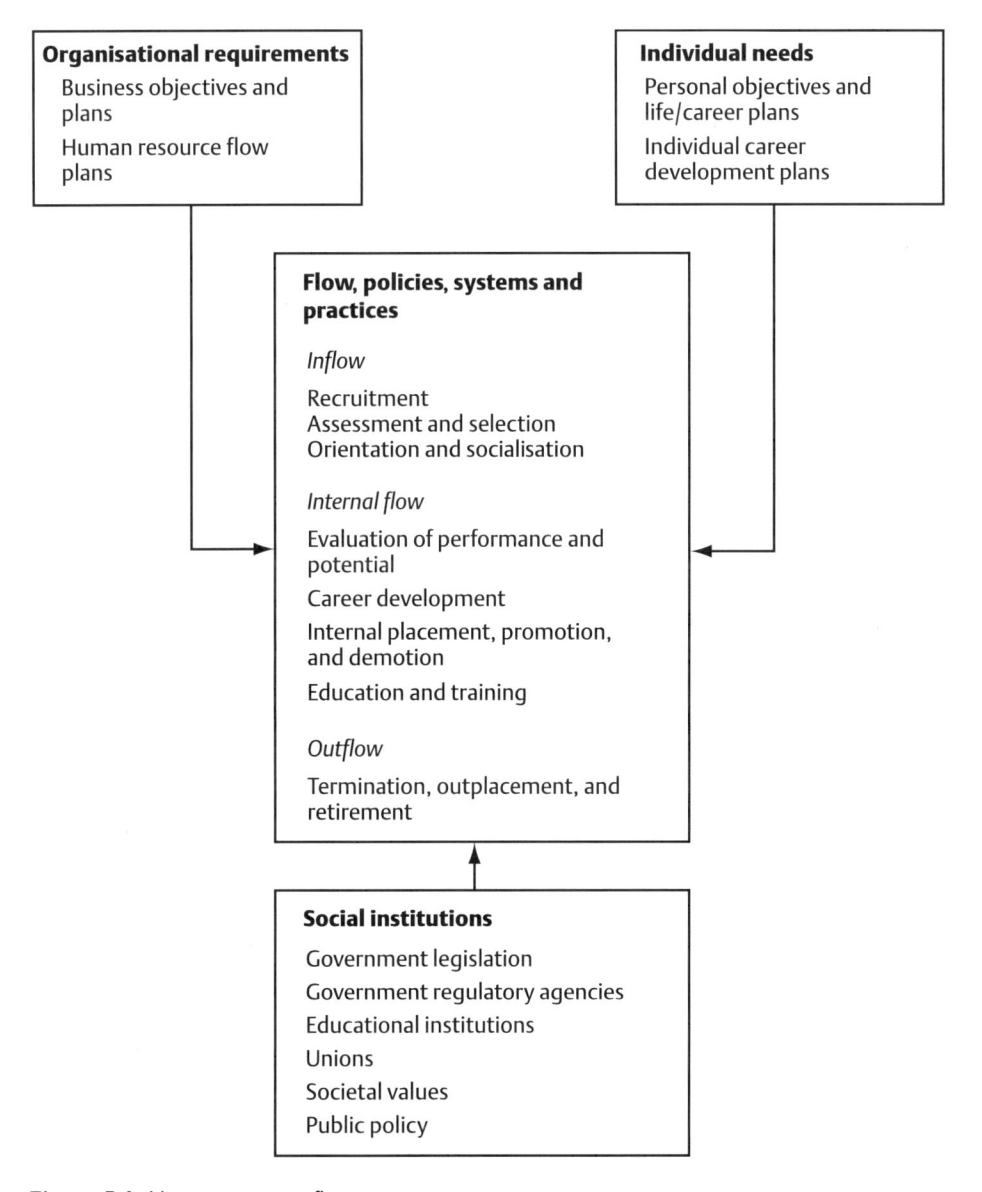

Figure 5.1 Human resource flow

Source: Based on ideas from Walker, J., *Human Resource Planning* (New York: McGraw-Hill, 1980). Reprinted with the permission of the Free Press, a Division of Simon & Schuster Inc., from Beer, M., Spector, B., Lawrence, P. R., Quinn Mills, D., and Walton, R. E., *Managing Human Assets* (figure 4.3, p. 99). Copyright © 1984 the Free Press.

The individual perspective—careers

Before looking at how flow policies affect organisations and society we first consider how employee resourcing affects individuals. This section discusses internal flow from the perspective of the individual and his or her evolving concept of a career at work. Employees experience human resource flow through the way it affects their employment conditions and career development. Careers can be short or long and many people will change careers several times during their working life. Everett Hughes in 1937 defined careers as having subjective and objective components.[4] Subjectively, individuals experience a sense of continuity of purpose and progression in skill or responsibility as they move through their careers. Often, people who feel their careers have been frustrated perceive that there could have been more development or change. In addition to the subjective sense of identity that can be gained from 'having a career', there is the objective view, by which one can plot the movement of the individual within the social order of the organisation, for example, from shopfloor worker to supervisor to middle manager.

Advocates of soft HRM have argued that careers should not be treated as the sole preserve of managerial and professional employees, but should be seen as being important to everyone. Careers are closely connected with individuals' experience of home and work life, and change in either of these two critical areas can cause people to alter their role expectations and career goals. An employee's sense of career is something that develops over time and has varying psychological meaning as career aspirations and expectations are modified. For example, in a study of UK managers and professionals nearing retirement, 48 per cent said that family and personal relationships were the most important thing to them at this stage of their life histories and careers.[5]

An individual's sense of identity is closely bound up with roles he or she plays at home and work. For example, a woman who is both an employee and a mother experiences conflicting demands on her time and energy that have to be managed daily. Success in performing her various roles will be affected by the relative importance that she and others attach to them. Our career preferences and choices are also affected by our personalities; in general, some individuals deeply value stability and security, while others place greater importance on novelty and change. Groups of people pass through similar phases of career expectation governed by common patterns of life history, the culture of organisations, and the norms of society. For instance, most young people in the initial stage of a career do not have the same family responsibilities that many older people have during their mid-life careers, when children and ageing parents are major domestic commitments.

Most people face obstacles and setbacks in their careers, and many employees, blue-collar and white-collar, change their jobs and even their occupations several times over their working lives. As people's experience of life changes over time, they adjust to some extent their concept of self and personal identity. There are some conventionally successful individuals whose careers progress relatively smoothly and develop in a linear and 'upwardly mobile' fashion. John Kotter's 1982 study of general managers in the USA found common factors for success; it seems to be connected with achievement at an early age and major responsibility being attained before the individual is in his or her mid-thirties.[6] However, managerial careers in the 1980s and 1990s have been less stable and predictable in developed countries than they were in the period between 1950 and 1980. Fundamental changes in government policy, especially concerning privatisation and deregulation (as discussed in chapter 2), have combined with greater competitive pressures, causing many large corporate organisations to flatten or 'de-layer' their managerial hierarchies, to 'downsize', and to subcontract what are considered peripheral services. One consequence of the reduction in levels of the organisational hierarchy for employees is that, in both the public and the private sectors, there is less incentive to seek hierarchical promotion. There now exists in organisations less opportunity for promotion, social advancement, and higher status than was available in the past. Reduced promotion prospects have been accompanied by fewer permanent contracts of employment and more part-time and fixed-term contracts. Such changes in employment prospects mean that employees either adapt their idea of what constitutes a career or become dissatisfied when their career expectations are not met.

Career satisfaction is a result of an individual's identification with home and work roles, performing them successfully, and being able to meet new challenges. In the work context, individual career satisfaction partly depends on the organisation's providing opportunities for employees to develop competence in a variety of roles. Charles Handy draws attention to the fact that a range of roles faces employees, in addition to the specific job roles allocated in their individual job descriptions.[7] During daily interaction, employees act in different contexts as subordinate, peer, and superior.

Career dissatisfaction will often result when ambitious and high-performing individuals outgrow their job roles and seek new challenges but their organisations are unwilling or unable to respond by introducing new opportunities. Tension and conflict may also be created because individuals' career aspirations change over time and may eventually no longer match organisational requirements. Career crisis can result from such mismatches, or when work and home lives are in serious conflict, or when the individual's job does not suit his or her abilities and personality. Crisis, as Handy reminds us, can be caused as much by role underload as by role overload.[8] A severe career crisis will often lead to job change, and if the crisis is not managed proactively by the individual, it can result in damaging psychological experiences such as long-term depression, 'burn-out', or inability to hold down a job for a reasonable length of time.

To help explain individual career choice and success and failure in careers, Ed Schein introduced the influential concept of 'career anchors' in 1978.[9] These are self-perceived attributes, motives, attitudes, and values that shape individual careers. Schein lists the following six career anchors: managerial competence (interpersonal, analytical, emotional), technical-functional competence, security, creativity, autonomy, and independence. Schein claimed that if these career anchors were present in employees' work, then they would be more satisfied with their careers and more committed to the organisation. To feel that they have managerial competence, employees must be able to interact effectively with other people, analyse situations clearly, and maintain a balanced emotional life. Technical-functional competence can be as broad as the skills of general management or as narrow as the specific competences of an engineer who maintains technical equipment. Schein's other career anchors, except for job security, assume an individualist orientation to work according to which an employee expects independence, creativity, and autonomy in, for example, determining tasks, prioritising and scheduling work, and evaluating the results. A more collectivist orientation to work would list alternative career anchors such as contributing to the group's purpose, working as a member of a team, and decision making by consultation and consensus. Schein pointed out that good planning of HR flow policies and employee development is a prerequisite to the existence and healthy functioning of career anchors in an organisation.

During the 1980s, in Australia and Western countries such as the USA and UK, it became more common for people to feel that stable careers no longer existed and that organisations were unable any longer to offer a job for life. In the mid-1990s, Herriot and Pemberton claimed that the very notion of career had fundamentally changed because the bargain between employer and employee that held in the 1960s and 1970s no longer applied.[10] Their research was concerned with managerial careers, although many of their points about the changing employment relationship apply to all employees in organisations where a contractual guarantee of lifelong employment and job security is no longer the norm. The authors say that the old deal has changed to a new deal.

Table 5.1 Old deal

You offered	Organisation offered
Loyalty—not leaving	Security of employment
Conformity—doing what you were asked	Promotion prospects
Commitment—going the extra mile	Training and development
Trust—they'll keep their promises	Care in trouble

Source: Herriot, P. and Pemberton, C., *New Deals: The Revolution in Managerial Careers* (1995), p. 17 Wiley. Reprinted by permission of John Wiley & Sons, Inc. Copyright c 1995 John Wiley & Sons.

The old deal was a relational contract whereby each party—employer and employee—learnt to trust one another over time (see table 5.1). Loyalty and organisational commitment were high wherever this trust existed, to the extent that each party would go the extra mile, even where there was no extrinsic benefit (for example, financial gain) to be had. For example, in the banking industry, it was not unknown for employers to help the families of loyal, long-serving employees who died suddenly by paying out a greater financial benefit than they were contractually obliged to render. Employees who were approaching retirement or who underperformed for significant periods of time would be accommodated and tolerated rather than summarily dismissed. On the employees' side, people have worked beyond contract, putting in long hours when necessary and forgoing offers of better jobs elsewhere or other benefits because of a sense of loyalty and commitment to the organisation. People usually entered at the bottom and stayed with the organisation throughout their careers. Blue-collar employees, graduates, and MBA students may have been hired at different entry levels. In general, older people were not asked to leave because legislation in the past made the costs of termination of employment prohibitive. Large corporations in Japan operated these systems, as did some companies in the West, such as *Fortune* 500 companies Hewlett Packard and IBM, until the late 1980s. Lifelong employment systems became less common in Australia and the West in general during the 1990s than they had been in the 1960s and 1970s. They are becoming the preserve of smaller and smaller categories of workers, even in corporations in Japan.

Increasing competitive pressures in general and change in national governments' policy in the face of multinational and national organisations have contributed to eroding the ability of employers to fulfil their side of the bargain under the terms of the old deal. Management style in the public sector has changed towards giving greater significance to value for money and towards facilitating private company services. Since the 1990s, professionals in the public and private sectors have been expected to be more 'businesslike' when dealing with clients. In industrial research and development, employment for technicians and scientists has generally become less secure as employers more frequently replace experienced employees as they reach middle age with younger people. These changes inevitably influence what has been called the 'psychological contract', which may be defined as the implicit beliefs about reciprocal obligations held by employers and employees.[11] The new deal, as proposed by Herriot and Pemberton, is a much more transactional relationship whereby each party weighs up the opportunities and costs of being in the relationship, adopting a short-term and less trusting attitude. The new deal is a less permanent psychological contract in which the two parties are unsure about what is being offered and what will be offered in the future (see table 5.2).

Table 5.2 New deal

You offer	Organisation offers
Long hours	High pay
Added responsibility	Rewards for performance
Broader skills	A job
Tolerance of change and ambiguity	

Source: Herriot, P. and Pemberton, C., *New Deals: The Revolution in Managerial Careers* (1995), pp. 19–20 Wiley. Reprinted by permission of John Wiley & Sons, Inc. Copyright c 1995 John Wiley & Sons.

Since the 1980s, many organisations, first in manufacturing and then in the service industries, have transformed the conditions of employment. In many instances, employees have perceived there to be two major sources of inequity during this change: procedural inequity in how new deals have been struck and distributive injustice in how rewards have been distributed. A prominent example of such inequity occurred in 1994 in the UK when, after privatisation of the utility British Gas, the chief executive, Cedric Brown, was awarded a 75 per cent increase in salary to £475 000 a year; shortly afterwards, 2600 showroom staff were warned that their salaries of £13 000 per annum were unrealistically high and redundancies could not be ruled out.[12]

The new deal, Herriot and Pemberton surmise, is a less happy relationship than the old deal. Unless it is managed better by both parties, they predict that the new deal will render organisations uncompetitive. They recommend that there be new, different deals to reflect the fact that organisations are no longer able to offer relational contracts and that employees want different things from their careers. They propose three main types of contracts that might better suit the new deal, for both parties: part-time contracts (with hours flexible to meet demand peaks), project contracts (with outcomes and completion dates specified but methods left open), and core contracts (with training flexible to meet organisational change requirements, but some security and employability for core workers).

Herriot and Pemberton note that the flexibility of part-time contracts is proving to be especially suitable to the career aspirations of unskilled and semi-skilled female employees and to early retirees who wish to continue working, but not full-time. They add to this list a small but growing group of part-time managers, who have been made redundant or who are unwilling to work in organisations that have significantly changed since they commenced their careers. The authors rename these part-time contracts 'lifestyle contracts' because they allow employees to more easily manage home and work responsibilities.

Project contracts are suited to people who are stimulated by careers with a technical focus, relatively unencumbered by organisational politics and the administrative duties typical of employment in the larger organisation. This type of contract is named the 'autonomy contract' because it offers employees independence, challenge, and the opportunity to concentrate on an area of expertise. Finally, core contracts are suited to people who have a 'managerial competence' career anchor (as described above) and therefore find motivation and job satisfaction in developing the general skills of the core employee. Organisations have to develop the skills of their core employees continuously to remain competitive and innovative, and so this contract is termed the 'development contract'.

Herriot and Pemberton observe that each of these types of contract is prone to difficulties for employer and employee, especially because employers will be tempted to renege on even this new deal by exploiting part-time workers, over-controlling project workers, and failing to develop the skills of core workers. They recommend that both parties continually monitor and renegotiate the contracts. Their hope is that, in future new deals, individual employees will offer the capability to learn and add value, while organisations will offer employability, a flexible contract, and individualised rewards.[13]

From the perspective of HRM, effective human resource flow means matching individual career needs with organisational needs. This first section has shown that the employees' sense of career is dynamic and affected by a variety of factors, some within and others outside the individual's control. Herriot and Pemberton's concept of new deals in employment illustrates that employee resourcing in an organisation is increasingly likely to be characterised by distinct agreements being applied to groups of people working under different contracts. Further, they warned that there are strong pressures on employers to act opportunistically in employee resourcing. New deals during the 1990s tended to negotiate a no compulsory redundancy pledge from employers in return for concessions from the workforce normally in terms of an agreement on new flexible work practices. Employment flexibility has been a major item in enterprise agreements for Australian banks and financial institutions. It has also been significant elsewhere; for example, the UK's biggest bank, Lloyds-TSB, promises a job for life as long as employees can prove they are flexible to change and agree to flexible work practices.[14]

The organisational perspective—four cultures

Organisational culture establishes norms and expectations of how people should be treated and serve the needs of the organisation. Culture affects employee resourcing by influencing the values and beliefs of owners, management, and other employees about which flow policies are appropriate. Research by Fons Trompenaars on culture illustrates the influence of organisational culture on employee resourcing. In 1993 Trompenaars proposed a framework for understanding cultural diversity in business.[15] He argued that cultural differences create four distinct corporate cultures, which he calls *family*, *Eiffel Tower*, *guided missile*, and *incubator*.

The *family culture* is dispersed among 'members of the family' (Trompenaars describes it as 'diffuse'), has parent figures in authority, is intuitive in its decision making, supports leadership from the top, and expects love and respect from its employees. HR flow policies are not clearly formalised and depend on decisions made by a few individuals at the top of the organisation. Senior management will demand loyalty and in return employees will demand to be treated like members of the family; however, flow policies in this culture will often be ambiguous and to some extent depend on who is considered by those in authority to be part of the family.

The *Eiffel Tower culture* is bureaucratic and mechanistic, placing more emphasis on rational efficiency and analytical skills than does the family culture. People are treated as human resources and are expected to follow organisational job descriptions, rules, and procedures. Flow policies in this culture are more likely to be formally laid down in writing. They are applied with a systematic logic that emphasises hierarchical status, office, and function more than attending to individuals and their feelings. Emphasis will be on procedural fairness in the implementation of rules and on distributive justice according to principles of rational efficiency of the organisation.

In the *guided missile culture*, work tasks are set as if they form part of a computer control system. This task-centred culture is tuned to altering its path according to feedback from the environment. The organisation is structured by projects with clearly specified goals, and employees are expected to become specialists or experts in their area of responsibility. Flow policies are established to achieve the completion of tasks and projects. Loyalty to a project will be seen as more important than loyalty to the organisation. Recruitment from the external labour market will be readily utilised when specialist expertise is lacking. Employees can expect to be managed by objectives and rewarded with performance-related pay. Promotion and development opportunities for the internal labour market will be based on previous project success, leading to high performers being offered assignments that are more challenging and entail more responsibility. A twin career track is consistent with this culture—one track for specialists, who don't want too much administrative responsibility, and one for general managers, who lose some of their technical currency to perform managerial duties.

The *incubator culture* is characterised by opportunity for personal growth and change. Relationships between employees are dynamic, energetic, and dispersed ('diffuse'). Management is carried out by example and through enthusiasm, with an emphasis on improvisation and joint creativity. Flow policies in this organisation are unlikely to be clearly articulated, the tendency being for employees to be recruited and laid off according to workload. Where creativity attracts business, the organisation will find it easy to recruit young and talented employees who seek the opportunity to work in a successful and creative environment. Where business is slack and employment vacancies exist in the external labour market, top management may formulate rudimentary flow policies in an effort to retain skilled and creative employees, and in readiness for an upturn in work.

Trompenaars's four cultures provide one explanation for why organisations do not have clearly defined human resource flow policies. A formulated, documented business strategy is likely to be present, at best, in two of the four organisational cultures, Eiffel Tower and guided missile, where there is an openness towards systematic methods. In the family and incubator cultures there is less interest in the accountability of top management and less preoccupation with decision making based on rational thinking. The belief system in these two cultures is more concerned with maintaining a sense of community based on loyalty and trust. In the family culture, loyalty is primarily to other family members, and in the incubator culture, trust comes about through shared work activity rather than loyalty being something owed to specific people. HR flow policies are therefore unlikely to be seen in these cultures as critical to running an organisation.

Trompenaars's framework for organisational culture helps us understand why employee resourcing has not routinely applied HR flow policies in the past. As far as the more recent situation is concerned, there is evidence that some organisations have been developing a simpler rationale for HR flow policies. During the 1990s many large organisations identified 'core competences', which were the skills deemed by top management to be critical for future success. From an organisational perspective, HR flow policies are designed to assist with the timely supply of the right quality of people to achieve an organisation's strategy. Once core competences are identified, they can be used by HR managers as guidelines for improving policy and practice in employee resourcing with the aim of improving the strategic value of the human resource and the competitiveness of the company.[16] The remainder of this section reviews one influential description of core competence.

Prahalad and Hamel analysed the success of Japanese corporations such as NEC, Canon, Honda, Sony, Yamaha, and Komatsu in comparison with the success of US organisations in cultivating and exploiting core competences to launch new, innovative products. They advised top management to think much more carefully about the relationship between competences and end products. In their 1990 *Harvard Business Review* article entitled 'The Core Competence of the Corporation', the authors use the analogy of a tree—the competences being the roots and the end products being the fruits.[17] Japanese corporations, the authors suggest, have understood better than US organisations how product innovation draws upon core competences. For example, Canon's laser and colour copiers and laser imagers are the result of having exploited competences in precision mechanics, fine optics, and microelectronics.

Prahalad and Hamel describe how the US company GTE was well positioned in the early 1980s to become a major competitor in the fast-developing information and communication industry. It was active in telecommunications and its operations relied on competences in a variety of areas, for example, telephones, semiconductors, and packet switching systems. They observe that in 1980, GTE's sales (US dollars) were nearly $10 billion while the sales of the Japanese company NEC in the same year were $4 billion. But by 1988, GTE's sales had grown to only $16.5 billion while NEC's had grown to $22 billion. What had happened? GTE had decided to focus on core competences in telephone operations, defence, and lighting products. The company was organised into strategic business units (SBUs) and took the decision to divest its products and core competences in televisions and semiconductors, and entered into joint ventures in switching, transmission, and digital systems. Meanwhile, NEC grew as a world leader in semi-conductors and became a first-tier competitor in telecommunication products and computers. Through its core competences, NEC was able to bridge the gap between telecommunications and office automation and produce a range of information and communication products, for example, mobile telephones, fax machines, and laptop computers.

The implication of Prahalad and Hamel's analysis for employee resourcing is that multidivisional organisations must facilitate the building of core competences. These competences enable the corporation to develop and innovate by utilising a variety of technologies and experiences from diverse product markets. HR flow that is restricted to developing products within separate, autonomous SBUs is less likely to engender core competences that in turn lead to creative development of new product markets. The authors suggest that Japanese corporations have been much more successful than Western corporations have in nurturing distinctive competences because they facilitate learning in the organisation across different product technologies.

So, according to Prahalad and Hamel, an employee resourcing challenge for modern corporations is to nurture core competences. They are the roots of success and cannot be assessed for their future usefulness on the basis of the current financial performance of product technologies within SBUs. Human resource flow policies that are based on a narrow portfolio investment analysis of SBU performance may be cost-effective in the short term, but can stifle an organisation's vision of the future and may even damage its capability to innovate.

The societal perspective—national culture

The societal perspective on employee resourcing is discussed in this section through reference to research on HRM and theory of national culture by Hofstede.

Chapter 1 discussed Brewster and Bournois's model of the European environment of HRM and Brewster's report on a survey of HRM in Europe. In this report

Brewster noted that there has been a trend in employee resourcing throughout Europe towards fewer 'standard' working contracts and more 'atypical working' (for example, part-time and short- and fixed-term contracts). As for what is happening specifically in the UK, Guest also reported that issuing fewer standard working contracts has become more common in some occupations, including HRM and personnel management.[18] More responsibility for HRM or personnel management has gone to line managers. Also, there has been an increase in the subcontracting of HR services and, in some organisations, devolvement of personnel management activity from central to local management. As was discussed in chapter 2, subcontracting of services in the Australian public sector has been pursued, and there has been an increase in subcontracting in all major Western European countries.[19]

The work of the influential writer on culture Geert Hofstede further explains the influence of national culture on employee resourcing and HR flow policies. During the 1970s, Hofstede conducted a study of national cultures. He researched 40 countries to determine empirically the differences in national culture, and he identified four dimensions that seemed to distinguish national cultures from each other: *power distance, uncertainty avoidance, individualism–collectivism,* and *masculinity*. He concluded that these four dimensions explain differences in the 'collective mental programming of people in different national cultures'.[20]

Power distance is the extent to which a society accepts an unequal distribution of power. High power-distance societies accept a large difference in status between superior and subordinate, whereas low power-distance societies expect the reverse. The Philippines and Mexico, for example, have high power distance, whereas Austria and Denmark have low power distance. *Uncertainty avoidance* is the degree to which a society attempts to avoid uncertainty in life through greater career stability, formal rules, intolerance of deviance, belief in absolute truth, and attainment of expertise. The cultures of Greece and Japan exhibit high uncertainty avoidance, whereas Singapore and Sweden have cultures with low avoidance. *Individualism–collectivism* is the degree to which a society is seen as being composed of individuals, whereas collectivism is characterised by a tighter social framework in which individual identity is bound up with that of the group (family, clan, organisation). The USA and Australia are high in individualism, whereas Pakistan and Thailand are high in collectivism. Finally, *masculinity* is the extent to which society favours the supposedly masculine values of assertiveness and acquisitiveness rather than the supposedly more feminine values of concern for people and quality of life. Japan and Australia are high in masculinity, whereas Scandinavian countries and the Netherlands are low.

HR flow policies can be strongly influenced by the national cultural assumptions within which the organisation operates. Flow policies operating on the basis of high power distance will seek to sustain hierarchical status differences between employees. The idea that 'boss is boss' is less likely to offend people who accept high power distance, and they will not be surprised by decision making routinely based on position rather than expertise, nor by unequal access to information and development opportunities. Flow policies constructed to support a culture high in uncertainty avoidance place more emphasis on career stability and predictability of future job advancement. Training and development in this culture occurs in regular phases, particularly before promotion to a higher position. In highly individualist cultures, flow policies that promote rapid turnover of employees and frequent recruitment from the external labour market will seem more natural than they would in collectivist cultures, in which greater recognition is commonly given to the family, and employers are held more responsible for contributing to the maintenance of stable, local-community relationships. Organisations functioning in a masculine culture will believe it is natural when devising flow policies to place higher emphasis on concern for task than on concern for people.

Hofstede's four dimensions of national culture help to explain different styles of management and the variety of practice in HR flow policies. The dimensions have been used here to illustrate how national culture can affect flow policies, although it is clear that they have implications stretching widely into many other areas of HRM. Societal influences on human resource flow are complex, but there are common trends that must be understood if managers and employers are to create and implement HR policy effectively. Likewise, for employees, an insight into the influence of culture and society, combined with self-insight, will help them to manage their careers and adapt to situations confidently so as to sustain their individual effectiveness and psychological well-being.

2 Managing human resource flow

Having looked at some of the issues and forces surrounding human resource flow policies, we now focus on HR flow itself and how it is managed in organisations. As internal flow has been covered in section 1 of this chapter, we focus here on inflow and outflow.

Managing inflow

Managing inflow chiefly concerns recruitment and selection, which are two separate but, obviously, linked processes. Recruitment is the process of attracting candidates for vacant jobs, and selection is the process of choosing the right person for the job from among a pool of candidates.[21] Recruitment and selection are an important part of achieving strategic goals and have significant impact on employment stability and employee turnover. In the past, managers have often avoided accurately informing recruits and longer-serving employees about the realities of their career prospects and likely progression within the organisation, with the result that many employees later become dissatisfied, having forged an ill-informed 'psychological contract' with their employer.

During the last two decades of the twentieth century, recruitment and selection systems have been used to stimulate organisational change.[22] Greater interest in the processes of selection has generally been accompanied by an increasing emphasis on the attitudes and behaviours of employees.[23] Organisations seeking to identify the best group of employees for achieving strategic change frequently specify the skills or competences they want.[24] Large organisations have introduced more assessment programs for identifying employees with career potential that fits the business strategy. These programs use biodata (individuals' life histories), psychometric testing (scientific measurement of personality and competences), and assessment centres (centres that administer structured tests and activities to assess employees' career potential and development needs, with occupational psychologists often included among the assessors).[25] These new and more 'scientific' systems of selection and recruitment have led to new methodologies of evaluation and assessment, particularly the competence-based approach, which is applied to a wide range of jobs and has been used to describe managerial work that has become more 'outward-looking, market-focused and team-oriented'.[26] In the Australian public sector, organisations have specified competences for improved customer care. Brisbane City Council has integrated customer service goals with its training and performance management schemes. Such initiatives have been recognised in awards from the Australian Customer Service Association. In one UK organisation, employees were expected to exhibit competence in achieving the key accountabilities of enterprise, customer care, and success; previously, this culture was said to have been dominated by the values of sobriety, caution, loyalty, respectability, thrift, and stability.[27]

The competences of employees have become important criteria for selection and recruitment.[28] They are being used to identify people who can cope with the present and future challenges of work;[29] however, they are only one part of the process of achieving a more productive internal organisation. In 1998, Paul Sparrow observed that Ford Motor Company and Lucas Industries made considerable improvements to the productivity of the workplace by attending not so much to competences but more carefully to work organisation and other factors influenced by management initiative.[30] Over a fifteen-year period, Ford reduced the number of workers needed to make a car per day from five to two. Lucas Industries' automotive manufacturing business reduced lead times from 55 days to twelve days.

Sparrow argues that with strategy, structure, and systems being changed to create new organisational design and with business processes such as just-in-time (JIT) and business process re-engineering (BPR) being radically rethought, less importance is being attached to the 'person–job fit'. Greater interest is now being shown in individuals' capacity to contribute to several fundamentally different business processes. Change in organisational design, therefore, is having an impact on resourcing along with other HRM policies and practices. Selection and recruitment are now concerned with identifying people who can cope with a new organisational environment in which:
- employees are exposed to new sources of information and new networks of relationships;
- there are changes to the roles that employees are expected to play;
- managers think differently about the tasks that need to be done;
- required decision-making processes are altered;

- the timespans of discretion before the consequence of an inappropriate decision becomes known are altered;
- the criteria for effectiveness, such as the judgment and leadership capabilities needed by employees, are altered;
- there are shifts in the actual work content and business process flow;
- the choice of performance-management criteria and measurement metrics is changing;
- there are changes to career aspirations, problems created by the natural inclination of people not to break the habits of their past and present roles, and significant shifts in their power, influence, and credibility.[31]

As new organisational design has tended to move away from bureaucratic and 'tall' (multi-layered), hierarchical structures, it has altered the design of jobs. Parker and Wall identify five common features of the content of these new jobs.[32] First, operational knowledge has become more critical as the new systems require greater flexibility and faster adaptation to change in workflow and quicker error detection. Second, employees find their work is more reliant on others' performance because buffers in the system such as spare stock, extra staff, supervisory management, and specialist inspectors have been removed. Third, the operations function has more contact with internal and external customers, increasing the importance of controlling the costs of machine downtime and eliminating inefficiencies and bottlenecks in workflow. Fourth, greater employee discretion and responsibility require higher-order cognitive competences, such as decision making and problem solving. Fifth, more attention is being paid to employees' social competences, especially their ability to work both independently and unsupervised and, when required, as members of a team, cooperating and communicating effectively. However, there is a lack of evidence for selection systems focusing on team competences. It is worth noting that although companies use sophisticated methods for selecting people for individual jobs they rarely use similarly systematic approaches for teams. Michael West et al. argue that organisations should improve the profile of their teams through incorporating more systematic methods of competence-based selection.[33]

In the more specific context of graduate recruitment and selection, graduates' ability to rate their own performance has been found to be a reliable predictor of success in the job. There is a difference in gender here, women being better than men at rating themselves accurately on their strengths and weaknesses.[34] A study of graduate selection in three European countries—the UK, the Netherlands, and France—found highly significant differences in the various selection methods. The methods used included traditional interviews, criterion-referenced interviews (interviews linked to behavioural anchors in which the interview focuses on candidates' past behaviours), situational interviews (also linked to behavioural anchors, but future-oriented), references, ability tests, personality tests, biodata, assessment centres, application forms, graphology (France and the Netherlands only), and astrology (France and the Netherlands only). The authors of the research study concluded that, similar to previous findings from research on management selection, while the more sophisticated techniques are being used in all three countries, some techniques with poor psychometric efficacy are still widespread.[35]

Research has shown that in the mid-1990s, employers neither adopted selection systems for teams nor preferred systems with strong psychometric efficacy. Further, the results showed that employers were not formulating plans for graduate recruitment and were therefore failing to address the increasing shortage of young recruits caused by the fall in birth rates since the 1970s.[36] There are many signs to show that there was an increased use of more selection tools during the last two decades of the twentieth century, but research by academics shows there is a lot more work to be done in making these systems more rigorous and in evaluating the effectiveness of different selection methods and the quality of assessors' judgments. Good selection and recruitment practices by an employer are also more likely to create a favourable impression of the organisation, improving its ability to attract and retain people. Some estimates say that reaction to the selection process accounts for 15–20 per cent of a candidate's decision on whether or not to accept a job offer.[37]

The remainder of this section on managing inflow provides some fundamental and practical guidelines on two commonly used methods of selection: face-to-face interviews and psychometric testing.

The face-to-face interview will probably continue to be the most commonly used method of selection because it provides an opportunity for both parties to find out more about each other and decide whether or not they want to work together. Interviewing has the advantage over other methods in that it is flexible and, although time-consuming, uses fewer resources than do some other popular assessment methods. Its disadvantages are that many people have poor interviewing skills and often don't know it. Psychological studies have shown that people tend to be attracted to others they see as like themselves,[38] so interviewers may end up choosing the person they feel they have most in common with rather than the person who is best for the job. The unstructured interview is said to be little better than chance, although many recruiters would be surprised to be told that their own unstructured interviewing is no better than a shake of the dice. Research shows interviewing on its own to be an ineffective way of selecting the best performers; however, its validity is increased when it is combined with other assessment methods directly related to present and future job requirements. Structured selection methods and training in interviewing technique can improve the quality of selection decisions.

In addition to interviewing, psychometric tests have come to be used more frequently since the 1980s as part of selection practice. Japanese corporations investing in Europe—for example, Toyota and Nissan—have been renowned for their rigorous, formal selection methods applied to all levels, including the shop-floor employee and office worker. The tests are not all new, and early versions have been utilised within the military and the public sector for some jobs for more than 50 years. A small industry has developed providing testing and assessment services, growing in the 1960s and 1970s in the USA and then in the UK. The use of assessment and development centres is now used in 50 per cent of major British

BOX 5.1

Effective interviewing

The structured interview, it should be remembered, is based on clearly identified competences that the candidate should possess to be successful in the job. The fundamental question then is which of the candidates meets the essential selection criteria. Time has to be allocated effectively and good rapport should be established to ensure that the candidates are all able to perform at their best. Maureen Guirdham has published guidelines for effective face-to-face interviewing, which are included in the example of a good-practice checklist shown below.[60]

Interviewers' checklist

The following items would be rated on a scale of 1 (very poor) to 5 (excellent) for effectiveness.

- Reception of candidates
- Room arrangements
- Introductory remarks created an open and businesslike climate
- Candidates were able to talk informally before transition to selection interview
- Chair described the job and the organisation thoroughly
- Interview plan
- Established an easy and informal relationship
- Did not plunge too quickly into demanding questions
- Asked patient and unhurried interview questions
- Interviewers appeared sincere and friendly
- Interviewers encouraged candidate to talk
- Asked open questions (i.e. many different answers might be given)
- Asked closed questions (i.e. when appropriate and requiring definite categorical answers)
- Asked probing questions (i.e. questions that follow up important issues and concerns)
- Asked hypothetical questions (i.e. what candidates would do given specific circumstances)
- Asked play-back questions (confirmed what the candidate was saying at critical junctures)
- Prevented candidate from glossing over important facts/issues
- Covered interview plan in enough detail
- Time management
- Analysed career of candidate
- Analysed strengths
- Analysed weaknesses
- Identified behaviour patterns

- Identified competences
- Identified attitudes
- Identified preferences
- Maintained pace
- Maintained direction
- Avoided making unnecessary, early conclusions
- Avoided leading questions
- Avoided discriminating questions
- Listening/talking ratio
- Recorded candidate's answers
- Encouraged candidate to ask questions towards the end of the interview
- Ensured candidate had the information needed to decide whether to accept job or not
- Made it clear what would happen next
- Ended the interview on the right note
- Had sufficient information on the interview to discuss all of the candidates thoroughly
- Feedback given to candidates on their performance, after interview.

Line and HR managers need to be aware of good practice in interviewing, and training in this technique of selection is important.

employing organisations, but, according to occupational psychologists and experts on assessment, unfortunately many practices are superficial, reducing the validity and reliability of these centres. Their adoption in Australian organisations must take into account their potential shortcomings. Common problems are lack of assessor training and guidance, lack of rationale for links between the exercises and the dimensions assessed, inadequate time devoted to activities and assessment, and insufficient validation of assessment instruments. There is also the danger that some tests are unfair and may lead to claims of unfair discrimination where it can be shown that they systematically discriminate, for example, against racial groups.[39]

There are two main types of psychometric test: reasoning and personality. The reasoning tests assess qualities such as aptitude, cognitive skill, ability, and intelligence. Personality tests examine how individuals behave and react to different situations, producing a profile of their personality traits, preferences, and attitudes. Cattell's 16PF (sixteen personality factors), Saville and Holdsworth's OPQ (Occupational Personality Questionnaire), and the Myers–Briggs Type Indicators have been used widely. These tests ask a variety of questions about individuals' likes and preferences, and often several questions addressing the same personality variable will be scattered throughout the questionnaire. Some tests incorporate questions to assess possible bias, such as a social desirability bias, whereby individuals tend to give what they believe is the socially desirable response. Also, the scoring key and analysis can determine a candidate's consistency and reliability of response, for example, the extent to which the respondent answers similar questions in the same way. Many of the questions are about basic values, attitudes, and preferences.

BOX 5.2

Gerald A. Cole lists some of the issues that must be considered before administering psychological tests.[61]

- Is such a test appropriate in the circumstances and will it provide the information that we are looking for in a candidate?
- Is a test to be used as an aid to short-listing or as an element in final selection?
- How will test evidence be weighed in comparison with other elements of the selection process?
- Is the test a fair one to use with the candidates in question, for example, does it unfairly discriminate against ethnic minorities or women?
- Should candidates be given an opportunity to prepare for the test beforehand?
- Will candidates be given feedback on their test results?
- How will confidentiality of test results be protected?
- Should the test(s) be administered and/or analysed by the organisation's own staff or by specialist consultants?
- What steps should be taken to monitor the use of tests and to assess their value and effectiveness?

In addition to ensuring fair and due process in selection decisions as recommended by Cole, some academics and occupational psychologists have recommended maintaining a degree of healthy scepticism about the extent to which one can be rigorous in what is a process of exchange of information and negotiation between prospective employer and employee. On this point, Sue Newell and Chris Rice offer the following salutary caution: 'Selection decisions are outcomes of human interpretations, conflicts, confusions, guesses and rationalisations rather than clear pictures unambiguously traced out on an engineer's drawing board.'[62]

Managing outflow

Whether an organisation is based in an economy such as Australia's, which is heavily influenced by short-term pressures created by the financial system, or in one such as Germany's, which is influenced by longer-term pressures, and whether it has an individualist or a collectivist culture, managers in countries throughout the world periodically find themselves under pressure to make reductions in the workforce. Early retirement and laying off low performers have been common methods of altering the age and competence profile of a workforce with the aim of reducing costs and retaining people believed to have an appropriate attitude to the changing work environment. Beer et al. observed that these outflow strategies are becoming more and more constrained by national employment legislation. There has been a rapid increase in legal action taken by individuals in the USA claiming unjustified discharge or discrimination. It is interesting to note, however, that the ratio of black unemployed men in 2001 was lower in the USA than in the UK, where black males are nearly five times more likely to be unemployed than white males, showing an uneven relationship can pertain between the extent of discrimination and amount of litigation. From their soft HRM perspective, Beer et al. therefore identify the central strategic dilemma of an organisation as balancing employees' need for job security and employment rights with the organisation's use of outflow as a means of cost reduction and renewal.[40] There follows a brief overview of the various ways of approaching outflow: lifelong employment, downward and lateral mobility, early retirement, and workforce reduction and redundancy.

Fewer companies offered lifelong employment in the 1990s. Even those employers that have used lifelong employment for core workers as part of a strategy of 'sophisticated' human relations, such as IBM and Hewlett Packard, are prone to reassess individuals' job security according to individual and organisational performance. Sophisticated approaches to human relations are typical of the newer, non-unionised industries such as the computer, electronics, and pharmaceutical industries, in which employees are retained through a range of modern personnel-management techniques and special incentives and rewards.[41] These sophisticated approaches are not, however, the general trend of the majority of non-unionised industries and their companies. Whether 'lifelong employment' really means lifelong employment is tested whenever there is a serious industry recession or exceptionally poor competitive performance. Some organisations, such as Ford, made lifelong employment commitments to core employees in the late 1980s and early 1990s in exchange for changed attitudes and flexibility of working practices and targets. However, while Ford Australia's Enterprise Agreement (2000) stresses the need for flexibility, there is no commitment as such to lifelong employment. The psychological contract is not an issue, though, that employers can risk burying, as demonstrated in research on knowledge workers in high technology and financial services industries, which found the psychological contract has a direct effect on employee commitment and intention to stay in the organisation.[42]

The process of rationalisation of human resources has been occurring over the last twenty years in most developed countries, including Australia, with significant influence on employee resourcing, particularly hierarchical promotion and long-term job security. In UK manufacturing companies such as British Aerospace, GEC's subsidiary company, Marconi Instruments, and elsewhere—for instance, in the retail, banking, and insurance industries—the reduction in the number of layers in the hierarchy from top management to the most junior employee has been from between thirteen and twenty levels down to as few as three levels. The 'delayering' process has also occurred in Australia, with layers of management being removed in over 40 per cent of large organisations during the periods 1993–95 and 1997–98. Beer et al. argue that where a company emphasises performance in the job over position in the status hierarchy, downward and lateral career movement (for example, where a division manager is asked to return to being head of a particular function, or a sales manager is requested to return to working in the field) will be easier to implement without causing fundamental loss of self-esteem.[43]

Early retirement at age 50 or 55 has been a common outflow strategy, often accompanied by compensation packages such as pension benefits similar to those normally received at retirement at age 60–65. For American companies in the 1980s, this was the most popular method of managing outflow in the attempt to revitalise their international competitiveness.[44] Since then, it has become a popular strategy for public sector restructuring in many countries.

Severe reduction of the workforce often has damaging consequences for the local labour market. Managing outflow in this way can be emotionally charged for both management and for employees. Local communities often suffer hardship and unrest until either new jobs become available or new businesses and industries develop in the region. The Hunter Valley in New South Wales is one region that has suffered, but is now seeking to replace traditional manufacturing companies with new viable businesses. Downsizing in manufacturing has had a negative effect on employment opportunities throughout many regions that were highly dependent on this and other old industries. Case study research on the practices of employment restructuring suggests that some variation exists in management style influenced by national culture: in four case organisations in Poland, managers generally adopted less harsh practices than their Western counterparts, but the researchers concluded that there would likely be a convergence towards Western practice.[45]

Managers who have been involved in major redundancy programs have often found that the employees who are retained by the organisation judge their employer as much by the way it treats the redundant and early-retired employees as by the way it treats them. There are codes of good practice for observing fair treatment and due process. The key to good practice in managing outflow is being able to maintain participative and open two-way communication and to resolve conflicts quickly and equitably. In some countries, much stricter procedural mechanisms have to be observed. For instance, in Germany there are much tighter institutional constraints and legislative requirements surrounding consultation with employees and their representatives than there are in the UK.[46]

Rationalisation of organisations, particularly 'downsizing', has been found in both the USA and Europe to force people down transitional career paths on which they experience strong emotions such as shock, disbelief, betrayal, animosity, lowered morale, guilt, higher stress, and fears over job security.[47] Kets de Vries and Balazs studied rationalisation in Europe and found it also has negative effects on managers, once the 'organisational memory' (the collective knowledge of the history of the organisation) and crucial HR skills are disrupted.[48] Their research found that some employees adjusted to the change by downplaying its emotional significance and forming a more cynical psychological contract. Others adjusted less successfully and displayed more emotion, attempting to 'get even' by withdrawal or reduced involvement. However, it is not only in the area of compulsory redundancy that self-esteem, organisational commitment, job satisfaction, and work motivation can be strongly affected. Herriot recommends that managers and HR practitioners pay more attention to individual well-being during any type of career transition, and he provides examples of how change in organisations and jobs forces such transitions:
- redundancy, demotion, or the move to part-time employment can damage self-esteem, threaten identity (for example, as breadwinner), and damage people's sense of agency;
- cross-functional moves can threaten professional identity, but conversely may add to self-esteem;

- promotions, role changes, and allocation to more prestigious projects may enhance self-esteem;
- promotions may, however, split work and home identity, since taking on a heavier workload may threaten one's identity as effective parent, spouse, or partner;
- the increased frequency of transitions may threaten the stability of our identity, since our capacity to incorporate the new roles into our notions of who we are may be stretched to the limit;
- our feeling of being in some sense in control of our lives can only be supported if we have a degree of choice about the 'whether', 'when', and 'what' of transitions.[49]

How an organisation manages HR outflow is a good indicator of its management style and culture. Managing outflow is a strong test of the skills and endurance of managers who are responsible for the process of making employees redundant, and for other means of moving people out of the organisation. Invariably, one also has to take into account that what is acceptable practice will differ to some extent according to national culture. For example, in South Korea, local companies have a tradition of not encouraging 'inter-firm mobility' (the practice of employees with significant work experience leaving one company and joining a competitor), and a study of downsizing during the mid-1990s recession found that US multinational corporations offered part-time contracts while Korean firms prohibited such arrangements.[50] Unfortunately, some companies and individuals have been insensitive to the psychological damage the realities of outflow can cause employees, and it is a major responsibility of the HR function to ensure that these transitions are handled effectively for the benefit of both the organisation and its employees. It is important that people working in HRM remember that the psychological contract is complex and multidimensional. It may include individual perceptions of: the work environment, job security, rewards, equity and leadership.[51]

3 Human resource planning

There is a range of quantitative methods available for HR planning and established statistical means of representing the inflow, internal flow, and outflow of human resources. New business strategies will demand new approaches to employee resourcing; for example, if a company acquires another company, it will have to identify those employees who are considered critical to the new organisation and those who are considered to duplicate resources. And strategies for entry into new markets or areas of business often prompt the development of HR plans for retaining and developing select groups of employees.

Quantitative techniques for planning human resources have been available for nearly 50 years; however, research evidence suggests that utilisation of HR planning techniques has been ad hoc.[52] The importance of HR planning in ensuring that the organisation has the human resources to achieve its strategic goals has long been asserted and this figures plainly, for example, in the UK Institute of Personnel and Development's definition of HR planning: 'The systematic and continuing process of analysing an organisation's human resource needs under changing conditions and developing personnel policies appropriate to the longer-term effectiveness of the organisation. It is an integral part of corporate planning and budgeting procedures since human resource costs and forecasts both affect and are affected by longer-term corporate plans.'[53]

Storey and Sisson argue that increasing uncertainty about conditions in the external environment, combined with the traditional reluctance of managers to plan human resources, bodes ill for increased use of strategic rational planning.[54] They observe that most HR planning methods have three key components: identifying the demand for labour, identifying the supply of labour, and reconciling supply and demand. The reconciliation process should be consistent with the business strategy.

Armstrong provides a number of practical examples of strategies leading to different HR plans.[55] 'Acquisition strategies' require the forecasting of HR needs. 'Retention strategies' entail planning how to retain the people the organisation wants to keep. 'Development strategies' (for example, multiskilling) involve describing how the skills and competences of employees will be increased to meet the needs of the organisation. 'Utilisation strategies' set targets for improving productivity and cost-effectiveness. 'Flexibility strategies' aim to develop more flexible work practices, and 'downsizing strategies' find ways in which numbers of employees can be reduced. A flexibility strategy used in the Australian retail industry has been to change casual positions to permanent part-time appointments, which cover a broad span of working hours on a monthly cycle. An example of a flexibility strategy implemented outside of Australia was NatWest Bank's launch in 1999 of new annualised-hours contracts to cover extended opening times without inflating the wages bill. The scheme covers 15 000 branch employees and means that employees work a set number of hours annually rather than a standard working day plus overtime. Salary packaging, according to remuneration consultants, has been used over recent years and in Australia and continues to be one way of not increasing the wages bill through exploiting tax benefits.[56]

Practical tools for planning and measuring HR flow are available and can be useful for assessing HR performance by making industry comparisons or benchmarking with 'best practice' organisations. One such tool is manpower planning, which is used at both the national and the organisational level. At the national level, it is primarily an activity of government and industry bodies. At the organisational level, it is essentially used to forecast workload and manpower. The techniques of manpower planning are numerical and include time series analysis (a quantitative method of measuring and representing how data varies over time), HR forecasts, and budgets.

Three common, organisational measures of HR flow are the turnover index, stability index, and survival rate. The turnover index measures wastage:

$$\frac{\text{Number of leavers in one year (or other specified period)}}{\text{Average number of employees during same period}} \times 100$$

The stability index measures the tendency for longer-serving employees to remain with the organisation:

$$\frac{\text{Number with one year's service or more}}{\text{Number employed one year ago}} \times 100$$

The survival rate plots the distribution curve of losses from entry groups of employees on a graph, time on the x axis, and percentage of leavers on the y axis.

John Bramham distinguishes manpower planning from human resource planning, saying, 'Planning for human resources is more focused on culture, attitude and employee development, the argument being that when these are in place financial and technical control of numbers and costs naturally follows.'[57]

However, this chapter has found little evidence that HRM reduces the need for manpower/HR planning; rather it suggests that management is missing the opportunity to implement HR planning and improve employees' understanding of their future role in the organisation. Clearer policy on HR flow should, through management's making long-term commitments to employees' careers and development, increase employee trust, resulting in higher performance at work.[58] Managers will less likely succeed in their long-term strategic goals where HR planning is given over to serving solely short-term financial considerations.

Further, in the context of global business and, specifically, transnational corporations (TNCs), organisations should be more systematic and informed about international human resource management (IHRM). The recruitment and development of international managers is a key challenge facing TNCs and there is a recent and growing research literature on this topic. The failure rates of expatriate managers, for example, have been studied and there are differences between countries in the reasons for failure. In US and UK transnationals research found, 'inability of spouse to adjust' to a new country and culture is the principal reason for managers failing to perform well, while in Japanese companies it is 'inability to cope with larger overseas responsibility'. TNCs need to take action on this and other relevant research to minimise the major causes of failure in resourcing and become more flexible to national differences and cultural preferences. There is also now more knowledge on the success factors for training and development, which TNCs have by and large neglected. Historically, they have preferred to develop home-country national managers exclusively and neglect managers from other countries.

The literature on IHRM highlights three important lessons linking employee resourcing with employee development: do not simply export parent-country training and development practices but adapt them; align development to the specific strategic needs in each country as well as the overall strategy of the firm; and encourage more transfers of managers between headquarters and other countries to develop management teams that have more global capabilities.[59]

Summary

In this chapter, three perspectives on human resource policies—individual, organisational, and societal—were discussed. Individuals' career progression and opportunities for development are reduced when there is little internal flow of human resources. Overall, there has been increased experimentation with different types of employment contract, sometimes known as 'new deals', which is one of the consequences of reduced collective-bargaining arrangements and a more individualised employment relationship. HR flow policies are influenced by the culture of the organisation, and Trompenaars's four corporate cultures was introduced to illustrate how some cultures accommodate formalised HR policy better than others. During the 1990s, managers in large organisations talked about core competences as a rationale for determining HR flow. Prahalad and Hamel suggested that competences will flourish better where there is a long-term orientation towards the potential of the company's different markets and innovative technologies. National culture has an influence on HR flow policy and to illustrate this it was argued that there has been greater pressure towards social partnership between government, employers, and unions in European countries than in the USA. Hofstede's four dimensions of national culture were discussed to explain how HR flow policies are influenced by the national cultural assumptions under which organisations operate.

Human resource policies were categorised into three areas—internal flow, inflow, and outflow—and it was argued that many organisations have been attempting to apply more systematic methods of recruitment and selection to improve the quality of internal flow, most notably through psychometric testing and competences. However, some organisations have been less effective in managing outflow, which is an area in which HR professionals should be more involved. Finally, formal methods and techniques of HR planning were discussed in order to increase awareness of their availability and the fact that they have been underutilised.

BOX 5.3

Case study—Adoption of competences in an Australian city council

In 2001, Bilby City Council conducted a review of HRM obstacles to meeting its local government service delivery targets. The report concluded that the council should review the potential of competence-based approaches for coping with increasing service levels while, at the same time, reducing its costs of delivery.

Bilby City Council is responsible for a budget of $800 million in 2002–03 and manages assets of over $7 billion. Its structure recently became more complex with the decision to create a new set of business units to increase its capacity to respond proactively to National Competition Policy, which encourages public sector organisations to seek quality provision of services. The intent is to achieve a judicious mixture of business methods and alternatives, utilising in tandem public and private sector efficiencies. Since adopting the 1997 purchaser/provider partnership approach, purchaser and provider roles have been separate parts of the organisation. The purpose of this separation was to ensure that business units within the organisation sought to maximise quality provision for ratepayers and other stakeholders, while minimising the costs of purchasing services. Recent moves have been towards partial re-integration of these two areas, in part because the downsizing phase and related business process redesign and redundancies during 1992–99 had been completed, leading to a period of modest growth in the total number of employees and a substantial expansion of the range and volume of services provision. It is most unlikely, however, that recruitment will increase much more in the foreseeable future given the continual pressure on costs and the fact that over 80 per cent of employees are permanent and full-time with less than 10 per cent of total employees in casual and contractor categories.

The most recent enterprise bargaining agreement instituted key performance indicators (KPIs) with 'stretch targets' linked to an employee bonus scheme. This initiative had been successful in achieving some productivity gains, but it was the general consensus among senior executives that something more creative would be required in the future to motivate everyone towards achieving new, even more ambitious goals.

Bilby City Council has been at the forefront of HRM initiatives in business process redesign, continuous improvement, and the learning organisation, although, for unclear reasons, it had more or less ignored the competences movement of the 1990s. The council did not use competences for recruitment or appraisal nor did it have a specification of 'core competences' of the organisation. Competences were included in a number of job specifications, but almost exclusively in terms of necessary attributes for successful, technical task performance. The report acknowledged that Bilby City Council's use of competences had been restricted to technical tasks, although this was understandable because minimum levels of technical proficiency are paramount for a number of its daily services, such as transport drivers and water engineers. Clearly, the uptake of competences had been low in comparison to private sector organisations, and fell well short of, for example, Athey and Orth's definition of the role and potential of competence-based approaches: 'A competency is a set of observable performance dimensions, including individual knowledge, skills, attitudes and behaviours, as well as collective team process, and organisational capabilities that are linked to high performance and provide the organisation with competitive advantage.'[63]

The competences literature suggests some problems may also be inherent in the organisational structure and systems of Bilby City Council. First, its subdivision into comparatively autonomous business units may mitigate against lateral communication and transfer of competences. Second, its traditional job analysis, predominantly relying upon role descriptions to define job specifications, places constraints on the extent of innovation and flexibility within and across jobs.

In significant ways, though, the organisation is suited to implementation of competence-based approaches in HRM. Bilby City Council has a clearly specified vision, mission statement and set of values. It is large and varied, having more than 1,500 employees and a well-defined organisation of jobs and job roles. These positions can be readily analysed by employees, consultants, and researchers to produce schedules of competences. Third, the organisation has a well-staffed department team of six full-time HR professionals, in addition to a number of part-time professionals and consultants reporting to senior executives and line managers.

Case study activities

1. Briscoe and Hall[64] suggest that three approaches to competences have predominated over recent years: (a) research-based (behavioural event interviews identifying keys to successful performance); (b) competences linked to the strategic direction of the organisation (strategy-based); and (c) competences linked to cultural values and norms (values-based). Assess the relative merits of each approach, and then, giving your reasons, make recommendations for Bilby City Council selecting one of the three approaches to competence.
2. In the light of information in the case study, specify what competences might be important for two types of job in Bilby City Council. Select one position from the management levels and one lower-level position in a customer-facing capacity.
3. Write a two-year detailed action plan for establishing competences in recruitment, appraisal and rewards, and covering all levels of employees.

Study questions

1. Discuss what, in your view, are the main issues for employee resourcing at the three levels of the individual, the organisation, and society.
2. How have careers changed in organisations? Write a ten-point list of principles and an agenda for employer action on career management and development.
3. What is the role of organisational culture in employee resourcing?
4. What is the role of national culture in employee resourcing?
5. What are the main issues in managing outflow? What skills do managers need to develop for the effective management of outflow?

Further reading

Barney, J., 'Strategic Human Resource Management within a Resource-Capability View of the Firm', *Journal of Management* (1991), 17, 1, pp. 99–120.
Kamoche, K., 'Strategic Human Resource Management within a Resource-Capability View of the Firm', *Journal of Management Studies* (1996), March, 33, 2, pp. 213–33.
Sandberg, J., 'Understanding Human Competence at Work: An Interpretive Approach', *The Academy of Management Journal* (2000), 43, 1, pp. 9–25.
Schuler, R. S., 'Human resource issues and activities in international joint ventures', *International Journal of Human Resource Management* (2001), 12, 1, February, pp. 1–52.

CHAPTER 6

Motivating Employees

CHAPTER CONTENTS

Introduction

1 Motivating individuals
   Content theories—what motivates employees
   Maslow's hierarchy of needs
   McClelland's three basic needs
   Herzberg's motivators and hygiene factors
   Process theories—how to motivate employees
   Latham and Locke's goal-directed theory
   Porter and Lawler's expectancy theory
   Bandura's self-efficacy theory
   Hackman and Oldham on job design
   Limitations of content and process theories

2 Motivating groups
   Equity theory
   Two theories of management motivation
   Limitations

Summary
   Case study—Motivating the team: the HR initiatives of a retail store supervisor
   Study questions
   Further reading

Introduction

The topic of this chapter, motivating employees, is linked to material in the following chapter on financial rewards, because paying employees is part of motivating them. However, we deal with employee motivation in depth in its own chapter because it is pivotal to the study of HRM and because different theories of what fundamentally motivates people at work underpin the various models of HRM. For example, as we saw in chapter 1, soft HRM adopts an approach of development and commitment in addressing motivation, while hard HRM concentrates more on controlling and using people as a means to the organisation's ends. Whatever their particular concept of HRM, its advocates claim it is an alternative approach to the traditional employment relationship, and therefore some understanding of the psychological theories of motivation will be helpful in evaluating HRM theory and practice. Motivation theory is significant to many social science disciplines and will help the reader determine how far HRM is capable of motivating employees in ways that are distinct from past approaches. A basic understanding of what motivates and what discourages employees is also a valuable underpinning to management practice. This chapter first covers motivating individuals and then motivating groups. The section on motivating groups discusses equity theory and two important theories of management motivation.

1 Motivating individuals

This section on motivating individuals gives an overview of several content theories and process theories of motivation. Content theories seek to explain *what* motivates employees; process theories explain *how* to motivate employees. Three content theories are described—Maslow's hierarchy of needs, McClelland's three basic needs, and Herzberg's motivators and hygiene factors. All three are 'need' theories, which means that they assume that individuals' motivation is driven by common and fundamental needs. Four process theories are then described: Latham and Locke's goal theory, Porter and Lawler's expectancy theory, Bandura's self-efficacy theory, and Hackman and Oldham's research on job design. At the end of this section, the limitations of content and process theories are discussed.

Content theories—what motivates employees

Maslow's hierarchy of needs
Abraham Maslow's hierarchy of five basic needs—physiological needs (food, water, sleep, oxygen, warmth, and freedom from pain), safety, social belonging, esteem, and self-actualisation—comprises lower- and higher-order needs.[1] Maslow claimed that as each level of need, starting with the lower-order needs, is gratified, we seek a higher-order need (see figure 6.1). We start by seeking to satisfy our physiological needs and when those are satiated, safety needs emerge, and so on. Social belonging,

esteem, and self-actualisation are growth needs—in other words, they are needed for growth beyond a basic level of existence. The two lower-order needs, physiological needs and safety, are deficiency needs. This means that if a deficiency arises at some point for whatever reason in the individual's supply of physiological necessities or feeling of physical safety, redressing this deficiency can temporarily become more important than fulfilling the higher-order needs. When all of the deficiency needs are again satisfied, the individual can again be motivated by growth needs, first seeking rewarding social relationships, then prestige, recognition, and achievement, and then the highest category of growth, self-actualisation, which is the desire for self-fulfilment through development of one's potential. This can be expressed in many different ways, including maternally/paternally, occupationally, and artistically.

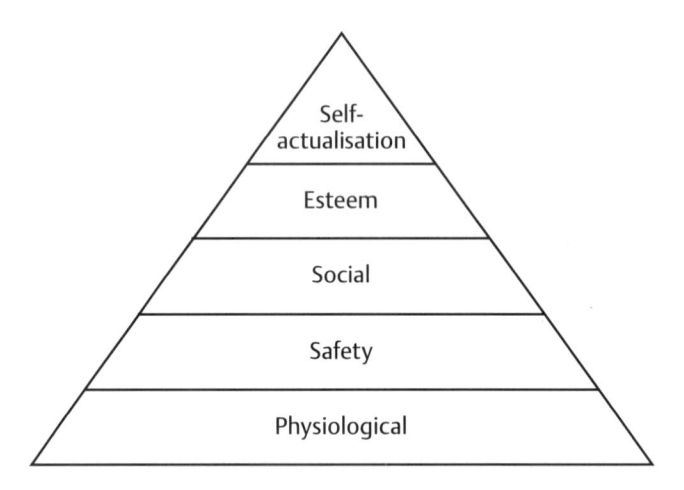

Figure 6.1 Maslow's hierarchy of needs

Source: Robbins, S., *Organizational Behaviour: Concepts, Controversies, Applications*, exhibit 5-2, p. 170. Copyright © 1998. Reprinted by permission of Prentice-Hall, Inc., Upper Saddle River, NJ.

Maslow's theory has long had appeal partly because it appears to be so readily applicable to most situations; however, on close inspection the attractiveness of the theory is its vagueness and difficulty to disprove.[2] The distinction it makes between lower-order needs (physiological, safety) and higher-order needs (social, esteem, self-actualisation) is one that has had intuitive appeal to students and business practitioners from different backgrounds and cultures partly because it is imprecise and open to a wide variety of interpretations.[3] Nevertheless, the hierarchy retains significance for business and management students by drawing attention to the prominent role of intrinsic motivation in ensuring that work is satisfying for employees.

McClelland's three basic needs
David McClelland's well-known theory of need motivation focuses on the needs of achievement, power, and affiliation.[4] People with a high need for achievement seek

jobs and tasks in which they have personal responsibility and can obtain quick feedback on their progress and attainment. High achievers are moderate risk takers, preferring the odds of success to be even or in their favour. They are not motivated by success that can be put down to good luck, preferring outcomes that they believe are a consequence of their own achievements. People with a high need for power seek situations where they can have power and influence over others. They like to be in positions of status and authority and frequently will aim to increase their influence over others in preference to concentrating on effective work performance. People with a high need for affiliation are motivated by being liked and accepted by others. They are most motivated in work situations where there is a high degree of cooperation and where greater priority is given to attaining mutual understanding among the group rather than to competition between individuals.

In summary: the achievement need is the drive to excel and to achieve according to standards set by others and by oneself; the need for power is the need to make others behave in ways they otherwise would not behave; and the need for affiliation is the desire for friendly interpersonal relationships. McClelland's research found that high achievers—who seek situations in which they gain personal responsibility, get feedback, and undertake moderate risks—are people who tend to be successful in entrepreneurial activities; however, they are not always the best general managers. It is the needs for power and affiliation, according to McClelland, that are related to managerial success, particularly in large organisations, the best general managers having a high need for power and a relatively low need for affiliation.

Herzberg's motivators and hygiene factors
In 1968, Frederick Herzberg published an article in the *Harvard Business Review* (*HBR*) that by 1987 had sold 1.2 million reprints, the largest sale of any article in *HBR*'s history. The article was republished in 1987 as an *HBR* Classic, entitled 'One More Time: How Do You Motivate Employees?' Herzberg suggests that the key to motivating employees lies in job design and job enrichment. He argues that there has been a series of myths about motivation and cites nine personnel practices that in his view are failed past attempts to instil motivation.

Reducing the time spent at work, he says, will not motivate employees because motivated people seek more hours of work, not fewer. Increasing wages, or reducing them in an economic depression, does not motivate people either. Fringe benefits, he suggests, have become an expectation and are unlikely to motivate. People take for granted having to work only five days a week and for less than ten hours a day. Furthermore, they see share options and medical cover as being almost a basic right of employment. Herzberg also criticises human-relations teaching in the business schools and companies of his time, implying that managers have become soft and employees more awkward, so that they have to be told to do something three times rather than doing it after being asked only once, as they would have done in the past. He also suggests that sensitivity training, improving two-way communication between managers and employees, job participation, and employee counselling are all failed attempts at motivation.

Past personnel initiatives have been unsuccessful because they do not reorganise the job. Only by doing this, Herzberg claims, will employees gain more of a sense of achievement, recognition, intrinsic satisfaction from work, responsibility, advancement, and personal learning and growth. Herzberg sees individuals as having two sets of basic needs. One set stems from the in-built drive to avoid pain and to satiate biological needs. The other set of needs is unique to human beings and is concerned with achievement, recognition for achievement, the work itself, responsibility, growth, and advancement. The first set of needs he calls hygiene factors, which are extrinsic to the work the employee does and include company policy and administration, supervision, interpersonal relationships, working conditions, salary, status, and security. The second set of needs comprise growth needs or motivating factors and are intrinsic to the work.

Herzberg's first article was based on twelve different research investigations that included in their samples low-level supervisors, professional women, agricultural administrators, men about to retire from management, hospital maintenance staff, manufacturing supervisors, nurses, food handlers, military officers, engineers, scientists, housekeepers, teachers, technicians, female assemblers, accountants, and foremen. In these studies, the employees were asked to describe positive and negative job events. Motivating factors (motivators) were found to be those that contributed to job satisfaction, and hygiene factors were those that, at best, meant employees would not be dissatisfied.

Herzberg criticised previous work on job design and enrichment for concentrating too greatly on horizontal job loading—loading employees with more tasks and more variety in their work—yet not including in the job any motivating factors that lead to an improved sense of achievement, recognition, responsibility, advancement, or growth over the longer term. Herzberg advises that organisations redesign their jobs so that they are more enriched with motivators. Jobs need to have vertical loading to be motivating (that is, any new component added to the job should build upward towards job satisfaction) and should be designed to make employees feel they have more responsibility and opportunity for growth.

Some of Herzberg's views are contentious and have been the subject of hot debate. His article bluntly recommends some very simple practices of management, for example: 'The argument for job enrichment can be summed up quite simply: if you have employees on a job, use them. If you can't use them on the job, get rid of them, either via automation or by selecting someone with lesser ability. If you can't use them and you can't get rid of them, you will have a motivation problem.'[5]

The 1987 *HBR* reprint concludes with a retrospective commentary on the original article, in which Herzberg defends his basic distinction between motivation factors and hygiene factors; however, he does suggest that the original article ignored the positive role played by organisational behaviourists[6] in reducing workplace tension, implying an admission that his article went too far in denigrating the positive contribution of management practice that is sensitive to human relations. He also presents further research evidence, found in a job-attitudes study conducted in six countries, supporting the importance of motivators. They were again found to be important in contributing to job satisfaction, while hygiene factors at best reduced the occurrence of job dissatisfaction.

Herzberg provides a model of job enrichment that is consistent with the recent focus on serving the customer and that highlights the contribution of learning and feeling in business performance. In the model, employees work closely together in serving clients and understanding and developing the product. Five ingredients are proposed as contributing to client- and product-focused learning and feeling: control over resources, self-scheduling, personal accountability, direct communication with authority, and direct feedback. Herzberg warns that personnel practices in the 1980s became too focused on hygiene factors and serving the bottom line. He suggests that the work ethic and the quality-of-work-life movement have succumbed to what he says are the abstract and emotionless fields of finance and marketing. Job enrichment, he asserts, is still the key to designing work that motivates employees.

Content theories of motivation identify what motivates human beings. Two of the content theories discussed here, Maslow's and Herzberg's, assume, first, that needs can be subdivided into higher- and lower-order needs and, second, that healthy and well-adjusted individuals will aspire to the fulfilment of higher-order needs once lower-order needs have been adequately satisfied. All three of the content theories discussed maintain an individualist conception of motivation and subordinate social contribution and belonging to individual achievement and 'self-actualisation'. These theories have been criticised for propounding a male-dominant perspective on motivation. They have been described as being too specific to the national culture in which they were developed[7] and for promoting a gender-specific view of reality that favours men by prioritising motivation in the workplace above motivation in other contexts, such as home and family.[8]

Process theories—how to motivate employees

Latham and Locke's goal-directed theory[9]
Latham and Locke in 1979 stated that the advantage of goal theory is that it has clear practical applications for managing and motivating people. They observe that most managers are not in a position to change people's personalities and the best they can do is to use incentives to direct employees' energies towards the goals of the organisation. Money, they say, is the primary incentive, but there are many others, such as participation in decision making, job enrichment, behaviour modification (using structured systems of incentives to modify employees' behaviour), and organisational development.

Latham and Locke reported on laboratory experiments showing that individuals who were given specific, challenging goals outperformed those who were given vague goals. These experiments also found that pay and performance feedback resulted in improved performance only where the feedback led the individuals to set themselves higher goals than they had before. The authors also reported studies they undertook to help supervisors improve the productivity of logging crews in North America. Giving logging crews specific production goals, such as the amount of wood to be felled and collected, was found to increase productivity—when it was combined with a supervisory presence on site. Crews left on their own without supervision tended to underperform. When there was an atmosphere of trust between managers and subordinates, crews given the most demanding goals were found to outperform others, having higher rates of productivity and lower rates of absenteeism, injury, and employee turnover.

Similar experiments by Latham and Locke with drivers loading trucks in a unionised US company found that when drivers set goals for attaining correct load capacity, large sums of money were saved for the company through reduction of waste. The researchers concluded that three steps should be followed to obtain the best results in goal-setting. First, goals must be specific rather than vague; clear time-limits must be set for goal accomplishment; and goals should be challenging and reachable. Second, managers must ensure that employees accept and remain committed to the goals. This is best achieved when there is an atmosphere of trust between managers and subordinates and when a supportive supervisory style is used. Non-supportive supervisory styles were found not to motivate employees towards goal commitment. The third step is to give employees support in the form of adequate resources, money, equipment, time, and help. The authors' finding was that goal-setting works best when it is combined with good managerial judgment and when production goals and employee-development goals are attended to.

Porter and Lawler's expectancy theory

Victor Vroom's book *Work and Motivation* is regarded by many as a landmark in the field of motivation.[10] His theory assumes that human behaviour is goal-directed and that work will be more motivating when it provides the opportunity for goal attainment and needs satisfaction. Vroom developed what is known as expectancy theory, in which motivation is a function of each individual's expectation that his or her behaviour will result in outcomes that have psychological value. It is predicted, according to expectancy theory, that individuals will behave in ways they think are likely to lead to rewards they value. Expectancy theory was developed to explain how individuals can be motivated when they have different values and priorities for rewards. The theory's recommendation for managers is that work should be designed so that effective performance leads to outcomes desired by employees. People will work hard if their labours achieve things they want, which can vary from extrinsic rewards such as a productivity bonus to intrinsic rewards such as the pleasure obtained purely from doing the task.

In 1968 Porter and Lawler devised a model of motivation based on Vroom's expectancy theory that has frequently been taught to managers.[11] The model describes a person's motivation as a function of three things: the attractiveness of the rewards, performance-to-reward expectancy, and effort-to-performance expectancy.

First, the perceived attractiveness of the rewards: motivation to exert effort is stimulated by the prospect of desired rewards. People must value the rewards in order to be motivated to perform. Rewards, as was first mentioned in chapter 1, can be either intrinsic or extrinsic. Those who are motivated by intrinsic rewards, such as challenging job assignments, will be motivated by the work itself more than will people who are primarily motivated by extrinsic rewards, such as money.

Second, performance-to-reward expectancy: this is the employee's expectation that if the desired performance is achieved, then desired rewards will be obtained. For example, if the employee's pay is linked to the financial performance of the organisation through a profit-sharing system and if the organisation consistently makes low profits, then the profit-sharing element of the reward system will not be very motivating.

Third, effort-to-performance expectancy: employees will make the necessary effort only when they believe there is a reasonable probability of achieving the target performance. For example, when working in a small team, the individual may believe his or her effort is likely to have a direct effect on the group. However, when the same individual is asked to help improve the overall profits of the whole company, which employs many thousands, this person may feel that his or her contribution won't make a significant difference to the company results. The larger the group, the less any one person feels that individual effort will affect overall performance. Effort-to-performance expectancies are influenced by ability and perception of role: any individual must be adequately educated and trained to accomplish the necessary tasks and should have a perception of his or her role that is sufficiently consistent with the performance actually required.

Porter and Lawler's revised version of Vroom's expectancy theory model is shown in figure 6.2. The model recognises that the perceived attractiveness of the extrinsic and intrinsic rewards offered by the organisation will depend on how much employees value them. It says that effort-to-performance expectancies will be moderated by ability, traits, and perceptions of role, and the level of effort applied will depend on individuals' ability, training, and role perceptions. Performance-to-reward expectancies will in turn be moderated by a sense of equity and a perception that the rewards are allocated fairly. If employees believe some individuals or groups have obtained an unfair proportion of the rewards, then the aggrieved will be less satisfied and less motivated to perform to the level required in the future. The jagged line between performance and rewards on the diagram is there to show that motivation is a function of the performance–reward relationship. Two of the feedback loops depicted represent the reinforcement and increase of motivation. First, achieving the performance and obtaining the reward strengthen an individual's belief that a similar outcome will recur in future. Second, the satisfaction from the reward strengthens motivation by increasing the individual's valuation of the reward.

The expectancy model does not include all of the factors that organisations must influence in order to motivate employees. Other important factors include the relationship between management and employees, development opportunities for employees, and meaningful work goals. Especially problematic for organisations has been sustaining a motivational link between rewards and performance. It is a complex link and it is often not easy to develop good measures of performance and

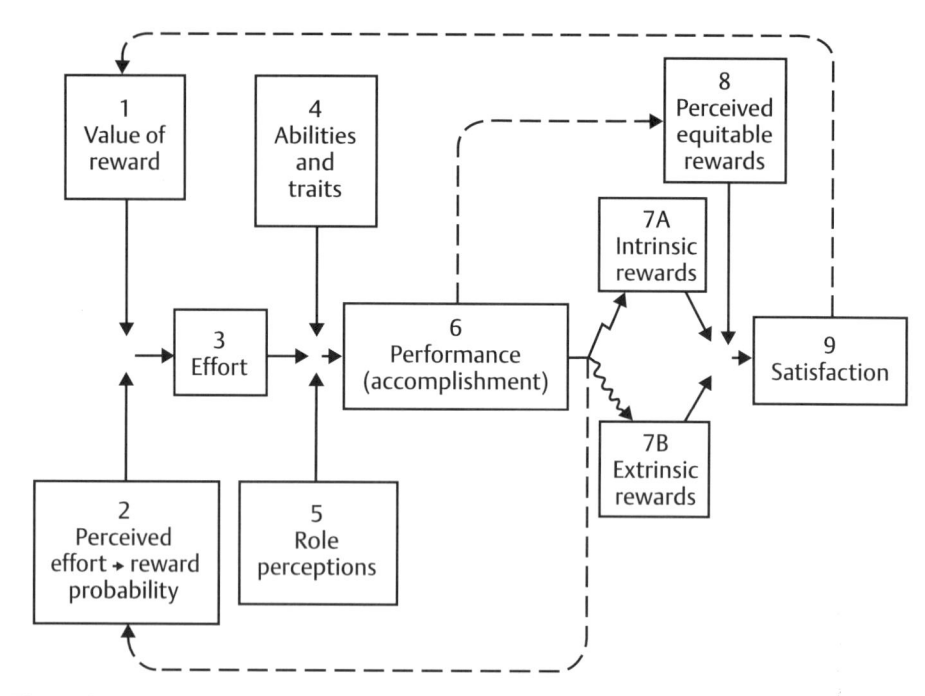

Figure 6.2 Porter and Lawler's model of Vroom's expectancy theory

Source: Pinder C. C., in V. H. Vroom and E. L. Deci (eds), *Management and Motivation*, 2nd edn (Harmondsworth: Penguin Books, 1992), p. 98.

to communicate the evaluation of individuals' performance in ways that are acceptable and motivating. Organisations frequently have difficulties in linking pay to performance. Trust must be sustained between management and employees, and the evaluation system for rewards has to be credible and visible if individuals are to be motivated. Otherwise, they will not believe that the extrinsic rewards promised will materialise upon delivery of effective performance.

Bandura's self-efficacy theory

Albert Bandura's self-efficacy theory is often quoted in the management literature.[12] It proposes that the main influence over behavioural change and motivation is self-efficacy, which is the strength of belief an individual has in his or her ability to achieve outcomes through behaviour. Bandura cites previous research showing that positive reinforcement of behaviour does not persuade individuals to act in a similar manner in the future unless they believe the same actions will again be rewarded.[13] Bandura says that mastery and effective performance are more influenced by high self-efficacy than they are by track record.

His theory states that people have the capacity to exceed their previous performance or to perform less well than they did before by holding different expectations of their own efficacy. Expectations of what degree of personal mastery they can achieve will influence both the point at which they start relying on coping behaviours (behaviours that appear in order to help someone get through a specific situation) and how long they will persist with them. The individuals' expectations of their own efficacy are a major determinant of what activity they will choose to work at, the amount of effort they will expend, and the length of time they will spend dealing with stressful situations. Efficacy expectations differ from task to task and, of course, from individual to individual. For example, individuals may have efficacy expectations of either broad or narrow magnitude, generality, and strength. Magnitude is the extent to which they believe in being able to perform ever more complex tasks. Generality is the sense of being able to master a range of situations. Strength is the degree to which individuals will cope with setbacks and failure.

Bandura's self-efficacy theory is a theory of social learning, being concerned primarily with how individual learning is affected by social factors such as maintaining self-confidence and making comparisons between oneself and other people. It suggests that four major sources of information are used by individuals in creating their sense of personal efficacy: *performance accomplishment*, *vicarious experience*, *verbal persuasion*, and *physiological states*. *Performance accomplishment* (in other words, success) raises expectations of mastery, while repeated failure lowers them. Once self-efficacy has been established, it tends to generalise to other situations. If the sense of self-efficacy is low, the individual's performances may be debilitated by preoccupations with personal inadequacies. Improved self-efficacy enables the individual to transfer effective behaviours to a wider range of situations and tasks.

Vicarious experience includes the experiences people have of seeing others perform well, sometimes under adverse conditions. By comparing themselves with others, people gain a heightened sense of self-efficacy; by seeing that others can do it, they believe they can too. Bandura says that efficacy expectations created solely by modelling them on other people's behaviour, however, are weaker and more vulnerable to change than is the experience of successful performance by oneself.

Verbal persuasion is known to have an important influence on people's sense of self-efficacy. Individuals can be encouraged to believe they will succeed through suggestion and coaching. This persuasion must take place in conditions that allow improvement and effective performance to occur; otherwise, the persuaders will be discredited in the eyes of the individuals learning to achieve mastery if they fail to perform effectively due to unfavourable conditions.

The *physiological state* that affects self-efficacy is emotional arousal, with high arousal usually debilitating performance. Increased levels of anxiety and fear will negatively influence individuals' sense of self-efficacy by provoking imagined threats that far exceed the actual threat of the situation. Self-efficacy is much more likely to improve where the individual feels that the successful performance was the result of skill rather than luck.

Bandura's theory of social learning helps to explain why some company training programs spend considerable time motivating employees to hold a high sense of self-efficacy. Perhaps the most surprising and important assertion of self-efficacy theory is that perceived self-efficacy proves to be a better predictor of behaviour than does past performance.

Hackman and Oldham on job design

Hackman and Oldham's research on job design follows in the tradition of expectancy theory with its assumption that individuals are motivated by outcomes that they value. It extends Porter and Lawler's work by identifying job characteristics likely to motivate individuals, although to different degrees according to their individual psychology and values. They argued in 1976, as did Herzberg when discussing job enrichment, that motivation is concerned with effective design of jobs and matching the correct people to the work required: 'When people are well matched with their jobs, it rarely is necessary to force, coerce, bribe, or trick them into working hard and trying to perform the job well. Instead, they try to do well because it is rewarding and satisfying to do so.'[14]

Hackman and Oldham recommend three conditions for internal motivation. First, the individual must have knowledge of the results of his or her work; otherwise, it will be difficult to be emotionally influenced by the outcomes. Second, the individual must experience responsibility for the results of work. People must be allowed to take initiative and feel pride in the results when they do well, and feel concern when goals are not achieved. Third, the individual must experience work as being meaningful. Hackman and Oldham say that when all three of these factors are present, strong internal work motivation will develop and is likely to persist. Their view is that motivation at work has more to do with the design of tasks and jobs than it has to do with individual dispositions.

The authors also suggest five job characteristics that lead individuals to experience their work as being meaningful, possessing responsibility, and enabling knowledge of results. The five characteristics are *skill variety*, *task identity*, *task significance*, *autonomy*, and *feedback from the job*. The first three lead to experiencing work as meaningful; the fourth, autonomy, leads to experiencing responsibility for outcomes of the work; and the fifth leads to knowing the actual results of the work (see figure 6.3).

Skill variety is the number of different skills required to do the work. *Task identity* is the extent to which the job has an identifiable beginning and end with a visible outcome. In other words, people must feel that they are doing more than a mundane, pointless task. *Task significance* is the degree to which the job is felt to affect other people's lives. Hackman and Oldham observe that the three different task characteristics may occur at quite different levels and still be meaningful to any one individual. For example, two out of these three characteristics may be quite low and yet the task may still be found to be motivating. For other employees, all three may have to be high before they will experience the work as meaningful. *Autonomy* is defined by the authors as 'the degree to which the job provides substantial freedom, independence, and discretion to the individual in scheduling the work and in determining the procedures to be used in carrying it out'.[15] As autonomy increases, individuals will feel more responsible for their work and also more accountable. However, there are limits as to how effective this can be for organisations' performance. A recent UK study of empowerment in organisations devolving responsibility downwards found it led to performance improvements only when there were high levels of variation in work requirements. Knowledge of results

Core job characteristics → Critical psychological states → Outcomes

Skill variety, Task identity, Task significance → Experienced meaningfulness of the work

Autonomy → Experienced responsibility for outcomes of the work

Feedback from job → Knowledge of the actual results of the work activities

→ High internal work motivation

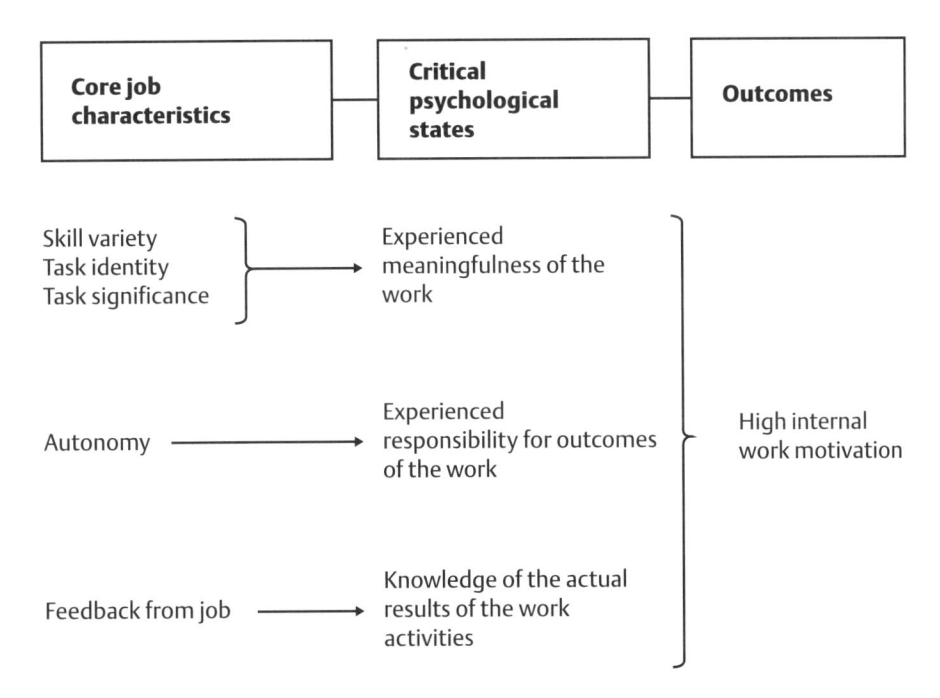

Figure 6.3 Hackman and Oldham's job characteristics

Source: Hackman, J. and Oldham, G., *Work Redesign* (Reading, MA: Addison-Wesley, 1980), figure 4.6, p. 90. Copyright © 1980 Addison Wesley Publishing Co., Inc. Reprinted by permission of Addison Wesley Longman.

comes through *job feedback*, either from people or via machine. The feedback must be directly linked to the job the individual is doing. Individual differences are important in determining how each employee is motivated by his or her work. Three characteristics seem to be especially important: the level of knowledge and skill; the psychological need for growth and personal learning (some have stronger growth needs than others); and the degree to which the individual is satisfied with the work context. People who are not satisfied with their pay, job security, co-workers, and supervisors will not respond as positively to jobs designed to be motivating. It is commonly thought that when employees are demotivated and dissatisfied, they are less likely to provide a satisfactory service for customers. There is some research evidence to support this; for example, a survey of employees' attitudes from the UK retail company Sainsbury's suggests that the more satisfied they are at work, the happier customers are with the service they receive. HRM has a role to play here, according to a recent study on human resources practices, organisational climate, and customer satisfaction, which found HRM practices can impact on service performance through their influence on organisational climate. Recent research on shopfloor workers in the retail industry found that managers might overemphasise marketing and customer service to such an extent that it can reduce employee motivation and organisational commitment through lowering their own psychological sense of well-being. Australian research on law firms has found that the provision of personal support, interesting tasks, autonomy at work, fair reward systems, and equitable career paths created the conditions most conducive to organisational success and the best service for clients.[16]

Limitations of content and process theories

Content and process theories of motivation can help managers understand how to better motivate their employees. The content theories, concentrating on what motivates people, show the importance of satisfying higher- and lower-order needs. Maslow's theory is said to be the theory of motivation most commonly known to managers. It was believed by Maslow, and later by Herzberg, that the hierarchy of needs specified universal needs that are consistent across different national cultures, but Hofstede's research on culture (discussed in chapter 5) shows that motivation will be influenced by cultural factors.[17] McClelland's needs theory argues strongly for the influence of culture when he says that a high need for achievement is brought about through upbringing. It is vital, he argues, that individuals be inculcated with these achievement values from an early age.

Maslow's hierarchy of needs is not clear, then, about the extent to which the higher- and lower-order needs are instinctual to all human beings and the degree to which they are culturally acquired by individuals in societies. Research by Alderfer managed to find some empirical support for the claim that the higher-order needs become more important as lower-order needs are satisfied. He also found that when individuals were prevented from obtaining higher-order needs, they regressed to seeking more satisfaction from a lower-order need rather than continuing to seek satisfaction at a higher level. This contradicts Maslow's theory, which proposes that once satisfaction is achieved at a lower level, individuals will be motivated to obtain satisfaction from a higher level. A practical example of regression would be a group of employees who were initially satisfied with their level of pay seeking more money for the same job after a period of time during which they failed to obtain satisfying interpersonal relationships within the workplace.[18] Salancik and Pfeffer observe that the overall research evidence supporting the hierarchy of needs is slight. The findings of research studies on the hierarchy can be explained by other theories that appear to be equally as plausible as Maslow's explanation.[19] Nevertheless, despite these shortcomings, content theories—and especially Maslow's—remain the best-known to people in business.

Process theories of motivation, whether primarily concerned with job satisfaction, general motivation, or job design, tend to be formulated in terms of expectancy theory. The theory is helpful to managers in reminding them that they must take account of individual differences between employees. The reward system, to an extent, must be capable of catering for employees' different needs and perceptions. Expectancy theory shows that individuals make different evaluations of actions, goal achievement, and the connections between actions and rewards. Expectancy theory is, however, a complex needs-satisfaction model of motivation that has been criticised for its lack of simplicity in guiding management action.[20] Process theories, from the point of view of guiding managerial practice, have the advantage over content theories by explaining how people are motivated. However, managers have found it difficult to ascertain how to implement expectancy theory in their organisations, and have often been sceptical of the benefit gained from doing so. Hackman and Oldham's theory of job design is a useful version of expectancy theory because it prescribes five specific areas of work organisation to which managers should attend and to which they often can attend in practice. Their theory concentrates attention on designing jobs so that improved processes of individual motivation are more likely to result.

Content and process theories of motivation are helpful for gaining a better understanding of how individuals can be motivated. However, they have been criticised for the limited extent to which their principles can be applied in practice, for being biased towards Western individualist culture, and for presenting, usually implicitly, a male-dominated view of work and family. This last criticism concerning gender bias argues that these motivation theories adopt an essentially male perspective whenever they assert that relationships with others are fundamentally of lower order and of less value than individual achievement.[21] To end this section on a more general point, the theories that have been discussed so far highlight individual differences of motivation and do not accord much significance to the role of the group and environmental factors.

2 Motivating groups

This second section reviews three theories that focus—more than those discussed so far—on the role played in motivation by the social group. It introduces equity, agency, and stewardship theories of motivation. Equity theory considers how an individual's motivation is influenced by his or her perception of the group. Agency and stewardship theories aim to explain what motivates groups, particularly management. They make assumptions about *how* managers should be motivated (process) on the basis of fundamentally different assumptions about human nature and *what* motivates management (content). The agency perspective is more consistent with hard HRM (controlling), and the stewardship perspective with soft HRM (employee commitment).

Equity theory

The equity theory of motivation aims to explain the way that employees agree to a 'fair rate for the job'. Adams says that individuals compare what they contribute to the employment relationship and what they receive from it in return. Contributions include effort, skills, training, and seniority, while returns are pay, fringe benefits, recognition, status, and promotion. Employees compare their contributions and returns with those of other employees and, if dissatisfied by the comparison, will reduce their effort, seek a pay rise or promotion, or attempt to reconcile their dissatisfaction either by rationalising the differences in contributions and returns between themselves and others as being fair or by selecting another reference group to compare themselves against.

Equity theory demonstrates that individuals are concerned not only with the total reward package they get but how this compares with what others who are in a similar position receive. Empirical research on equity theory shows that employees are motivated by a sense of distributive justice; that is, employees are more motivated where they perceive rewards to be fairly distributed among people. A recent study in Australia found that equity in the cost of living and pay levels in comparable organisations were two criteria important to the majority of respondents.[22]

Adams studied how people responded to others being paid more or less than themselves and found that they will do one of six things:

1. People will maximise returns that they value (because these are what are most important).
2. They will minimise contributions that require effort and change.
3. They will resist changes that are a strong challenge to their self-concept and self-esteem.
4. They will resist changing themselves more than they will resist reconsidering the equity of others' contributions and returns.
5. They will quit their jobs only when they perceive there to be a very high level of inequity and when they can find no other means of reducing the sense of unfairness. If the inequity is felt less strongly, absenteeism results.
6. Once the individual has established a sense of what is fair, this viewpoint becomes stable over time and part of the individual's sense of security.[23]

Jaques recommended that pay must pass the 'felt fair' principle. Employees have standards for what constitutes fair payment that are shared unconsciously among the work population of any given country. When an individual assesses his or her pay against that of another employee, that employee's pay must be in line with what is thought to be a fair rate for the job, and the individual must be perceived by others as capable of performing the job.[24] Armstrong observes that this 'felt fair' principle is one of the most common methods used for determining employee rewards.[25] The principle is applied in collective agreements, where they still exist, between management and trade unions at national, regional, and local levels of bargaining. It is also applied in negotiating an individual's rewards. The same basic principle applies in employment contracts, whatever the size of the business, although what is felt to be fair by employers and employees in a large multinational organisation can be very different from what is felt to be fair in a small local business. What is felt fair will also differ by region and by country. It is common for employers to offer higher rates of pay in more prosperous areas. Employees who are doing the same job in Sydney will often expect to be paid more than those working in other regions where the cost of living is lower. Even in occupations where there are fixed national rates of pay, there may be extras, such as cost of living weighting allowance. At the country level, different expectations and customary practices will influence what is thought to be a fair reward. In Thailand, for example, large domestic companies automatically increase pay annually to match the rate of inflation. Torrington and Chee Huat examined some of the differences in human resource management that play an important role in determining employees' expectations in South-East Asian countries.[26] In Singapore, all employers are required to contribute to the Central Provident Fund, which is a mandatory savings scheme providing for retirement and medical benefits. Singaporean employees' contributions are high compared with contributions in other countries, and a worker coming to live in Singapore may take time to adjust to accept that the higher contribution rates are fair.

Two theories of management motivation

Agency and stewardship theories are two contrasting views of what motivates management. Agency theory has hard HRM's emphasis on control and rewarding required behaviour, and stewardship theory has soft HRM's attention to employee commitment and influence.

Agency theory is an economic theory that has been widely used in management education and training within business schools. Agency theory predicts that owners (or 'principals') and managers (or 'agents') will behave differently in serving their own interests and that these will differ from each other: principals seek to maximise their wealth and managers follow their own interests, which will not always be consistent with principals' interests. The theory advises owners to motivate managers to serve the interests of owners' capital by rewarding and controlling the managers to pursue the owners' interests.

Gomez-Mejia and Balkin have criticised agency theory for being too managerialist and for recommending that managers treat employees as objects.[27] The theory is highly instrumentalist in that it views employees as a means to management's ends rather than as having legitimate ends of their own. Agency theory is, however, reasonably effective in explaining the differential reward systems found in the UK and USA for senior managers and other employees. In most organisations, managers receive higher pay than other employees do, and better fringe benefits, often enjoying privileged access to more company shares, larger profit-related payments, and higher performance bonuses. These differences in the reward system are in response to a range of factors; nevertheless they can be seen as empirical evidence supporting agency theory's proposition that principals (owners) seek to ensure that their agents (managers) identify with principals' needs.

Agency theory assumes principals and agents have divergent interests that must be curbed by controls. It assumes that agents are highly competitive, individualistic, opportunistic, and self-serving. Davis, Schoorman, and Donaldson argue that those assumptions can be reversed to depict subordinates as collectivist, pro-organisational, and worthy of trust.[28] They argue that while agency theory provides a useful way of explaining how divergent interests can be better aligned through proper monitoring and a well-planned reward system, further theory is needed that takes a broader view than this restrictive economic perspective.

Stewardship theory states the reverse of agency theory, saying that top managers, as stewards, or custodians, are motivated in the best interests of their principals.[29] Stewards place a higher value on cooperation than they do on independently seeking their own interests. They prefer cooperation to conflict and are rational, usually thinking sensibly and judiciously about what is expected of them. They are collectivist in orientation rather than individualist and therefore work towards the best interests of the group rather than selfishly seeking to satisfy their own needs in preference to those of other people. Stewardship theory warns against too much control over managers (acting as stewards) by principals because it reduces motivation and can hinder pro-organisational behaviour by the stewards. Managers' autonomy, it proposes, should be extended because they can be trusted. The two theories are very different in motivational terms: agency theory focuses on extrinsic rewards, which have a measurable market value, and stewardship theory focuses on intrinsic rewards, which are less easily quantified.

Stewardship theory, recalling Maslow and McClelland, is particularly interested in the higher-order needs of growth, achievement, affiliation, and self-actualisation. In stewardship theory, people who are motivated by higher-order needs are more likely to become stewards. Stewards are motivated by intrinsic factors more than by extrinsic factors; identify highly with the organisation; have high value commitments, being sincere about their ethical responsibility and work duties; will use their personal power rather than institutional power when influencing others; will try to involve employees rather than simply control them; survive better in collectivist cultures than in individualist cultures; and prefer to use lower power distance rather than high power distance (as discussed in chapter 5) in managing others. Davis et al. suggest that managers following the principles of stewardship theory will maximise the performance of the firm and minimise costs.[30]

Limitations

Equity theory is a theory of individual motivation that predicts that individuals will make different assessments about the equity of their rewards at work. It is a theory about how groups are motivated insofar as it assumes that individual motivation is fundamentally connected with judgments about the equity with which other comparable people or reference groups are treated. Equity theory predicts that an employee is motivated or discouraged by judgments about the distributive justice of rewards. It is a more altruistic theory of human nature than expectancy theory. Equity theory predicts that individuals will seek to maximise equity so that a higher piece-rate worker (one who receives, for example, 50 cents per unit rather than 25 cents per unit) would feel motivated to produce less output and higher-quality work than workers on the lower rate would. In this way, the individual hopes to restore equity in the group by personally achieving a lower rate combined with high-quality work that requires a high degree of effort. Expectancy theory, on the other hand, is a hedonistic theory predicting that the individual rewarded with a higher piece rate would seek to maximise satisfaction by greater output and do so without additional attention to the quality of the work. Research on equity theory has found that employees can be subdivided into two groups, those who are relatively altruistic and behave consistently with the theory and those who are relatively less altruistic and behave more hedonistically.[31]

Agency and stewardship theories are relevant to an understanding of how individuals are motivated by interests common to the group. These theories are concerned primarily with two groups: owners and managers. Agency theory is an economic theory that implies a unitarist organisation can be achieved through controlling and motivating managers to behave in the interests of owners. The theory assumes that owners' and managers' interests are in conflict but that they can be aligned more closely through appropriate controls and incentives. Stewardship theory is more collectivist than agency theory and assumes unitarism is a natural condition for a proportion of the human population. The theory predicts that through the appropriate controls and cultural context, owners will maximise managers' capability to look after owners' interests. In short, it is based on the assumption that shared interests are already managers' natural inclination.

The core content of both theories has less to say about motivation of non-managerial employees, who form the bulk of the workforce in most organisations. The two theories are therefore difficult to generalise into guidelines for HR policy and practice, although as was mentioned in the previous section, agency theory has a general affinity with hard HRM because both are based on the philosophy that human beings are rational, calculating, and self-interested beings. There is also a similarity in the assumptions of stewardship theory with soft HRM because both assume that managers will be highly committed to owners' interests whenever importance is attached to the collective interest and steps are taken to engender trust. Agency and stewardship theories are of limited application to the broader external political environment and lack substantive historical justification. One of their most frequently quoted limiting assumptions is that motivation is determined by rational processes of decision making, even though there is considerable evidence that people often are constrained by the options open to them in the social environment and do not habitually make decisions by a rational consideration of alternatives.[32] However, this should not become a justification for extreme and irrational methods of motivation. Unfortunately, there are occasional incidents of excessive attempts at motivating employees; for example, in July 1998 trainees in a major insurance company were encouraged to walk over hot coals with the result that seven of them needed hospital treatment. Another hot coals exercise held in February 2002 during an annual three-day team-building conference of KFC managers at Port Stephens (New South Wales), reportedly designed to encourage self-confidence and bonding, resulted in 30 participants having their feet burned.[33]

Summary

In this chapter, three content theories of motivation were discussed and it was noted that they all suggest that people are motivated by higher-order and lower-order needs. It was found that whereas soft HRM aims to motivate employees by appealing to higher-order needs, hard HRM places less importance on the fulfilment of higher-order needs by concentrating specifically on motivating people only insofar as it is a means of serving the organisation's strategy. The three content theories and the four process theories that were introduced represent motivation from the perspective of individual psychology and some, such as Hackman and Oldham's theory of job design, contain prescriptions for implementing HRM. Equity theory describes how individuals are motivated by comparing themselves to other people, and the concept of what constitutes fair treatment and remuneration continues to be an important component of pay surveys and decisions on rewards policy. Agency and stakeholder theory describes ways that managers should be controlled and motivated, but is of limited application to motivating non-managerial employees. Agency theory is arguably a product of Western, individualist business thinking, stewardship theory being better suited to collectivist orientations or culture, for example, Japanese management practices. From the industrial relations perspective, all of the motivation theories discussed tend to play down fundamental tensions and differences of interest between owners, management, and employees.

BOX 6.1

Case study—Motivating the team: the HR initiatives of a retail store supervisor

Introduction
Murrays is a specialist food-store chain: its stores tend to be smaller than those of the major players in the food retailing industry, Coles and Woolworths. Murrays' major competitors are small, specialist retailers. The company has never deviated from its policy of being a provider to profitable niche markets, particularly in middle-class areas. Many of the newer stores are located in fashionable inner suburbs, but do not compete head-on with the big players, which during the 1980s and 1990s tended to be located in shopping malls and in middle suburban areas. However, the company has retained a strong base of inner city stores and expects more competition from the growing numbers of small retailers. Distribution takes place from the central warehouse in three major cities and many of the stores are located in the wealthier areas of New South Wales, Victoria, and Queensland.

Each Murrays store has a common structure and is divided into separate sections of food goods, fruit and vegetables, fish, meat and delicatessen, bakery, and general grocery products. The company's mission statement makes clear its belief that success is based on the provision of quality produce, a variety of food goods, value for money, honesty, and high standards of service.

Appointment of new supervisor
Imagine you are studying for an undergraduate degree at university and, in addition, have undertaken part-time employment in order to make some money and gain work experience. You have been working for a month in your local Murrays store.

Before commencing employment you attended a short management training course. You were appointed weekend supervisor for the fruit and vegetable section. Currently, you are working two evenings a week and all day every Saturday.

Poor motivation in the store
The fruit and vegetable section suffers from poor standards of produce presentation and poor quality and inadequate levels of stock. The store has a small number of full-time staff who generally are of mature age; however, a considerable contribution to the work effort is made up by 'weekenders', who are usually teenagers from the local schools. Weekenders work at Murrays part time during weekday evenings and all day on Saturdays.

There were approximately twelve part-time staff, or weekenders, at the time you were appointed. Immediately after your first week, the low morale of staff became obvious. General standards of discipline among the weekenders were inadequate, including an unsatisfactory level of personal presentation. A cursory inspection of employees' records also revealed the level of absenteeism to be quite high. At the end of your first month, you attended a management meeting at which you found out that the store had serious business problems: financial targets were not being met and levels of produce wastage were too high. You felt that some change was required, but before taking action decided to make a written assessment of the problems you would have to tackle in the fruit and vegetable section.

The heart of these problems, you were sure, lay in human resource management shortcomings. There were no serious difficulties with delivery by suppliers, nor was there a problem with the quality of incoming goods on arrival at the store. You summarised the store's difficulties as requiring action in three key areas.

First, Murrays has a top-down management style and systems that are felt to be oppressive by almost all of the employees. The main complaint is that there is a lack of two-way communication between the employees and their section managers and, further up the organisation, between the employees and the assistant branch manager. Second, although the store's workforce is divided into teams, a general lack of team spirit is evident. This has caused people to feel discouraged and that they lack direction. Third, your conversations with people have made it clear that there is a general lack of training, making it difficult for them to do their jobs properly.

You decided to divide your assessment of the HR problems into two main areas: those which, specifically in the fruit and vegetable section, could be tackled extensively by your own management initiative, and could likewise be dealt with successfully by other section managers, and then those areas that required the implementation of solutions involving higher levels of management.

You appreciated the need for everyone in the Murrays store to work as a team and implement storewide changes; however, you also were aware how much of an influence you personally could have on improving morale. You decided to get started with training the weekenders more effectively. Murrays already had quite a strong training program in place; the problem was that nobody in your store seemed to know about it except the few new weekend supervisors who had been trained for their jobs. The program for weekenders took the form of a short module focused on particular topics, followed by a small number of questions to check trainees' understanding of the material.

You introduced the training program for the weekenders working in fruit and vegetables and obtained permission for them to be released from their duties for half an hour each week during work time. The new training program was supported by your own vigorous presence on the shopfloor. The pay-off in HR terms was immediate: your weekenders became more capable of doing their jobs and started to take more initiative, particularly with ordering of stock and presentation of goods. By the end of your third month, there were improved financial results in your section in the form of increased sales and significantly lower levels of stock wastage.

Case study activity
Analyse employee motivation in the Murrays case by applying theories of motivation.

Study questions

1. Define what is a content theory of motivation. Compare and contrast the three content theories discussed in the chapter: Maslow, McClelland, and Herzberg.
2. Define what is a process theory of motivation. Compare and contrast the four process theories discussed in the chapter: Latham and Locke, Porter and Lawler, Bandura, and Hackman and Oldham.
3. Evaluate hard and soft HRM using content theories of motivation and then using process theories of motivation.
4. Analyse Storey's twenty-five-item checklist on HRM and personnel management (see chapter 1) by classifying the items according to concepts from agency and stewardship theory.
5. Select two theories of motivation and explain how they can be used to improve policy and practice in HRM.

Further reading

Armstrong, M., *A Handbook of Human Resource Management Practice*, 8th edn (London: Kogan Page, 2001).
Davis, J. H., Schoorman, F. D., and Donaldson, L., 'Toward a stewardship theory of management', *Academy of Management Review* (1997), 22, 1, pp. 20–47.
Vroom, V. H. and Deci, E. L. (eds), *Management and Motivation*, 2nd edn (Harmondsworth: Penguin Books, 1992)
Wilson, F. M., *Organizational Behaviour and Gender* (Maidenhead: McGraw-Hill, 1995), chapter 4, pp. 125–51.

CHAPTER 7

Financial Rewards and Performance Management

CHAPTER CONTENTS

Introduction

1 Financial rewards
Reward systems
Pay structures and systems
Rewards for individual or group performance
Rewards for organisational performance
Top management pay

2 Performance management
The four components
Performance appraisal
Kaplan and Norton's balanced scorecard
HRM practices and outcomes

Summary
Case study—Performance appraisal in a car manufacturing plant
Study questions
Further reading

Introduction

Chapter 3 on trade unions and industrial relations described how, in Australia, national and local systems of collective bargaining for pay determination are less common from the 1990s onwards than they were in the 1970s. The reduction in collective bargaining arrangements has been accompanied by increased implementation of individualised rewards and performance-related pay. The new structures and systems of rewards for individual, group, and organisational performance have been accompanied by greater experimentation in formal systems of what is called 'performance management'. This chapter provides an overview of the different types of financial reward, as we have already explored the issues of non-financial reward extensively in the context of motivating individuals and groups in chapter 6. It also introduces the concept of performance management, ending with an overview of Guest's suggested links between HRM and performance.

1 Financial rewards

Reward systems

Figure 7.1, taken from Michael Armstrong, shows the main processes of financial rewards. As the top of the diagram depicts, reward strategy has to be consistent with human resource (or personnel) strategy, which should be in line with business strategy. The implementation of a reward strategy will feed modifications back to the human resource strategy, which in turn should lead to some modification of the business strategy. At the next level of the diagram, we see that the implementation of the reward strategy has three basic components: financial rewards, performance management, and non-financial rewards. The non-financial reward processes are designed to motivate employees through recognition, responsibility, achievement, development, and growth. According to this model, these motivators should be outcomes of the performance management processes and, following the arrows of the diagram, lead to improved individual and team performance and, from there, to improved organisational effectiveness.

The performance-management process also, as shown, feeds into the reward of variable pay, especially pay according to performance. Armstrong subdivides financial reward processes into three key areas: base pay, employee benefits, and variable pay. Base pay is determined through job evaluation studies and pay surveys that inform the pay structure. Employee benefits (such as company pensions and health care schemes) and variable pay (for example, profit sharing and bonus payments) are determined according to minimum standards set by national legislation and influenced by the requirements of Australia's taxation system and by custom and practice within the organisation. All three taken together make up the total remuneration received by the individual. Where the financial reward system is motivating, improved individual and team performance should result.

FINANCIAL REWARDS AND PERFORMANCE MANAGEMENT | 143

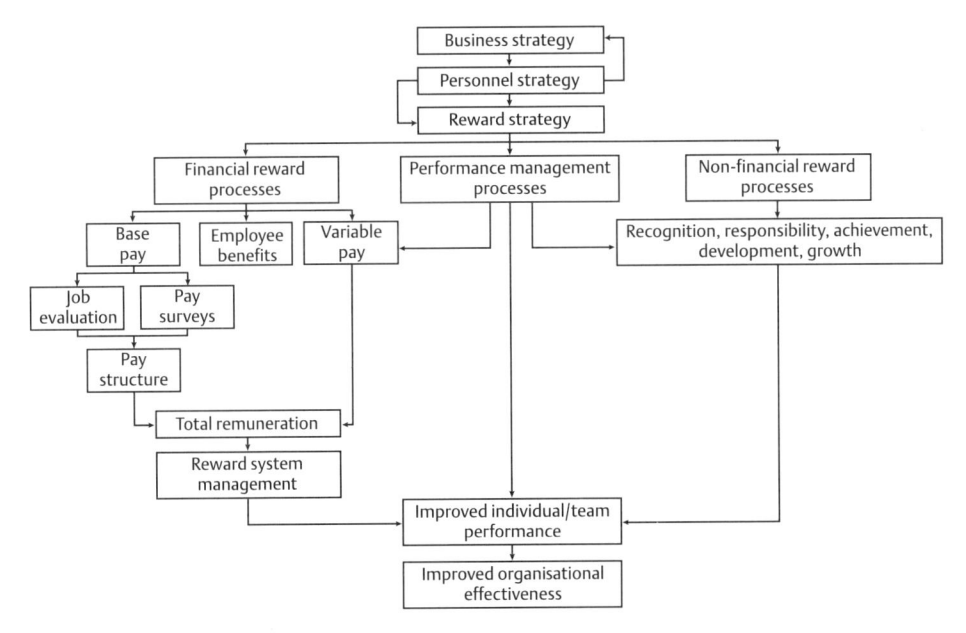

Figure 7.1 The reward system

Source: Armstrong, M., *Employee Reward* (1996), figure 1, p. 7, reproduced with the permission of the publisher, the Institute of Personnel and Development.

Government and employers' attitudes towards rewards have been changing over the last twenty years. Armstrong characterises these trends as a move away from hierarchical and rigid pay structures towards more team-based and flexible systems. His representation of recent reward trends is reproduced in table 7.1. The older systems, on the left of the table, tend to award pay according to narrowly defined jobs. The main way of obtaining more pay is through promotion; there is only some emphasis on performance-related pay, rewards tending to be consolidated around base pay. More recent trends in reward-management systems have emphasised skill and competence development; personnel development plans are a common component of these systems. However, there has been less evidence of competences playing a fundamental role in organisations' pay systems, except for those engaging in organisational transformation and culture change. In Australia, until 1996, competence-based systems for pay and career advancement were implemented at national and state levels through the training reform agenda, which applied competences to restructuring of industrial awards, pay rates and job classifications.[1] There have also been concerted efforts to increase employees' cooperation with each other through job evaluation processes that identify 'job families' (see the section on pay structures below) and overlapping categories. Broad-banded pay structures and increased focus on team-based pay are two important trends in the new reward systems (see table 7.1). These approaches aim to involve employees in determining the structure of the reward systems and have the objective of aligning employees' attitudes more closely with the performance goals of the organisation. However, it is debatable whether they form part of a new and distinct approach to HRM or are just a continuation of longer-term endeavours by management to link pay more closely to individual and organisational performance.[2] During the 1980s and 1990s, in Australia and countries such as the USA and the UK, innovations in rewards systems, particularly performance-related pay, have been implemented so as to distinguish good performers from the rest, making output and productivity the focus rather than position in the organisation.[3]

Table 7.1 Reward trends

From	To
Narrowly defined jobs and job standards	Broader generic roles—emphasis on competence and continuous development
Inflexible job evaluation systems sizing tasks, rewarding non-adaptive behaviour and empire-building and encouraging point-grabbing	Flexible job evaluation processes assessing the value added by people in their roles, often within job families
Hierarchical and rigid pay structures in which the only way to get on is to move up. Focus is on the next promotion	Broad-banded pay structures where the emphasis is on flexibility, career development pay and continuous improvement. Focus is on the next challenge
Emphasis on individual performance-related pay	More focus on team performance through team-based pay
Consolidation of rewards into base pay	More emphasis on 'at risk' pay

Source: Armstrong, M., *Employee Reward* (1996), table 1, p. 19, reproduced with the permission of the publisher, the Institute of Personnel and Development.

Pay structures and systems

No matter how important job satisfaction and other intrinsic rewards are, the essential reward employees receive for their work is pay. Many pay structures and systems have been developed and any system, in practice, is something of a compromise between the different interests of employees and pressures from the external environment. This section is based on Armstrong's material on pay structures and pay systems. Pay structures are, as their name suggests, different structures for determining the pay for individuals and groups of employees. Pay systems are the processes of paying employees within a given structure. We now give a brief overview of each type of structure and system; as pay is a major element in the employment relationship, it is important to be familiar with these.

Pay structures

Any pay structure will have certain characteristics that it rewards in preference to others. Graded and broad-banded pay structures place more significance on such factors as length of employment with the organisation (tenure) and progression through the organisational hierarchy. Structures such as individual pay range, job families, spot rates, and rate for age give more weight to, respectively, market rates combined with individual characteristics, occupation and expertise, external market rates of pay for particular jobs, and pay adjusted for age. Pay curves, pay spines, and integrated pay attempt to reconcile rewarding superior past performance with providing future opportunity for improved performance and potential for increased rewards for employees who were not top-rated but may be next time there is a pay review. All pay structures therefore possess some rationale and some bias as to what constitutes equitable treatment in rewarding employees.

Graded
A conventional graded pay structure consists of a sequence of job grades into which jobs of equivalent value are fitted. Each grade has a pay range or band, offering the employee scope for progression within his or her grade (see figure 7.2).

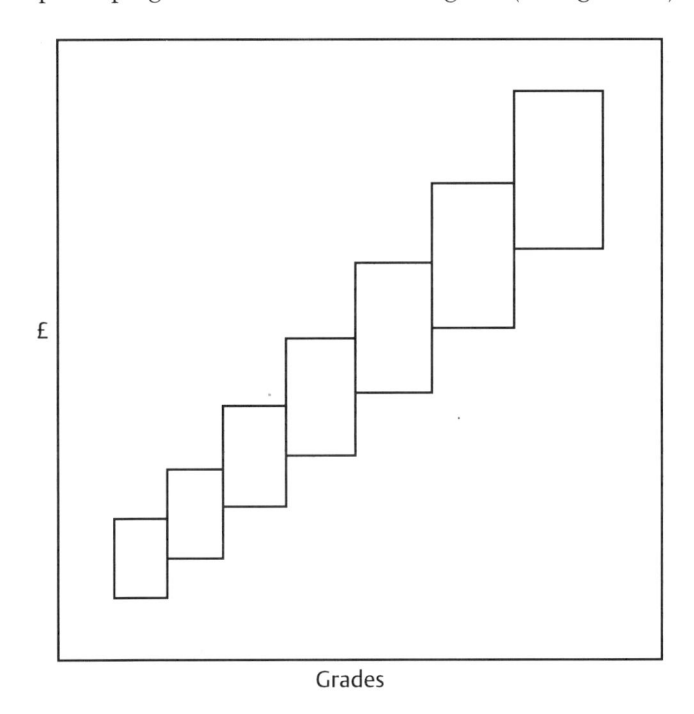

Figure 7.2 A typical graded pay structure

Source: Armstrong, M., *Employee Reward* (1996), figure 13, p. 197, reproduced with the permission of the publisher, the Institute of Personnel and Development.

Broad-banded
The recent trend has been towards reducing the number of grades and increasing the discretionary range (the range of the amount of pay or bonus an employer can award) within grades. The pay range, or band, within each grade can be made broader, and

these broad-banded pay structures are used where the organisation does not want to reinforce a sense of hierarchy through the pay system. Broad-banded structures allow for considerable overlap between different occupations and levels of responsibility, albeit with the maximum obtainable amount of pay usually still increasing as one progresses through the bands and being consistent with increased management responsibility. The key difference between graded and broad-banded structures is that the latter are simpler and more flexible (see figure 7.3).

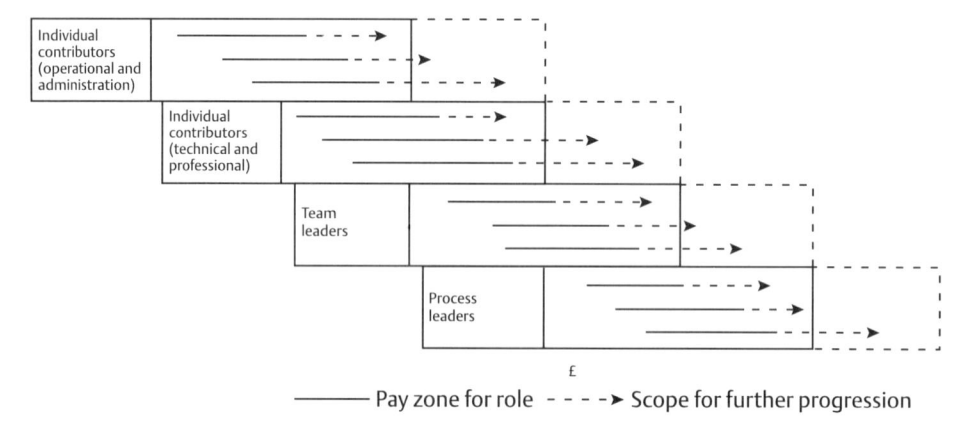

Figure 7.3 A broad-banded structure

Source: Armstrong, M., Employee Reward (1996), figure 14, p. 198, reproduced with the permission of the publisher, the Institute of Personnel and Development.

Individual pay range
Individual pay range structures specify a separate pay range for each job within categories such as senior management, middle management, and team leaders. The midpoint of the pay structure tends to be aligned with market rates, enabling the organisation to compete effectively with rates of pay in comparable organisations.

Job families
Job-family structures consist of separate pay structures for job families, which are groups of jobs evaluated as being equivalent. Each job family has its own structure that may be graded in terms of skills, competences, or responsibilities. Job-family structures allow the flexibility of being able to respond to market rates; however, a disadvantage is that they can create tensions between groups of employees who do not accept the groupings.

Pay curves
Pay curves, sometimes called maturity or progression curves, provide different pay progression tracks according to skill, competence, responsibility, and performance. Exceptional performers are placed on a higher pay curve than are merely effective

performers. The pay curve for effective performers may stop at, for example, Band 2, with only exceptional performers progressing to Band 3. Exceptional performers receive very high pay in comparison to typical market rates (see figure 7.4).

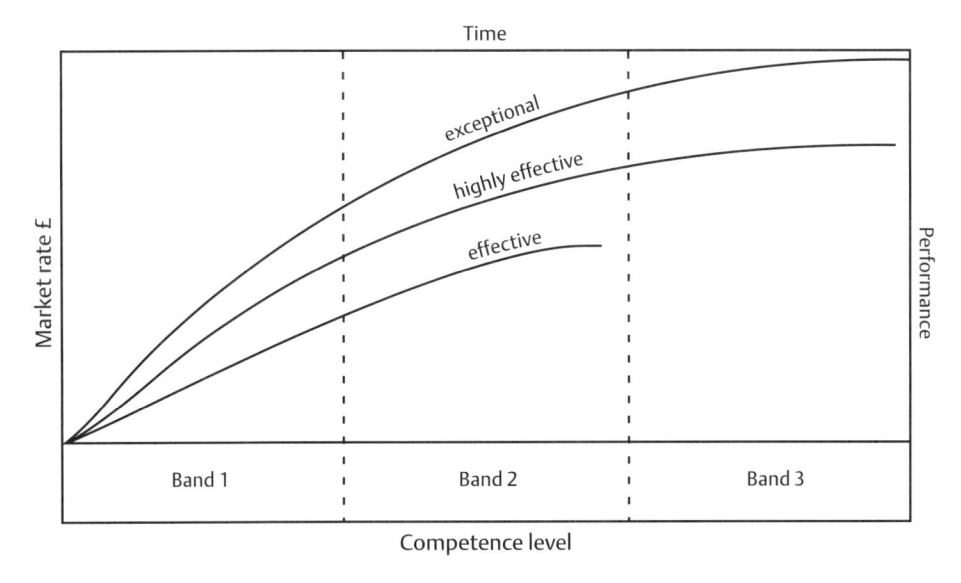

Figure 7.4 A competence and performance-related pay curve

Source: Armstrong, M., *Employee Reward* (1996), figure 16, p. 201, reproduced with the permission of the publisher, the Institute of Personnel and Development.

Spot rate
Spot rate or individual job rate structures use separate rates for particular jobs. These structures are used by organisations that emphasise the management's prerogative to pay whatever they wish and are useful for attracting employees with valuable skills.

Pay spines
Pay spines have been common in the public sector and in voluntary organisations. The various grades are organised along a single pay spine. Individuals are paid according to their grade and their point on the spine. A move to a point higher up the spine can be awarded for performance or additional responsibilities (see figure 7.5).

Integrated pay structures
Integrated pay structures have become more popular and have been introduced to facilitate flexible working arrangements by reducing the barriers created by occupational and hierarchical pay structures. They have been commonly used during organisational change, especially in cases of delayering the organisational

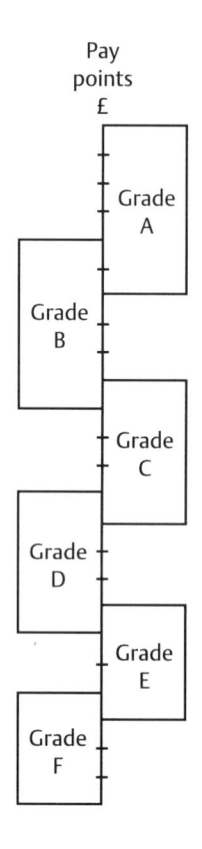

Figure 7.5 A pay spine

Source: Armstrong, M., *Employee Reward* (1996), figure 17, p. 202, reproduced with the permission of the publisher, the Institute of Personnel and Development.

hierarchy and downsizing. They also have been implemented whenever the company philosophy has moved towards single-status employment policies, whereby the organisation deliberately reduces hierarchical status distinctions between employees to improve communication. These policies have often attempted to mimic either Japanese management practices or the HRM single-status policies of some US firms. For example, the BHP Coal Pty Ltd Enterprise Agreement (2001), covering all staff employees, stipulates there will be no demarcation of work, and staff employees may be required to perform production and engineering tasks. To give another example of single-status conditions, in 1987 the UK cable manufacturer Optical Fibres introduced a pay policy of no distinction between clerical and manufacturing workers so that all employees were to be paid a salary rather than manufacturing workers being paid according to number of hours worked.[4] The introduction of new technologies in the workplace has also spurred a move towards a more integrated pay structure with the aim of encouraging greater cooperation, communication, task sharing, flexible practices, and skill development.

Rate for age
Rate-for-age scales link pay to the age of employees and have become relatively uncommon, although they are still used with the younger workforce, particularly young adults on formal training schemes. In Australia, workers under eighteen years of age are paid at lower rates than those who are older. Only recently, in the late 1990s, was a minimum wage established in the UK, which similarly included a scaling factor for young adult employees, whereby they receive a lower minimum wage than the standard.

Payment systems
This section reviews payment systems, commencing with the time-rate system, which is one of the most common. The other systems are divided into two categories, those that reward individual or group performance and those that reward organisational performance.

Time rates
Time-rate systems reward the employee for a unit of attendance at work—an hour, day, week, month, or year. Time rates are one of the most commonly used pay systems. They are relatively simple and cheap to administer and help managers forecast human resource costs. They have the advantage of being easily understood by employees, although a criticism from the perspective of HRM would be that they do not motivate performance well because there is little incentive to improve productivity or efficiency. Nevertheless, they have remained a popular payment system in Australia, the USA and UK since the 1990s.

Rewards for individual or group performance

Individual piecework
Individual piecework (straight piecework) schemes reward individuals directly according to their work output and have been common in agriculture for hundreds of years, although it is only in the last two centuries that individual productivity has been directly and routinely tied to monetary payment. Piecework remuneration was common in, for example, the European wool and textile trade during medieval times and in manufacturing industry since the beginning of the Industrial Revolution, although it is less common now in Australia, the USA and the UK than it was at the beginning of the twentieth century. The advantages of piecework systems are that they are simple to understand and make it easy for employees to predict their earnings according to their rate of work. From the employers' perspective, piecework motivates individuals to work quickly and labour costs are directly related to the pace of work and its consequent level of productivity. A disadvantage of individual piecework systems for employers is that the quality of work often suffers from the rush to obtain high rates of output. For employees, piecework may cause undue stress and poor health after a sustained period of work.

Work-measured schemes

In work-measured schemes, which became popular in the 1950s and 1960s, first in the USA then in the UK, jobs or their component tasks are measured and a standard time is established for performing them. These schemes reward employees for performance above the standard. They have the advantage that pay is related to productivity, the employee being expected to perform to at least the standard rate of time allowed for the job. The employee has the incentive to work harder than the standard rate, and also has the flexibility of being able to vary output according to circumstances and motivation. For a work-measured scheme to be effective, it is vital that the work be measured accurately, because employees have an incentive to exaggerate the time necessary to perform tasks in order to make incentive payments easier to obtain. These schemes did not find such a receptive environment in Australia, where the system of industrial awards discouraged these types of pay incentive.

Measured day work

Measured day work schemes use techniques of work measurement to determine the level of performance expected of an employee and then set an appropriate level of payment.[5] Measured day work schemes were popular in the 1960s and 1970s in the UK, when it was important for management to secure predictable levels of productivity to meet market demand. Under measured day work, the employees' pay includes an incentive payment that assumes output will be in accordance with the rate agreed. These schemes were often the subject of collective bargaining and negotiation between management and unions, and the incentive payment was given in advance, therefore obliging employees to achieve the agreed rate of productivity. They were not a significant form of reward in Australia because productivity issues only attained a similar degree of prominence during the 1980s.

The advantages of measured day work schemes from managers' point of view are that they retain freedom to deploy the workforce in the most efficient way and they encourage a high and steady rate of output. These schemes have, in the past, recognised and rewarded differentials between occupational groups of employees—for example, skilled and semi-skilled workers. This was often felt to be vitally important by unions and their members. The disadvantages of these schemes are that there is no direct individual incentive for high performance and little encouragement for innovation or improved methods of working. The individual has no control over earnings because there is no direct relationship between the individual effort made and the rewards obtained.

Group or team incentives

Group incentive schemes reward the group or team with a cash payment for production output that meets an agreed target. The payment may be an equal amount to each individual or it may be made on an agreed proportional basis. Group or team incentives are a form of piecework incentive scheme that is nowadays regarded by managers as being too difficult to control.[6] These payment by results (PBR) schemes have the advantage of encouraging group discipline and teamwork, but they have the disadvantage that output can be restricted by the group because it is individual employees who determine what level of earnings they wish to achieve. This incentive scheme—in common with individual piecework, work measured, and measured day work—stresses rates and levels of productivity, whereas many companies now have to concentrate as much on quality as on quantity. Recent case study research on team performance—in small and medium-sized firms, pharmaceutical companies, and two call centres of large organisations—found that the more successful team initiatives paid close attention to recruitment, selection, training, and rewards. In some of the companies, unforeseen difficulties were encountered in establishing appropriate pay levels; therefore, team incentives and team-based pay should be planned before new teams are created. The tendency is for there to be less use of HRM in small and medium-sized enterprises, although according to one study of Australian SMEs there has been 'moderate' uptake.[7]

Individual and group bonuses
Bonuses are granted in addition to base salary and paid to either individuals or groups as a reward for achievement or for completion of a project. Many reward systems incorporate individual and group bonus schemes. The advantage of individual bonus schemes is that if individuals are motivated by the bonuses to achieve targets, the schemes can be relatively easy to administer. Individual bonus systems become difficult to operate where the outputs of work are intangible, as is typical of most services, and bonus schemes can encourage individualistic and uncooperative behaviours. The advantages of group bonus schemes are that teamwork is promoted and achievement of group targets is reinforced through the rewards system. The disadvantage of these schemes is that by their very nature they can reduce individual motivation to a sole concern for achieving bonuses.

Performance-related pay
Performance-related pay (PRP) can be defined as 'a system in which an individual's increase in salary is solely or mainly dependent on his/her appraisal or merit rating'.[8] This rating may take into consideration not only individual output but 'other indicators of performance such as quality, flexibility, contribution to team working and ability to hit targets'.[9]

PRP systems differ from the older systems of payment by results, commission, and bonus schemes in that they assess the outputs of work and employee behaviour. These systems enjoyed a growing popularity during the 1980s, concurrent with the move towards greater individualisation of the employment relationship and away from collectivism, with many seeing PRP as a key practice of HRM.[10] An advantage of PRP is that effective, individual performance can be elicited through the rewards system: high performers are paid more than low performers are. But organisations implementing these schemes have found some common stumbling blocks: they are costly to run, employees concentrate on their objectives related to pay rather than the whole job, and they have the potential to create a sense of inequity within the organisation if employees feel that managers have rewarded through favouritism rather than objective judgment of performance.[11] Researchers from the

London School of Economics and Political Science found that performance-related pay in the civil service, hospitals, and schools has made a minority of staff work harder, but at the cost of lower morale and poorer relationships caused by greater resentment towards managers. Similarly, an examination of performance-based pay in the Australian public service found that linking pay to individual performance had negative effects on teamwork, was highly subjective in operation, gave managers excessive prerogative, and led to inadequate measurement and feedback. One factor likely to increase a PRP scheme's likelihood of success, therefore, is an effective process of performance assessment sustaining a sense of equity and good working relationships. Performance-related pay appears to be more commonplace in US and British companies than it is in Australia, and in the public sector, it has often been associated with privatisation.[12]

Skill-based and competence-based pay
Skilled-based and competence-based pay schemes differ from the other pay systems discussed so far because they concentrate on the performance capabilities and inputs made by the employee, with the exception of some competence systems that are purely outcome-based. Sometimes these schemes will include rewards for employees' personal competences, which in effect can be similar to older versions of merit pay, whereby employees were rewarded retrospectively for personal merit (that is, behavioural traits and other inputs) rather than being directly rewarded for the outcomes of work.

For the purpose of this chapter, skill-based and competence-based systems are treated as being the same, although it is acknowledged there are differences between them. Competence-based systems are a more recent development, defining required standards of employee behaviour and performance. They are a deliberate attempt to motivate high performance,[13] or to ensure that performance meets an agreed level and occupational standard. National Competency Training Schedules are often specified and approved by the Industry Training Assistance Boards and the Australian National Training Authority. In the UK, Industry Lead Bodies and the National Council for Vocational Qualifications play a similar role. Skill-based approaches are an older system and, as with the competence-based approaches, have traditionally concentrated on inputs that can be assessed by qualifications or by observing behaviour or making inferences on the basis of work outputs. Skills, therefore, can be inferred either from individual behaviour, as interpersonal skills are, or from the results of the employee's applying technical/occupational skills to work tasks. In practice, the terms 'skill' and 'competence' have often been confused.[14] In the context of job analysis, Armstrong proposes treating skills separately as 'inputs', and competences as 'behaviours' and 'achievement'. He distinguishes between 'knowledge and skills', which are inputs (what the employee has to be able to know and do); behaviour, which consists of 'process competences' (how the employee is expected to behave); and achievement, which consists of 'output competences' (what the employee is expected to achieve).[15]

In the 1980s and 1990s, these systems of pay were used by organisations to encourage employees to develop their skills and competences. An employment trends survey published in 1998, conducted by the Confederation of British Industry (CBI) and the William Mercer consultancy, involving over 670 employers and 2.4 million employees, found that two-thirds of firms were using competences as part of the means of determining pay. This probably exaggerates the extent that competences are an integral part of the pay system in countries such as Australia and the UK, and especially within small and medium-size enterprises.[16] Organisational downsizing and delayering frequently have had the short-term result of intensifying employees' work and broadening their responsibilities. Some companies switched away from performance-based systems of pay to emphasise more greatly the acquisition of new skills and competences with the aim of stimulating employees to behave and develop in ways consistent with the planned direction of organisational change. The skills and competences that are rewarded can be very broad, ranging from soft skills/competences, such as teamwork and communicating with customers, to technical skills, such as operating new technology and systems. In the computer and information industries, Unisys and IBM are two examples of companies that during the early 1990s implemented skill-based and competence-based pay systems. Recent competence-based systems have covered a wider range of behaviours and attributes than skill-based systems do,[17] rewarding inputs such as teamwork, customer orientation, innovation practices, accountability, and motivation.

IBM, during the turbulent worldwide business conditions of the early 1990s, adopted a broad-band pay system sensitive to market pay rates and then combined it with a pay element emphasising development and employability. A central purpose of many skill-based and competence-based systems has been to stress that employees must continuously improve their work practices and develop themselves, therefore maximising both the competitiveness of the organisation and their own employability. These demanding systems are in stark contrast to the older pay systems, which traditionally emphasised internal promotion and encouraged employees to assume there was a job for life in the organisation.

Cafeteria or flexible benefit systems
Cafeteria or flexible benefit systems have become popular in the USA and UK because they give employees more choice in determining their remuneration packages. They focus on variable pay rather than basic pay, by concentrating on benefit packages. Since the introduction of enterprise bargaining, greater focus has been placed on flexible remuneration including superannuation, health care, and mortgage repayments. This has been notably popular in the welfare sector; for example, Gold Coast Skill Centre Enterprise Agreement (1999) permits a maximum of 30 per cent of salary to be taken as a non-salary benefit. To take another industry sector—retailing—BHS Ltd (British Home Stores) was one of the first companies in the UK to introduce a cafeteria pay system that provided managers with the opportunity to choose from different levels of life insurance cover, private medical care, annual holiday entitlement, disability insurance, and other benefits. Advantages of cafeteria systems, from the employer's perspective, are that they are flexible and, when well managed, can be tax effective and reduce employer risks and liabilities during insurance claims because the employer has offered the employee clear choices

over pay and benefits. Salary packaging has been a popular new element of rewards in Australia offering tax and purchasing benefits to employees. The threat of litigation has been an increasingly significant issue in the USA and, to a somewhat lesser but growing extent, in Australia and the UK, where individual employees are becoming more litigious in disputes with their organisations, sometimes winning substantial court settlements that are very costly to the employer.

Rewards for organisational performance

Gainsharing

Gainsharing is a bonus plan that gives employees a share of the financial gain made by the organisation's improved performance. It is an alternative to the individualised rewards of performance-related pay, relating rewards to organisational performance. The potential advantages of gainsharing are that it allows employees to have control over their work and encourages teamwork and cooperation. If productivity rises and the organisation gains, then everyone gains. These schemes intend to focus employees' attention on the key issues influencing organisational performance. A gainsharing scheme operates on a formula agreed between management and employees whereby everyone shares in the gains resulting from effective work performance. Modern versions are most often based on measures of value-added performance, calculated by deducting expenditure on materials and purchased services from sales.

Profit sharing

With profit sharing, employees are paid a proportion of the organisation's pre-tax profits. Governments can use taxation reform to make profit-sharing schemes more attractive to employers. The UK Conservative governments of the 1980s were keen to encourage companies to use profit sharing as a means of educating people to become more conscious of the profitability of their employing organisation. There was not an equivalent impetus towards profit sharing by Australian governments during the 1980s, although discount share offers were made to employees of Australian privatising companies during the 1990s. The tax relief on these schemes meant that Australian employers could provide extra benefits to employees without increasing company contributions. Traditionally, profit-related pay schemes in the UK were not formal schemes approved by the Inland Revenue, the UK's taxation authority. Non-Inland Revenue approved profit-sharing schemes awarded eligible employees cash from a pool, according to a formula that was at the discretion of the company and did not have to be published. Profit-sharing schemes in Australia have sometimes been established as part of enterprise agreements, for example, Victoria-based Water Wheel Flour Mills (1994), and Boral Window Systems' (Geebung, Brisbane 2000) Enterprise Agreement, which undertakes to develop a profit-sharing system in the future. In the 1980s, with the tax incentive from the UK Inland Revenue, it became possible to award UK employees approximately 3–6 per cent profit-related pay on top of their salaries without having to pay any tax on that element of pay. The maximum amount allowed in any one year has been £3000 or 10 per cent of total pay, whichever is greater.

UK Inland Revenue approved profit-sharing schemes allocate profits to a trust fund that obtains shares in the organisation for employees. The 1978 Finance Act (UK) made provisions for companies to distribute shares to employees free of charge. The period between shares being obtained by the employees and the actual release of payments to them can be prolonged. Further, stock market fluctuations make the eventual worth of the shares uncertain. These difficulties reduce the extent of employees' belief that there is a direct relationship between their own efforts and the eventual profitability of the organisation, and have been mentioned in some Australian enterprise bargaining agreements as a problem of employee perception.

Save-as-you-earn
The UK Conservative governments (1979–97) were also supportive of save-as-you-earn (SAYE) schemes. UK Inland Revenue–approved save-as-you-earn (SAYE) employee share-option schemes made it easier and more tax efficient for UK organisations to buy shares for full-time employees, who have the opportunity to cash in their shares after an agreed period of time. The 1980 Finance Act (UK) enabled employees to have options to buy, hold, and sell shares. Schemes required employees to save for five or seven years, but more recently it has become possible for employees to sell their shares after only three years. In Australia, enterprise bargaining has acted as a significant catalyst to profit sharing, while salary sacrificing (whereby employees give up part of their salary, in exchange for a particular benefit, such as child care) has also become increasingly popular. Both can provide employees with short-term tax advantages. The management of these schemes, particularly in large organisations, has become quite complex, and the administration costs alone amount to many thousands of dollars. Recently companies have become increasingly concerned that as the tax relief is withdrawn from these schemes, the total rewards bill will increase substantially.

A key purpose of schemes that reward organisational performance is to make employees and managers more profit-conscious and to align their interests with those of the company. A disadvantage of profit sharing, employee share-option schemes, and salary packaging is their complexity, which renders them difficult for employees to understand. Some corporate employers have been engaged in profit sharing and employee share-option schemes for some years—for example, large organisations in Australia such as Bovis Lend Lease, Mobil, and SPC; and UK corporate organisations such as BT (telecommunications), Barclays (banking), Sainsbury's, and Tesco (retailing). Many of these organisations have had to set up administration and information services to make sure that employees are well informed and involved. Research studies of some of these schemes have found that they do not strongly motivate employees to perform better at work,[18] although they are motivating to some extent, for example, through increasing job satisfaction.[19] The extent to which employees feel personally rewarded by the schemes is strongly moderated by other factors, such as individual preferences for participation[20] and position in the organisational hierarchy.[21] Some research suggests that motivation is moderated by the extent to which the individual is intrinsically or extrinsically motivated.[22] Employees who are extrinsically motivated are thought to be satisfied only when the actual reward is calculated to be a fair return on effort. Intrinsically motivated employees tend to be more satisfied with the fact that the schemes facilitate wide employee ownership and, in general, they will make less precise assessments of the actual financial benefit they derive from the schemes.

Final remark on pay structures and payment systems
As mentioned earlier, time-rate systems have remained popular partly because they are a comparatively simple means of rewarding employees and are less likely to lead to disagreement over the amount awarded. John Storey contrasts personnel management with HRM on the issue of pay (see Storey's twenty-five-item checklist in chapter 1), saying that a personnel management approach rewards employees according to fixed grades but HRM uses performance-related pay. John Purcell has summarised performance-based pay systems in two dimensions: the type of performance and the unit of performance rewarded.[23] The type of performance he categorises as either output or input, with the majority of performance-based pay systems rewarding output performance. The unit of performance he subdivides into individual and collective systems. Individual systems include piecework, commission, individual bonus, individual performance-related pay, skill-based pay, and merit pay. Collective systems include measured day work, team bonus, profit sharing, gainsharing, and employee share-ownership schemes. Purcell's summary of types of performance-based pay system is shown in table 7.2.

Table 7.2 Purcell's types of performance-pay system

Type of performance	Unit of performance	
	Individual	Collective
Output	Piecework	Measured day work
	Commission	Team bonus
	Individual bonus	Profit sharing
	Individual performance-related pay	Gainsharing
Input	Skill-based pay	Employee share-ownership schemes
	Merit pay	

Source: Purcell, J. (1993), unpublished, cited by Kessler, I., 'Reward Systems', in J. Storey (ed.), *Human Resource Management: A Critical Text* (London: Routledge, 1995), p. 256

Occasionally, organisations have completely changed their pay structures and systems in an attempt to signal change and encourage new employee behaviours and attitudes. Australian Workplace Agreements (AWAs)—such as AWAs in Bundaberg Brewed Drinks Pty Ltd—have provided a major avenue for employers seeking to transform organisational culture and employee attitudes. Pay levels may even go up and down in different parts of the company. In Australia, McDonald's has argued in the media, and elsewhere, for reduced wage rates in order to create more employment opportunities. By contrast, in the UK, McDonald's launched new initiatives on pay and career prospects in a massive recruitment drive and battle against Burger King for UK market share. Both companies had been paying well below the Low Pay Commission's minimum level and were said to be anxious not to be caught in negative publicity that would reinforce the 'McJob' image.[24] However, the majority of organisations' structures and systems have evolved over time, with pay structures being modified and systems progressively becoming more complex as management seeks to motivate and reward employees for improved organisation performance.

Top management pay

Traditionally, managers have been paid more than most of their subordinates. The structures and systems for rewarding managers are similar to those for rewarding employees, although for management in many companies there is a wider range of schemes available, related to profit sharing, performance bonuses, share options, pensions, and other benefits. Executive share schemes specifically give executives options to acquire shares at fixed prices. These schemes aim to give executives a stronger sense of ownership of their organisations and more closely align their interests with those of the shareholders (see the section on agency theory in chapter 6). Some of these schemes have been very generous, providing managers with as much as, or more than, the value of their annual pay packages. The gap between employees' pay and top managers' pay has widened in developed countries such as Australia, the USA and the UK. This occurred noticeably during the 1980s, when directors' pay rose, in real terms, considerably faster than employees' pay did. In the UK, according to the National Institute for Economic and Social Research, during the period 1985–90 directors' pay increased by 77 per cent, while employees' pay increased by only 17 per cent. In Australia, since the 1980s, executive salaries have outperformed those of wage-earning employees, and there has been a significant increase in inequality of wealth and income. In the USA, the salaries of chief executive officers (CEOs) have consistently outstripped those of most employees over the past two decades, while the lowest paid have fallen consistently behind, as the real value of the minimum wage fell during the 1990s to only 80 per cent of the value it had during the mid-1970s. Clearly, Australian CEO compensation, which is increasing at twice the rate of average weekly income in Australia, is following trends set in the UK and the USA.[25]

Management of executives' rewards became a frequently debated issue during the 1990s and in the UK led to the publication of three influential reports: the Cadbury Report (1993), the House of Commons Employment Select Committee's Report (1995), and the Greenbury Report (1995). However, in Australia there have been no comparable high-profile government investigations. These reports have advised greater control over executives' rewards by increasing the transparency of the reward systems through measures including tighter service contracts, use of remuneration committees involving non-executive directors, and wider publication of the remuneration policy for directors, including publication of the amount of their individual remuneration.

2 Performance management

Performance management is an approach used by organisations to try to achieve strategic goals consistently through better formal and informal motivation, monitoring, evaluating, and rewarding of performance. Performance management systems grew in popularity during the 1980s because they were thought to facilitate rigorous specification of performance standards and measures and increase the likelihood of achieving organisational goals at a time when organisations needed to respond to increasingly competitive business conditions. They were also a move away from collectivism towards greater individualisation of the employment relationship. They have remained very popular in the private and in the public sector and continue to be promoted by consultancies.[26]

During the 1990s there was increased interest among HRM practitioners and researchers in high-performance or high-commitment practices, and there is evidence for a link between adoption of high-performance HR practices and superior organisational performance. US researchers Pfeffer and Huselid claim that adoption of their best practices, when combined with long-term commitment and consistent performance measurement according to high standards, will result in superior performance.[27] David Guest sees Huselid's work as a potential breakthrough for HRM theory and practice:

> Using company market value as the key indicator, he [Huselid] found that firms with significantly above-average scores on the index of high-performance work practices (in technical terms, this meant one standard deviation above the mean) provided an extra market value per employee of between £10 000 and £40 000. On this basis, an investment in HR pays off handsomely.
>
> Given these seemingly huge financial benefits, what are the specific practices that provide such an advantage? One thing is clear from all of the research: there is no value in investing heavily in specific practices. Performance-related pay, psychometric tests in selection or extensive training will not in themselves bring bottom-line results. The key lies in having the right 'bundle' of practices—and the challenge for personnel managers is to find it.[28]

However, Stephen Wood observes that UK companies are failing to derive benefit from high-commitment management because they do not implement the practices consistently and over the longer term. These companies are underachieving by taking the classic British short-term and piecemeal approach to strategy. Lack of international comparison studies on high-commitment management render it difficult to qualify how much his criticisms apply to Australia; however, a related study of high-involvement management in Australian manufacturing companies certainly highlights the importance of strategic HRM. To achieve high commitment within the organisation, its authors recommend implementation of effective consultation and participation arrangements within the overall context of enterprise bargaining. Guest (2001) proposes making a theoretical distinction relevant to HR practitioners and researchers alike, that distinguishes more clearly the different senses of HRM and its outcomes: high-*performance* practices; high-*commitment* practices; and high-*commitment & flexibility* practices.[29]

The four components

In 1996, Marchington and Wilkinson proposed four principal components of performance management (see figure 7.6). Performance management is a continuous process whereby employees know the performance expectations for their work and are supported by managers and their peers to achieve these expectations. This informal and formal support should occur consistently throughout the year. All individual performance is formally reviewed and appraised once or twice a year. Following the formal appraisal interview, actions are decided by employee and manager that aim to achieve new levels of performance, to implement training programs and other development initiatives, and to find ways of resolving performance difficulties or failures. In large organisations—for example, public sector local authorities—follow-up actions include the management of absenteeism.

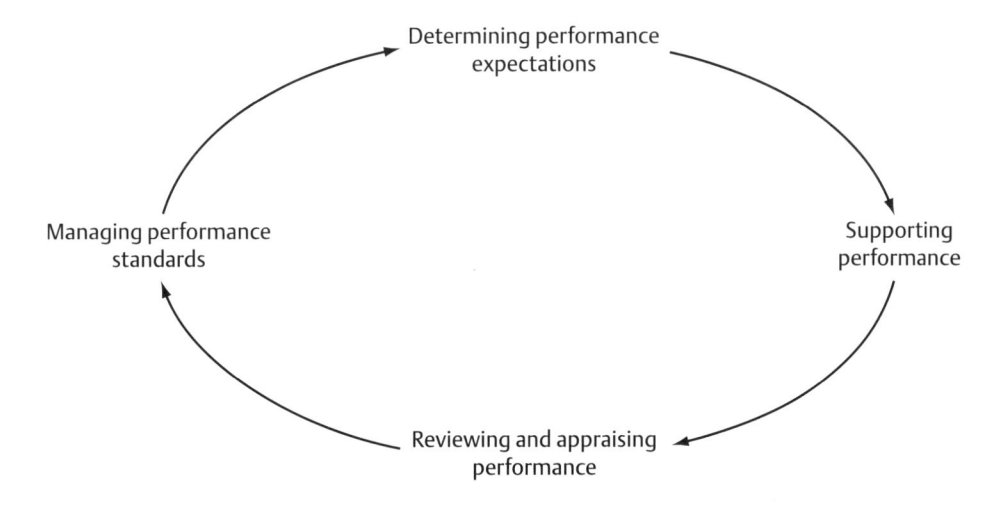

Figure 7.6 Four components of performance management

Source: Marchington, M. and Wilkinson, A., *Core Personnel and Development*, (1996), figure 5, p. 135, reproduced with the permission of the publisher, the Institute of Personnel and Development.

Connock stresses that performance management places great emphasis on the future and on achievement using 'SMART' objectives and targets (specific, measurable, achievable, realistic, time-constrained).[30] The process places importance on setting key accountabilities, agreeing to future objectives for them, agreeing on measures and standards to be obtained, and assigning time-scales and priorities. Formal, sophisticated monitoring techniques also play an important role in performance management, as shown by the Fourth Workplace Employee Relations Survey (1998). The survey found that there is a group of HR practices associated with performance management: psychometric testing, use of employee attitude surveys, and performance appraisal. Feedback on absenteeism, for example, is important because employees have been found to often underestimate their own and overestimate others' absence. The most recent Australian Workplace Industrial Relations Survey (AWIRS, 1995)[31] found that the great majority of workplaces (76 per cent) had increased their use of performance-monitoring measures (including benchmarking, key performance measures, and labour productivity), whereas only 5 per cent had reduced their use of such measures. Performance management systems use formal employee appraisal as a central component, but they should not be seen as appraisal under a new name. These systems include a number of human resource activities, and typical features include well-communicated mission statements, regular communication on progress according to business plans, integration with quality-management policies, a clear focus on senior managers' performance, use of performance-related rewards, and a strong emphasis on training and development tailored to achieve performance expectations.

The demerger of ICI into ICI and Zeneca led to new systems of performance management in the two demerged companies. ICI introduced what was known as the 'Triple A' project (accountability, achievement, autonomy), which was designed to manage individual performance, making it more closely aligned with the strategic needs of the business. Employees working in the new system were said to be better informed about their accountabilities and their achievements according to objectives and targets, and learned to work with newly devolved responsibilities and within devolved budgets. In February 1998, ICI Australia changed its name to Orica; it first became an independent Australasian company in July 1997.[32]

Performance appraisal

Performance appraisal is not only a central component of any performance-management system but also the main, formal method of setting, measuring, and achieving performance expectations. Anderson defines performance appraisal as involving:
- The systematic review of the performance of staff on a written basis at regular time intervals; and
- Holding of appraisal interviews at which staff have the opportunity to discuss performance issues, past, present and future, on a one-to-one basis, with their immediate line manager.[33]

FINANCIAL REWARDS AND PERFORMANCE MANAGEMENT | 161

Harrison suggests that performance appraisal used within performance-management systems requires four activities, as shown in figure 7.7, which are part of the role of all line managers.[34] The manager must appraise and review the past; conduct the performance-appraisal interview; plan the future and agree on performance targets and development plans; and follow up the interview with future action.

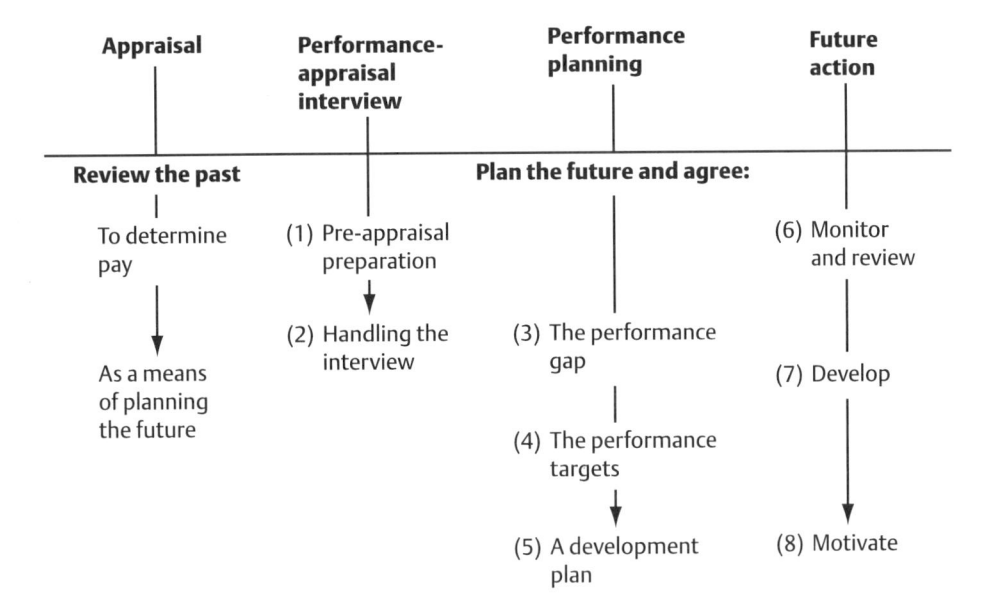

Appraisal	Performance-appraisal interview	Performance planning	Future action
Review the past	**Plan the future and agree:**		
To determine pay	(1) Pre-appraisal preparation		(6) Monitor and review
As a means of planning the future	(2) Handling the interview	(3) The performance gap	(7) Develop
		(4) The performance targets	
		(5) A development plan	(8) Motivate

Figure 7.7 The manager's role in performance management

Source: Harrison, R., *Human Resource Management: Issues and Strategies* (1993), figure 10.3, p. 262. Reprinted by permission of Pearson Education Limited.

The immediate line manager is not always the person who acts as the appraiser. In some armed forces, the manager's manager has taken on the appraiser's role, it being assumed that he or she holds a more impartial view of the employee's performance. A common problem with appraisal by the manager's manager is that the higher-level manager is not always well acquainted with the employee's day-to-day work, aspirations, or performance. Most appraisals that aim to involve employees and to be 'transparent systems' (in which personal records and judgments are open to inspection by the appraised individual) incorporate self-appraisal as a necessary component of the review process. In Australia, self-appraisal has proved popular, but most often as a prelude to appraisal by an immediate manager.[35]

Other less commonly used appraisal methods are 'upward appraisal', whereby subordinates make the appraisal. This approach has been used successfully in large organisations such as Australian universities where students evaluate the performance of lecturers and in British retail companies where all of the employees periodically appraise their managers. Peer appraisal has found more popularity in the professions, such as lawyers in partnership firms and doctors in general medical practices.[36] Research suggests that 'multi-appraisal' methods, which are the most comprehensive because data are collected from all around an employee (a '360-degree appraisal'), sometimes from inside and outside the organisation, provide a fuller picture and limit the danger of distortion from using one perspective.[37] Since the early 1990s, 360-degree feedback is said to have been adopted in the USA and UK, across a range of public- and private-sector organisations involving subordinates, peers, superiors, and sometimes customers and suppliers. The 360-degree appraisal approach has mainly been used as a development tool enabling individuals to better identify their strengths and weaknesses as others see them, but there are signs that organisations are incorporating it with performance appraisal and some are seeking to link it with pay. However, Australia appears to have been less quick to adopt this innovation despite its growing popularity elsewhere. Research on a task-based 360-degree appraisal system assessing Australian and Singaporean managers based in the retail and construction industries suggests that its outcomes may not always be overwhelmingly positive for the majority of appraisees. It found a tendency for the appraisal results to become polarised into two groups: an elite group of managers and the rest.[38]

The appraisal process can never be a fail-safe system because its effectiveness continually depends upon the participants' behaving cooperatively and sensitively. Exploratory research on a sample of Australian managers and employees found that formal performance-appraisal interviews often did not add much to the ongoing feedback already given by managers to their subordinates.[39] Grint describes some of the common distortions likely to occur when assessing performance.[40] Under the 'halo effect' the appraiser overestimates performance because he or she likes the individual. Under the 'horn effect' the reverse applies. Other common distortions include the 'crony effect', under which appraisal is not objective for fear of damaging personal or family relationships. Attempts to implement appraisal in some of the countries of the Middle East and Asia, such as Bahrain and Thailand, have met with difficulties caused by complex networks of personal and family relationships in the workplace. Another problem, the 'Veblen effect', is a distortion that results from the appraiser's tendency to rate individuals as average because it is easier to award people average appraisal ratings than it is to discuss and agree on a range of ratings from high performance to low performance. Also, appraisers can be reluctant to rate appraisees objectively because employees become disillusioned by what they perceive to be adverse and unfair criticism. These problems can be resolved to some extent by proper training of managers and employees in the appraisal process, particularly by developing their skills in getting the best out of the written reviews and the face-to-face interview. Appraisal systems have to be sensitive to norms of national culture and may have to be implemented in different ways. A research investigation on performance appraisal comparing practice in Hong Kong and the UK found that British appraisals were more participative and less directive than Hong Kong appraisals. Investigation of supervisory appraisal by Hong Kong Chinese and US managers working in Hong Kong and US companies found that Hong Kong managers based in Hong Kong companies were least supportive of subordinate evaluation for executive appraisal.[41]

Fletcher and Williams say that appraisal is often difficult to implement effectively because it requires managers to perform adequately in two potentially contradictory roles, those of 'judge' and 'helper'.[42] These assessment and development roles in appraisal systems have been known for many years. McGregor described appraisal as having three objectives. First, there is an administrative objective, which is judgmental about the employee's career, such as determining who gets promoted and rewarded (the 'judge' role). Second, appraisals have the objective of being informative—making judgments about an employee's performance, strengths, and weaknesses. Third, as well as performing this judgmental function of categorising individuals, appraisals must be motivational, creating learning experiences that motivate employees to develop themselves and improve their performance (the 'helper' role).[43]

To summarise, four essential elements of performance management are:
1. setting individual objectives that support achieving the business strategy;
2. performance appraisal;
3. review of pay and rewards, including performance-related pay; and
4. organisational capability review—the performance-management system must influence the business strategy.[44]

Kaplan and Norton's balanced scorecard

One innovation in performance management that has attracted the attention of senior management in companies[45] and that satisfies the features listed above is Kaplan and Norton's version of the 'balanced scorecard',[46] a management system designed to encourage what the authors call 'breakthrough performance' in product, process, customer, and market development. The scorecard presents four different perspectives on performance measurement: financial, customer, internal business, and innovation and learning. Kaplan and Norton say that, in the past, managers failed to utilise this range of perspectives and have stuck too closely to short-term financial measures such as return on investment (ROI), sales growth, and operating income. These financial measures are important, but in terms of the 'balanced scorecard' they represent just one-quarter of the picture. The scorecard or the financial measures should be used, they say, as a means of bench-marking performance on projects and in new growth businesses.

Figure 7.8 shows that the balanced scorecard is a management process involving four main steps. First is deciding the vision of the future. Second is determining how this vision can become a competitive advantage for the organisation as seen from four perspectives: shareholders, customers, internal management processes, and ability to innovate and grow. The third step is determining from these four perspectives the critical success factors, and the final step is identifying the critical measurements for ascertaining how far along the organisation is on the path to success.

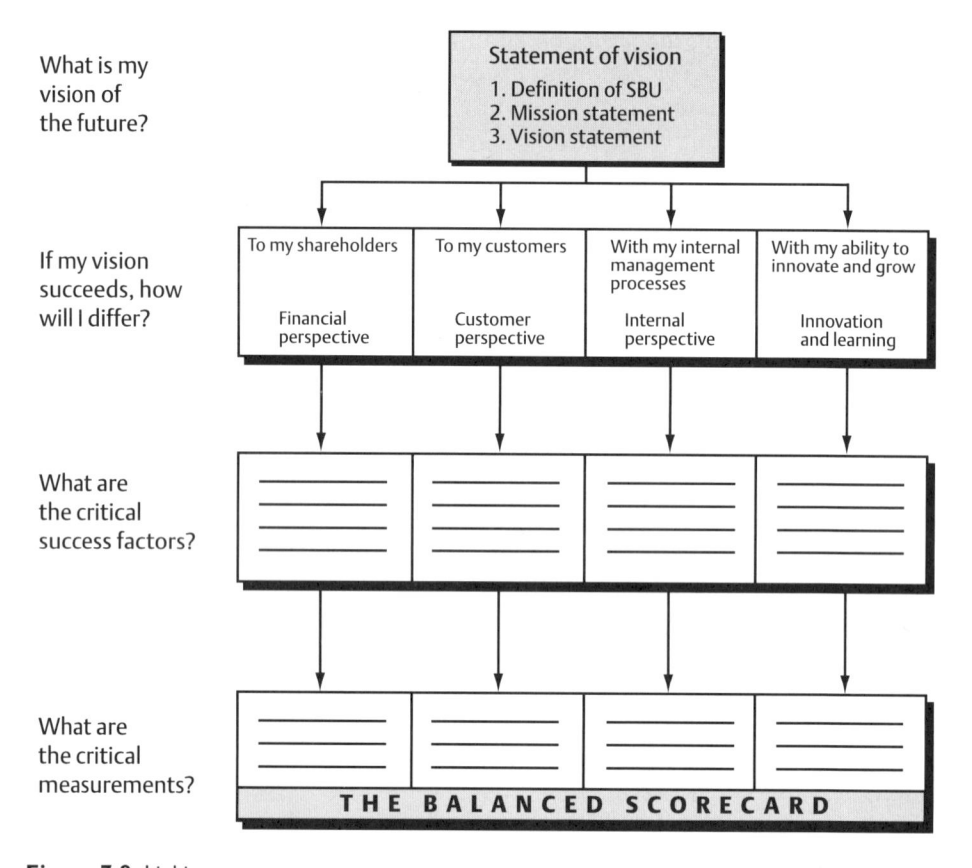

Figure 7.8 Linking measurements to strategy

Column labels (top, left to right):
- What is my vision of the future? → Statement of vision: 1. Definition of SBU; 2. Mission statement; 3. Vision statement
- If my vision succeeds, how will I differ? → To my shareholders (Financial perspective); To my customers (Customer perspective); With my internal management processes (Internal perspective); With my ability to innovate and grow (Innovation and learning)
- What are the critical success factors?
- What are the critical measurements?

THE BALANCED SCORECARD

Source: Kaplan, R. S. and Norton, D. P., 'Begin by Linking Measurements to Strategy', *Harvard Business Review* (1993), September–October, p. 139. Reprinted by permission. Copyright © 1993 the President and Fellows of Harvard.

Kaplan and Norton give several examples of the balanced scorecard in practice. One case study involves a US company called Rockwater, a subsidiary of a global engineering and construction company, Brown & Root/Halliburton. The measures used by organisations depend on the critical success factors identified in the balanced scorecard. For Rockwater, from the financial perspective, critical measurements included return on capital employed (ROCE), cash flow, and sales backlog. From the customer perspective, measures included customer ranking surveys, the customer satisfaction index, market share, and the pricing index. From the internal business perspective, critical measurements included hours spent with customers on new work, success rates of tenders, amount of rework required, and success in project performance, particularly meeting new customer needs. From the innovation and learning perspective, measures included staff attitude survey results, percentage of revenue from new services, revenue per employee, and employee suggestions. Kaplan and Norton's approach has been said to be influential, with 60 per cent of the top 100 UK companies confirming that they use the balanced scorecard.[47]

HRM practices and outcomes

David Guest, whose soft HRM model was introduced in chapter 1, says that people will take HRM more seriously when research delivers better evidence for the linkage between HRM and organisational performance.[48] Guest criticises previous research for not paying enough attention to the nature of organisational performance and for not providing a strong rationale for specific HR practices. He recommends that better theories of performance be created, citing the balanced scorecard (introduced in the preceding section) and the expectancy theory of motivation (discussed in chapter 6). Recent research on HRM in the world automotive industry found that high individual performance depends on three factors: skill, effort, and appropriate role perception; all three were originally proposed in expectancy theory.[49]

Reminiscent of his own earlier prescriptive model, Guest suggests three HRM outcomes are linked to practices: quality, commitment, and flexibility. Quality outcomes are linked to practices concerned with selection, development, and quality. Commitment is linked to employee relations, promotion, and rewards. Flexibility links with structural characteristics and with formal and informal communication and teamwork. The detail of the HRM practices linked to outcomes is laid out in figure 7.9.

Practices	Outcomes
Selection Socialisation Training and development Quality improvement programs	Skills and ability (Quality)
Single status Job security International promotion Individualised reward systems	Effort/motivation (Commitment)
Communication Employee involvement Teamwork Job design Flexible job descriptions	Role structure and perception (Flexibility)

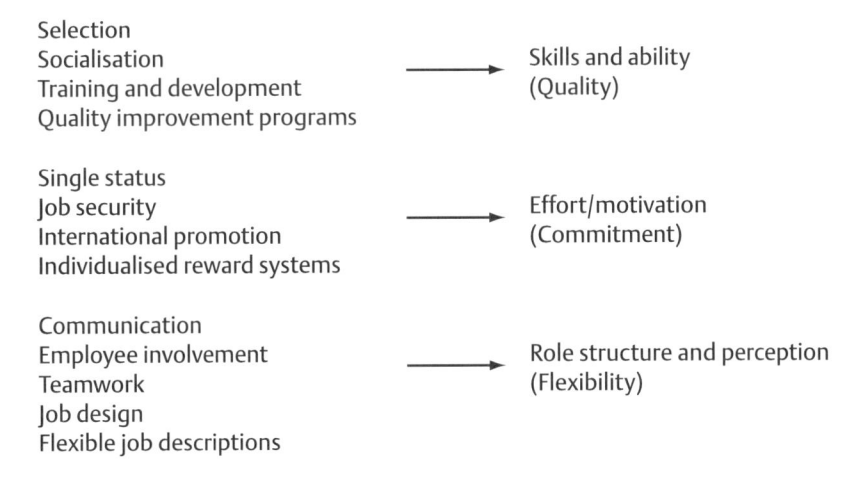

Figure 7.9 HRM and performance

Source: Guest, D. E., 'Human Resource Management and Performance: a Review and Research Agenda', *International Journal of Human Resource Management* (1997), p. 269. Reprinted with permission of Taylor & Francis Ltd. www.tandf.co.uk/journals

Reviewing empirical research on the link between HRM and performance, Guest comes to the conclusion that, first, higher performance outcomes are more likely where HR practices are linked to business strategy and the external environment.[50] Second, most strongly supported of all in a growing number of research studies is the link between high-performance HRM practices and better organisational performance as indicated by productivity, labour turnover, or financial indicators.

Third, there is some evidence for superior performance where coherent groups of practices are deliberately applied. This is known as the HRM 'bundles' approach, which aims to achieve high performance by utilising mutually reinforcing clusters or 'bundles' of HRM practice.

Summary

This chapter reviewed ways of financially rewarding employees and identified some of their strengths and weaknesses. Payment structures and systems reward different aspects of employees' work. Some structures are comparatively simple, such as graded pay structures, and have tended to measure performance only periodically and prior to salary progression. Others, such as pay curves, are more complex and depend on more frequent measures of performance in calculating the amount of reward due.

Similarly, some systems of pay are comparatively simple—for example, time rates have worked with very rudimentary records of attendance—while others are more complex, such as work-measured and performance-related pay systems. Most systems focus on rewarding either individual or group or organisational performance. Performance-related pay requires making individual distinctions between employees based on their performance for the purpose of allocating different proportions of pay. Group bonus schemes reward groups of employees for having achieved targets. Gainsharing and SAYE schemes establish a fixed proportion for employees who are then rewarded an equal or proportional share of the returns from the performance of their organisation. The way that employees are paid reveals assumptions about what is to be valued and who is to be rewarded. The structures and systems make important statements about how pay should and can motivate performance in the workplace.

BOX 7.1

Case study—Performance appraisal in a car manufacturing plant

Introduction
Imagine you have been working for one year in a major car manufacturing plant. You are a team leader working on the production line and your appraisal interview is due in three weeks' time. You will be appraised by your line manager. The system is an open one insofar as all of the written documentation is available to you, your line manager, and the line personnel manager. You are reflecting on what you have done before you commit your ideas to paper.

Appraisee's brief

Your team, along with others in the company, has been asked to come up with ways of introducing quality improvements and cost savings. One project you worked on for your part of the production line was very successful. Your team estimated that it was costing the company $100 000 per year to revamp the car floor mat. The mats were getting scratched during assembly and the minimum repair cost was $75 per vehicle. Your team has cut that area of waste down to zero, simply by introducing a rubber mat that could be laid on top of the floor mat, thus preventing any scratching and waste. Your team's cost projection is that if this innovation is introduced for other teams it could lead to savings in the region of $50 000 a year.

You have enjoyed your first year as team leader: the job is challenging and you have twelve people to manage on a daily basis.

Your team has responsibility for talking directly to suppliers wherever there are improvements that can be made. The relationship between shop floor employees and management is generally felt to be good, and the organisation is flatter and less hierarchical than it used to be. There no longer seems to be the 'us and them' mentality that characterised the plant ten years ago. Your team is highly committed to productivity and quality targets, and everyone feels they all are in the same boat. Your team is aware of the increasingly competitive global markets, and the management style emphasises that employees must work smarter and not just harder. The team is informed by line management communications, personnel and employee involvement, as well as you and your fellow workers, about new business challenges and how to meet them through achieving weekly and monthly targets.

You have had some opportunity for self-development; for example, you gave a presentation on team briefing to another manufacturing company at their annual conference. Also, you have met the managing director, who periodically visits the track to talk directly with shop floor employees and listen to issues they want to discuss.

Formal team briefings are held weekly. All of the team leaders meet beforehand for a management meeting and briefing from a representative of senior management. The team leaders then go back to brief their own teams at the start of the shift. These meetings take approximately 20 minutes and team leaders present an update on the situation, then set and review targets for the coming week and ensuing months. The briefing is a two-way communication process: members are expected to participate and raise any issues they want to with the group.

Your team's composition has changed recently, through the reintroduction of a Saturday morning shift, which had been abandoned during an earlier downturn in demand when production had to be reduced. The changes have caused some difficulties because the three members who had to leave in order to join another shift were well liked and part of a very positive working relationship. Your team is now having to learn how to work with three new people and morale is not as high as it was over the last year. Time has been spent properly inducting the new team members, and although the group is not yet as cohesive as it should be, you are confident that over the next few weeks, with on-the-job development and effective management on your part, the team will mould once again into a high-performing work group.

For one month, your team had a graduate engineer who was working for you as part of a government-supported training scheme. He observed from an outsider's perspective some basic improvements that could be made to the work processes, which your team enthusiastically listened to and quickly adopted. One straightforward innovation that has saved time and money is that the team now takes car seat parts in batches of two or three rather than one at a time. Another innovation suggested by the graduate engineer was to get maintenance to paint more red lines on the floor to guide stacker trucks. The new lines prevent trucks from parking too close to your team. Although no accident had yet happened, this proactive approach to health and safety is strongly encouraged by the company.

Your line manager has been very helpful and you have enjoyed working with her on planning tasks, reviewing production schedules, and identifying training and development needs for the team. You are ambitious and want to enrol for a part-time diploma in management at your local university. However, this will mean taking some time off work and having a member of the team act as team leader. There was another person trained and experienced as a team leader, but he was one of the three who recently left. So, there is no one in the team trained in that position, although two individuals have come forward, but you have not yet had time to discuss with your line manager the on-the-job development and training these two members require.

The management style in your company, according to the long-serving members of the team, used to be somewhat autocratic. The culture has changed and now is participative and open. People on the shop floor say that they feel more confident and able to talk both to managers and to employees from other parts of the plant. They are ready to voice their own opinions, listen to others' criticism, and act positively and decisively. High standards of communication and performance are expected of everyone, and teams likewise expect proper support from their team leaders and adequate resources to undertake the goals set for them.

One team member has noticed that there are no internal telephone directory entries for many people employed by component supplier firms even though they are considered part of the company for quality-management reasons. The company has already been dealing with this issue centrally through the purchasing and supply department. However, one individual in your team is convinced it would be better for the team to compose its own list. You appreciate how time-consuming it will be to set about compiling and updating a list of relevant external telephone numbers and telephone extensions. Given the current workload your team is facing, it does not make sense for the task to be done locally. You are aware that this team member is a highly enthusiastic individual who sometimes reacts oversensitively to setback and failure. His personality is such that he can become easily disappointed. You have managed to delay him from starting on his telephone project, but have not yet been able to tell him directly that it is not feasible. When you last broached the topic with him, he used it as an opportunity to sell you the idea rather than listen to your explanation of the impracticality of his proposal. Furthermore, there is a new empowerment program under way in the company and you do not want to risk being seen as acting negatively towards this new HR initiative. You discussed the telephone directory project with your line manager before talking to the team member, but although you followed her advice it did not lead to the result she had predicted.

The team members have reviewed their working relationship and the overall atmosphere within the team. After a full and frank exchange, they concluded that members were able to express their feelings and that their ideas were being taken up by the company, particularly through the suggestion scheme. They were positive about incorporating the three new members and everybody endorsed the quality-management targets, saying they made the team's priorities clearer.

New targets for reducing waste have been introduced by the company and the team is pleased with its results. Very few items that are the team's direct responsibility have had to be scrapped; however, some scrap items have been coming from further up the line. The team has been effective in identifying these scrap items and sending them back to their originators, although this has sometimes negatively affected your team's output. You know that some influential members of the team feel that you have not done enough to ensure the scrap items aren't dumped on the team again in the future. You have talked about the scrap problem with the other team leaders responsible and also separately with your own line manager. It is likely that the scrap problem will continue until new software is installed for controlling the carousel, thus enabling changes to the work process. At present, some of the other teams are having to work weekend overtime to make up for lost time caused by faults identified in the computer software.

Overall, you have enjoyed your first year as team leader and are keen to get ahead. You appreciate that you have at least another year of hard work as team leader before promotion is likely. You are looking forward to your appraisal interview and hope that your line manager will make it clear what your next step will be in your career with the organisation.

Case study activities

1   In this case study organisation, the appraisal process involves the appraiser and appraisee both completing the same form independently beforehand, and then meeting to develop a combined, agreed formal record of the appraisal meeting. In small groups, construct an easy-to-use and informative appraisal form that is identical for appraiser and appraisee. Spend some time consulting textbooks, employees, appraisal training videos, and company web sites to ascertain what appraisal forms should look like in terms of good practice. Discuss the forms produced by your groups, selecting the best one for the role-play. The appraisal form should include opportunity for covering sections on:

> a achievement of objectives/targets over the previous twelve months
> b way of working
> c dealing with people
> d objectives/targets for the next twelve months
> e other issues
> f development goals and action plan.
> 2 On the basis of the case study information above, complete the appraisal forms and, with a colleague acting as your line manager, role-play the appraisal interview.

Study questions

1 Define and explain three payment structures of your choice. Discuss the difficulties likely to be encountered from moving from one pay structure to another.
2 Define two payment systems of your choice, one based on rewarding individual performance and the other on rewarding organisational performance. Explain the likely benefits and drawbacks of their joint implementation.
3 Discuss how alternative payment structures and systems might suit different organisations operating within different markets.
4 Define performance management and discuss how far it is consistent with models and frameworks of HRM introduced in chapter 1.
5 Write a short report recommending, for a selected case organisation, how Kaplan and Norton's balanced scorecard should be integrated with HR policy and practice.

Further reading

Armstrong, M., *Employee Reward*, 2nd edn (London: Institute of Personnel and Development, 1999).
Armstrong, M., *Performance Management*, 2nd edn (London: Kogan Page, 2000).
Marshall, V. and Wood, R. E., 'The dynamics of effective performance appraisal: an integrated model', *Asia Pacific Journal of Human Resources* (2000), 38, 3, pp. 62–90.
Stiles, P., Gratton, L., Truss, C., Hope-Hailey, V., and McGovern, P., 'Performance Management and the Psychological Contract', *Human Resource Management Journal* (1997), 7, 1, pp. 57–66

CHAPTER 8

Learning and Development

CHAPTER CONTENTS

Introduction

1 What are learning and development?
The importance of employee development
Definitions
HRM versus personnel management perspectives

2 Creating the learning organisation
Innovations in training and development
The learning company
The learning cycle
Individual learning styles
Organisational learning

3 Employee development
Thinking more broadly about development
Outdoor development
Technology-based learning and open learning
Management development

Summary
Case study—Smarna Gora Holdings
Study questions
Further reading

Introduction

This chapter focuses on innovative ideas and practices in employee learning and development. First, it identifies the importance accorded to learning and development within human resource management, then investigates ways of creating a 'learning organisation', and finally examines current policy and practice in employee development.

Chapters 2, 3, and 4 on the context of HRM described how difficult it is for managers to maintain a long-term perspective on employee development and have shown it to be strongly influenced by national policy and by funding of education and training provision through state-subsidised institutions. There are obstacles to implementing the learning organisation; chapter 2 on the environment of HRM clarified the particular problems of the Australian context for employee training and development. In general, there is less of an institutional framework for training in the Australian system than in Germany, for example, where there is greater legislative support and more frequent partnerships between education providers and employers. Furthermore, it is difficult to plan and invest in training employees because there are strong pressures on management to reduce costs wherever possible and to deliver short-term financial returns. Compounding the demanding financial performance requirements faced by companies is the fact that Australian financial institutions prefer to lend money on a short-term basis, making it still more difficult to invest in human assets, particularly whenever the return on the investment is either long-term or difficult to quantify. Private sector employers in Australia traditionally have not sought to compete by long-term investment in employee development, preferring when possible to use lower skilled and lower cost labour or to recruit trained people directly from the external labour market.[1] As a destination for many immigrants, Australia has systematically targeted skill shortage areas as part of its immigration policy, which to some extent has reduced the pressure felt by government and employers to adopt a long-term training approach for all employees. A coherent and strategic approach to training and development is difficult enough to achieve in any company, but even more so in the Australian environment. A comparison study by Deery, Walsh, and Knox (2001) of employee relations practices and outcomes for unionised and non-unionised workplaces in Australia found that non-unionised workplaces compared unfavourably on a number of dimensions:

> These included the use of innovative work practices, joint consultative committees and grievance procedures. Moreover, non-union workplaces were far less committed to the provision of family leave and to policies designed to assist with gender equality. Furthermore, they had demonstrably poorer employee relations outcomes in terms of their dismissal and labour turnover rates. However, in the areas of training, staff appraisals, employee communications and the use of meetings their practices and procedures were not significantly different from those of unionised workplaces. On the other hand, non-union workplaces were decidedly more individualistic in their contractual, remunerative, and bargaining arrangements.[2]

Many of the criticisms showing the Australian environment to be inimical to developing human resources also apply to the USA and the UK. From an industrial relations perspective, Kochan and Osterman argue that Japanese and German corporations have been better than US firms at institutionalising human resource practices that lead to competitive advantage.[3] They are sharply critical of the North American institutional context, observing that there are particular obstacles for small and medium-sized employers (SMEs) who wish to compete by fostering a highly skilled, highly paid workforce. The labour market environment offers SMEs few incentives to train all of their employees to the highest level, for fear of loss of the HR investment to poaching by competitors. In contrast to overseas competitors, US, UK, and Australian employers are often isolated from each other and relationships with key trading partners and international competitors are adversarial, low-trust, and hostile. The net result of these circumstances is that they promote short-term thinking and a limited investment in human resources.

Adoption of human resource practices, and their sustainability, is heavily influenced by macro-factors, particularly capital markets, corporate governance structures, institutional infrastructure, and government policies. Kochan and Osterman argue that US management has not in the past paid sufficient attention to the macro-factors of the American environment, tending to concentrate on issues concerning product markets, labour markets, technology, competition strategy, managerial values, and the distribution of power within the organisation. They suggest that there is a link between HR and performance. The process begins with high investment in human capital and superior organisational practices, leading ultimately to a competitive society with high living standards. They say the following about their model, shown in figure 8.1:

> The key argument is that achieving competitiveness at high standards of living requires a high rate of growth in productivity, product innovation, and adaptability to changing markets. This in turn requires corporate strategies that give high priority to developing and fully utilizing the skills of the work force. Finally, the gains of improved productivity must be distributed in an equitable fashion to the multiple stakeholders who helped create them and reinvested in ways that ensure future generations improved standards of living.[4]

Kochan and Osterman's model assumes that for wealth to be created, productivity must be improved; this includes increasing the efficiency of firms and the economy in utilising scarce resources. If enterprises are to be competitive in the global marketplace, products must be continuously improved according to the quality standards that are important to customers, and time-to-market must be rapid and responsive. Their concept of productivity is broader than simply efficiency, also implying enlarging the capability of firms and the economy as a whole to innovate and utilise new technologies. Ways of developing a more highly skilled workforce, through the practices of the learning organisation and training and developing employees to become more innovative, are discussed in this chapter.

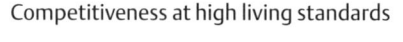

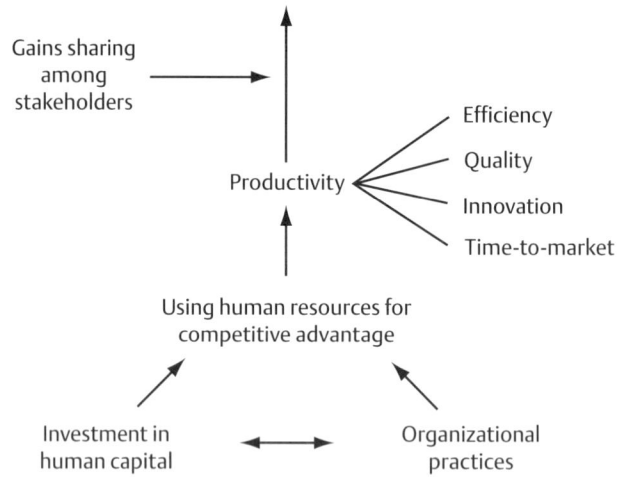

Figure 8.1 Human resources and national competitiveness

Source: Kochan, T. A. and Osterman, P., *The Mutual Gains Enterprise* (1994), p. 6. Copyright © 1994 by the President and Fellows of Harvard College, Boston, MA; all rights reserved. Reprinted by permission of Harvard Business School Press.

Fundamental change towards 'learning organisations' seems unlikely at the time of writing. One of the preconditions for it is for greater influence to be applied at the level of the state and on financial institutions to facilitate and respect employees' long-term learning and development. Creating a high-skills economy involves more than simply ensuring skill supply for the nation's skill needs; it means addressing major structural issues such as the role of business networks, research and development, investment, and product innovation.[5] This chapter acknowledges the difficulties employees face in seeking better opportunities for learning and development, and does not pretend that learning and development will often be at the top of a line manager's agenda when he or she is facing short-term business pressures. The chapter also informs the reader about innovations in learning and development over the last 30 years and, most importantly, offers insight into what might be achieved.

1 What are learning and development?

The importance of employee development

There are strong arguments for improving learning and development in organisations. Learning and development have been said to be indispensable components of strategic human resource management,[6] as well as a means of reducing uncertainty in the market-place and achieving organisational goals.[7] Harrison's definition of employee development assumes that the main point of development is to help the organisation achieve its mission and business goals, as is proposed in hard HRM:

> Employee development as part of the organisation's overall human resource strategy means the skilful provision and organisation of learning experiences in the workplace in order that performance can be improved, that work goals can be achieved and that, through enhancing the skills, knowledge, learning ability, and enthusiasm of people at every level, there can be continuous organisational as well as individual growth. Employee development must, therefore, be part of a wider strategy for the business, aligned with the organisation's corporate mission and goals.[8]

Research suggests that the argument that employee learning must be linked to business strategy is consistent with the views of many business managers.[9] Even in companies striving to be learning organisations that go so far as to promote some individual learning and education separable from the direct needs of the business, top management would tend to agree with Harrison's perspective. For example, the General Motors Holden Enterprise Agreement (2001) specifies the necessity of integration of individual competence development with company continuous improvement goals.[10]

Definitions

To understand what we mean by 'learning' and 'development' in the organisational context, we need to define the commonly used terms 'learning', 'training', and 'education'. There are a variety of processes of learning and it takes place in many different contexts. Learning can be defined as 'the process whereby individuals acquire knowledge, skills and attitudes through experience, reflection, study or instruction'.[11]

Training tends to be defined more narrowly than is learning or education, and can be defined as 'a planned and systematic effort to modify or develop knowledge/skill/attitude through "learning" experience, to achieve effective performance in an activity or range of activities'.[12]

Education, which is commonly more broadly defined, can be seen as 'a process and a series of activities which aim at enabling an individual to assimilate and develop knowledge, skills, values and understanding that are not simply related to a narrow field of activity but allow a broad range of problems to be defined, analysed and solved'.[13]

So, according to a broad interpretation of education, its purpose is to provide individuals with an understanding of the traditions, ideas, and values important to the society in which they live and to help them acquire and develop skills in learning, creativity, and communication. A difficulty that all three of the above definitions are said to have in common is that they are rooted in an individualist conceptualisation of the world. That is to say, they concentrate on the individual to the exclusion of more collectivist concepts of learning, such as learning in teams, organisations, and the community.

HRM versus personnel management perspectives

HRM and personnel management perspectives on employee development are different: personnel management concentrates on controlled access to courses and formal training interventions that occur off the job, whereas HRM is more concerned with creating learning companies. Storey includes 'training and development' as one of his twenty-five points of difference and one of the key 'levers' in managing the human resource (see chapter 1). Overall, Storey's levers for HRM emphasise managing individuals and the culture of the organisation. Teamwork, managing climate and culture, having fewer pay grades, and wide-ranging cultural, structural, and personnel strategies are all part of the new HRM approach. In any one company, it should be remembered, most of these levers were once management aspirations or plans under implementation rather than organisational reality.[14] Storey and Sisson have voiced concern over education and training practice in the UK, arguing that there is a gap between the rhetoric—'people are our greatest asset'—and the reality, namely that the UK is not a 'development-oriented, flexible, well-motivated, efficiently operating, highly skilled and well-paid economy'.[15] Some surveys provide evidence in support of their argument, showing that numerical and financial flexibility initiatives in the form of irregular employment contracts strongly outweigh the development of multi-skilling. Several researchers have suggested that, with the proliferation of casual employment, a similar pattern exists in Australia.[16] Sectors of the economy that are union-free have in general failed to introduce new HR initiatives and contracting-out of services has not often led to improved HRM. Storey and Sisson recommend that a better balance should be sought between individualism and collectivism in managing human resources and industrial relations. Development of employees' skills and careers has become a focal point for recent industrial unrest and this may lead to more development opportunities within some companies where unions are influential or where individual grievances lead to significant employee-relations problems. These problems could be resolved in the future by a more proactive policy on employee development. An example of individual grievances erupting into collective action in a non-unionised company is the strike by cast members of the Disneyland Paris parade (including those portraying the big-name Disney characters Snow White and the Seven Dwarfs, Mickey and Minnie Mouse, and Goofy), which made newspaper headlines in the summer of 1998. The action lasted for one month but did not spread further throughout the non-unionised workforce. The major complaint was that the company was not providing the performers with development opportunities in ballet skills to enhance their careers and increase their employability.[17]

Storey and Sisson conclude that employee trust, commitment, and capability must be continuously improved to attain a high-quality workforce. Storey is unconvinced that HRM can ever be 'owned' by line management working in devolved business units with no strategic HRM and a climate dominated by short-term targets.[18] He optimistically suggests that the recent trends towards business process re-engineering, zero-based budgeting, outsourcing, and focusing on core processes will lead to less bureaucracy in organisations—and unavoidably challenge managers to rediscover the basic tenets of HRM. Future organisational success depends on a consistent and coherent approach to HRM, particularly the basics such as the human resource cycle of recruitment and selection, appraisal, development, and rewards. Management therefore must adopt a long-term perspective, and responsibilities for provision of HR/IR must be clearer and more effectively coordinated at the various levels of the organisation than they have been in the past. Storey and Sisson have argued, however, that this is extremely difficult and therefore managers interested in working towards the learning organisation should be realistic about what can be achieved in the short term.

2 Creating the learning organisation

Creating the learning organisation is a strategy for sustainable development in which more organisations may take a greater interest in the future, but as yet it is still mainly a vision of what might be. It is claimed to be not simply a new way of training individuals, but an approach to wider processes of learning that enable continuous transformation of the organisation.[19] Pedler et al. have been influential in disseminating the learning organisation concept and they define learning at the 'whole organisation level' as follows: 'A learning company is an organization that facilitates the learning of all its members and continuously transforms itself.'[20] By 'members' of the organisation they mean the full range of key stakeholders: 'employees, owners, customers, suppliers, neighbours, the environment and even competitors'.[21]

Innovations in training and development

This section traces the antecedents of the learning company concept, based on work by Pedler et al. In developed countries during the 1950s, when labour was often in short supply, training was either given only where needed in response to a specific problem or centred around the pursuit of qualifications and skills for promotion purposes.[22] By the mid-1960s, systematic approaches to training were becoming more common, particularly in large organisations, which were further encouraged to formalise training provision following the establishment of the Industry Training Boards (ITBs). In the UK, the Industrial Training Act of 1964 created the system whereby industry boards had power to raise a levy from companies to fund training. Companies were expected to produce training plans and reports. The ITBs played an important role in promoting better formal organisation and improved design of training programs, and, at their height, there were 27 boards covering training arrangements for 15 million employees. Unfortunately, companies were reported to find them too bureaucratic and inflexible. The systematic approach to training continued into the 1970s but often failed to produce desired outcomes because, so Pedler and his co-authors claim, it was unworkable.[23] As a consequence of its impracticality, employees became discouraged and felt undervalued. The systematic approach uses rational methods of planning, preparing, delivering, assessing, and evaluating training. It draws on models of learning and instruction[24] and operates on the assumption that outcomes should be specified, measured, and assessed. Where the training intervention fails, corrective action must be applied. Action might be, for example, improved planning, redesign of the content, or use of different systems and techniques of delivery.

Another development movement is organisational development (OD), which has been more prevalent in the USA than in Australia and focuses on transforming individuals to help them become more open to personal learning and change, more emotionally sensitive, and more effective in dealing with people.[25] OD is a long-term approach to improving the organisation's change processes, problem solving, and renewal. It is carried out with the help of internal or external consultants who assist management and employees in problem solving. The OD interventions pay attention to the interpersonal behaviour of individuals and groups, particularly their emotions and feelings, and expect people to become more open-minded, tolerant of each other, and better communicators. The OD program is based on the integrity of the individual, and the consultants often have backgrounds and training in such fields as counselling and psychotherapy.[26]

A few large multinational corporations have experimented with the OD movement, but Pettigrew reports that OD has been only marginally successful because it is too different from the attitudes and behaviour of dominant management cultures.[27] The chemicals and plastics company ICI (now Orica in Australia), for example, tried to implement OD methods. While its culture differed from site to site of the company, it tended to be either bureaucratic or technocratic, and neither of these cultures is amenable to OD interventions. Bureaucracies are generally too inflexible and hierarchical to allow the learning organisation to flourish. Technocracies are also unreceptive because they value too much the technical expertise and rational decision making of elite groups, thus failing to encourage the commitment, communication, and involvement of employees. Interestingly, in June 1993, ICI demerged its pharmaceutical business into a separately owned company, Zeneca, in recognition that the industries in which ICI as a whole competed were such different businesses that the pharmaceutical area was considered better off separately owned and managed. The general opinion of management and financial commentators is that both companies have since consistently benefited from going their separate ways.

Pedler et al. argued that by the 1980s, three different approaches to learning and development were evident. First, the OD approach was still being used in some companies but was failing to deliver long-term significant benefits. Second, self-development and action learning were generally being used as an excuse for lack of real support for training and development. Self-development, when applied with clear commitment from top management, aims to solve poor transfer of training by developing more motivated and self-directed employees. The approach was based on learner-centredness and the learner having control over the processes of learning. The aim is to gain improved transfer of learning to the workplace; formal training and development interventions, although important, are not the main objective of facilitators and trainers. They instead aim to empower people to learn from their actions and to act on their learning.[28] Typical roles of the manager or trainer in facilitating individual employees' self-development are those of instructor, coach, or mentor. Which role is selected depends on its appropriateness for learning. Instructing helps individuals best when they need directing, coaching is best when some guidance is required, and mentoring is called for when development takes place over a long period of time. Mentors offer support and experience, and often, but not always, are of higher positional authority in the organisation than the individual being mentored. Action learning is a technique pioneered by Reg Revans, involving tailor-made management development based on real-life problems.[29] A common approach is to form a small group into an 'action learning set' and provide an opportunity for reflecting on a major project or projects occurring over several weeks or months. The projects are based on real workplace problems and have objectives derived from needs of the business that have been identified by senior management. The third approach to learning and development in the 1980s came about when there was a lot of excitement and enthusiasm generated by the American management gurus making pleas to top executives to change their organisations' cultures and to create excellent companies.[30] Unfortunately, it did not significantly alter employees' exposure to training and development,[31] and the claims that financial performance could be improved by adopting 'excellent company' practices have been in doubt since the research was first published.[32]

According to Pedler et al., the problem with all of these approaches—OD, self-development and action learning, and excellent company cultures—was that it was felt that companies were making too many changes with too little effect.[33] Interest grew during the 1980s in quality management and Japanese management practices, partly because they were seen to be integral to Japanese companies' business success. Inspection of these practices showed formal on-the-job training to be very important. However, many other important management considerations were also raised that were not so much about training or development interventions as about making a concerted and collective approach to continuous improvement of the organisation. Japanese management practices seemed to be able to develop employees who would work with high organisational commitment, high involvement, and low conflict with management. In recent years, the more idealistic Western perceptions of Japanese practices have undeniably become rather tarnished following the impacts of the 1997 Asian economic crisis and deflation in Japan's economy. One of the most high-profile Japanese entrants to the Australian economy, the major retailer Daimaru, opened two large stores (Melbourne with 760 employees, Gold Coast with 250 employees) during the 1990s. However, in September 2001, it announced it was closing its Australian operations, largely as a consequence of fierce cost-cutting competition by retailers in the Japanese domestic market.

Pedler et al. represented graphically the historical occurrence of innovation in training and development as a timeline, shown in figure 8.2. The reader should note that the Pedler et al. representation of the move from systematic training methods to the learning company concentrates on the history of innovation in training and development and has been discussed for that reason. Their timeline identifies the development of new ideas over time, but should not be taken out of this context, which would be to accord a more significant role to these innovative approaches than they actually have had on employee development within most Australian workplaces, and elsewhere.

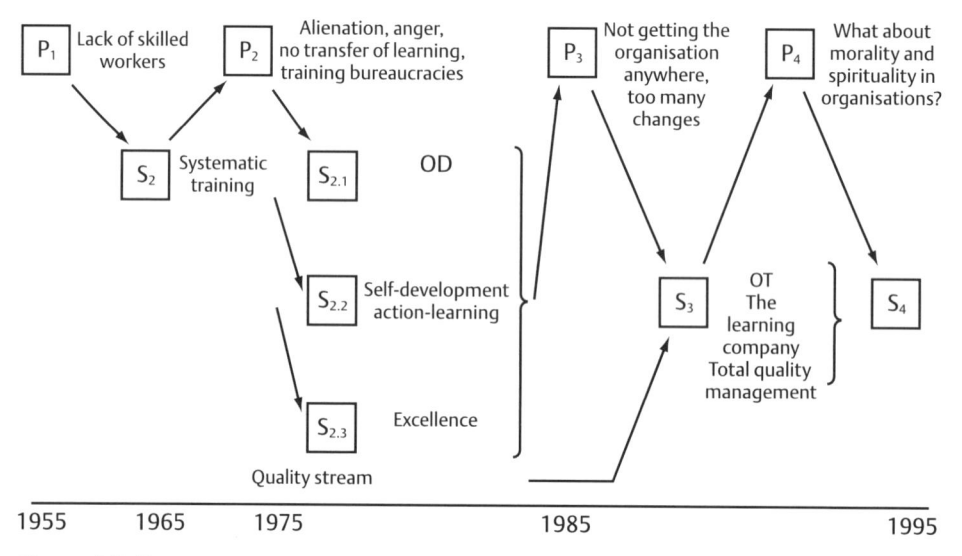

Figure 8.2 From systematic training to the learning company

Source: Pedler, M., Burgoyne, J., and Boydell, T. (1991) *The Learning Company: A Strategy for Sustainable Development* (Maidenhead: McGraw-Hill), figure 2.9, p. 17. Reproduced with the kind permission of McGraw-Hill Publishing Company.

The learning company

The learning company is a set of aspirations rather than a reality and represents a synthesis of ideas for development, including self-development, action learning, OD, quality management, and organisational transformation (OT). Various writers have proposed ground rules for becoming more like a learning company; Pedler et al. propose eleven, organised under five general categories, shown in box 8.1.

In the USA, Peter Senge and his colleagues from the Massachusetts Institute of Technology have worked with many executives in helping their companies to become learning organisations. Senge recommends that organisations encourage more adaptive and generative learning.[34] Adaptive learning is important for adapting to changes in the environment and has become particularly important for bureaucratic organisations, which have generally been slow to react to external change.

BOX 8.1

How companies become learning companies

Strategy
1 The learning approach to strategy
Strategy and direction are regularly updated. Policy and strategy are structured as learning processes. Experimentation, frequent modification, and feedback.
2 Participative policy making
All members participate so that policy making is significantly influenced by stakeholders. Use of appraisal and career planning discussions for policy development within an organisational climate that encourages employees to express conflicting views and differences.

Looking in
3 Informating
Information, databases, and communication systems are used in the company for a variety of learning purposes. Readily available information on departments/sections is made accessible through use of computers. Information technology is used to facilitate understanding and decision making.
4 Formative accounting and control
Systems of accounting and reporting are structured to assist learning. Everyone feels responsible and accountable for work group/unit. Accounting and finance are advisory and the system encourages individuals to undertake risks involving venture capital.
5 Internal exchange
Cooperation between groups (e.g. departments) within the organisation; treating each other as internal customers and ensuring that goods and services are delivered according to agreement, on time and at the right cost.
6 Reward flexibility
Discussion of and experimentation with reward systems. All participate in determining the reward system and the basic values underpinning it, and there is shared use of flexible work practices, enabling individuals to make different contributions and be rewarded accordingly.

Structures
7 Enabling structures
Experimentation with new forms of organisational structure. Structure and rules are regularly discussed, reviewed, and changed. Appraisal is focused on developmental aspects with careers flexibly structured to allow for experimentation, growth, and adaptation.

> **Looking out**
>
> *8 Boundary workers as environmental scanners*
> All employees monitor and report on activities and events outside of the company. Company regularly receives intelligence reports on the economy, markets, technological developments, and world trends. Internal meetings regularly review the business environment and external meetings are frequently held with stakeholders (e.g. customers, suppliers, and community members). Learning events and meetings with business partners.
>
> *9 Inter-company learning*
> Employees go on job attachments to work for a specified period of time for business partners. Participation in joint ventures with partners to develop new products and markets. Use of benchmarking to learn best practice from other industries.
>
> **Learning opportunities**
>
> *10 Learning climate*
> A positive attitude to the principles of continuous improvement. Employees are always trying to learn and do better, including learning from what went wrong. People take time to question their own practices and will get others to help them when needed. Differences of all sorts are recognised and positively valued as essential to learning and creativity.
>
> *11 Self-development opportunities for all*
> Open-access, resource-based learning available for employees and external stakeholders. People are encouraged to be active self-developers. Appraisal and career planning concentrate on identifying and exploring individual learning needs. Self-development budgets are used.
>
> Source: Pedler, M., Burgoyne, J., and Boydell, T., *The Learning Company: A Strategy for Sustainable Development* (1991), figure 3.1, pp. 26–7. Reproduced with the kind permission of McGraw-Hill Publishing Company.

Generative learning is particularly important for creating new ideas, products, and processes, for example, in new product development, innovation, and quality management. Senge cites the Japanese corporations of the 1980s as being effective in both adaptive and generative learning. He recommends three critical processes for building learning organisations: building shared visions, uncovering and challenging mental models, and engaging in systems thinking.

Building shared visions is a continuous process involving the distribution of leadership skills among a number of employees and the creation of shared visions by communicating, analysing, and blending individual visions. Uncovering and testing mental models is a discipline that aims to challenge assumptions within organisations, with the aim of encouraging learning. False assumptions need to be questioned and managers have to become more skilled in understanding and exploring other points of view. Senge says that managers learn to be good at advocating their preferred viewpoint but must be able to balance their presentation and persuasion skills with the ability to enquire meaningfully into others' views and opinions. This means being able to distinguish what Argyris and Schon call 'espoused theory' from 'theory in use'.[35] The espoused theory is what people in organisations claim to be the theory that the organisation operates under, while the theory in use is the ideas they actually use. For most individuals part of the solution in more successfully uncovering and testing mental models is to recognise and defuse defensive routines. These are routines that we all use to avoid plain speaking or uncomfortable issues; often, these defensive routines destroy full and frank discussion. By 'engaging in systems thinking', Senge means focusing systematically on underlying trends and forces of change. This is the ability to see interrelationships and dynamic complexity and ultimately to identify solutions. Senge says that good leaders often are systems thinkers capable of focusing on high-leverage changes, that is, changes that require minimum effort but lead to significant improvement.

The learning cycle

The learning organisation is based on individual and organisational change (organisational change will be covered in detail in chapter 9) and creating the conditions for better learning. It is more collectivist than are traditional learning theory and instructional design, which have roots in disciplines such as information science and cognitive and developmental psychology. Dixon proposes that there is an 'organisational learning cycle', a way that we can learn collectively.[36] Dixon's cycle borrows heavily from work by Kolb, who is best known for his theory of individual,

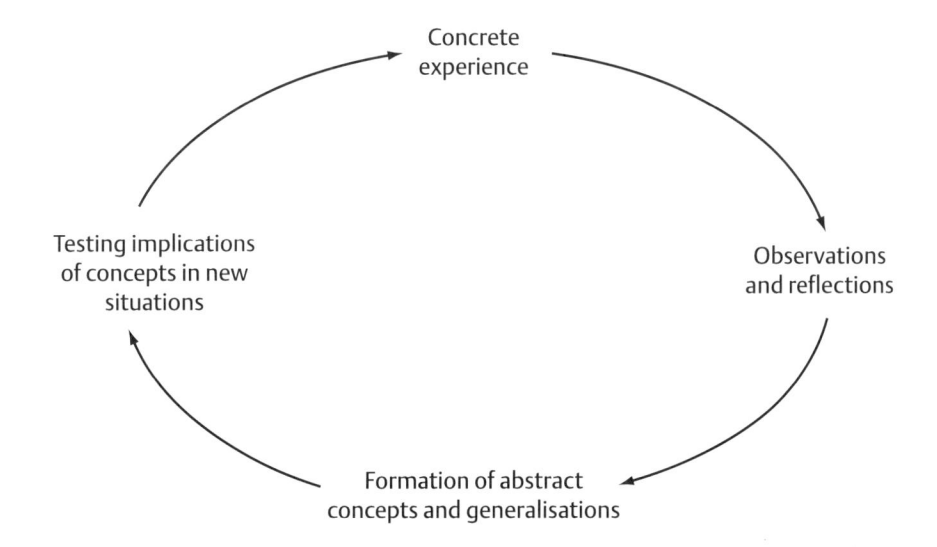

Figure 8.3 Kolb's experiential learning cycle

Source: Kolb, D. A., 'Management and the Learning Process', in K. Starkey (ed.), *How Organizations Learn* (London: Thomson Publications, 1996), pp. 270–87 (see p. 271).

experiential learning.[37] Dixon's and Kolb's learning cycles are both four-stage processes of continuously revising and creating knowledge.

Kolb's experiential learning cycle suggests that an individual's learning progresses through four stages: concrete experience, reflective observation, abstract conceptualisation, and active experimentation (see figure 8.3).[38] The first stage requires generating ideas through experience. During the second stage the individual integrates and reflects on the experience. The third stage involves drawing conclusions and abstracting lessons or concepts from the material experienced and reflected upon. The fourth stage involves testing out theories or ideas, which then returns the individual to seeking more concrete experience, and so on. In a perfect world, Kolb says, the individual would have a balance of abilities consistent with his or her four stages of the learning cycle.[39]

In reality, most people develop learning styles that emphasise some abilities over others.[40] For example, a finance manager with strong mathematical skills may prefer abstract conceptualisation and active experimentation, while a sales manager may have greater interest in learning from concrete experience and reflective observation. This is not to say that one should be too quick to stereotype people or occupations; within any group there will be a range of abilities and preferences. One of the main roles of the learning styles in employee development has been to improve individuals' learning and their interpersonal communication by making them more aware of their own and others' learning styles.

Individual learning styles

Honey and Mumford propose a model similar to Kolb's in which individuals have a mixture of four learning styles, normally with a preference for one or two of the styles.[41] Honey and Mumford's learning styles questionnaire (LSQ) and Kolb's learning styles inventory (LSI) are both diagnostic tests to help individuals identify their strengths, weaknesses, and development needs. The four learning styles, based on Kolb's theory of stages in the learning cycle, are: activist, reflector, theorist, and pragmatist (figure 8.4). Box 8.2 provides a short definition of each style along with its potential strengths and weaknesses.

No learning style has a monopoly of the virtues, and the strengths of each of the learning styles are not appropriate for all situations. What is a strength in one situation may become a weakness in another. This is one reason why, when a group works as a team, it is often able to perform better than solitary experts. A good example of this is what happened during a week of team-building exercises in a major car company when engineers pitted their wits against those of groups of non-specialists from a variety of disciplines (operations, finance, IT, purchasing, and so on) in performing specific tasks. The engineers were shocked to find they didn't perform tasks involving a significant engineering element as well as the non-specialists did. The hard lesson for them was that better teamwork, using a range of learning styles to implement the full learning cycle, is a real strength and the possession of professional occupational expertise is not sufficient on its own.[42]

LEARNING AND DEVELOPMENT | 185

```
              Activist
                ___
              /     \
  Pragmatist |       | Reflector
              \ ___ /
              Theorist
```

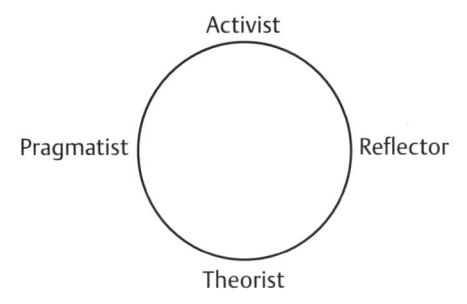

Figure 8.4 Honey and Mumford's four learning styles

Source: This model is based on the Honey and Mumford learning cycle, in P. Honey and A. Mumford, *The Manual of Learning Styles*, 3rd edn (1992); The Learning Styles Questionnaire 80 item version (2000) and The Learning Styles Helper's Guide (2000). It is reproduced here with the kind permission of the publisher, Peter Honey Publications Ltd. www.peterhoney.com

---

BOX 8.2

Strengths and weakness of the four learning styles

Activist
Strengths
Sociable, open-minded, welcomes challenge, highly involved, prefers here-and-now
Weaknesses
Bored by implementation details and the longer term, always seeks the limelight

Reflector
Strengths
Good listener, tolerant, sees different perspectives, postpones judgment, cautious
Weaknesses
Takes a back seat in meetings, low profile, distant

Theorist
Strengths
Integrates observations with theory, rational, objective, analytical
Weaknesses
Perfectionist, detached, impatient with subjective and intuitive thinking

Pragmatist
Strengths
Experimenter, quick to adopt and try out new ideas, practical, down-to-earth
Weaknesses
Impatient with theory, impatient with open-ended discussion

Organisational learning

As was mentioned in the section on the learning cycle, Dixon's organisational learning cycle is geared to the collective organisation and not individuals.[43] Kolb's learning cycle was developed to represent individuals' learning, but was modified by Dixon to represent organisational learning. Dixon's cycle, which contains four stages similar to Kolb's, is shown in figure 8.5.

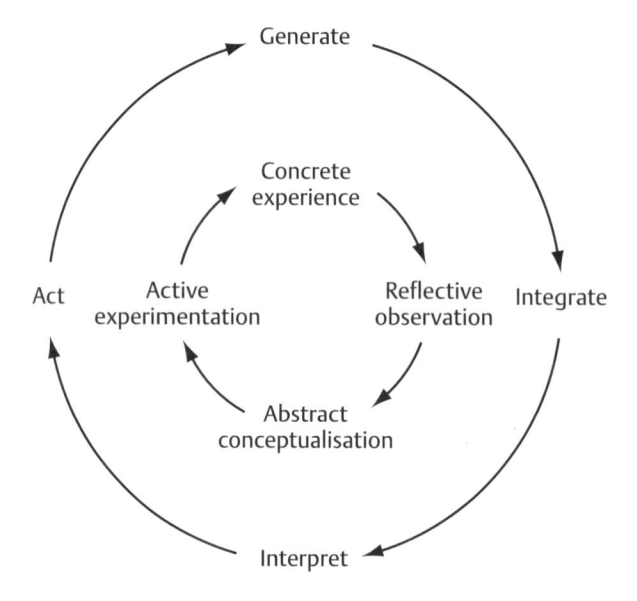

Figure 8.5 Dixon's and Kolb's learning cycles

Source: Dixon, N. M., *The Organizational Learning Cycle* (McGraw-Hill, 1994), figure 4.2, p. 46.

In Dixon's organisational learning cycle, information is widely generated by utilising the external and internal environments. It is collected continually and from multiple sources. Internally, it is generated by experimentation, analysis of mistakes and successes, and the use of data for self-correction. Further, research and development is not the exclusive preserve of an isolated R&D department, but is conducted by line management. Information is integrated into the organisational context by disseminating it accurately and in a timely manner. The flow of information is unimpeded and employees are rewarded for accurate reporting on what they have found rather than for just saying what they think they are expected to say. Information sharing is encouraged through job design that focuses on multi-skilling and multi-functioning. Where possible, staff positions such as personnel and marketing are integrated with line management. Information is collectively interpreted by encouraging all employees to discuss their different interpretations with each other. Rather than funnelling information to a conclusion, individuals are expected to be more open-minded, flexible, and questioning of their own points of view. Frequent interactions, keeping the organisation limited in size, and treating everyone equally are other methods of collective interpretation. In summary, everything is held to be open to question. Action is taken giving authority and control to the local level of the organisation. This is done according to centrally agreed, critical specifications. There are no penalties for failure, when taking reasonable risks, and the reward system uses profit sharing and stimulates committed and innovative action.

The organisational learning cycle depends on a supportive organisational structure and culture; further, it assumes individuals will be motivated to learn. Western companies have been criticised in the past for encouraging functionally divided careers that have motivated ambitious managers and employees to work for the good of their own work group and function rather than to the strategic benefit of the company. Ford of Europe, a US-owned company operating in Europe, had an organisational structure described as 'functional chimneys'. The functional structure encouraged vertical communication and a high degree of specialisation in areas such as finance, accounting, and product planning, but had the negative effect of making Ford employees internally competitive rather than focused as one group serving its car markets. Competition from overseas manufacturers, particularly Asian car manufacturers, became more intense in the late 1970s and the 1980s, forcing Ford executives to reconsider the effectiveness of their business strategies and of the internal organisation. As is often the case for companies across the world, it takes a big shock caused by a development in the external environment to persuade managers of the need to act quickly and make fundamental changes.[44]

Starkey and McKinlay have researched Ford of Europe's improvement of the product development process. In short, Ford's costs were too high and the time-scale too long. Japanese companies such as Mazda, Toyota, and Honda were identified as leaders in product development and their approach was very different from Ford's. These Japanese companies were more integrated and cross-functional organisations using distinct management practices (see section 3 of chapter 1). Ford learnt a lot from Mazda by having a 25 per cent equity stake in the company. It learnt from Mazda's successful practice of simultaneous engineering, judged to be a new approach and a step beyond matrix management (a popular form of organisation for innovation and project management in the engineering industry), because it operated with a tighter coordination of product development and manufacturing. In 1989, Ford was facing the need to reduce its new product cycle time by eighteen months just to become competitive. Ford had had problems in the past with either manufacturing dominating and compromising product design or, vice versa, product design remaining aloof from manufacturing, leading to inefficiencies and operational problems. Both problems were caused by compartmentalised thinking and a failure of functional integration. In Australia, the car industry was the subject of a systematic process of rationalisation, whereby the number of manufacturers was reduced to four (Holden, Ford, Toyota, and Mitsubishi) during the 1990s, within the context of award restructuring, automation, and the introduction of various quality control initiatives. The overall policy goal of this process was to achieve 'world class' standards designed to increase Australia's vehicle exports substantially—a goal that has been achieved, to a considerable extent. To illustrate, between 1999 and 2000, vehicle exports from Australia rose by 38 per cent overall and there were particular success stories, such as $1 billion in sales to Saudi Arabia.[45]

Mazda stressed four factors for successful simultaneous engineering: communication between product development and manufacturing; formal cooperation including cross-functional careers; team culture and shared responsibility; and customer-driven processes. Following Mazda's example, an important part of the development process is to facilitate increased lateral communication and decreased functional separation. Employee development in Ford will be of strategic benefit only where it can stimulate improved innovation and new ways of working. Separate and isolated employee development programs will not take the company far enough in the highly competitive car market. Employee development must occur in improved cross-functional work environments and reinforce new structures of organisational learning. Managers and employees must learn to cooperate and integrate their activities more effectively rather than coexist under conditions of internal competition, isolation, and status divisions. The evidence then is that the structure and culture of Japanese corporations have been more successful than those of Western companies in facilitating some aspects typical of the learning organisation, such as information sharing throughout the company, on-the-job learning, teamwork, and routine development of subordinates by managers. Results from the Australian Workplace Industrial Relations Survey (1995), on Australian and foreign-owned multinational companies, reveal different preferences for HRM in US, Japanese, and British firms. US firms, for instance, show less propensity to acknowledge unions than do Australian and British firms.

Since the late 1990s, interest in Japanese management methods has waned somewhat as the performance of Japan's global corporations has been influenced by the economic crisis in Asia and periodic downturns in specific industries such as the high tech slump leading to workforce reductions in companies such as Fujitsu. Some aspects of the learning organisation, such as information sharing, have continued to be promoted in the knowledge management arena, which has grown in popularity in the management domain since the mid-1990s. Employers have been encouraged by consultants and professional associations to consider more carefully how they manage flows of knowledge inside and outside of the organisation. Some of this work involves innovative HR and IT practices and other parts of knowledge management continue long-standing themes within business management, such as encouraging more informal communication and forming groups that span hierarchical and functional divides within the organisation.

3 Employee development

Thinking more broadly about development

HRM claims to have a more proactive approach to employee development than personnel management does. HRM is said to view promoting and facilitating continuous learning as everybody's responsibility. In the past, the separate training function of the organisation was considered responsible for learning and development, it being almost exclusively the duty of a small department staffed by a training manager and trainers. In some companies, training has been seen as part of the personnel function, and line managers have tended to avoid responsibility for identifying development needs and supporting training and development. In the learning organisation, employee development does not centre exclusively upon the training or personnel department; rather, as in HRM, it is considered the responsibility of everyone in the organisation, and particularly line management.

An important part of the management of employee development is to decide what tasks are the responsibilities of which party—employees, their line managers, or, where it exists, the training department. The training or HR department will provide for some needs; others will be best met by contracting external providers. For example, it may be found to be more cost-effective and time-saving to pay a specialist training consultancy to run a two-day training course on assertiveness skills rather than to 'upskill' the in-house trainers to be able to deliver it themselves. In HRM, training and development have a big role to play in innovation.[46] Much of the employees' development will be informal and occur through on-the-job learning; however, there is often additional need for structured, off-the-job learning programs. Trainers and HR facilitators are now most frequently encouraged to develop their role as change agents in managing change (see chapter 9). The trainers must therefore be highly flexible and supportive of innovation, and some of them will play major parts in organisation-wide change through partnership with managers, idea generation, and sponsoring and 'orchestrating' innovation. Here, facilitation and coordination skills are more important than imparting instruction or assessing individuals' skills.

Research on innovation in organisations has found that major technological changes frequently come from outside the industry; mature product markets and their leading companies generally don't spawn the new breakthrough product that undercuts them.[47] The transistor, for example, was not a product of companies that were manufacturing vacuum tubes. There are some companies—although they are unusual—that seek to innovate continuously, such as 3M, which has a business mission committed to developing new products that are first to market. These are high-investment products that often have high profit margin sales for a comparatively short and fixed period of time. 3M knows that profitable innovation most often comes from listening to customers and having an internal organisation that can learn, acquire promising small entrepreneurial technology companies, and enter into joint ventures with business partners. For years, 3M has encouraged lateral and informal communication as well as using the formal organisation structure for funding ideas and promoting product champions.[48] Galbraith recommends that, if organisations wish to innovate, they must attend to four design components: structure, processes, reward systems, and people. The structure must encourage idea generators, sponsors, and orchestrators. It must be differentiated enough to allow variability of ideas and activities and possess small pools or 'reservations' of resources. The processes must involve planning ahead for innovation, idea generating, blending ideas, and managing innovative products. The reward system should provide opportunities, autonomy, promotion, and recognition for individuals and groups who are successful innovators. Finally, Galbraith says, people must be selected and encouraged to self-select and then the necessary training and development must be provided.

Occupational health and safety (OHS) issues are an area for innovation in organisations, but they rarely receive much media attention in Australia. Nevertheless, very important training and development issues arise from OHS, and not least because work-related deaths, accidents, and illness are an endemic problem, causing personal tragedies, disruption to work and families, and major financial losses.[49] Certain industries (for example, mining, construction, and agriculture) have chronically high rates of fatal and non-fatal injury, arising from use of vehicles or tools, and from people falling or being struck by objects.[50] Despite the seriousness of OHS issues, though, Australia lacks a comprehensive, consistent national OHS database, with information being collected mainly at the state level or on specific OHS problems. There is only one example of a national surveillance system for a single work-related disorder—the National Occupational Health and Safety Commission (NOHSC) Mesothelioma Register, which provides details of all reported cases of malignant mesothelioma, the disease caused by exposure to asbestos and the incidence of which (and associated legal cases) has risen steadily over recent years.[51]

OHS issues involve various areas of expertise, including occupational therapists, rehabilitation counsellors, psychologists, social workers, human resource managers, industrial relations specialists, lawyers, judges, policy makers, ergonomists, and engineers. OHS is concerned with the prevention of workplace death, injury, and illness, and with the rehabilitation and compensation of victims. More holistic perspectives on OHS seek to address the interrelationships between health and safety at work and broader issues of social, physical and psychological well-being.[52] The effectiveness of OHS strategies is influenced by the strength of legislation; the presence of OHS policies and the monitoring of standards; levels of compliance, enforcement, and prosecutions; and compensation schemes and rehabilitation provisions.

The factors or conditions that produce OHS problems are numerous and frequently interconnected. They include:

- *Various hazards*—these may be physical (for example, fire), chemical (for example, noxious waste), biological (for example, contaminated blood), or electromagnetic (for example, radiation from computer monitors); the working environment (for example, poor lighting or excessive noise); poorly designed jobs (for example, unnecessarily repetitive work); inadequate ergonomics (for example, badly designed office furniture); lack of personal security (for example, walking to car parks or public transport through unlit areas); workplace organisation (for example, assembly line production); organisational change (such as downsizing); management practices (for example, highly authoritarian management styles); bullying (which may range from personal criticism to physical violence); harassment[53] (which includes sexual and other forms of harassment); inadequate training or education for the work being performed (for example, the use of potentially dangerous machinery); physical violence of various kinds; shift work;

both overwork and underwork; low pay; job insecurity; poor working and/or reporting relationships; role ambiguity (lack of clarity on the responsibilities of one job in relation to others); travel and commuting.
- *The changing character of the contemporary workplace*—decentralisation of pay and conditions, more casual and contract work, greater incidence of organisational change and reduced job security—has a direct impact on health and safety.[54] Employees have to cope with greater uncertainty and associated stress than was once the case. Working arrangements have also become considerably more diverse and less predictable. For example, increasing pressures for extended hours of operation, or even 24-hour operation, in a number of industries (for example, hospitality) have encouraged the spread of shift work. For many employees, it is an integral element of the work they do—approximately 18 per cent of all employees are shift workers. Varieties of shift work include permanent night or late shifts, rotating shifts, and blocks of two or more weeks' working at a time. Although some types of shift work may offer some potential benefits to employees, shift work can cause serious work–family problems—such as difficulties in arranging child care, which is rarely available outside 'normal' working hours. Shift workers also experience a higher incidence of various health problems than workers with more 'regular' working hours.[55]
- *Work intensification*—Australians are working considerably longer hours than people in several other developed economies—an average of 1860 hours in 2000, as compared to, for example, Norway (1376 hours) and Germany (1480 hours) and the UK (1708 hours), although we should not ignore that the US average was 1877 hours. A recent article in *HR Monthly*, however, questions the extent of overwork in Australia, observing that overtime work has not changed for people outside the white-collar workforce over the seven-year period prior to 2001.[56] Work intensification has become a major issue, and many enterprise or individual agreements require employees to work over an increased span of hours. Australia also lacks any legislation on maximum working hours, which means that some workers may be working 80 or more hours in one week.

Such factors can produce significant stress, a phenomenon that in itself is nothing new, but has only in recent decades been recognised and addressed as a serious workplace problem. In its simplest terms, stress is caused by *stressors*—events or situations that generate psychological and/or physiological reactions in individuals. Stress is not necessarily harmful, since we often require certain levels of stress to perform effectively. However, 'abnormal' stress levels (which vary according to the individual concerned) can produce severely damaging psychological and/or physiological effects. The main sources of stress are: (1) work-related, (2) personal, and (3) general (for example, economic recession). Stress levels are cumulative, with stress in one area compounding stress in others. There are two main strategies for dealing with workplace stress: stress reduction, which requires control of the stressors, and requires dealing with organisational issues; and stress management, which involves dealing with the individual manifestations or symptoms. Often, a combination of both approaches is used.

Australia's OHS legislation has a patchwork character, and is primarily the province of the states. There has been long-running debate on the extent to which OHS should be the subject of legal regulation or should be left to self-regulation by organisations. The 'Robens Model' of self-regulation, arising from a Committee of Inquiry under Lord Robens in the UK during the early 1970s, has been a major influence on Australian legislation over recent decades. One of the most important characteristics of Robens-style legislation in Australia has been the 'general duty' of responsibility for health and safety, which covers employers, employees, contractors, labour hire agency workers, suppliers, and manufacturers. Employers have a duty of care to their employees, as well as to contractors or agency workers who also use the premises. This duty includes: the provision of a safe, healthy workplace and facilities (for example, dining areas), appropriate maintenance of equipment and the working environment (such as air conditioning), effective information, training and supervision in relevant languages on workplace health and safety issues (for example, potential hazards); the maintenance of relevant OHS records; and regular monitoring of safety standards and employee health. Employees, contractors, and agency workers are legally obliged to use safety equipment where provided, to follow relevant safety procedures, and to avoid putting others at risk. Any breach of duty is a criminal offence.

Government OHS inspectors have an important role in ensuring observance of OHS regulations. They have the authority to issue improvement notices on dutyholders, requiring them to rectify a problem that breaches OHS regulations. Improvement notices are designed to achieve changes over a protracted period. They may also issue prohibition notices, to address immediate problems: an inspector may prohibit a particular workplace practice until any associated risks have been eliminated. Failure to comply is an offence for which individuals and organisations are liable to fines of varying amounts, according to the jurisdiction and severity of the offence.

Health and safety committees and representatives occupy an important role in Robens-style self-regulation. Joint union–management OHS committees, which deal with policy and strategy issues, as well as designated OHS representatives (who conduct OHS inspections and can point out specific problems requiring immediate attention), can ensure that OHS issues are dealt with in any process of organisational change. They are useful for analysing and evaluating the OHS implications of new technology and work techniques before they are implemented. OHS management plans, in this respect, are reasonably open, evolving strategies with related OHS procedures.

Direct assistance to the victims of workplace sickness and injury has taken two main forms: compensation and rehabilitation. Workers' compensation systems have been designed to provide financial support for employees who are victims of work-related injury or illness. Compensation schemes were introduced in the early decades of the twentieth century. They have often been the focus of considerable controversy, largely arising from government concerns over costs.[57] During the 1980s, the states introduced legislation to make compensation schemes more effective, comprehensive, and integrated. However, workers' compensation schemes have remained a politically sensitive issue. This sensitivity was revealed most dramatically in June 2001, when there was a workers' blockade of the NSW State Parliament, in protest against changes to the state's workers' compensation scheme. The Labor government introduced legislation intended to reduce the number of common law claims for compensation, which had resulted in a significant number of high pay-outs, contributing to the scheme's deficit of over $2 billion and to rapidly increasing workers' compensation premiums.

Effective occupational rehabilitation schemes can substantially reduce the adverse personal, organisational, and financial effects of occupational illness or injury. Occupational rehabilitation schemes are designed to maintain affected workers within their workplace or to provide them, after a period off work, with new employment either with their original employer or a new employer. Where workers are unable to return to their previous jobs, due to injury or illness, it is often possible to redeploy them to other positions.

Overall, OHS has often been seen as a less than fundamental issue by organisations. However, from a more strategic perspective, it can be argued that OHS should be seen as an integral part of organisational decision-making. Among the benefits that can be achieved through comprehensive OHS policies and plans are higher productivity due to less time being lost through sickness or injury, enhanced employee commitment and organisational morale, and reduced absenteeism and turnover.[58] Health and safety issues should be taken into account in designing management structures, workplaces, and jobs, as well as in employee recruitment, training, and development. Involvement of management, employees, and unions is likely to help ensure organisational accountability for OHS performance, identifying actual and potential problems and developing appropriate strategies to deal with them.

The next three parts of this section review current innovations in the policy and practice of employee development: outdoor development to promote teamwork and organisational commitment, open learning methods and training-technology tools to improve employees' access to learning and development, and the use of competences in employee development.

Outdoor development

Outdoor development courses have been used in some companies (for example, Fujitsu) for inculcating teams with company values or as part of induction for new recruits. The learning activities on these courses aim to motivate employees and develop their skills in leadership, teamwork, problem solving, decision making, and creativity. There are a number of specialist providers of this type of training; however, to be successful, programs must be carefully planned and properly supported in the workplace, including making sure that a critical mass of employees obtain places. Experienced companies aim to maximise the benefits of these programs by ensuring that the facilitators and trainers running them are well informed about the company's strategy, culture, and employee attitudes. Managers of the employees attending these courses give pre-course briefings and post-course feedback and organise follow-up activities to ensure the maximum transfer of learning back into the workplace. If these activities are not performed, the outdoor development will not be appropriately contextualised and participants will complain that the outdoor events were not relevant or, more disappointing still, that expectations were raised and then not met back at work. Marchington and Wilkinson report problems with outdoor development where programs have been poorly managed and inadequately supported by employing organisations.[59] They also quote some of the ground rules for increasing the chances of success:

- integration with other training activity and with organisational goals;
- clear and achievable objectives, which are monitored and relate to the workplace; these need to be established in conjunction with the outdoor trainers;
- rigorous checks on safety offered by providers;
- tutors and trainers who are skilled at undertaking ongoing reviews of the courses, both of a structured and unstructured nature;
- programs tailored to individual and company needs;
- a sense of ownership on the part of the participants.[60]

Jones has examined a number of the claims for outdoor management development and argues that one of its most potent strengths is in improving individuals' ability to learn.[61] Jones cautions against counter-productive outdoor development, for example, sessions that unnecessarily reinforce status relationships at work, often resulting in an overassertion of power and authority of the organisational hierarchy.

Technology-based learning and open learning

Large corporations and financial institutions began to experiment on a larger scale with open, flexible, and distance learning methods in the 1980s. Organisations such as Qantas have used computers for training since the 1970s, for example, flight simulators for pilots. Computer technology platforms have become increasingly more capable of delivering high-quality multimedia presentations that respond flexibly to individual queries, answers, and decisions. Training technologies that use computers and audiovisual machines have a history of usage and experimentation in education and training that dates back over the last four decades. The 1960s saw the development of the instructional design movement and audiovisual learning programs, which were generally better resourced in the USA. It was the period when 'teaching machines' were introduced, the more sophisticated ones being controlled by computer. There was a great deal of interest in the use of educational television, film, overhead projectors, and 35 mm slide displays. The 1970s brought video cassettes and, when the price of photocopying machines declined, greater use of photocopied handouts for routine training purposes. The 1980s saw more sophisticated software programming and the use of more powerful microcomputers. It was a decade when interactive video (computer-controlled videodiscs) had a brief heyday in large company training by providing an advanced form of computer-based training and utilising a range of video, graphics, and audio material. The 1980s were a decade of experimentation and a period of government-funded projects in new software technologies, especially artificial intelligence.

Since the early 1990s there has been a continued improvement in the use of the technologies of the 1980s in both work and home environments. Personal computers (PCs) are much more prevalent in offices, educational institutions, and training organisations. Multimedia capabilities have become more available through improved technologies in Windows and hypermedia software, computer graphics interfaces, and in-built CD peripheral devices. Children are developing IT literacy skills as a normal part of their upbringing, with mobile phones, Internet resources, home computer games, and widespread availability of PCs in schools. Over the last decade there has been a steadily increasing usage of advanced multimedia technologies in large companies and in the home. Training technologies can be flexible to a range of learning aims in basic technical skills and 'soft' or 'people' skills (for example, interpersonal communication). Computer-based training offers a learning experience in which the path that the learner takes through the material can be highly individualised yet restricted so that all users ultimately achieve the final objectives. On the one hand, training technologies can help in 'closed' tasks; for example, a bank employee can learn how to process a customer payment involving ten to twenty steps that have to be learnt and practised until the employee is competent. On the other hand, the learning might be more open-ended: individuals or groups browsing through a large database of stills, video clips, and computer simulations to acquaint themselves with an area of a country or a complex plant or piece of CMC machinery, for example.

Open learning centres were established as new facilities in many large companies and education institutions during the 1980s and 1990s. Qantas College Online (QCO) was established in 1996–97 to provide corporate online training and development, and is currently producing hundreds of course completions per month. Depending on how they are defined, open learning facilities can be traced back to open-access education and training technologies of the 1960s or further back to correspondence courses, institutes, specialist libraries, and societies of the nineteenth century. Derek Rowntree suggests that open learning can be considered in two different contexts—philosophy and method:

- A philosophy: a set of beliefs about teaching and learning that involve reducing barriers to access and giving learners control over learning.
- A method: a set of techniques for teaching and learning. Open learning using self-study materials and a range of media such as print, audio cassettes, television, computers, and so on.[62]

National provision of open learning in the UK was begun by some noteworthy institutions that have given an opportunity to learn to people who otherwise would not have been able to study on traditional, formal programs. A number of other countries have a wealth of experience and expertise in open and distance learning, particularly Australia, the USA, and Canada, where large distances have rendered it impractical for some rural populations to pursue traditional face-to-face methods of education. In the UK, the Open University (OU) was established in 1971 to provide distance learning, supplemented by occasional workshops and summer schools. Nearly two million people have studied with the OU. It has a worldwide reputation for its high-quality course materials developed by teams of specialists and its flexible system of credit-based undergraduate degrees, diplomas, and certificates. Some companies such as BT, Prudential Corporation, and Price Waterhouse (now PriceWaterhouse Coopers) began to experiment more with training technologies in open and distance learning during the 1980s.[63] Australia has a long tradition of distance learning, with many universities having run substantial external studies programs for several decades. In 1991, this tradition went a step further with the establishment of Open Learning Australia (OLA), a government-sponsored initiative to broaden educational access. As a private company initially funded by the Commonwealth, OLA adopted print, radio, and audiovisual technologies for its 'flexible learning' formats. The increasing geographical spread of many large organisations' operations, combined with improvements in hardware and software, have encouraged managers' interest in technology-based training. For example, several Australian universities and TAFE colleges offer management courses that can be completed through online learning, from anywhere in the world.

The media technologies used for open learning over the last decade are more sophisticated and versatile than the products available in the 1960s. Reynolds and Iwinski recommend using the term 'technology-based learning' (TBL), in preference to 'technology-based training', to cover the full variety of information and communication technologies.[64] Many of the uses for TBL involve informal and unplanned learning through media such as interactive media, video and computer teleconferencing, simulators, and virtual reality devices. The use of Internet and Intranet (Internet services exclusive to one organisation and its chosen partners) has grown rapidly since the early 1990s. Companies such as Telstra and BP have made creative and intensive use of computer databases, computer conferencing, and Intranet services to promote 'breakthrough advances' in learning by employees. In the words of BP chief executive John Browne, 'Leadership is all about catalysing learning as well as better performance.'[65] Large organisations have had a leading role in the development and distribution of TBL in Australia. It has been used for several years in diverse industries, including telecommunications (Telstra), banking (Westpac), oil (BP, Shell), and air transport (Qantas). Governments play a critical role in financing and promoting new technologies in training through institutions. Australian government departments at state and federal levels have been strongly involved with vocational education and training (VET) providers in the implementation of TBL initiatives, particularly through the Australian National Training Authority (ANTA) flexible delivery implementation plan.

The use of computer-based technologies for training and development has become popular in Australian organisations, particularly in some public sector agencies and the finance sector. For example, the use of CD-ROM training packages can enable employees to update or expand their skills at their own pace. Some private sector companies, such as Mincom, offer computer-based training programs that can be tailored to meet the needs of individual organisations.

Management development

HRM places more importance on management development than did traditional personnel management; hence this last part of section 3 reviews recent initiatives in management development and particularly the competence movement. Storey's twenty-five-item checklist (see chapter 1) advises, from the viewpoint of HRM, that line management use transformational leadership and that general, business, and line managers be the key HR decision makers.[66] Under HRM, managers' core skills are those of facilitation rather than negotiation. In later work Storey says increased activity in the field of management development has raised as many questions as it has answered. How, he asks, should management development be conceptualised? What are the main methods and techniques? What are management competences and how effective has the Management Charter Initiative been since it was launched in 1988? What factors influence the provision and effectiveness of management development? There was change in management practice during the 1980s and 1990s in the UK, notably a growth in direct communication practices by managers such as face-to-face communication, briefings, and meetings. Analysis of findings from the Australian Workplace Industrial Relations Survey (1995) on multinational companies in Australia found that British firms made significantly greater use of a range of HR policies and practices than Australian establishments, including formal written selection procedures, appraisal, performance-related pay schemes, and mechanisms for grievance resolution. Nevertheless, employee direct participation initiatives are widespread in Australia, although they have not led to substantially enhanced employee discretion in the workplace.[67]

Under conditions of greater instability and increased global competition, Storey argues, managers capable of reliable and efficient performance, high conformity, cost reduction, and what are called 'satisficing' behaviours ('social pleasers') do not have enough capabilities to ensure a well-managed organisation. Other competences of a more entrepreneurial and flexible nature are now sought after, particularly at the higher levels of the organisation. An idea of what these new competences might be can be gained from Gareth Morgan's research study, reported in his book *Riding the Waves of Change*.[68] His study of emerging managerial competences was funded by Shell Canada and involved senior executives, twenty of whom participated in a round-table forum. The competences they identified were: reading the environment, proactive management, leadership and vision, HRM, promoting creativity, learning and innovation, skills of remote management (particularly facilitation and empowerment), using information technology as a transformative force, managing complexity, and developing contextual competences (particularly building alliances and social responsibility). The interested reader is advised to consult the book for more detail on the scope and content of these proposed competences. Reading the environment requires competence in scanning and gathering intelligence, forecasting, scenario planning, and identifying key points of change. Human resource management, they argue, involves valuing people as key resources, developing abilities during organisational change, getting the best out of specialist and generalist qualities, and managing in an environment where all managers and employees are, ultimately, equals.

Management development during the 1980s became more connected than it previously had been with managing organisational change (see chapter 9), the reduction of middle management, and its replacement by work teams that are tightly performance-managed.[69] These management development programs have had common aims, such as making managers more innovative, risk-taking, and 'businesslike'.[70] Facilitators of change have sought to make managers aware of the change in company values and the need to concentrate on providing quality customer services at competitive prices. The methods of delivery have normally combined formal and informal methods of development. Managers have had to attend change conferences and undertake formal training in adopting new values, work methods, and systems. Informally, it is known that those who are most likely to survive in the organisation are those able to enact the new values with commitment and responsibility.

While there are some opportunities for promotion in organisations, there has been a general delayering of the management hierarchy and downsizing, meaning that development is a required part of the job and not something done only to managers who either lack necessary skills or who are being developed for promotion. Many of the methods and techniques used in management development apply equally to other employees. Indeed, if organisations develop the competencies of their managers, they must similarly advance the attitudes and skills of subordinate employees; otherwise problems of communication and skill shortages will result further down the line. As noted in section 1 of this chapter, some companies, aspiring to learning-organisation status, have implemented ambitious employee development and assistance programs to ensure everyone in the organisation is receptive to learning new skills and ideas and improving themselves.[71]

Other countries have different traditions of management development. The American approach involves provision of formal business education in colleges and universities with a very high output of MBA graduates.[72] The French have favoured recruiting top management material from élite schools, known as Grandes Écoles, and the Germans have pursued in-depth technical and university education with relatively little emphasis on formal business qualifications, until more recently. The MBA degree was not available in German universities in the 1980s and early 1990s and the few who studied for it did so through collaboration with foreign providers such as Henley Management College, Cranfield University, and the Open University. In Germany, MBA courses are now more popular and have a stronger reputation than in the 1990s. The Japanese approach favours recruiting 'raw material' from top universities and then training managers in-company over the years through a process of continuous development, with developing the competencies of one's subordinates being a key role of the Japanese manager.[73] The Japanese and German approaches have both traditionally favoured strong internal labour markets for management development, which leads to high likelihood of promotion from within the organisation and routine, planned employee development of the core workforce.

The importance attached to competence development for management is usually traced back to a number of reports of the mid-1980s, saying what many people in business had for some time been acutely aware of—that managers were receiving inadequate formal and informal development.[74] It is hard to quantify informal development, but easier to measure formal development (for instance, in number of training days per year). During the time of those reports, managers in the UK were receiving approximately one day of training a year on average, although provision was highly skewed, with the majority receiving none. The amount of training for managers in most developed countries grew in the 1990s, although Australia and the UK lagged behind major competitors.[75] Today, an employee in a professional occupation is five times more likely to receive training than an unskilled employee, and very few companies have been consistent over recent years in resourcing management training.[76] The amount of formal training input is only one measure of management development, which says nothing directly about the quality and effectiveness of the provision, but it is at least one indicator showing that, overall, provision is gradually improving in Australia and elsewhere.

The competence movement in education and training has been a national government policy priority in Australia and the UK since the latter half of the 1980s. Competences are a way of specifying capabilities that can be assessed and developed according to nationally agreed criteria. They are a method of rationally planning and detailing the attainments of individuals and, ultimately, the whole workforce. Their purpose is to ensure a more competent workforce capable of performing competitively in global and domestic markets. Functional management competences have been criticised for being too generic and non-specific, and for being too bureaucratic and over-rational, particularly the high workload created in assessment activity. However, the movement is little more than fifteen years old and its immediate intellectual forebears stretch back over just twenty years.[77]

BOX 8.3

The Management Charter Initiative

The Australian approach to management competence development has been strongly influenced by standards of competence published by the Management Charter Initiative (MCI). The MCI was launched in 1988 by the Confederation of Business and Industry (CBI), the British Institute of Management (BIM), and government organisations. It is responsible for improving and assessing management functional competences and has developed national occupational standards for managers. These standards are a nationally recognised and accredited system for developing more effective managers in the workplace.

Sections of the MCI standards have been adopted by employer and education organisations in Australia. There are seven key roles in the MCI occupational standards for managers and each is divided into units. The units subdivide into elements, which themselves consist of performance criteria together with underpinning knowledge and understanding. Assessment of the standards is primarily work-based and involves testing the knowledge and understanding required for consistent performance. The assessor essentially wants to know what a manager can do and that he or she can perform competently.

In summary, the standards consist of:
- Key Roles
- Units
- Elements
- Performance criteria
  (underpinning knowledge and understanding)

The seven key roles are:

A: Manage activities
B: Manage resources
C: Manage people
D: Manage information
E: Manage energy
F: Manage quality
G: Manage projects

There is space here to give details on only one example.

Key role C: Manage people

This role describes the work of managers in getting the most from their teams. It covers recruiting, training, building the team, allocating and evaluating work, and dealing with people problems. It also includes managing oneself and managing relations with others at work.

Units

C1 Manage yourself
C2 Develop your own resources
C3 Enhance your own performance
C4 Create effective working relationships
C5 Develop productive working relationships
C6 Enhance productive working relationships
C7 Contribute to the selection of personnel for activities
C8 Select personnel for activities
C9 Contribute to the development of teams and individuals
C10 Develop teams and individuals to enhance performance
C11 Develop management teams
C12 Lead the work of teams and individuals to achieve their objectives
C13 Manage the performance of teams and individuals
C14 Delegate work to others
C15 Respond to poor performance of teams and individuals

C16 Deal with poor performance in your team
C17 Redeploy personnel and make redundancies.

Source: *What are Management Standards?—An Introduction*, Management standards information pack, Management Charter Initiative (1997), MCI, London.

The standards can be assessed at different NVQ levels of qualification. Level 3 is for practising managers or supervisors, and levels 4 and 5 for higher-level managers. At different levels some units are mandatory and some are optional, thus providing some choice for individuals with different job responsibilities and career goals.

The assessment criteria are straightforward and assessors often scrutinise the manager at the level of an element because it contains a group of related performances. The manager is assessed according to one of three judgments: competent, insufficient evidence, and not yet competent. If the candidate is competent in an element, then he or she will move on to other elements or units of the standards. If there is insufficient evidence, then more evidence has to be gathered before the assessor can make a judgment. If the result is 'not yet competent', then more learning and development has to take place before new dates for assessment are agreed. The assessment methodology is criterion-based, meaning that, to pass, a candidate must meet an objective standard of competence that is nationally specified and understood. It is not a norm-based system by which an arbitrary number below average attainment fail whatever the objective standard of the whole group.

Australia has been active in new forms of vocational education and training for nearly twenty years. From 1983, under the Hawke government, the ALP–ACTU Accord provided a framework for a systematic approach to vocational education and training (VET) and skills formation. Three reports provided considerable impetus for this approach and the development of the 'Training Reform Agenda'. First, the Kirby Report (Report of the Committee into Labour Market Programs, 1985) proposed an approach to education and training that focused on the development of a more 'skilled society', whereby the presence of a highly skilled workforce would attract greater investment. Second, the Karmel Report (Quality of Education in Australia—Report of the Review Committee, 1985) proposed a greater focus on the school-to-work transition, and an increased commitment to the provision of broad-based education and training. Finally, the combined ACTU and Trades Development Council (TDC) report, Australia Reconstructed (1987), influenced by Scandinavian examples, saw the need for government to ensure better labour market adjustment through education and training programs that sought to encourage the movement of employees from declining to expanding industries. There was a generally tripartite approach to training and education reform: a work practices summit in September 1986, involving government, business, and unions led on to the process of award restructuring, whereby more structured career paths were to be related to skills formation and multiskilling (the performance of a broader range of tasks by workers). VET was to emerge as a competence-based system, with its credentials formalised in the Australian Vocational Training Certificate, designed to provide a national approach to both assist and respond to economic restructuring, a major feature of the Hawke government's 'clever country' campaign. The Keating government's *One Nation* statement, however, represented a less interventionist approach and a shift towards neo-liberalism, which had been growing for several years. The training system was to become more market-oriented, and there was to be a reduced focus on industry policy. Under the Liberal–National coalition government, this shift was accelerated and the tripartite approach was abandoned, as training and education were turned over to private providers and to market demand, rather than being focused on national policy objectives.[78]

There has been interest in the UK competence-based approach from other countries, including France, Germany, and Japan. The Australian Institute of Management offers a Graduate Certificate in Management Competence (GCMC). This program comprises five management units—managing, leading, and developing people; managing finance; managing information; managing operations; and managing strategy—adapted from the British MCI middle and senior level competences. Recent research evidence has found that social competences (for example, punctuality, loyalty, creativity, customer orientation, responsibility, and cooperation) are an area that employers are paying greater attention to by selecting and developing employees using a 'fit to team' attitudinal model rather than a 'fit to job' functional model.[79] Case study research of organisational learning in Fiat, Motorola, Mutual Investment Corporation, and Électricité de France found it was stimulated by influential managers' recognition of the difference between what was significant and what had been achieved in the past and their identification of which resources needed to be further developed. The authors recommend that learning should link intangible human resources (for example, knowledge, skills, and expertise) to core competences.[80]

Summary

The learning organisation is a set of aspirations rather than a reality. Theories of the learning organisation make recommendations on improving employee development to benefit individuals and their employing organisations. Innovations in training and development have been discussed in this chapter. Three such innovations—systematic training, OD, and action learning—notwithstanding their longevity have not been especially influential for the majority of organisations and have all come under criticism from employers for being ineffectual and expensive. Specific tools for employee development—the learning cycle and learning styles— have been described. They continue to be applied in the twenty-first century by some companies in certain aspects of training and development, and are part of the formal strategic plans of some Australian public sector organisations, for example

Gold Coast City Council. More recently, Kolb's learning cycle has been extended by Dixon into a practitioner framework for organisational learning, but has had considerably less impact on managers interested in the learning organisation[81] than did earlier work by Senge and Pedler et al.

The use of open learning and training technologies has had slow but continuous development in training and education since the late 1970s, but one of the major reasons for their longevity is the attractiveness to employers of their claims to reduce education and training costs, especially the number of people employed in delivery. The competences approach used in employee resourcing (especially for selection and recruitment), as discussed in section 2 of chapter 5, has also been a recent innovation in employee development. We concentrated on one example of the use of functional competences for management development, but the standards approach has not been as influential during fifteen years of initiatives as its main proponent had hoped. Employers have tended to concentrate more on attitudinal competences rather than functional standards, partly because attitudinal competences are more often specific to the internal labour market of the employing organisation while vocational standards of competence are said to be less specific to the employing organisation and furthermore are generic, portable qualifications in the external labour market.[82]

This chapter has acknowledged the difficulty of creating learning organisations in practice and characterised past innovations in training and development as tending to be short-lived and of limited influence. Nevertheless, the learning model offers a challenging vision of the future—a new organisational culture, a philosophy of lifelong learning, and long-term investment in people.

BOX 8.4

Case study—New pressures for learning and development in the fork-lift truck factory of Smarna Gora Holdings

This case study is a good example of much broader employee development needs that arose when a company found itself changing its business from trading within a socialist economy to operating in a transitional capitalist economy and being exposed to global market competition. The case compares the company's situation at the end of the socialist era in 1990 with its situation in 2001.

1990

The company has a total of 2000 employees and is divided into five different factories: turbine (water, electricity production), pump (water), industrial equipment (presses, hydraulic equipment), fork-lift truck, and work factory (cranes, cement, mechanical parts). The fork-lift truck factory has 250 employees and is organised into four departments: construction, commercial, finance, and technical. The commercial department is divided into buying and selling. The technical department is divided into planning, production, storage, and maintenance.

In 1990, the company was functioning within the socialist system, which focused on production. It is based in Slovenia, which at the time was a state of Yugoslavia. Igor Pavlin, the manager for the factory's operations, said: 'There was no planning done at the organisational level and no emphasis on markets nor much on management. There was no client orientation and no need to compete with European countries. The market was almost exclusively Yugoslavia.'

Consumption was greater than production and there was no strong need to invest in new product development. The majority of investment went into the construction department. Organisational commitment was low, with lower-level employees not feeling much responsibility for their work or the organisation. Management did not help the situation by placing low importance on efficient methods of working. As for industrial relations, the syndicate structure (trade union) was very strong in influencing how the organisation was run and the system of management was strongly paternalistic, making additional assets available for the factory's use so that employees could rent company houses and travel to company holiday sites.

2001

There has been considerable downsizing and rationalisation of Smarna Gora Holdings and the number of factories has been reduced since 1990. The turbine and pump factories have been combined and so have industrial equipment and the work factory.

In the fork-lift truck factory the commercial department has combined buying and selling to reduce the number of employees and to simplify horizontal communication across the organisation. Storage has been moved from the technical department to the commercial department. The number of employees has been reduced to 130 and the work is now directed by the commercial department rather than the emphasis being on production. Managers, with employees, have agreed on the mission and vision of the factory. It is documented and available to everybody.

Smarna Gora Holdings has a good reputation in other Eastern European countries and there are initiatives being taken with the turbine section of the recently formed turbine and pump factory to raise the profile of the company in Western markets to gain a market share. The company is developing a global orientation and making strong use of previous trading relationships with countries such as Iran and India.

Igor Pavlin said the company is about to create a new managerial post for human resource management that will have ambitious targets for employee development over the next three years. Igor explained the challenges facing the new manager:

> Changing the culture involves changing the mindset of the employees. For example, in construction there are now six new types of fork-lift truck which require additional skills and experience within the company. The workforce needs training and education to meet the changing technology requirements. Skill shortages have become apparent in

some of the semi-skilled and skilled jobs, like turning and welding. The whole operation has to meet higher quality standards—ISO 9001—and work with more complex technologies. The departments have to attend to improving teamwork and are addressing difficulties in recruitment and training needs of the existing workforce, particularly additional knowledge, both technical and managerial. Job responsibilities and tasks have been enlarged as a result of the reduced number of people employed in the business. New computer systems are being introduced and modifications being made to be compatible with ISO 9001.

The financial situation has been precarious across the new countries of the former Yugoslavia, due to the war and internal political difficulties associated with the dismantling of the socialist state. The national market was closed during the war, but following the end of the Milosevic period of rule it has been predicted that the market will improve steadily over the next three years. The long-term outlook for the country in terms of increased tourism and more small- and medium-sized-business investment, particularly from immediate neighbours such as Italy and Austria, is an optimistic one. There were some problems in the mid-1990s leading to strikes by the workers, said to be prompted by the unions. One national syndicate organised a work stoppage for two hours in order to obtain and negotiate the divulgence of more information by employers. Employee involvement and participation remain significant issues; however, industrial relations unrest in terms of strikes seems to be less critical today than it was in the mid-to-late 1990s.

There have been ongoing cash-flow problems for five years relating to difficulties in raising finance through the banks, with risk countries not making payments according to schedule (for instance, two-month repayment periods have increased to a staggering two years), and a general reduction in productivity. Igor explained the problematic employment conditions of the workforce, which he saw as likely to continue unless the factory's products become more competitive on the export market and employees change their job attitudes, especially their work commitment and skill development. Igor was positive about the capability of the factory to succeed in its growing international markets, although he was fully aware of the very great human resource difficulties and challenges that lay ahead:

A few years back, around 1997, the workers had lower wages than in previous years, equivalent to about 500 Deutschmarks a month. There still are fewer fringe benefits than in those times, and they work harder and longer, although their overtime payments are not late like they were in 1997. Inevitably, with the rising cost of housing and accommodation, some of our employees will continue to live ten to fifty kilometres outside of Ljubljana [the city where the factory is based]. Our concern is that compared to those who live nearby, they don't identify as strongly as we would like with the strategic needs of the organisation. We need greater organisational commitment and better skills for the competitive marketplace.

Case study activities

1 Identify the positive and negative pressures on learning and development in the fork-lift truck factory of Smarna Gora Holdings. Ensure your answer covers both external and internal pressures, and characterises both change and continuity between 1990 and 2001.
2 Write a ten-point plan for both management and employee development in Smarna Gora Holdings over the next five years. Ensure that you order your points for priority of action.

Study questions

1 List some of the innovations that have occurred in training and development and outline their strengths and weaknesses.
2 Analyse the relationship between Kolb's, Honey and Mumford's, and Dixon's theories of learning.
3 Select an organisation in which you or a colleague have worked. Using the Pedler, Burgoyne, and Boydell framework, assess how far it approximates a learning organisation.
4 Write a detailed training and development rationale for technology-based learning and open learning in an organisation that you have studied. Include the following issues: cost benefits, speed of response, flexibility of delivery, ease of use, individualisation of learning, and creating the learning organisation.
5 Find out more information about competences and standards of competence. Devise a career and competence-development plan for yourself and the group, assuming you are in the employment of your choice over the coming five to ten years.

Further reading

Hargadon, A. B. and Sutton, R. I., 'Technology Brokering and Innovation in a Product Development Firm', *Administrative Science Quarterly* (1997), 42, pp. 716–49.
Kamoche, K. and Mueller, F., 'Human Resource Management and the Appropriation-Learning Perspective', *Human Relations* (1998), 51, 8, pp. 1033–60.
Senge, P., *The Fifth Discipline: The Art and Practice of the Learning Organization* (New York: Doubleday/Currency, 1990).
Starkey, K., *How Organizations Learn* (London: International Thomson Business Press, 1996).

CHAPTER 9

Managing Change

CHAPTER CONTENTS

Introduction

1 From organisational structure to organisational culture

2 Strong cultures and excellent cultures

3 Frameworks of change
Lewin's force field analysis
Reger et al. on reframing the organisation
Burns on personal change

4 Implementing change
Nadler and Tushman
Todd Jick

5 The role of the HR function

Summary
Case study—O'Keefe Centre
Study questions
Further reading

Introduction

Human resource specialists nowadays are said to be giving more time to diagnosing, planning, facilitating, and reinforcing organisational change than they have in the past. Organisational change can be minor and smooth or major and transformational. Chapter 2 explained how, in the 1990s, many public sector organisations in Australia were privatised or partly privatised, and large companies underwent major restructuring often accompanied by reduction of the workforce. Increased uncertainty in domestic and world markets and increased threats of loss of business due to fiercer competition have put pressure on management to be effective in managing internal organisational change. Managing change has been a central concern in Australia for government and the public sector, implementing rolling programs of financial change, new systems of public sector management, and substantial downsizing of the public sector. Managing change has also become a critical issue in many countries across the world as a consequence of increased activity by national governments in restructuring, contracting out, and privatisation of public sector services.[1] Likewise, companies have found themselves under greater pressure since the 1980s to initiate major programs of organisational change, raising questions about how the process should be managed.

In chapter 3 we examined the nature of industrial relations in Australia, identifying the move away from centralised regulation and wage fixation. Since the 1980s, greater importance has been attached to enterprise-level bargaining and regulation, and private and public sector managers are often assigned roles as leaders of organisational change, which raises questions about how change is being achieved. In this chapter, we review some of the influential literature on managing change. Many of the frameworks of change outlined below are compatible with the philosophy of HRM and unilateral regulation. For example, in Storey's twenty-five-point framework (see chapter 1) under 'HRM' two of the points are that managers should show transformational leadership and manage the climate and culture of the organisation. The majority of the guidelines for managing change discussed in this chapter adopt a managerialist and unitarist perspective, but are reviewed with the expectation that the reader will discuss these critically and understand them in conjunction with ideas and perspectives on HRM presented in previous chapters.

Chapter 9 is divided into five sections. In the first two sections, we review the developing debate in the management literature since the 1980s and its change of emphasis away from a preoccupation with optimal organisational structure towards more interest in changing the organisational culture. Next, three frameworks of change are introduced; then we explore some of the widely known work on the scale and implementation of change. Finally, the role of the HR function in the management of organisational change is briefly evaluated.

1 From organisational structure to organisational culture

In the 1970s, it was commonplace for practitioners and academics in the management field to stress the importance of organisational structure. In 1962 in the USA,

Chandler researched companies' historical growth and diversification into multi-divisional firms and concluded that 'structure follows strategy'.[2] By this he meant that how the company is organised to achieve its goals (structure) must be consistent with the business strategy. In the UK, the well-known Aston school undertook studies of specific dimensions of organisational structure, such as specialisation, standardisation, formalisation, centralisation, and configuration.[3] Research of this nature was full of discussion about what constituted optimal and suboptimal structure of an organisation's systems, procedures, plans, and controls.

By the beginning of the 1980s, Japanese manufacturing companies had made significant inroads into traditional US and European domestic markets, particularly in the automotive and consumer electronics industries. These Japanese businesses were achieving success through higher productivity, better quality, lower cost, and a quicker responsiveness to customers. Although much of the Japanese quality philosophy had originated in the USA with 'quality gurus' such as W. Edwards Deming and Joseph M. Juran,[4] the operations and quality systems of these companies were different to those in the West, and, overall, the Japanese industry structure and the national and organisational cultures were distinctive in many ways. Some Western business leaders who visited Japanese companies in the late 1970s and early 1980s were strongly influenced by what they saw and were convinced their companies would have to change if they were to survive in the increasingly competitive world market-place.[5]

In the 1980s, partly in response to the rising power of the economies of the Pacific Rim, the focus of interest in management consultancy and writing moved from issues of organisational structure[6] to organisational culture. Ed Schein from the Massachusetts Institute of Technology defines the culture of an organisation or group as: 'A pattern of shared basic assumptions that the group learned as it solved its problems of external adaptation and internal integration, that has worked well enough to be considered valid and, therefore, to be taught to new members as the correct way to perceive, think, and feel in relation to those problems.'[7]

Schein goes on to say that his concept of culture involves understanding how groups socialise new members into the group, identifying the behaviours that groups nurture and reward, and appreciating that large organisations will have a corporate culture and subcultures. Schein believes that leaders can create group culture, as did Deal and Kennedy, whose advice on changing organisational culture met a clear need among senior executives in the 1980s when many companies in the USA and other developed countries were suffering a crisis of business confidence in their traditional home markets.[8] Deal and Kennedy's perspective on culture change concentrates on the more symbolic aspects of management, highlighting differences in national and organisational cultures and extolling the virtues of charismatic leadership, entrepreneurialism, vision and values, rites and rituals of corporate life, and 'the way we do things around here'.

Deal and Kennedy proposed a new challenge to management and employees, asking them to think about their organisations as 'strong' and 'weak' cultures. America's great companies were not merely organisations, they said, but successful, human institutions. The high performers were 'strong culture' companies, for example, Caterpillar Tractor, General Electric, DuPont, Price Waterhouse, 3M, IBM,

Procter & Gamble, Hewlett-Packard, and Johnson & Johnson. Deal and Kennedy said that high-performing companies owe their success to the development of a strong culture and listed five situations when change is necessary and the culture needs reshaping; the first two in particular, relating to the environment, were perceived to be significant in the 1980s:

- when the environment is undergoing fundamental change, and the company has always been highly value-driven;
- when the industry is highly competitive and the environment changes quickly;
- when the company is mediocre, or worse;
- when the company is truly at the threshold of becoming a large corporation— a *Fortune* 1000-scale corporate giant;
- when the company is growing very rapidly.[9]

It has often been said that only when a dramatic change occurs in the external environment do companies become motivated to undertake large-scale organisational change. Pettigrew's study of the ICI corporation is a good example of the importance of the external environment in persuading people to recognise the need for change.[10] Pettigrew found that it was not until the organisation was facing a substantial crisis (in the early 1980s) threatening its long-term existence that fundamental change started to occur, on that occasion under the leadership of John Harvey-Jones.

In some respects, ICI had a strong culture already, but it had become inappropriate when the environment changed fundamentally. Its culture was felt by managers such as Harvey-Jones to be too elitist, bureaucratic, and inward-looking to remain a major player in the world chemicals industry. The need to adapt had been recognised within parts of the company for years, but ICI's organisation development programs and other change initiatives had received half-hearted support from top management and were insufficient to stimulate substantial change. The external environment became the determining factor when the growing threat to the company's business interests was ultimately recognised in the form of reduced profitability and the worst losses ICI had ever experienced.

During the 1980s, consistent with the move towards unilateral regulation of the employment relationship, top management paid more attention to ensuring managers were visible to the rest of the workforce in implementing change. The greater significance accorded to managers in leading change reinforced the message that joint regulation was no longer practical because it was an obstacle to visionary leadership and the exercise of management prerogative.

2 Strong cultures and excellent cultures

One line of thinking on managing change, which emerged in the USA during the 1980s, is that its essence lies in managing the organisational culture. A variety of high-performing US corporations were considered by some researchers from Harvard Business School and the consulting company McKinsey to be successful because they had the right culture. Peters and Waterman popularised the approach of managing culture in their book *In Search of Excellence*.[11] The 'excellent company' and 'strong culture' approaches come from the same group of people.[12] As well as having the same origins, both approaches are committed to the concept of 'transformational' leadership and effective cultural management.

Advocates of the 'excellent-company' approach became increasingly convinced by the argument that strong culture is a major key to business success, although events over the ensuing years have called this into question as some of their 'excellent' companies have experienced difficulties. For example, 'Walt Disney was to produce a string of films that were failures, Caterpillar experienced declining demand for its heavy plant machinery, and Atari, the name once synonymous with computer games, almost disappeared entirely.'[13] The excellent-company study has been criticised for not being very thorough in terms of research design;[14] nevertheless, the eight attributes that Peters and Waterman said make an excellent company have remained influential. One measure of the considerable interest at the time in the excellent-company approach was that, at the height of its popularity, the book was selling more copies than the Bible. A possible explanation for its appeal lies in the eight attributes' cultural acceptability to US organisations. The attributes emphasise qualities of individualism, autonomy, medium-to-low power distance (as explained in section 1 of chapter 5), and tolerance of ambiguity. The 'excellent company' attributes are as follows:

1. a bias for action—getting on with it;
2. close to the customer—understanding and responding to what the customer wants;
3. autonomy and entrepreneurship—fostering leaders and innovators;
4. productivity through people—treating employees as the root source of quality and productivity gain;
5. hands-on, value driven—being close to the job, no matter what one's job status;
6. 'stick to the knitting'—doing things you know how to do well;
7. a simple form, lean staff—keeping the organisational structure simple, with few corporate staff;
8. simultaneous loose–tight properties—pushing autonomy right down to the shop floor while a few core values (e.g. reliability) are rigidly adhered to.[15]

The eight attributes are general enough to be open to a variety of interpretations on what constitutes excellence, thus facilitating alternative ways that top managers could see the excellent company concept as being relevant, at least in part, to their own organisation. Peters and Waterman's case descriptions are situated in diverse industries with exemplary companies ranging from, for example, 3M, a manufacturing company with a long-standing reputation for first-to-market product innovation, to McDonald's, a company famous for its successful global operations in fast food. Peters and Waterman believed American organisations had become too bureaucratic and overcentralised. Top management concentrated too exclusively on rational, top-down decision making and achieving short-term results; consequently, so they argued, companies were failing to win real commitment from their employees. The message from Peters and Waterman was that employees' commitment has to be won through treating them as valued assets.[16] In short, they believed employees will respond positively to the soft HRM approach, or, in Tom Peters' words, 'It all comes down to people.'[17]

> ## BOX 9.1
>
> ### A recipe for successful change
> Based on their experience of private and public sector organisations, Terrence Deal and Allan Kennedy formulated the following 'how-to' of successful organisational change.
>
> Position a hero in charge of the process. A strong leader must be put in place to lead the change. The selected person must have the necessary vision and tenacity to take the process through to completion and be someone whom employees will come to see as a hero.
>
> Recognise a threat from outside. Strong-minded individuals won't be enough unless they can point to circumstances that show the need for change. The external business environment can have a strong influence on how far employees are prepared to accept change. The threat of competition and factors in the external environment must be communicated to motivate cultural change and persuade people to leave old customs and practices behind.
>
> Make transition rituals the pivotal elements of change. Often, the culture change is a radical departure from old ways of doing things and people need time to 'mourn' the loss of the old and learn to appreciate the new. This period of transition is necessary and should not be ignored. Transitions should be facilitated by the organisation.
>
> Provide transition training in new values and behaviour. The company must provide opportunities for training and acculturation to the new set of values normally involving changes in attitudes and behaviours. Often, to mark the inception of the new culture, different language and symbols used for communication within the organisation are encouraged.
>
> It is vital that organisational change be led by members of the organisation; otherwise employees will question the extent of management commitment. However, it is common for consulting firms to assist with diagnosing, planning, and facilitating change. Deal and Kennedy recommend the use of outsiders, using the colourful phrase 'Bring in outside shamans'. They can add valuable experience gained from working on analogous programs with other companies; in addition, they bring an outside perspective and help to give more objectivity to what are often emotionally charged events.
>
> Major programs usually involve changes in organisational structure. Change to the structure leads to new formal systems and changed procedures, redistributes power within the organisation, and reinforces new ways of working. Using the language of cultural change, Deal and Kennedy recommend that organisations 'build tangible symbols of the new directions'. Naturally, when such changes involve job loss, employees worry about their security. Too much angst and anxiety and a lack of trust can lower morale and productivity in the company.[50] Therefore, they argue,

the 'people side' of the change process must be paid adequate attention if it is to be successful over the long term. Insist, Deal and Kennedy say, on the importance of security in transition. This requires making what are perceived to be reasonable or even generous redundancy settlements. It involves re-establishing a sense of security through clearly communicated plans and redundancy programs, primarily through top manager's remaining true to their word so that employees know where they stand and can then plan accordingly. The organisation needs to make sure that it pays good attention to those whom it wants to retain; otherwise they will feel like 'survivors of the wreckage rather than winners of the game'.

Deal and Kennedy's book is primarily targeted at management and advises managers to exercise the management prerogative through exemplary leadership and by managing the culture of the organisation. As the authors summarise it: 'Sometimes, change is necessary and not all bad, although it is almost always risky, expensive, and time-consuming. Indeed, the difficult part of change is changing the culture. But cultures can be changed if the managers who would change them are sensitive enough to the key cultural attributes—heroes, values, rituals—that must be affected if the change is to succeed.'

Source: Deal and Kennedy, *Corporate Cultures: The Rites and Rituals of Corporate Life* (1982), p. 176.

3 Frameworks of change

Frameworks of the process of change are of importance to general managers and HRM practitioners because they want to achieve results as smoothly and quickly as possible. Frameworks are equally important to academics, as they help them to understand the causes, reasons, and processes of change. This section reviews three frameworks utilised by consultants, general managers, and HR practitioners for managing change. The first, by Kurt Lewin, is fifty years old and continues to be used by some of the UK's major companies during change conferences and training events.[18]

Lewin's force field analysis

Kurt Lewin's force field analysis[19] is one of the early frameworks of change used in the management field and is still a popular tool, but it has been criticised for oversimplifying the change process, which it undoubtedly does. More complex frameworks of change are available, for example, processual analysis.[20] These other academic approaches to organisational change are well worth becoming acquainted with but are beyond the scope of this chapter, which focuses on unitarist approaches to managing change (interested readers should consult the list of further reading at the end of the chapter).

Kurt Lewin had an interest in models of change that used dynamic and topographical concepts derived from physics and mathematics (topographical concepts involve detailed description and map-like representation). He is one of the most frequently quoted people on the subject of change and his Three Steps framework of force field analysis is a normative description of people's tendency to resist change (see figure 9.1).[21] His approach assumes people naturally resist change but can be persuaded to change when the causes of their resistance are dealt with appropriately. This section concentrates primarily on the individual factors leading to resistance to change; however, the broader structural and political factors are just as important and should be identified in addition to analysing organisational change using the force field approach.

Lewin's framework portrays change as a dynamic process in which individuals have to progress through three stages: unfreezing, which means recognising the need for change; changing, which means overcoming and reducing the 'forces of resistance' and utilising and strengthening 'driving forces'; and refreezing, which means habituating the change (see figure 9.2).

The application of Lewin's force field theory to management practice is simpler than his original academic psychological research[22] and incorporates more recent concepts from psychology on individual change. These and other ideas from the management literature are now discussed in the remainder of this section. The Three Steps approach argues that the change process naturally involves dealing with people's resistance. We all develop habits in our daily tasks and sometimes these behaviour patterns interfere with our recognising the need for change. Once the individual shows a readiness to alter his or her behaviour or at least has acknowledged the need for change, the change agent (i.e. the person or group pushing for the change) can assist the process of change in two main ways: first, by overcoming and reducing the forces of resistance and, second, by strengthening the driving forces. The change will be all the easier to implement where it involves a definition of the employees' role that is consistent with social, cultural, and legal expectations commonly held by the work group.[23] Generally, change programs progress more effectively when they are able to appeal to cultural values already held by the group as a means of motivating them to do things differently.

In organisations, employees will often psychologically resist change when it involves altering their work values and self-concept; for example, some professionals find marketing and administration duties unsatisfying when they take up time that could have been spent executing professional work. Many professionals in the public and in the private sector are facing increased responsibility for marketing and administration and some of them are unsure how much of their newly defined role they should accept.[24] Their reluctance to change is partly a consequence of their occupational commitment to professional work; their unwillingness to take on more duties is rarely just a case of irrational resistance.[25]

Change can increase the amount of uncertainty felt by employees and becomes problematic whenever they are unclear about what is wanted from them. Resistance to change occurs when it creates too much role incompatibility for employees.[26] For example, expecting shop-floor workers to communicate with a larger number of

MANAGING CHANGE | 215

Force Field Analysis Worksheet

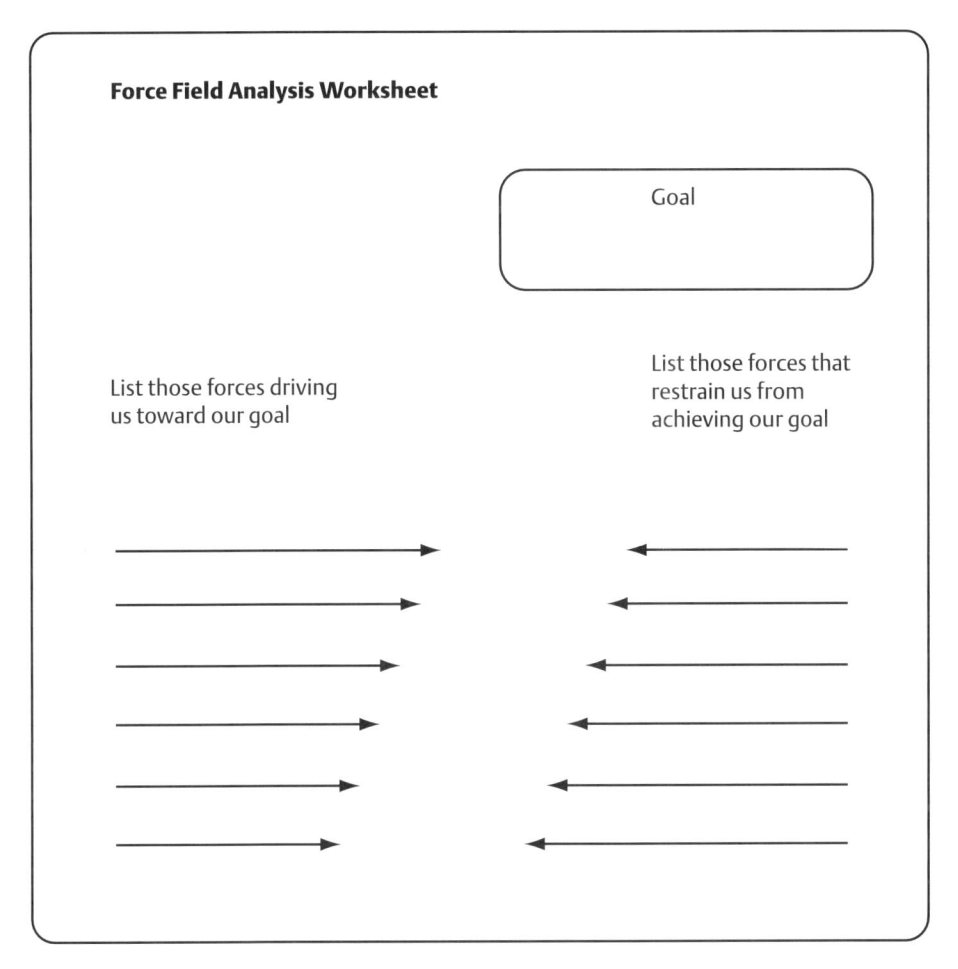

Goal

List those forces driving us toward our goal

List those forces that restrain us from achieving our goal

Figure 9.1 Force field analysis

Source: Based on Lewin, K. 'Frontiers in Group Dynamics', *Human Relations* (1947), 1, pp. 5–42, and Lewin, K., *Field Theory in Social Science* (New York: Harper, 1951).

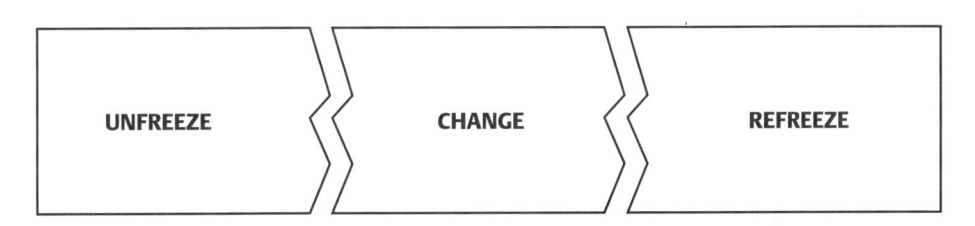

UNFREEZE → **CHANGE** → **REFREEZE**

Figure 9.2 The change process

Source: Based on Lewin, K. 'Frontiers in Group Dynamics', *Human Relations* (1947), 1, pp. 5–42, and Lewin, K., *Field Theory in Social Science* (New York: Harper, 1951).

teams and managers in the plant will mean they have to adopt a broader role set; that is, they will have to cooperate with various groups and learn to behave and respond to different expectations. Some employees will find developing a broader set of relationships at work to be a stimulating new challenge and personally fulfilling; however, others may find these new relationships to be incompatible with their more restricted concept of self, and experience increased role strain and stress.

People adopt various strategies for resolving role problems that they feel to be stressful, and some psychological coping mechanisms act as blocks to personal change. Three of the more common coping mechanisms are repression, withdrawal, and rationalisation.[27] Repression occurs when individuals force the unpleasant issue away from consciousness into the subconscious; withdrawal occurs when individuals physically or psychologically distance themselves from unpleasant circumstances (for example, absenteeism, poor participation in meetings); and rationalisation happens when individuals fabricate stories to justify actions that require explanation, substantially avoiding or altering the truth.

If the change program creates unclear role expectations, this too leads to uncertainty and resistance. Therefore, effective change agents will identify in advance any areas of potential uncertainty and make clear how people's work is to be evaluated, what the scope is for advancement and responsibility, and exactly what the new expectations are of individual employees' performance.[28] Effective change programs should take account of the fact that some people have a higher tolerance of stress than others do. The management of individual stress has become recognised as a higher priority for managers, who have seen it as a more significant employee-relations problem in the 1990s than working days lost through industrial disputes.

Marchington and Wilkinson estimate that 30–40 per cent of all sickness absence is stress-related. By 1994 the CBI and Percom survey reported that 171 million working days were lost in the UK through sickness, compared with half a million lost through industrial disputes. A study in Singapore of turnover in nursing found stress directly influenced employee departure intentions. The AWIRS (1995) survey found that 50 per cent of employees reported increased stress over the previous twelve months. A survey of 10 000 employees across a variety of industries, conducted in 1997 for the ACTU, found that the most commonly reported sources of stress were: management issues (including lack of consultation and communication), increased workload, job insecurity and lack of career opportunities, organisational change and restructuring, and inadequate staff and resources.[29]

Resistance to change also has to be seen in this light because people who are 'resistant' are not necessarily being stubborn but may be slower in having 'insight' into the situation. Resistance is sometimes portrayed by consultants and managers as the result of employee weakness, and individuals may be stereotyped and called saboteurs, shirkers, dinosaurs, ostriches, loony lefties, and so on. Such stereotyping of resistant groups of people occurs more openly in spoken dialogue and the news media than it does in textbooks, and is a means of representing resistance as both irrational and destructive to the collective good. Stereotyping can prevent the voicing of fundamental issues and ignore valid alternatives and directions for change. For example, the stereotyped groups may believe, rightly or wrongly, that they are not participating sufficiently in processes of organisational decision making that affect their lives or they may have interests and cherished values that are threatened by the change, but could be better accommodated.

Reger et al. on reframing the organisation

Recent attempts to establish Total Quality Management in US and UK companies have drawn attention to obstacles to institutionalising change (the last of Lewin's Three Steps) created by the difficulty of habituating employees to new ways of working. Reger, Gustafson, Demarie, and Mullane have written about why implementing total quality is easier said than done.[30] Reger et al. argue that fundamental change is most likely to be successful where the proposed change is aligned with people's positive beliefs about the organisation's ideal identity. If the change fits with people's idea of where they would like the organisation to be, then they are more likely to support it wholeheartedly. On the other hand, if the radical improvements threaten people's core values and they see the change as attacking what they cherish in the organisation, then they will resist it.

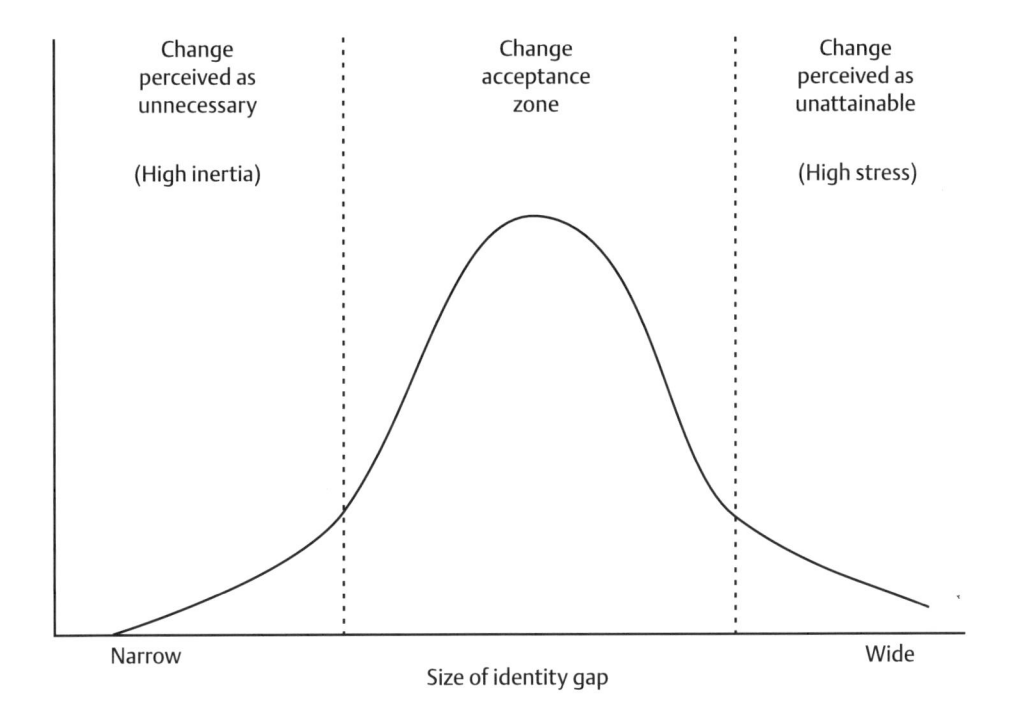

Figure 9.3 Reger et al., on reframing the organisation

Source: Reger, R. K., Gustafson, L. T., Demarie, S. M., and Mullane, J. V., 'Reframing the organisation: why implementing total quality is easier said than done', *Academy of Management Review* (1994), 19, 3, figure 3, p. 576. Republished with permission of Academy of Management. Reproduced by permission of the publisher via Copyright Clearance Center, Inc.

Managers have two options in this situation, say Reger et al.: either to change people's sense of what is ideal or to change their sense of what the current situation is. Their framework of change calls for balance. On the one hand, change must be of sufficient magnitude to overcome what is called cognitive inertia; in other words, people must consider it worth doing and not perceive it to be pointless. However, on the other hand, change must not seem so great that it offers a future that people think is overly idealistic or impossible to achieve. The art, they say, lies in getting the change to fall in between the two extremes and within what the authors call the 'change acceptance zone' (see figure 9.3).

One strength of considering the 'probability of change acceptance' is that it encourages management to plan the implementation of TQM by taking into account the likely extent of employee acceptance and resistance. A limitation is that it presents employees' acceptance of change within a framework that has an implicit preference for unilateral regulation and does not take sufficient account of the extent that TQM may, for example, be felt by employees to be benefiting large shareholders more than themselves. This occurs when TQM comes to be perceived as work intensification for no concrete reward, rather than viewed as a work philosophy for improving product and service quality in order to increase the competitiveness of the organisation.[31]

Burns on personal change

With the aim of promoting psychological well-being in the workplace, Robert Burns advises that employees, and managers especially, should learn to cope more effectively with change.[32] Burns offers a concept of change seen in terms of personal adaptation, recommending that we get to know ourselves better and develop more effective personal strategies for coping with stress. Humans, he says, generally prefer stability but nowadays everyone must become more skilled in living under rapidly changing conditions of work. Common stress factors on the job should be identified and, where possible, sources of stress reduced and proactively managed by the organisation. Burns lists the following as having the potential to cause stress:
- thwarted career development
- lack of job security
- too much or too little work/responsibility
- inability to adapt to new work practices
- boring/meaningless work
- little support from management
- lack of required skills
- inability to use existing skills
- inadequate training/reskilling
- lack of involvement in decision making
- lack of socio-emotional support/counselling

- rumours about future change
- uncertainty about the future.[33]

Ultimately, dealing with stress is the responsibility of each individual. Colleagues, friends, family, and experts can all help by offering information and emotional support. Burns advises positive self-management, including relaxation techniques to reduce tension, proper diet, exercise, sleep, and time management. It is especially important, he says, that we build our self-confidence and confront anxieties and fears by increasing our capability to remove negative and self-defeating thoughts. Burns observes that while it is not possible to predict how an individual will react to change, there is a distinct and recognisable pattern of responses known as the transition curve (see figure 9.4).

One strength of the transition curve is that it assumes positive change is attainable, but that the process of change involves negative periods during the transition when individuals commonly experience loss of confidence, grieving, and disappointment. It attempts to encourage people to be more patient and understand that fundamental learning and change are accompanied by a period of transition in which performance often deteriorates, but only temporarily. A limitation of the transition curve, in direct opposition to its strength, is that by representing change as a linear series of events it does not encourage people to reflect upon the cyclical nature of processes, nor does it effectively represent the ebb and flow of recurrent themes.

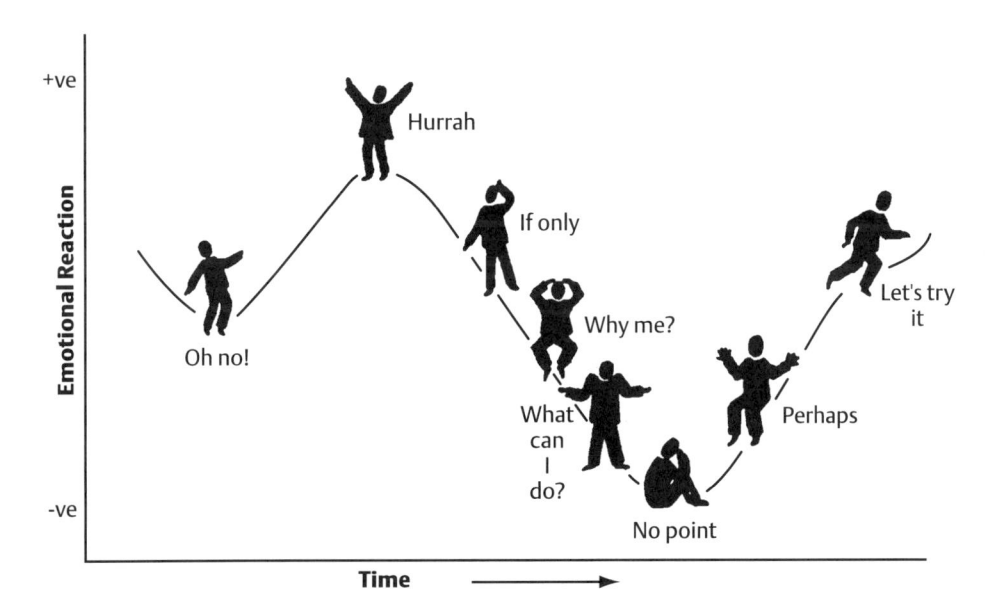

Figure 9.4 The transition curve

Source: Burns, R., *Managing People in Changing Times—Coping with Change in the Workplace—a Practical Guide* (London: Allen & Unwin, 1993), figure 1, p. 21.

4 Implementing change

We have identified the growing interest in managing change among managers and within the HR function, and have reviewed three frameworks of change. This section now turns to guidelines for implementing change.

Nadler and Tushman

Since the 1980s in the USA, the UK and Australia, many large organisations have restructured, delayered, and implemented planned change.[34] In an *Academy of Management* article on large-scale organisational change, Nadler and Tushman propose four types of organisational change: tuning, adaptation, reorientation, and re-creation (see figure 9.5). These types vary according to the scope of change (either incremental or strategic) and the relationship of the change to external events (either an anticipatory or a reactive relationship).

	Incremental	Strategic
Anticipatory	Tuning	Reorientation
Reactive	Adaptation	Re-creation

Figure 9.5 Nadler and Tushman's four types of organisational change

Source: Nadler, D. A. and Tushman, M. L., 'Organisational frame bending: principles for managing reorientation', Academy of Management, Executive Magazine (1989), vol. 3, no. 3, pp. 194–204, exhibit 2. Republished with permission of Academy of Management. Reproduced by permission of the publisher via Copyright Clearance Center, Inc.

Incremental change is a change to only one element of the organisation and is consistent with existing plans and practices—for example, changing the company pay and rewards system to adapt to new developments in the external labour market. Strategic change constitutes change that affects the whole organisation and marks a reshaping or even a breaking away from previous approaches. An example of this would be breaking out of the conceptualisation of the product-market environment within which the company has historically operated. Anticipatory change is, as the phrase suggests, change made by the organisation in anticipation of events occurring in the external environment, such as government rules being simplified and repealed to deregulate trade in an industry sector. The deregulation of the air freight business and consequent growth of operations for companies such as Federal Express is one example of this. Reactive change is simply where the organisation reacts to events in the environment—for example, a response by a major retail company to the unanticipated signalling of a price war by a key competitor.

The four types of organisational change shown in the four boxes comprise either an incremental or a strategic scope and either an anticipatory or a reactive relationship to external events. Tuning is anticipatory and incremental and as such involves the lowest intensity of 'shock' and discontinuity. According to Nadler and Tushman, it is a way of increasing efficiency and is not a response to an immediate problem. Adaptation is reactive and incremental and has the second-lowest intensity of shock. It is a response to external events but does not involve fundamental change throughout the organisation. The two strategic scopes of change have higher relative intensity, re-creation often bringing the biggest shock—because it is unanticipated and unplanned—and reorientation the second-biggest shock. Reorientation is a change made with the luxury of time afforded by having anticipated events and is described as 'frame-bending' change, whereas re-creation marks a radical departure from the past and is 'frame-breaking'.

Todd Jick

Professor Todd Jick, in a Harvard Business School teaching case study on implementing change, proposes three roles for those involved in the change: change strategists, change implementers, and change recipients.[35] The change strategists are responsible for the early work: they identify the need for change, create a vision of the desired outcome, decide what change is feasible, and choose who should sponsor and defend it. The change implementers make it happen and shape, enable, orchestrate, and facilitate successful progress. The change recipients are the institutionalisers of the change who have to adopt and adapt.

Jick offers ten 'commandments' for implementing change:
1. analyse the organisation and its need for change;
2. create a shared vision and common direction;
3. separate from the past;
4. create a sense of urgency;
5. support a strong leader role;
6. line up political sponsorship;
7. craft an implementation plan;
8. develop enabling structures;
9. communicate, involve people, and be honest;
10. reinforce and institutionalise change.[36]

When following the first commandment, 'analyse the organisation and its need for change', the change strategists, Jick recommends, should examine the forces for and against change (as in Lewin's force field analysis). He gives further advice:
- explain change plans fully;
- skilfully present plans;
- make information readily available;

- make sure plans include benefits for end users and for the corporation;
- spend extra time talking;
- ask for additional feedback from the workforce;
- start small and simple;
- arrange for a quick, positive, visible payoff;
- publicise successes.[37]

Given that this is a textbook on HRM, it is also worth drawing attention to Jick's advice for the ninth commandment, 'communicate, involve people, and be honest'. Jick recommends that employees be prepared for both positive and negative effects of change.[38] This should be done by encouraging dialogue between management and employees. The employee preparation should:

- be brief and concise;
- describe where the organisation is now, where it needs to go, and how it will get to the desired state;
- identify who will implement and who will be affected by the change;
- address timing and pacing issues regarding implementation;
- explain the change's success criteria, the intended evaluation procedures, and the related rewards;
- identify key things that will not be changing;
- predict some of the negative aspects that targets should anticipate;
- convey the sponsors' commitment to the change;
- explain how people will be kept informed throughout the change process;
- be presented in such a manner that it capitalises on the diversity of the communication styles of the audience.

The aspiration of the above list is illustrated by the following quotation from a well-known practitioner of change, Jack Welch, CEO of General Electric: 'The best companies now know, without a doubt, where productivity—real and limitless productivity—comes from. It comes from challenged, empowered, excited, rewarded teams of people. It comes from engaging every single mind in the organization, making everyone part of the action, and allowing everyone to have a voice—a role—in the success of the enterprise. Doing so raises productivity not incrementally, but by multiples.'[39]

Change, then, needs to be managed if organisations are to survive and prosper over time.[40] Arguably, it is only by winning and nurturing the commitment of employees that change will be sustained in organisations. Managers and employees act within an organisational structure and culture that they inherit, work with, and re-create. Some will re-create their organisation anew; others will replicate it as before.

5 The role of the HR function

Both hard and soft versions of HRM theoretically portray human resources as potentially valuable strategic assets, and since the first HRM texts of the 1980s, new theories have been proposed on how to develop human potential and obtain competitive advantage through human resources.[41] In practice, as this book repeatedly emphasises, Australian, US and UK companies have been more influenced by short-term considerations than have Japanese companies, traditionally known for their long-term vision. Paradoxically, though, since the late 1990s, it is the Japanese multinational companies that are being eclipsed by US companies as 'trend-setters' in progressive HRM and in the contingent response to the environment that leads to superior performance.[42] In-depth studies of working conditions in Japanese-owned companies operating in the UK have found positive responses to Japanese management practices from some employees, but the balance of the recent evidence has been that workers are concerned about the consequence of these practices in relation to health and safety, intensity of work, understaffing, and rigidly standardised jobs. Interestingly, all of the Japanese car manufacturers operating in the UK now recognise a union; Honda was the last with workers voting in 2001 in favour of recognition for the Amalgamated Engineering and Electrical Union (AEEU).[43] However, this is not to say that companies from other countries are able to transfer their HRM practices across cultures completely. For example, a study of Dundee NCR (Scotland) found that recruitment, training, pay, benefits, and pensions followed US parent company policy but other areas of HR policy and practice were adapted to suit the local environment. Differences in tax laws and national legislation also can restrict the degree of uniformity of HR policies. For example, Enron employees in the USA lost their pension schemes, which were largely tied up in Enron company shares, but the situation was less severe for UK employees where pension schemes are permitted to invest only up to 5 per cent in shares.[44]

Marchington and Wilkinson observe that responsibility for HRM[45] has over recent years been split up and handed to a wider range of people outside the traditional personnel department. In 2002 there are more consultants than were available to senior and line managers twenty years earlier. There are more large, multidisciplinary firms, notably management consultancies and the consultancy arms of the major accountancy practices, specialist HR consultancies, independent consultants, academics, and professional groups and associations such as the Australian Human Resources Institute, Australian Chamber of Commerce and Industry, and the Australian Institute of Management—all with interests in advising on HRM. Companies are now more willing to pay for consultancy services, and one important consequence of the greater availability of expertise is the need for employed practitioners of personnel management and HR to be able to compete against external providers. Partial outsourcing of HR in global organisations through the creation of shared services centres is becoming more commonplace. Standard Chartered Bank recently established such a centre for transactional HR information: resistance to its implementation was apparently least in Singapore, then Hong Kong, and greatest in London. If the trend continues, in-house HR practitioners will have to become more capable of winning competitive tenders and develop their skills in quantifying the business benefits of their activities. They will also more often have to prove themselves skilled in understanding, assessing and motivating employees, in comparison with alternative HR providers.[46] They need to be more effective in persuading top management of their understanding of the business and, in general, improve their credibility with line management.

The problem of personnel or HR function credibility is not new,[47] but some academics who have researched HRM for over ten years are cautiously optimistic. Tyson and Fell say that the HR function has become more split up among several groups.[48] The new HRM in organisations is more likely to consist of high-level (strategic) change agents, internal and external consultants working in partnership with line management, and basic administrators serving line management demand. They warn against making extreme predictions, whether euphoric or pessimistic, and recommend we look for new forms of capitalist organisations, featuring, for example, a changed stakeholder role for shareholders with a broader, ethical, and environmental responsibility.

Summary

This chapter reviewed the growth of interest in organisational culture and discussed three frameworks for managing change and two for implementing change. Senior and middle managers have a vital role to play in establishing the organisational culture and managing the process of change, but ultimately success relies just as much on all employees as it does on the actions of individual managers. These frameworks all have in common the assignment of more responsible and proactive behaviour, especially for management, which is in accordance with the spirit of HRM conveyed in Storey's twenty-five-point contrasting of personnel management with HRM (see chapter 1). The disadvantage of the frameworks and guidelines on managing change is that by concentrating on leadership by managers and portraying employees as passive recipients or resisters, they tend to ignore the potential of employees' contribution. Lack of opportunity to participate in decision making and low employee involvement in the organisation can damage employee morale and motivation. When opportunities for employees are not available, over time they will become less motivated and less committed to the organisation and its strategy. It is worth mentioning here that the Fourth Workplace Employee Relations Survey (1998) found that a group of HR practices—training, teamworking, supervisors trained in employee relations matters, and problem-solving groups—were statistically associated with each other, which can be construed as positive evidence for an HRM approach to employee participation and involvement in decision making. Some recent research on leadership argues strongly that leadership is less about 'wonderman' or 'wonderwoman' than it is about the ability to support others, helping them to remove barriers and work towards a joint vision.[49] Chapters 5–8 have all presented theories and proposals for effective HRM on topics partially addressed in the guidelines on managing change discussed in this chapter—for example: facilitating employability, enabling career development, improving the motivational content of work, maintaining equitable pay arrangements, ensuring supportive performance management, and fostering a culture of learning and employee development. The frameworks on change covered in this chapter were intended by their originators to be short statements of principles and thus are unable to attend in depth to many critical issues that arise during organisational change. Therefore, managers and HR practitioners who attempt to apply the frameworks and guidelines presented in this chapter without insight into their limitations run the risk of oversimplifying and underestimating a variety of factors that contribute to effective HRM during the management of change. However, one important advantage of the frameworks and literature reviewed in this chapter is that, overall, they encourage managers to assume personal responsibility and accountability for managing change; and they attach high priority to the need for managers to be clear about both the *direction* and the *process* of organisational change.

BOX 9.2

Case study—O'Keefe Centre

O'Keefe Centre was opened in 1968 to provide a varied program of entertainment events for the citizens of a large regional town. Situated in the heart of a wealthy suburban area, the centre became a focus of activity, and attracted little direct competition in the region. It had the full support of the local council, the state government, and the local people, who enjoyed its high profile as a centre for civic functions and concerts.

O'Keefe had good occupancy rates throughout the 1970s, providing a venue for pop groups and high-quality orchestras. Problems began to arise in the mid-1980s when competition intensified, occupancy rates began to drop, and the local authority became less supportive of utilising the venue and meeting the rising costs. With the introduction of compulsory competitive tendering (CCT) in the 1990s for a range of local government services, O'Keefe diversified its business. Duncan Arnold, the general manager, led the organisation into new ventures, including exhibitions, conferences, private hire, and weddings; however, little business planning or marketing was undertaken and the business was generated in an ad hoc and reactive manner.

Arnold was very aware of the deteriorating performance of O'Keefe, having managed the organisation since its heyday in the late 1970s. He was an actor by profession and a sociable man with an outgoing personality, but was nearing retirement age and did not possess the motivation or experience to turn the organisation around. O'Keefe had engaged in outsourcing for catering, cleaning, and portering services, but following the success of the in-house bid there was no substantial change in working practices or performance.

The organisation drifted during the mid-to-late 1980s and failed to adapt to change in the entertainment industry. It had diversified into a range of activities, several of which were not making a profit. The total income of the centre improved slightly during this period, but by the end of the 1980s, with high unemployment and a national recession, the organisation again fell into crisis. In the early 1990s, a review was undertaken by the director of community and leisure and it was agreed that the O'Keefe Centre had a continuing role to play in the market as a service provider, but that it must become more commercially viable.

Duncan Arnold retired in 1997. The centre had an acting general manager for two years, a new general manager, Anne Roberts, was appointed in 1999. She had had a career in the leisure and retail industries. Roberts undertook an audit of the venue and analysed its structure, operations, culture, and resources. Shortly after commencing the audit, Roberts appointed a marketing manager, Trent Shaw, who had experience in conference and exhibitions work, a professional MBA qualification, and was a member of the Australian Marketing Institute. This was the first full-time marketing manager for O'Keefe Centre and Shaw shared Roberts' enthusiasm for its business potential.

A marketing plan was developed, and the core areas of business were identified and their markets targeted and segmented. It was agreed by the senior management that O'Keefe would become a focal point for business conferences and events and that the private-hire business would be expanded.

These services were planned to generate income, a proportion being used to assist the promotion of an enhanced and competitive entertainment program. Having developed a clear vision of the way forward, Roberts acknowledged that her top-down, directive management style would be successful only in the early stages of the process of change. In fact, over an eighteen-month period, a number of management initiatives were successfully implemented, but through discussion and consultation with employees.

Following an employee conference, the first ever to be held, as well as open group discussions using a firm of local HR consultants as external facilitators, a new corporate strategy was devised and documented. The organisation was restructured into business areas and service teams. The service contract was revised and was retendered. New systems, targets, and controls were established. A new corporate identity was adopted using a local PR and advertising firm, and the first up-to-date and networked IT system was installed by the local council's outsourced IT services provider.

Income generated from two profitable education and IT conferences held during Roberts' first two years at O'Keefe Centre provided the much needed revenue for reinvestment. The IT conference was first identified by one of the junior employees as something that O'Keefe could do every bit as well as the conference organisers based in Melbourne. By offering a location near the city, well-connected with good road and rail links, Roberts and her marketing manager successfully undercut the existing conference providers. O'Keefe Centre was upgraded at a cost of $1 500 000 for refurbishment and infrastructure improvements. The building was improved to provide customers, visitors, and promoters with facilities that were modern and practical. The investment raised the profile of the venue in the minds of two important stakeholders, the local council and the local business community.

After the first eighteen months of Roberts' tenure as general manager, resistance to change was still evident among some of the employees and local councillors. A small group of senior employees still possessed a strong power base from which to influence particularly the longer-serving employees of the O'Keefe Centre. Their shared belief was that the change was temporary and could be 'sat out'. This blockage to change was tackled by holding team-building sessions outside the workplace and following them up with identification of training needs and subsequent development activity. Personal management support was given to those experiencing greatest difficulty in adapting to the new way of doing things. Some of the councillors were uncomfortable with Roberts' strategy of going down the commercial road, partly because it involved a loss of special privileges. However, in business terms, O'Keefe survived its internal differences and the local politics, returning impressive business results during the period 2000–02.

Occupancy rates rose 37 per cent, with 400 events being held each year. Market share was up by 16 per cent and costs down by 19 per cent. The budget was balanced and a profit on subsidy achieved. Since 1999, O'Keefe has consolidated the change in employee attitudes as well as behaviour, and better teamwork is evident throughout. As for the customer, market research surveys show an improvement in the centre's reputation.

Case study activities
1. Write a set of ten OHP transparencies analysing the process of change at the O'Keefe Centre in terms of the three stages of change described by Lewin (recognising the need for change, change, and habituating the change).
2. Analyse the implementation of change at the O'Keefe Centre using Todd Jick's ten commandments (discussed in section 4 of this chapter) or Kotter's eight-stage framework (see figure 9.7).

Study questions

1. Why is an understanding of the external environment and organisational culture important for achieving major organisational change?
2. Describe two different examples of excellent companies. In what respects and to what degree do their cultures differ?[51]
3. Identify a major organisational change and conduct a force field analysis by drawing up a list of the forces driving the organisation towards its goal and a list of those forces that are restraining managers from achieving their goal.
4. In what ways can individuals resist organisational change and how in your view should this resistance be managed?
5. Compare and contrast Todd Jick's ten commandments (see section 4 of this chapter) with the guidelines from either Patrick Dawson's processual approach to organisational change (figure 9.6) or Kotter's eight-stage process (figure 9.7).

1   Maintain an overview of the dynamic and long-term process of change, and appreciate that major change takes time;

2   Recognise that the transition process is unlikely to be marked by a line of continual improvement from beginning to end;

3   Be aware of and understand the context in which change takes place;

4   Ensure that change strategies are culturally sensitive and do not underestimate the strength of existing cultures;

5   Consider the value of having a champion of change;

6   Affirm that the substance of the change is fully understood;

7   Train staff in the use of new equipment, techniques or procedures;

8   Ensure senior management commitment and support;

9   Develop a committed and local management team;

10 Ensure that supervisors are part of major change programs;

11 Gain trade union support;

12 Spend time developing good employee relations;

13 Clearly communicate the intentions of change to employees;

14 Provide appropriate funding arrangements;

15 Take a total organisational approach to managing transitions.

Figure 9.6 Patrick Dawson, Organisational Change: A Processual Approach

Source: Dawson, P., *Organizational Change: A Processual Approach* (1994), chapter 10, 'Conclusion: Managing transitions in modern organizations', p. 179.

1	**Establishing a sense of urgency**
	■ Examining the market and competitive realities
	■ Identifying and discussing crises, potential crises, or major opportunities

↓

2	**Creating the guiding coalition**
	■ Putting together a group with enough power to lead the change
	■ Getting the group to work together like a team

↓

3	**Developing a vision and strategy**
	■ Creating a vision to help direct the change effort
	■ Developing strategies for achieving that vision

↓

4	**Communicating the change vision**
	■ Using every vehicle possible constantly to communicate the new vision and strategies
	■ Having the guiding coalition model the behaviour expected of employees

↓

5	**Empowering broad-based action**
	■ Getting rid of obstacles
	■ Changing systems or structures that undermine the change vision
	■ Encouraging risk taking and non-traditional ideas, activities, and actions

↓

6	**Generating short-term wins**
	■ Planning for visible improvements in performance, or 'wins'
	■ Creating those wins
	■ Visibly recognizing and rewarding people who made the wins possible

↓

7	**Consolidating gains and producing more change**
	■ Using increased credibility to change all systems, structures, and policies that don't fit together and don't fit the transformation vision
	■ Hiring, promoting, and developing people who can implement the change vision
	■ Reinvigorating the process with new projects, themes, and change agents

↓

8	**Anchoring new approaches in the culture**
	■ Creating better performance through customer- and productivity-oriented behaviour, more and better leadership, and more effective management
	■ Articulating the connections between new behaviours and organisational success
	■ Developing means to ensure leadership development and succession

Figure 9.7 The eight-stage process of creating major change

Source: Kotter, J. P., *Leading Change*, p. 21. Reprinted by permission of Harvard Business School Press. Copyright © 1996 by the President and Fellows of Harvard College.

Further reading

Dawson, P., *Organizational Change: A Processual Approach* (London: Paul Chapman Publishing Ltd, 1994).

Deal, T. E. and Kennedy, A., *Corporate Cultures: The Rites and Rituals of Corporate Life* (London: Penguin Books, 1982).

Kotter, J. P., *Leading Change* (Boston, MA: Harvard Business School Press, 1996).

Tourish, D. and Pinnington, A., 'Transformational leadership, corporate cultism and the spirituality paradigm: An unholy trinity in the workplace?', *Human Relations* (2002), 55, 2, pp. 147–72.

PART 4
Future Developments

CHAPTER 10

Conclusion

This book has investigated the meaning of human resource management and has reviewed the evidence concerning its practice. In this final chapter, we briefly review key elements of HRM and consider potential lines of development in the future.

At the beginning of the book we introduced and discussed different models of HRM. There continue to be differences of opinion on what constitutes HRM and disagreement on the extent to which it is a welcome and progressive philosophy and approach. Indeed, many of those who wrote radical critiques of personnel management and HRM in the 1980s and 1990s continue to draw attention to HRM's contradictions, and some have become more rather than less critical of its role in work, organisations, and society. To quote one example of this scepticism of the benefits of HRM: 'The unctuous rhetorical blandishments of Human Resource Management (HRM) coexist successfully with the harsh legitimations of Business Process Reengineering (BPR), while there is no inconsistency in simultaneously promoting teamwork, delayering, commitment, flexibility, loyalty, individualism, greed, empowerment and surveillance.'[1]

So HRM continues to have strong critics, but it also has its advocates. Clearly, the ethical implications of HRM and the role of business ethics must be given more consideration. On this topic, a recent survey in Australia found high levels of disagreement among HR managers on a range of ethical issues.[2] Marchington and Wilkinson suggest that one way forward for organisations is to adopt a 'best practice' model of personnel and development, but at the same time they caution against excessive optimism, noting that genuine pursuit of best practice will require people to be 'deviant innovators' rather than 'conformist innovators'.[3] These terms were originally used by Karen Legge more than twenty years ago to characterise different roles of the personnel management function.[4] If best practice HRM is to be achieved over the long term, then innovation will have to be against the grain of what is traditionally expected in organisations and it will require courage and persistence on the part of a significant group of innovators, which, in practice, seems improbable given the fact that both the HR and the personnel professional have generally been more acceptable in the conformist innovator role.[5]

Some recent research on HRM, primarily from the USA, does provide evidence for a link between coherent HR practice and superior organisational performance. As was mentioned in chapter 7, research conducted during the 1990s found that HRM policies and practices can have a significant influence on company performance. Mark Huselid's study of approximately a 1,000 firms has moved the 'HRM and performance' debate forward by uncovering empirical evidence that HRM practices have affected employee turnover, employee productivity, and corporate and financial performance.[6] Brian Becker and Barry Gerhart's review of the recent conceptual and empirical research concludes that HRM is most influential when the HR system has high internal and external fit. By internal fit, they mean that the components of HRM complement and support each other; and by external fit, that there is a consistent match with the developmental stage and strategy of the organisation and particularly operating and strategic objectives. They claim that HRM must be properly aligned if it is to solve business problems and support operational and strategic initiatives. HR managers are at a crossroads, they argue: either they take up the challenge and stimulate improved HRM, resulting in added value for their companies, or the HR function will be outsourced by disenchanted senior managers.[7] The question is whether outsourcing HRM will make the achievement of strategic goals even more difficult. Longitudinal study of organisational change in Kraft Jacob Suchard (part of the Philip Morris Corporation) found centralised rather than decentralised HRM systems to be effective.[8] More UK companies are outsourcing the HRM function: for example, Prudential Financial has outsourced its HRM in a ten-year deal worth US$700 million, and Cable and Wireless (C&W) has outsourced the bulk of its HRM as a means of reducing cost. Since HRM is not seen by many organisations as a 'core' function, its outsourcing is seen as a method of reducing administrative costs, saving time, and drawing on greater expertise from external specialists. Evidence from the USA indicates that the great majority of organisations have outsourced at least one of their HR functions (for example, recruitment, development), and in Australia HR has been identified as the corporate function that Australian organisations are most likely to outsource.[9]

Although it is apparent that there is no universal agreement on what HRM is in theory or in practice, it is clear that the models introduced in chapter 1 share some common features. First, all of the models emphasise the importance of managing labour in a 'strategic' way. That is, they stress the need to integrate the management of people with the long-term goals of the business. A second common feature among the models is that they are based on a unitarist ideology, which plays down the potential for conflict within organisations and instead stresses common interests between management and employees. Third, advocates of HRM are optimistic about the social consequences for employees, as well as for managers, of an organisation adopting HRM. In particular, they stress the opportunities that HRM offers for employees to develop their skills and contribute to decision making.

One theme of this book has been that, though there has been considerable interest in HRM among practitioners, the evidence suggests that it has not taken root in as coherent a way as might appear at first sight. Many of the practices associated with HRM—such as sophisticated recruitment and selection, performance-related pay, teamwork, and employee involvement—have undoubtedly become more widespread. Furthermore, other developments, such as the growth of training initiatives and the decline in collective representation, are consistent with a move towards HRM. However, while the significance of these developments should not be denied, the evidence does not suggest that HRM in Australia has been implemented in a strategic way. It is worthwhile also remembering that countries have had different historical backgrounds and approaches to HRM. American academic George Strauss argues that the US approach has remained more akin to personnel management and observes the term HRM was used there as early as in the 1960s, whereas it became fashionable in Australia and the UK some fifteen years later.[10]

In part, HRM in practice in Australia reflects actual tensions and contradictions within the models of HRM. For example, two practices commonly considered to be components of the HRM approach are teamwork and pay linked to individual performance. It is clear that these two practices may on occasion be in tension with one another, and an employee may be more concerned with maximising his or her own performance and contingent rewards than with meeting the complete range of goals of the team. As we have shown, particularly in chapter 2, there are also potential tensions and contradictions between HRM and its environment. National institutions and culture also affect the implementation of HRM.

Despite various initiatives on empowerment and employee involvement, many managers have been reluctant to accord genuine influence to employees in decision making, believing decision making on key issues to be the preserve of managers alone.[11] It will take more than textbooks on HRM such as this one to persuade them otherwise, and the piecemeal way that HRM has been implemented arguably owes much to the uncertainties of the environment in which organisations operate. For many firms the last twenty years have been a period of rapid technological change characterised by significant turbulence in the international economy. Intensified demands for greater international competitiveness, including cost efficiencies and more flexible workplaces, have led to major change, which has brought HRM agendas to prominence. Numerous initiatives have been pursued, delivering some benefits for managers and employees. Commentators on HRM's impact say that there are signs that HRM has attained a secure foothold, offering some important advances in areas such as resource-based competitiveness and core competences.[12] Storey warns, however, that the prospects of strategic HRM are not strong in companies organised into devolved business units where line managers are continuously subject to stringent short-term profit targets and expected to treat employees primarily as a cost.[13]

In chapter 2, we explored the contemporary environment of HRM in Australia, focusing on the impact of the range of social, economic, and political factors captured by the term 'internationalisation'. The global dominance of transnational corporations and the emergence of major trading blocs have been accompanied by pressures for privatisation and the withdrawal of government from regulation of markets. Greatly increased labour force participation by women, mainly in the service sector, and the decline of traditionally 'male' areas of employment, such as manufacturing and mining, have brought major changes to jobs and who performs them. In conjunction with the related rise of unemployment and 'irregular' or 'atypical' employment, the contemporary working environment has become characterised by uncertainty, unpredictability, and organisational change. In this context, HRM strategies have become more attractive to managers. Yet while HRM rhetoric has achieved widespread popularity, the strategic implementation of HRM in Australian organisations is less apparent.

The available evidence also suggests an orientation towards 'hard' HRM goals of cost-efficiency, numerical flexibility, and managerial prerogative, rather than 'soft' HRM goals such as commitment, motivation, training, and development. On this topic, chapter 2 went on to review the progress of training and skills formation in Australia, in relation to governmental efforts to encourage a more systematic national approach, under the Hawke Labor government's 'clever country' banner. We saw how various initiatives achieved limited success, and how the Howard coalition government has pursued a more market-oriented approach to training and development. A particular concern has been the decline—through privatisation, downsizing, and outsourcing—of the public sector, which has historically performed a leading training role in Australia. The character of the public sector has been changed to a considerable extent, with the introduction of 'new' managerial models derived mainly from the private sector and strongly influenced by HRM.

In chapter 3, we examined another intensely political area of HRM interest—industrial relations. The chapter addressed the historical development of Australia's highly distinctive industrial relations system, including such central features as industrial awards, the role of trade unions, and the concept of a 'living wage'. The chapter went on to illustrate how Australia's trade union movement has sought to forge a new identity and purpose for itself, especially during the era of the ALP–ACTU Accord. Through 'strategic unionism', the union movement has sought to contribute to national policy formation and address the problem of declining union membership. In doing so, it has adopted a more conciliatory approach to industrial relations, albeit one that still acknowledges the potential for conflict in the employer–employee relationship.

Since the late 1980s a process of decentralisation and deregulation of industrial relations has been occurring, amid demands for greater workplace flexibility and productivity. Chapter 3 charted how this process gained momentum under the Labor government, but did not lead to an abandonment of the industrial award system. The chapter concluded with discussion of the Howard government's industrial agenda, including the *Workplace Relations Act 1996*, and its most radical innovation, Australian Workplace Agreements. While acknowledging that the coalition government's industrial relations plans have been curtailed to some extent by political and industrial constraints, the chapter indicated that pressures for further decentralisation and deregulation continue. The future of trade unions will be a primary focus of debate. Both the Prime Minister, John Howard, and his Minister for Workplace Relations, Tony Abbott, stressed, in the wake of their November 2001 election victory, that industrial relations would be the government's most crucial policy area for its third term.[14]

Chapter 4 provided an overview of labour law, itself very complex, highly political, and closely related to industrial relations. Australian labour law has been characterised by the prominent roles given to unions and centralised conciliation and arbitration to settle industrial disputes. The chapter showed how the Constitution has limited the extent of Commonwealth powers in industrial relations and created overlaps between Commonwealth and state jurisdictions. We noted how labour law has become more complex, as various types of agreement, both collective and individual, have been added to the award system. Legislative changes in recent years have weakened the roles of unions and centralised conciliation and arbitration. Industrial awards have been stripped back to 'safety net' provisions, to protect the lowest-paid workers, and the Workplace Relations Act has introduced greater 'flexibility' into the employment relationship. Unitarist approaches to HRM tend to support such initiatives, since they encourage employers and employees to negotiate pay and conditions directly. Pluralist approaches to HRM are usually less sanguine, however, since they highlight the considerable power differences between individual employers and employees.

We also described the growth of women's employment, and casual and part-time jobs. In the final section of the chapter, we examined the introduction of employment equity legislation and how it has also been changed in recent years. Yet equity initiatives may be undermined by a polarisation of pay and conditions within the labour market, as a result of decentralisation and deregulation. The future of labour law, like contemporary workplaces and employment, is today characterised by greater uncertainty and unpredictability.

In chapter 5, we saw that in Australia and in many other countries there has been increased experimentation with different types of employment contract, which has influenced organisations' HR inflow, internal flow, and outflow. Further, significant growth in casual and short-term employment has placed constraints on the extent to which employees in these categories receive training and development in organisation-specific expertise. The number of casual employees in Australia has doubled over the last two decades such that more than one-quarter of employees are employed on a casual basis. Some surveys have found that this group is especially concerned about the comparatively poor promotion, social, and training opportunities available.[15] Employers continue to place emphasis on achievement of individualised employment relationships and there has been a general move towards more flexible forms of work, increasing the need for supervisors and middle managers to be skilled in many of the basics of HRM. Managers' day-to-day contact with employees contracted on a short-term basis places an onus on them to have expertise in: recruitment and selection, induction, training-needs analysis, informal coaching and development, communicating performance expectations, motivation, and managing relationships, including the final phase up to termination of employment. For some of these HR activities, external consultants and in-house HR professionals have the primary responsibility, but managers will still find themselves in frequent face-to-face contact with temporary employees. These managers' overall attitudes and behaviours may have a significant influence on relationships at work likely to impact on productivity levels and employee satisfaction. The more that employment relations become individualised, the greater the need for managers to be skilled in HRM. As was discussed at length in chapter 5, the extent of actual improvement will depend on a range of factors, including the overall receptiveness of Australian culture and organisational cultures to more professional human resource management of individual employment relationships.

During the mid-1980s, interest from employers grew in the potential contribution of competences for selecting, training, and developing employees. The competence movement has been a varied one, lasting throughout the 1990s and showing few signs of abating. At industry and occupational levels, the standards-based competence movement has specified, trialled, and implemented comprehensive 'statements of competence'. These include performance criteria and expected outcomes that demonstrate a standard of achievement. A wide range of stakeholders has been involved in developing these standards, including public servants, industry and trade union representatives, employer associations, occupational specialists, and HR professionals. At the organisational level, managers and consultants have formulated core competences identifying strategic advantages—human, financial, and physical—possessed by the organisation. Major organisational change programs have frequently been accompanied by reviews of competences leading to board-level approval of a shortlist of core competences deemed essential for survival and growth. At the individual level, work inspired by people such as Boyatzis, members of the McBer Consultancy, and Schroder, has identified personal competences thought to be associated with people of superior performance. It has led to movements such as the high performance managerial competencies approach that has been used extensively in a few of the larger corporations for employee assessment and development.[16]

In recent years, it has become more commonplace for Australian organisations to incorporate lists of competences in selection criteria and in performance appraisal documentation. Managers therefore need to develop further their understanding of competence-based approaches, and appreciate their limitations and their strengths for selection and assessment. This area has traditionally been the province of specialists, particularly occupational psychologists. It seems reasonable to predict that as Australian organisations become more sophisticated in competence-based approaches to job placement and career development, then their employees will demand more of managers, expecting them to be proficient in demonstrating, explaining, and assessing competence.

In chapter 6, it was shown how motivating individuals and motivating groups requires taking into account that all employees, regardless of status, have wide-ranging needs. This implies that managers who stereotype employees' motivations will fail to understand what drives and satisfies people. Attitude surveys and research studies on perceptions often reveal that managers are less accurate in estimating their employees' motivations and feelings than they assume.[17] In the long term, employee motivation is likely to be sustained and improved through two-way communication. Theories of motivation present a varied justification for regularly updating and reviewing HRM policies and practices. They assume that cooperative relationships between management and employees can be achieved, and this will be facilitated when employees feel that their personal circumstances of work are fair and secure. The trend towards more individualised and performance-related forms of reward therefore means that, to enhance workforce motivation, HRM must maintain a sense of distributive justice among employees.

Chapter 7 on financial rewards and performance management showed that there has been growing interest among employers in making reward structures more closely linked to market considerations and managerial judgment. Consequently, pay structures have tended in one sense to become more simplified in order to allow latitude for judgment. Pay systems, on the other hand, have become more complex and numerous when employers have sought to increase the contingent element in financial rewards through establishing systems of performance-based pay, group bonuses, team bonuses, profit sharing, and so on. The trend towards individualised pay and conditions, with the move away from industrial awards, means that Australian managers will have to become more skilled in performance-management techniques of informing, mentoring, coaching, monitoring, and appraising employee development, and ensuring achievement of goals. In coming years, their organisations will also need to implement more sophisticated technological systems for efficient administration of rewards. Human resource information systems have slowly become more popular in large corporations and a number of HR software providers now offer generic and customised systems for human resource management.[18]

In chapter 8, we reviewed several training innovations developed in the USA and the UK such as systematic training, organisational development (OD), action learning, open learning, and the learning organisation. There is evidence that open learning and technology-based training are not passing fads. They will continue to be implemented by large corporations whenever considerations of cost, geography, or individual accessibility favour them over more conventional methods. This is not to say that uptake will be extensive even when needs have been identified. An example of underutilisation of an existing technology is teleworking and telecommuting, where there is research evidence to suggest its incidence has been greatly overestimated, in Australia and elsewhere.[19] We acknowledge that traditional and innovative methods of learning and development owe their continuing viability to sufficient levels of financial and human resources. It has now become more common in Australia to focus on major private sector companies when seeking out new models of training and development since their comparative demise in public sector organisations. Universities and business schools have become more market-oriented in their provision and delivery of courses on technology and business education, for example, the Master of Business Administration (MBA). Nevertheless, the worlds of higher education and business have some way to go before they can be said to be creating a highly skilled workforce in an internationally competitive economy. Recently, the topics of knowledge management and entrepreneurship have created considerable interest among government, companies, and academia. Some of their recommendations encourage employers to consider practical and significant ways that work organisation can be improved through use of IT and other ways such as redesigning the use of space to facilitate knowledge transfer. Randall Schuler has recently emphasised the significance of both knowledge flow and learning in international joint ventures.[20] It is worthwhile pausing to note that many of the aspirations of the learning organisation are yet to be achieved, and they continue to signal some of the ways in which knowledge can be managed and entrepreneurial behaviour stimulated. Employers and HR professionals can benefit from making a careful assessment of how their employees can participate more in management decision-making, be better informed about the organisation and its competitors, and be encouraged to learn and be empowered to take reasonable risks.

In chapter 9, we concluded that managers should be clear about both the direction and the process of change. Theories of transformational change and cultural change often promote charismatic leadership qualities as being fundamental to successful change.[21] Leaders who are perceived as being charismatic and visionary have powerful means at their disposal for motivating others. People often attribute to these leaders special capacity for insight, unusual organisational ability, and strong human qualities of compassion. The downside, however, can be that some senior executives are better at promoting themselves and selling their vision than in encouraging employees to participate and share their ideas. This can lead to cynicism, as in this example from research on the management of change in an insurance company: 'If I walked out of here and got hit by a bus, they could get someone else to do this job tomorrow. Everyone's dispensable ... They wouldn't like us all to get hit by the same bus at the same time. That would be very inconvenient.'[22]

Tolerating and sharing differences between employees can be difficult, particularly when organisations are undergoing radical change. Effective transformational leadership accepts a degree of conflict in the workplace and actually sees it as an important part of the change process. Intolerant managers who routinely seek to impose conformity to one set of values and norms are less likely to motivate and inspire their workforce in the long term. In other words, we argue that employees are more than mere 'change recipients', and to treat them purely in that way is likely to damage their morale and motivation. Todd Jick's recommendation to 'communicate, involve people and be honest' encapsulates the importance of valuing people as more than simply human resources. In the complex, international environment of business, it is likely that Australian managers will in the future continue to find themselves in positions of responsibility working under conditions of economic uncertainty. They will have to take on leadership roles for achieving business targets and face difficult situations in their relationships with employees, who sometimes will be resistant to change. One of our central arguments is that managers will only get the best out of their employees when they communicate genuine concern for their active involvement and participation. The literature on culture and change frameworks discussed in chapter 9 customarily espouses both strong leadership and inclusive approaches to employees. However, in the real world of business, people can easily fall into the trap of seeing the importance of leadership while needing to be reminded of the significance of the value of participation.

What then of the future? A detailed analysis of what may happen in this century is beyond the scope of this concluding chapter, but we would like to highlight certain important issues for Australia over the next few years.

It has become a truism to state that Australia is a 'new' country with the oldest surviving civilisation in the world, an indigenous population that has lived here continuously for at least 40 000 years. It was only in the 1960s that all indigenous peoples achieved the right to vote, despite decades of campaigning, and only in 1993 was the doctrine of *terra nullius* (whereby Australia was defined as uninhabited territory prior to British occupation) finally overturned with the High Court's 'Mabo' judgment, giving the land rights movement considerable impetus.

As a modern nation, having been created in January 1901 from the amalgamation of six colonies, Australia is only just over a century old. From having been a distant outpost of the British Empire, Australia moved during the middle of the twentieth century towards identification with the USA as its most important ally. Then, since the 1970s, Australia has been oriented more towards Asia, especially in economic terms, as first Japan and then other Asian nations emerged as important trading partners. Similarly, whereas once the great majority of immigrants were from the UK, during the post-World War II period there was a considerable influx of migrants from non-English-speaking nations, particularly in southern and Eastern Europe, and subsequently from Asian nations, such as Vietnam and Taiwan. Australia today is a very different country from what it was even 30 years ago, when there was still a 'White Australia' policy, the notion of multiculturalism was yet to emerge, and relatively few women were in the formal workforce. Today, the country is among the most socially and ethnically diverse in the world and women have made substantial, albeit still partial, advances in employment. As we have illustrated throughout this book, the field of work has been changed substantially in recent decades—to a significant extent in response to Australia's changing position in the world more generally. HRM has an important part to play in the management of diverse groups of employees, and managing diversity is likely to continue to be an important area for HR practitioners and researchers.[23]

For most of its economic history, Australia was able to rely to a considerable extent on agriculture and mining, although it has long had a significant manufacturing sector, which following Federation received quite a high level of protection from foreign competition. Since the 1970s, however, there has been a steady reduction of tariff protection and the service sector has become increasingly important to the country's economy. While Bob Hawke stated that Australia could no longer rely on being the 'lucky country' (a phrase originally used ironically by Donald Horne in the 1960s), an offhand comment by then Treasurer, Paul Keating, that the country was in danger of becoming a 'banana republic' encapsulated some of the fears that many Australians held about being left behind in the pursuit of 'international competitiveness'.

As we saw in the opening chapters of this book, the introduction of HRM techniques was in large part a response to these concerns. We have documented how the main HRM models have emerged mainly from the USA, but we have also sought to locate the implementation of HRM strategies within the context of Australia's distinctive social, political, and economic development. For example, 'internationalisation' has had impacts here that differ from those in other countries, raising certain questions about the implementation of HRM within Australian contexts. Which models are most appropriate socially, politically, and economically? How should HRM be adapted to suit Australian conditions? For example, Australia's industrial relations history of centralised wage fixing and a strong role for unions, in which concepts such as the 'living wage' and 'comparative wage justice' have been so important, may render an HRM model that assumes unrestricted managerial prerogative, the absence of unions, and relatively unregulated wages and conditions, of limited value. How do we develop strategies that are relevant to the Australia of today? Answers to these questions are beyond the scope of this book. However, we hope it has provided some resources that may be drawn upon to address them further.

Human resource management originated in the USA as a set of proposals for optimising the management of employees. Its principles and ideas spread quickly, becoming accepted by some practitioners and academics in countries such as Australia and the UK. During the 1990s, HRM was advocated more concertedly by senior managers in major corporations. David Guest has argued that HRM's strongest advocates have been believers in an American Dream of rugged individualism, a meritocratic society, equal opportunity, democratic leadership, and McGregor's (1960) Theory Y approach to management.[24] The extent to which HRM remains an attractive set of principles and practices might depend, therefore, on how far one ascribes to myths consistent with the American Dream. Guest argues that HRM has the strongest appeal for American managers and suggests that other myths may resonate more with managers from other countries. Models of social partnership between government, employers, and trade unions have been more popular and persistent in Europe than in the USA. In some Asian countries such as South Korea, which prior to democratisation in 1987 suppressed trade unions, there has been reform, and employers have had to learn to negotiate with trade unions.[25] Similarly, Australia has a complex industrial relations heritage and a history of bouts of government enthusiasm for principles of social democracy that have been influenced by countries such as Sweden. In recent years Australia has experienced three periods of Liberal–National federal government that have stimulated a move towards more *laissez-faire* economic and social policy. Indeed, the Howard government and some large corporations have been antipathetic to major involvement by trade unions in many key workplace matters.

People's attitudes towards the issues of unitarism, strategic integration, and HRM's social goals will influence which model of HRM is seen as most appropriate. This book has been written with the aim of informing the debate on the future of HRM. We hope it will play some part in encouraging employers and employees to create fairer, happier, and more successful places of work.

Glossary

affirmative action
In Australia, the term 'affirmative action' has been used specifically to refer to legislation, policies, and strategies designed to reduce gender inequities in the workforce. The most important legislation in this regard was the *Affirmative Action (Equal Employment Opportunity for Women) Act 1986*. However, the *Equal Opportunity for Women in the Workplace Act 1999* removed references to 'affirmative action' on the grounds that it had undesirable associations with quota systems.

agency
The freedom to act from choice and with individual responsibility. Agency results wherever individuals have the ability to act on their intentions. Agency is their capability to behave according to individual choice. Whenever individuals have choice over how to behave, they should assume that moral judgments may reasonably be made by others about their actions.

agency theory
Agency theory addresses how owners of capital and businesses control the management of their enterprises. The theory says that owners (principals) must control and give incentives to managers (agents) so as to ensure that agents' behaviour is consistent with the principals' interests. Agency theory has been dominant in the financial economics literature during recent years.[1]

allowable matters
The *Workplace Relations Act 1996* stipulated that, from 1 July 1998, all federal awards should be restricted to *no more than* twenty 'allowable matters'. Managerial prerogative was extended, as the employer could unilaterally assert conditions on a particular matter. These provisions have subsequently been the focus of considerable legal debate.

ambit
The claims made by the parties in industrial negotiations usually contain an element of ambit (that is, a demand well in excess of what the parties could reasonably be expected to attain), allowing the parties to reach a settlement within the range set by their initial claims.

anti-discrimination
Legislation has been introduced in federal and state jurisdictions to prevent direct and indirect discrimination on several bases, including gender, race, ethnicity, sexual preference, marital status, disability, or pregnancy. For example, federal industrial agreements and awards contain a statutory anti-discrimination clause.

arbitration
　The process whereby an industrial tribunal makes a determination designed to resolve a dispute between employer and employees (usually represented by a union). The determination must fall within the respective claims of the two parties—it can also be appealed to the Federal Court—and leads to the establishment of an industrial award. Occasionally, the tribunal may have to make judgments on disputes between different employers or between different unions.

atypical employment
　See 'irregular employment' below.

Australian Chamber of Commerce and Industry (ACCI)
　Peak employer body, based on state and local chambers of commerce and industry.

Australian Council of Trade Unions (ACTU)
　The peak body of the Australian trade union movement, which plays an important role in wage cases, union strategy, and policy formation.

Australian Industrial Relations Commission (AIRC)
　The formally independent tribunal that exercises the federal conciliation and arbitration powers established by the Constitution. The commission produces awards that set down minimum pay and conditions for specific industries. It also oversees and facilitates enterprise bargaining negotiations, deals with unfair dismissal claims, and the operations of unions and employer associations.

Australian Labor Party
　Founded in 1891, originally as the political 'wing' of the labour movement. Since then, it has been the main party on the Left of the political spectrum, although it has for many years renounced any claims to being a socialist party.

Australian Workplace Agreements (AWAs)
　Established by the *Workplace Relations Act 1996*, these are individual agreements made directly between an employer and an employee, stipulating wages and/or conditions for the job. Once they have been approved by the OEA or the AIRC (if they meet the 'no disadvantage test' or are exempted from it), AWAs replace the relevant award for the job. While employees may seek advice from 'third parties', most AWAs have been established without 'third party' (most importantly, union) involvement. Prospective employees who refuse to sign an AWA can legally be refused employment. Similar types of agreement also exist in several state jurisdictions.

behaviour modification
　Behaviour modification is concerned with changing behaviour through rewards. The original term for behaviour modification is 'operant conditioning', which comes from reinforcement theory. Robert Vecchio argues that expectancy theory of motivation and reinforcement theory are similar theories of motivation and rewards.[2]

casual employees
　There is no single, universally accepted definition of casual employees. However, they are generally seen as not having access to the entitlements received by full-time and part-time employees (such as holiday and sick pay), and as being

able to be dismissed or to leave on notice of one day or less. Casual employees usually receive a 'casual loading' to compensate for their lack of entitlements and job security.

centralisation
The degree to which the authority to make certain decisions is located at the top of the management hierarchy.[3]

certified agreement (CA)
A collective agreement regulating wages and/or conditions between an employer and a group of employees, and a union or number of unions, achieved through enterprise bargaining. To become ratified under federal law, an agreement must pass the global 'no disadvantage test', which in theory means that wages and/or conditions should not be worse than those contained in the relevant award.

collective bargaining
In Australia, unions have been the main agents for collective bargaining, which involves the negotiation of a collective agreement covering all employees in a particular occupation, industry or enterprise.

collectivism/ist
A collectivist approach is characterised by an emphasis on the needs of the group. Collectivism is the opposite of individualism. Within collectivist approaches, there are different motivational bases for working collectively.[4] See 'individualism/ist' below.

collectivist national culture
Geert Hofstede defined collectivist national cultures as comprising in-groups (relatives, clan, organisations) and out-groups. Members of the in-group expect to be looked after and, in exchange, they offer loyalty to the group. The collectivist culture exhibits some of the following features:

- In society, people are born into extended families or clans who protect them in exchange for loyalty.
- 'We' consciousness holds sway.
- Identity is based in the social system.
- There is emotional dependence of the individual on organisations and institutions.
- The involvement with organisations is moral.
- The emphasis is on belonging to organisations; membership is the ideal.
- Private life is invaded by organisations and clans to which one belongs; opinions are predetermined.
- Expertise, order, duty, and security are provided by the organisation or clan.
- Friendships are predetermined by stable social relationships, but there is a need for prestige within these relationships.
- Belief is placed in group decisions.
- Value standards differ for in-groups and out-groups (particularism).[5]

See 'individualist national culture' below.

common rule award
A common rule award, in the industrial relations context, extends to all employers and employees in an industry or occupation. Due to the constitutional

limitations of the federal conciliation and arbitration power, common rule awards are virtually impossible in the federal jurisdiction, although they are possible under state jurisdictions.

comparative wage justice

The principle of comparative wage justice (CWJ) was established through Justice Higgins' 'Harvester' judgment. Broadly, it stipulates that equivalent work should receive similar pay and conditions. Yet until recent decades, this principle was confined mainly to white, male, full-time workers. As an important concept in Australian wage fixation, the principle of comparative wage justice states that work requiring similar skills and attributes, performed in different industries, should be paid at broadly similar rates. The concept has been significant with respect to gender equity, as it has been used in efforts to ensure that work in industries in which the majority of workers are women is paid at comparable rates to work in industries in which the majority of workers are men.

compliance

In order to ensure the honouring of entitlements to wages and conditions—as contained in awards, agreements, and industrial legislation—mechanisms (such as industrial inspectorates) are designed to achieve compliance—that is, the due observance of these entitlements. However, in practice, such mechanisms are often weak and it is usually left to employees and unions to identify non-observance and to ensure that correct wages and conditions are maintained.

conciliation

The process whereby an industrial tribunal seeks to settle a dispute between parties through advice, consultation, and encouraging further negotiation.

conciliation and arbitration power

Section 51(xxxv) of the Constitution contains the conciliation and arbitration power, enabling the Commonwealth Parliament to enact legislation on industrial disputes that occur in more than one state.

configuration

The 'shape' of the organisation's role structure—for example, whether the management chain of command is long or short, whether superiors have a limited span of control (relatively few subordinates) or a broad span of control (a relatively large number of subordinates), and whether there is a large or small percentage of specialised or support personnel. 'Configuration' is a blanket term used to cover all three variables.[6]

content theories

Content theories of motivation focus on what motivates behaviour. Maslow's frequently cited hierarchy of needs is a content theory.[7] See 'process theories' below.

contingent employment

See 'irregular employment' below.

contracting out

See 'outsourcing' below.

core–periphery

Managerial strategy characteristic of the 'post-Fordist' era. The number of 'core', permanent employees is reduced to a minimum, while a 'periphery' of short-term, part-time or casual employees is used to meet the need for numerical 'flexibility'.

corporations power

Section 51(xx) of the Constitution enables the Commonwealth Parliament to make laws relating to the operation of foreign corporations, and trading and financial corporations operating within Australia. In recent years, this power has been used to regulate employment conditions.

decentralisation

The process, beginning in the late 1980s, whereby the setting of pay and conditions has been moved to a significant extent from the federal or state system of industrial awards to enterprise-level negotiations or individual bargaining. The process of industrial relations decentralisation and deregulation has also meant that pay and conditions are less circumscribed by legal prescriptions. The reduced role of the conciliation and arbitration system, as industrial awards have been reduced to 'safety net' provisions, has also meant that unions have had to change significantly.

deregulation

Usually associated with decentralisation, this is the process whereby labour law and the industrial relations system have a reduced role in regulating employment. Greater 'flexibility' is now open to employers and employees to vary pay, conditions, and entitlements—usually through 'trading off' pay, conditions, or entitlements against one another (for example, working a longer spread of hours in order to have time off for child-care commitments).

descriptive models

Descriptive models of HRM describe what HRM is, and try to reflect exactly what has happened or is happening when it is implemented. Karen Legge subdivides descriptive models of HRM into two types: descriptive-functional and descriptive-behavioural. Descriptive-functional models state what *is* rather than what *should be* the function of HRM. Descriptive-behavioural models state more precisely what are the actual behaviours of specialists and managers engaged in HRM activities.[8] See 'prescriptive models' below.

distributive justice

Distributive justice is the fairness of judgments made about an individual or individuals. It is an important concept in pay bargaining and equity theory of motivation.[9]

diversification strategy

Diversification is an organisation's expansion into new products, services, and markets. The growth is managed by dividing the company into separate business units. It has become less common for companies to grow by unrelated diversification; rather, they tend to seek diversification that exploits interrelationships between, for example, tangible similarities in product technology or intangible similarities in skills and services.[10]

dual labour market

Primarily refers to the division of jobs and industries into predominantly 'male' and 'female' areas of employment, with the latter usually having poorer pay and conditions. Segmentation also occurs with respect to race, ethnicity, and various social factors.

employee

An important definition, as employee status confers certain rights and entitlements not available to subcontractors. An employee is a person who provides labour for an employer and receives remuneration as wages, salary, commission, tips, piece rates, or payment in kind. Less scrupulous employers can use the subcontractor or self-employed status to deny that workers are employees. This tactic is used to avoid payment of appropriate rates of pay and observance of employee rights and entitlements. However, the industrial courts can recognise that a particular relationship is an employer–employee relationship, even if it purports to be otherwise.

employer

Person or organisation hiring employees in return for remuneration of some kind. Sometimes, the employment relationship is disguised through the use of contractor-type relationships, as detailed above.

enterprise bargaining (EB)

During the 1990s, enterprise bargaining was introduced to Australian industrial relations. The enterprise bargaining process requires negotiations to be conducted between an employer on one side, and a union, group of unions, or group of employees on the other, to establish pay and conditions for a stipulated period within a specific enterprise (which may cover a number of workplaces). This process leads to an enterprise bargaining agreement (or certified agreement) that is binding on both parties.

equal employment opportunity (EEO)

A set of policies and legislation designed to eliminate barriers to more equitable outcomes in the workplace. There are various equity groups who experience direct and indirect discrimination, including women, Aboriginal and Torres Strait Islander people, gay and lesbian people, and people with disabilities.

external labour market

The external labour market consists of human resources not employed directly by the organisation. It comprises different groups of employees who, according to their occupational group and the economic demand for their labour, experience different degrees of bargaining power and of the value of their labour input. Recruitment of individuals direct from the external labour market rather than development of employees in the internal labour market has been a common approach by small and medium-sized businesses. The external labour market is used by the organisation as a source of temporary employment including primary workers (such as individuals with high skills, the self-employed, and subcontractors) and secondary workers (typically individuals with low-level skills and other less essential groups). Workers in the external labour market and from the primary group may find themselves in a relatively powerful bargaining position.[11]

The more highly skilled workers may be in great demand, and may choose to remain outside of mainstream organisational life in order to maintain greater control over their own lives, as well as earn larger amounts of money for their efforts. Obviously, some of the more successful consultants would fall into this category, as would other individuals whose skills are in demand (e.g. information technology specialists).[12]

See 'internal labour market' below.

extrinsic rewards

Extrinsic rewards are rewards that do not come as an inherent part of performing the work itself. Workers perform the job in order to gain some external desired commodity. Examples of extrinsic rewards are pay, bonuses, overtime pay, paid holiday leave, membership in pension or other financial schemes, and prizes and awards. See 'intrinsic rewards' below.

Federal Court

The Federal Court (Industrial Division), established in 1977, has the responsibility to interpret awards, enforce awards and orders of the Federal Commission, and resolve problems internal to registered organisations (e.g. disputes on the conduct of union elections). Some forms of industrial dispute can be taken to the Supreme Court and to local or magistrate's courts.

flexibility

Flexibility in the workplace assumes two main forms: (1) functional, which indicates that employees are able to develop a variety of skills that make the organisation more adaptable to change; and (2) numerical, which refers to the capacity to vary on short notice the number of employees, usually through the use of casual employees or contract workers.

flexibility (psychological contract)

Psychological contracts are resistant to change. Flexibility can therefore be hard to achieve in practice whenever it means breaking with previous custom and practice.[13]

Fordism

Fordism referred initially to the process of mass production introduced in Henry Ford's automobile factories in the earlier part of the twentieth century. Used more broadly, the term refers to the post–World War II era in the developed economies of near-full employment (primarily male and full-time), steady economic growth, stability of financial institutions, and growing public expenditure.

formalisation

The degree to which instructions, procedures, etc. are written down.[14]

freedom of association

Traditionally, this term referred to the right to belong to a union without harassment, threats, or dismissal from employers, governments, or their agents. The freedom of association, enshrined in the International Labour Organisation's conventions, is seen as a basic sign of a democratic society. The *Workplace Relations Act 1996* also incorporated the idea of freedom *not* to belong to a union or employer association, in order to eliminate preference clauses in awards and agreements, or any 'compulsory unionism'.

full-time workers

People who are paid for 35 hours a week or more of work (in one or more jobs) within a particular time period.

hard HRM

Hard HRM focuses on managing human resources in line with business strategy and on treating people primarily as an economic resource:

The 'hard' model stresses HRM's focus on the crucial importance of the close integration of human resources policies, systems and activities with business strategy, on such HR systems being used 'to drive the strategic objectives of the organization', as Fombrun et al. (1987) put it ... In essence, then, the 'hard' model emphasises the 'quantitative, calculative and business strategic aspects of managing the headcount resource in as "rational" a way as for any other economic factor' (Storey, 1987). Its focus is ultimately human *resource management.*[15]

See 'soft HRM' below.

head of power

All Commonwealth legislation must be authorised by one or more constitutional 'heads of power'. With respect to industrial relations and employment, the most important head of power is the conciliation and arbitration power. However, other heads of power are sometimes used, including the public service power, the incidental power, the territories power, the trade and commerce power, and the defence power.

hygiene factors

Herzberg developed a two-factor theory of motivation from his studies of job satisfaction. Interviewees who took part in the study were asked to describe job-related events in which their satisfaction had improved or declined. The hygiene factors included job security, company policies, interpersonal relations, and working conditions. They could not motivate a worker to achieve higher levels of performance, but could create great dissatisfaction when not attended to.[16]

individualism/ist

An individualist approach is characterised by an emphasis on the needs of individuals. Individualism is the opposite of collectivism (see separate entry above). Storey and Bacon propose criteria contrasting individualism with collectivism. Where individualism is high, industrial relations will be oriented towards non-unionism, the work organisation will place high importance on autonomy, and the division of labour will be high. The employment contract will be tailored to individual terms and conditions, and rewards will be according to individual skills and performance. Job security and career planning will be low, as will individuals' identification with collective myths, symbols, and values.[17]

Karen Legge argues that 'soft' HRM is torn between promoting the contrasting ethics of individualism and collectivism.[18]

individualist national culture

Geert Hofstede defined national individualist cultures as comprising a loosely knit social framework. People are expected to take care of themselves and their immediate family members. The individualist culture exhibits some of the following features:
- In society, everybody is supposed to take care of himself/herself and his/her immediate family.
- 'I' consciousness holds sway.
- Identity is based in the individual.
- There is emotional independence of the individual from organisations or institutions.
- The involvement with organisations is calculative.
- The emphasis is on individual initiative and achievement; leadership is the ideal.
- Everybody has a right to a private life and opinion.
- Autonomy, variety, pleasure, and individual financial security are sought in the system.
- The need is for specific friendships.
- Belief is placed in individual decisions.
- Value standards should apply to all (universalism).[19]

See 'collectivist national culture' above.

instrumental/ist

To behave in an instrumental way is to act in order to achieve outcomes rather than doing something for the sake of it or for some higher-order purpose. To treat people instrumentally is to treat them as means to achieving ends rather than treating them as ends in themselves. Vroom's theory of motivation includes instrumentality, by which, according to Vroom, work-related outcomes have valence for individuals. Valence is an expected level of satisfaction and/or dissatisfaction. Motivation is influenced, Vroom says, by the extent to which the individual perceives that the outcomes of his or her actions will be a means to (that is, instrumental in) achieving satisfaction.[20]

internal labour market

The internal labour market consists of human resources that are employed by the organisation, in contrast to the external labour market (see separate entry above), which comprises human resources outside the organisation's employ. The value of human resources on the internal labour market depends partly on how easy they are to replace by similar labour from the external labour market. Organisations often recognise the different economic values attached to distinct occupational groups. Development of the internal labour market is evident particularly in lifetime employment systems, which have been typical of large Japanese corporations. However, even in organisations that practise lifetime employment, the internal labour market is most often segmented into different groups of employees. Primary and secondary groups of workers and different associated approaches to the management and planning of the employment relationship are evident in corporations in the East and in the West.[21]

intrinsic rewards
  Intrinsic rewards are those rewards employees gain simply by performing the work itself, such as self-esteem, pride, a sense of challenge, or enjoyment.

  Intrinsically motivated behavior is operationally defined as choice behavior which is exhibited for no apparent external reward. The psychological basis of this is in people's need to be competent and self-determining ... In other words, people behave in ways which they think allow them to feel competent and self-determining in relation to their environment.[22]

  See 'extrinsic rewards' above.

irregular (non-standard, contingent or atypical) employment
  Refers to those jobs that do not conform to the traditional, full-time model of employment. The term(s) may be used to encompass a variety of employment situations ranging from permanent, part-time work (which has a considerable degree of job security) to more peripheral or insecure employment, most notably casual work.

just-in-time (JIT)
  Just-in-time production produces goods as and when the market requires them. Its operation usually requires sustaining multiple dependency relationships between organisations, systems, and employees:

  There are a number of critical elements to JIT production. Given, that, ideally, products are produced at a rate perfectly matched to market demand, at least one of two conditions is implied if production is to be performed at the last minute. Either demand is uniform—or at least predictable—and so plans can be made in advance, or the production process itself must be inherently very responsive ...[23]

labour force
  All members of the population who are officially classified as in employment or actively seeking employment.

labour market
  The dynamic set of structures and relationships comprising jobs, potential jobs, applicants and potential applicants. There are internal labour markets, which refer to the situation within organisations or enterprises, and external labour markets, which refer to the broader situation, within regions, states or the nation.

living wage
  The concept, initially devised by Justice Higgins, that all (at the time, male) employees were entitled to wages that gave them a life of 'frugal comfort'. The concept of 'living wage' is still used in campaigns by unions and the ACTU.

log of claims
  A set of demands on pay and conditions served usually by a union upon an employer or employer association. If the employer (the respondent) rejects the log of claims, an industrial dispute has begun.

managerialism/ist
An approach to the planning, organisation, control, and administration of work that gives the concerns and interests of managers priority to such an extent that it sometimes will exclude legitimate issues facing other stakeholders. HRM is said to be more managerialist than personnel management because it emphasises the role of managers over and above the role of personnel or HR specialists. Barbara Townley distinguishes HRM from personnel management on the basis of the former being more managerialist than the latter:

A primary distinction is the separation of planning or directive roles ('human resource management') from an essentially secondary information control function ('personnel management or administration'). The latter is regarded as an aid for management designed to enhance rational decision-making. HRM is promoted as a central organizational concern, associated with a long-term perspective, and strategic integration with business planning. Emphasis is placed on the role of employees as a valued resource, an ethos informing organizational culture and corporate goals. HRM stresses coherence in employee relations policies to ensure a strategic response for competitive advantage. Much more managerialist in focus, HRM is an area of senior management responsibility and line management implementation. HRM is now very closely tied with the strategic management and leadership literature, and from this adopts the themes of the importance of planning and the imposition of control over change in an era of uncertainty ... [24]

managerial prerogative
The presumed 'right' of employers to control 'their' workforces (for example, to hire and fire) as they see fit.

matrix management
Matrix management is based on a structure that involves dual lines of authority combining functional and product organisation.[25]

motivator/motivating factors
Herzberg developed a two-factor theory of motivation from his studies of job satisfaction. Interviewees who took part in the study were asked to describe job-related events in which their satisfaction had improved or declined. Work satisfaction seemed to improve according to the content of the job:

The satisfiers usually pertained to the content of the job and included such factors as career advancement, recognition, sense of responsibility, and feelings of achievement.[26]

mutual obligation
A notion introduced by the Howard government, largely associated with its 'Work for the Dole' scheme. 'Mutual obligation' refers to the idea that recipients of government welfare should meet certain legal obligations, in return for the provision of social welfare benefits and access to training or education.

need theories
Need-satisfaction models of motivation assume that people have basic, stable, relatively unchanging needs that must be attended to and managed in the

workplace. This assumption is helpful only in situations where individuals' needs are stable.[27]

'no disadvantage' test

A test to be applied to collective and individual agreements by the OEA or the AIRC: agreements should not disadvantage employees in relation to the relevant award. The 'no disadvantage' test, however, is a 'global', not a line-by-line test. Therefore, agreements can provide poorer pay and conditions if the OEA or AIRC decides they offer some 'trade-off' (such as hours flexibility). Also, an agreement may be ratified even if it fails the test, but a 'public interest' can be identified (for example, enabling a company to trade out of temporary difficulties through payment of lower wages).

non-standard employment

See 'irregular employment'.

normative

Normative approaches reflect or establish standard ways of behaving. These values or norms set expectations for individuals and groups. Models of 'hard' HRM by Fombrun, Tichy, and Devanna (1984) and 'soft' HRM by Beer, Spector, Lawrence, Quinn Mills, and Walton (1984), and by Guest (1997) are all examples of normative models.[28]

Office of the Employment Advocate (OEA)

Established under the *Workplace Relations Act 1996*, the role of the OEA is to oversee and ratify AWAs, to provide advice and assistance to employers and employees, and to publicise the supposed benefits of individual and enterprise agreements.

organisational behaviour

Stephen Robbins defines organisational behaviour (OB) in the following way:

Organizational behavior ... is a field of study that investigates the impact that individuals, groups, and structure have on behavior within organizations for the purpose of applying such knowledge toward improving an organization's effectiveness. That's a lot of words, so let's break it down.

Organizational behavior is a field of study. That statement means that it is a distinct area of expertise with a common body of knowledge. What does it study? It studies three determinants of behavior in organizations: individuals, groups, and structure. In addition, OB applies the knowledge gained about individuals, groups, and the effect of structure on behavior in order to make organizations work more effectively.

To sum up our definition, OB is concerned with the study of what people do in an organization and how that behavior affects the performance of the organization. And because OB is specifically concerned with employment-related situations, you should not be surprised to find that it emphasises behavior as related to jobs, work, absenteeism, employment turnover, productivity, human performance, and management.

There is increasing agreement as to the components or topics that constitute the subject area of OB. Although there is still considerable debate as to the relative importance of each, there appears to be general agreement that OB includes the core topics of motivation, leader behavior and power, interpersonal communication, group structure and processes, learning, attitude development and perception, change processes, conflict, work design, and work stress.[29]

organisation development (OD)
OD is the name given to planned change interventions that are intended to improve organisational effectiveness and employee well-being:

This improvement to the way an organisation functions is carried out with the help of a 'change agent' (internal or external consultant) who assists the organisation in defining a given problem, gathering data, discussing the implications of the data, and recommending action. Interventions may focus on the interpersonal behaviour of individuals, groups and/or wider structural and technical improvements …[30]

outsourcing (contracting out)
As many public and private sector organisations have engaged in extensive downsizing, in order to concentrate on their 'core' businesses, so they have looked to external contractors to carry out 'non-core' functions. Questions have been raised about the benefits of outsourcing or contracting out—for example, in the airline industry, where potential safety problems have been identified.

part-time employees
Employees who typically work fewer than 35 hours in a week, although the number of hours is usually much fewer.

pluralist
Pluralist perspectives assume organisations are composed of coalitions of interest groups that possess potential for conflict.[31] See 'unitarist/unitary' below.

post-Fordism
'Post-Fordism' is a term broadly used to refer to strategies designed to achieve greater 'flexibility' (both functional and numerical) in workplace organisation.

power distance
Power distance is the extent to which power is distributed unevenly among members of a group or organisation. Some national cultures accept large power distance while others value small power distance.

small power distance
- Inequality in society should be minimised.
- All people should be interdependent.
- Hierarchy means an inequality of roles, established for convenience.
- Superiors consider subordinates to be 'people like me'.
- Subordinates consider superiors to be 'people like me'.
- Superiors are accessible.
- The use of power should be legitimate and is subject to judgment as to whether it is good or evil.
- All should have equal rights.
- Those in power should try to look less powerful than they are.
- The system is to blame.
- The way to change a social system is to redistribute power.
- People at various power levels feel less threatened and more prepared to trust people.

- Latent harmony exists between the powerful and the powerless.
- Cooperation among the powerless can be based on solidarity.

large power distance
- There should be an order of inequality in this world in which everybody has a rightful place; high and low are protected by this order.
- A few people should be independent; most should be dependent.
- Hierarchy means existential inequality.
- Superiors consider subordinates to be a different kind of people.
- Subordinates consider superiors as a different kind of people.
- Superiors are inaccessible.
- Power is a basic fact of society that antedates good or evil. Its legitimacy is irrelevant.
- Power-holders are entitled to privileges.
- Those in power should try to look as powerful as possible.
- The underdog is to blame.
- The way to change a social system is to dethrone those in power.
- Other people are a potential threat to one's power and can rarely be trusted.
- Latent conflict exists between the powerful and the powerless.
- Cooperation among the powerless is difficult to attain because of their low-faith-in-people norm.[32]

prescriptive models
Prescriptive models of HRM are designed to authoritatively impose on others what should be the case and what should be done. Prescriptive research-based models make hypothetical claims that if certain pre-conditions are met then outcomes that are specified within the model will be achieved. The advantage of prescriptive models of HRM according to some researchers is that they are more open to scientific test than are descriptive or critical models. David Guest's model of HRM is prescriptive and proposes that when policies and practices are established in a way that is consistent with the model and integrated with the business strategy, this will lead to desirable outcomes for HRM, people, and the organisation.[33] See 'descriptive models' above.

process theories
Process theories of motivation concentrate on how rewards control behaviour. These theories focus on the dynamics, or process aspects, of work motivation. Expectancy, equity, reinforcement, and social learning theories are examples of process theories.[34]

See 'content theories' above.

relational
A relational contract of employment is one that is long term, such as those associated with lifetime employment systems and clan-based organisations. More permanent contracts of employment are predicted by Williamson to be preferable where there is high uncertainty in terms of monitoring productivity and quality, high frequency of exchange, and asset specificity.[35]

respondent
The recipient of a log of claims, usually the employer or employer association. To be covered by an industrial award, an employer (or an employer association to which the employer belongs) must be named in the award document.

roping-in award
 The AIRC can extend the coverage of an existing award by extending it to include other employers as respondents ('roping in').

safety net review
 The *Workplace Relations Act 1996* stipulates that the AIRC has to ensure that awards provide a 'safety net' of minimum pay and conditions. This is done through safety net reviews, initiated usually by the ACTU making a case for a wage increase due to changes in social and economic conditions.

social learning theory
 Social learning theories of motivation link social expectations, behaviour, and rewards:[36]

 People develop expectations about their capacity to behave in certain ways and the probability that their behavior will result in rewards. When a person meets a standard of behavior, that person rewards himself or herself with increased personal satisfaction and enhanced self-image.[37]

soft HRM
 Soft HRM focuses on developing employees' skills and achieving employee commitment and trust:

 In contrast [to hard HRM; see separate entry above], the soft 'developmental humanism' model, while still emphasising the importance of integrating HR policies with business objectives, sees this as involving treating employees as valued assets, a source of competitive advantage through their commitment, adaptability and high quality (of skills, performance and so on) ... Employees are proactive rather than passive inputs into productive processes; they are capable of 'development', worthy of 'trust' and 'collaboration', to be achieved through 'participation' and 'informed choice' ... The stress is therefore on generating commitment via 'communication, motivation and leadership' ... If employees' commitment will yield 'better economic performance', it is also sought as a route to 'greater human development' ... In this model, then, the focus is on HR policies to deliver 'resourceful' humans ... on *human resource* management.[38]

specialisation
 The degree to which an organisation's activities are divided into specialised roles.[39]

standardisation
 The degree to which an organisation lays down standard rules and procedures.[40]

strategic business units (SBUs)
 Individual units within an organisation, each emphasising a key competitive area of business. The organisational structure comprises businesses defined according to key points of competitive leverage.[41]

total quality control (TQC)
 A quality assurance system in which quality is considered the responsibility of all employees in the organisation. Products and services are planned and produced in response to customer requirements by using integrated, efficient work systems:

... [T]he total quality concept (also referred to as company-wide quality control) is frequently assumed to be Japanese in origin. In fact, the idea may be traced to an American, J. M. Juran, a specialist in quality control who was invited to Japan in 1954 by a branch of JUSE (the Japanese Union of Scientists and Engineers). Juran's philosophy was that quality control should be conducted as an integral part of management control, in contrast with the traditional situation in which responsibility for product quality was vested in the hands of a quality control department, which acted as a 'policeman' to production. Between 1955 and 1960, these ideas spawned the company-wide quality control movement ...[42]

total quality management (TQM)

Total quality management aims to ensure quality for the customer through the rigorous application of principles and practices of quality management. TQM must be part of the organisational culture and have a fundamental influence on human resource management policies if it is to be effective. TQM, therefore, has implications for how human resources are organised and managed.

Interestingly, some of the most advanced philosophies of quality management (such as TQM) tend to focus, like HRM, as much if not more on the quality of managers and managerial performance as on that of non-management employees ... They are also strongly associated with the redesign of organisation structures, 'delayering' of extended management hierarchies and a redefinition of middle and junior management roles.[43]

transactional

A transactional relationship is one focused on a short-term exchange between two parties. Transaction cost economists are interested in how contracts can maximise efficiency. A market-based contract is transactional and fixed-term. In recent years employers have experimented more with transactional contracts of employment.[44]

transnational corporation

In this text, we use the term 'transnational corporation' (TNC) to refer to major corporations that operate across several countries. The term 'multinational corporation' (MNC) is also often used to refer to these corporations. The use of 'MNC' suggests that these corporations have multiple locations with no centre, whereas the use of 'TNC', as used in publications of the United Nations, among others, suggests that these corporations have a centre in their home country but have operations in other (host) countries.

unitarist/unitary

Unitarist perspectives assume an identity of interest between management and employees:

In contrast [to the pluralist perspective; see separate entry above], the unitary perspective asserts that top management presides over a unified authority and loyalty structure based on the common interests and values shared by all members of the organisation. There is thus no rational basis for conflict between management and employees, and trade union organisation is viewed as unnecessary or illegitimate. It follows that conflictual industrial relations can be explained only by past or present management failings, such as poor communications, or by the actions of irrational or subversive trade unions in exploiting them. In the latter circumstances, the reassertion of management prerogative would be justified through the imposition of economic or legal sanctions on unions.[45]

Notes

1. Hill, C. W. L. and Jones, T. M., 'Stakeholder–Agency Theory', *Journal of Management Studies* (1992), 29, 2, March, pp. 131–54.
2. Vecchio, R. P., *Organizational Behavior*, 3rd edn (Fort Worth, TX: Dryden Press, 1995).
3. Pugh, D. S., 'The Measurement of Organization Structures: Does Context Determine Form?', in D. S. Pugh (ed.), *Organization Theory: Selected Readings*, 3rd edn (London: Penguin Books, 1990), p. 46.
4. Eby, L. T. and Dobbins, G. H., 'Collectivistic Orientation in Teams: An Individual and Group-Level Analysis', *Journal of Organizational Behavior* (1997), vol. 18, p. 277.
5. Hofstede, G., 'Motivation, Leadership and Organization: Do American Theories Apply Abroad?', *Organizational Dynamics* (1980), Summer, p. 48.
6. Pugh, 'The Measurement of Organization Structures', p. 46.
7. Maslow, A. H., 'A Theory of Human Motivation', *Psychological Review* (1943), 50, pp. 370–96.
8. Legge, K., *Human Resource Management: Rhetorics and Realities* (Basingstoke: Macmillan Business, 1995), pp. 4–6.
9. Vecchio, R. P., *Organizational Behavior*, p. 201.
10. Porter, M., *Competitive Advantage: Creating and Sustaining Superior Performance* (New York: Macmillan, Free Press, 1985), p. 378.
11. Loveridge, R. and Mok, A., *Theories of Labour Market Segmentation: A Critique* (The Hague: Martinus Nijhoff, 1979), p. 123.
12. Marchington, M. and Wilkinson, A., *Core Personnel and Development* (London: Institute of Personnel and Development, 1996), p. 29.
13. Gomez-Mejia, L. R., Balkin, D. B., and Cardy, R., *Managing Human Resources* (Englewood Cliffs, NJ: Prentice-Hall, 1995), p. 396.
14. Pugh, 'The Measurement of Organization Structures', p. 46.
15. Legge, K., 'HRM: Rhetoric, Reality and Hidden Agendas', in J. Storey (ed.), *Human Resource Management: A Critical Text* (London: Routledge, 1995), pp. 34–5.
16. Vecchio, R. P., *Organizational Behavior*, p. 191.
17. Storey, J. and Bacon, N., with J. Edmonds and P. Wyatt, 'The "New Agenda" and Human Resource Management: A Roundtable Discussion with John Edmonds', *Human Resource Management Journal* (1993), 4, 1, pp. 63–70.
18. Legge, *Human Resource Management* (1995), pp. 130–1.
19. Hofstede, 'Motivation, Leadership and Organization', p. 48.
20. Vroom, V. H. and Deci, E. L. (eds), *Management and Motivation*, 2nd edn (London: Penguin Books, 1992), p. 92.
21. Bratton, J. and Gold, J., *Human Resource Management: Theory and Practice* (Basingstoke: Macmillan, 1994), pp. 133–4.
22. Shapira, Z., 'Expectancy Determinants of Intrinsically Motivated Behavior', abridged from the *Journal of Personality and Social Psychology* (1976), vol. 34, pp. 235–44, in V. H. Vroom and E. L. Deci (eds), *Management and Motivation*, 2nd edn (London: Penguin Books, 1992), p. 106.
23. Oliver, N. and Wilkinson, B., *The Japanization of British Industry*, 2nd edn (Oxford: Blackwell, 1992), pp. 25–6.
24. Townley, B., *Reframing Human Resource Management: Power, Ethics and the Subject at Work* (London: Sage, 1994), pp. 14–15.
25. Robbins, S. P., *Organizational Behavior: Concepts, Controversies, Applications*, 8th edn (Upper Saddle River, NJ: Prentice-Hall, 1998), pp. 490–1.
26. Vecchio, *Organizational Behavior* (1995), p. 191.

27 Salancik, G. R. and Pfeffer, J., 'An Examination of Need-Satisfaction Models of Job Attitudes', abridged from G. R. Salancik and J. Pfeffer, 'An Examination of Need-Satisfaction Models of Job Attitudes', *Administrative Science Quarterly* (1977), 22, pp. 427-56, in V. H. Vroom and E. L. Deci (eds), *Management and Motivation*, 2nd edn (London: Penguin Books, 1992), p. 206.
28 Legge, K. *Human Resource Management* (1995), pp. 64-5.
29 Robbins, *Organizational Behavior*, pp. 7-9.
30 Inns, D., 'Organisation Development as a Journey', in C. Oswick and D. Grant (eds), *Organisation Development: Metaphorical Explorations* (London: Pitman Publishing 1996), pp. 21-2.
31 Clark, J. and Winchester, D., 'Management and Trade Unions', in K. Sisson (ed.), *Personnel Management: A Comprehensive Guide to Theory & Practice in Britain* (1994), p. 695.
32 Hofstede, 'Motivation, Leadership and Organization', p. 46.
33 Guest, D. E., 'Human Resource Management and Industrial Relations', *Journal of Management Studies* (1987), 24, 5, pp. 503-21.
34 Vecchio, *Organizational Behavior*, p. 204.
35 Williamson, O. E., *Markets and Hierarchies: Analysis and Anti-trust Implications* (New York: Free Press, 1975).
36 Bandura, A., 'Self-Efficacy: Toward a Unifying Theory of Behavioral Change', *Psychological Review* (1977), vol. 84, pp. 191-215, in V. H. Vroom and E. L. Deci (eds), *Management and Motivation*, 2nd edn (London: Penguin Books, 1992), pp. 78-89.
37 Vecchio, *Organizational Behavior*, p. 207.
38 Legge, 'HRM: Rhetoric, Reality and Hidden Agendas' (1995), p. 35.
39 Pugh, 'The Measurement of Organization Structures', p. 46.
40 Pugh, 'The Measurement of Organization Structures', p. 46.
41 Goold, M. and Campbell, A., *Strategies and Styles: The Role of the Centre in Managing Diversified Corporations* (Oxford: Blackwell Business, 1987), p. 180.
42 Oliver, N. and Wilkinson, B., *The Japanization of British Industry*, pp. 20-1.
43 Clark, J., 'Personnel Management, Human Resource Management and Technical Change', in J. Clark (ed.), *Human Resource Management and Technical Change* (London: Sage, 1993), p. 5.
44 Guest, D. E., 'Beyond HRM: Commitment and the Contract Culture', in P. Sparrow and M. Marchington (eds), *Human Resource Management: The New Agenda* (1998), pp. 31-57.
45 Clark and Winchester, 'Management and Trade Unions', pp. 695-6.

Notes

1 What is HRM?

1. Beer, M., Spector, B., Lawrence, P. R., Quinn Mills, D., and Walton, R. E., *Managing Human Assets* (New York: Free Press, 1984); Beer, M. and Spector, B., 'Corporate wide transformations in human resource management', in R. E. Walton and P. R. Lawrence (eds), *Human Resource Management—Trends and Challenges* (Boston: Harvard Business School Press, 1985). It should be noted that the term 'soft HRM' was coined by John Storey in 1988.
2. Guest, D. E., 'Human Resource Management and Industrial Relations', *Journal of Management Studies* (1987), 24, 5, pp. 503–21. Truss et al. (1997) (full publication details provided in bibliography) argue that Guest's model combines hard and soft HRM, the primary hard element being strategic integration.
3. Bratton, J. and Gold, J., *Human Resource Management: Theory and Practice* (Basingstoke: Macmillan, 1994), pp. 23–6; Keenoy, T., 'HRM: Rhetoric, Reality and Contradiction', *International Journal of Human Resource Management* (1990), 1, 3, pp. 363–84; Keenoy, T., 'HRM: a case of the wolf in sheep's clothing?', *Personnel Review* (1990), 19, 2, pp. 3–9.
4. Fombrun, C. J., Tichy, N. M., and Devanna, M. A., *Strategic Human Resource Management* (New York: John Wiley & Sons, 1984).
5. Legge, K., *Human Resource Management: Rhetorics and Realities* (Basingstoke: Macmillan, 1995).
6. Storey, J., 'Developments in the management of human resources: an interim report', *Warwick Papers in International Relations* (University of Warwick, November, 1987); Storey, J., *Developments in the Management of Human Resources* (Oxford: Blackwell, 1992); Beardwell, I. and Holden, L., *Human Resource Management: A Contemporary Perspective*, 2nd edn (London: Financial Times, Pitman Publishing, 1997).
7. Devanna, M. A., Fombrun, C. J., and Tichy, N. M., 'A Framework for Strategic Human Resource Management', in C. J. Fombrun, N. M. Tichy, and M. A. Devanna (eds), *Strategic Human Resource Management* (New York: John Wiley & Sons, 1984), pp. 33–51.
8. Devanna, M. A., Fombrun, C. J., and Tichy, N. M., 'A Framework for Strategic Human Resource Management', in C. J. Fombrun, N. M. Tichy, and M. A. Devanna (eds), *Strategic Human Resource Management* (New York: John Wiley & Sons, 1984), p. 34.
9. Fombrun et al. (pp. 36–9) developed their concept of HRM through discussion of some of the well-known literature on management style, organisational structure, and strategy, notably Mayo (1933), Chandler (1962), and Galbraith and Nathanson (1978) (full publication details provided in bibliography).
10. Devanna et al., 'A Framework for Strategic Human Resource Management', p. 41.
11. Kramar, R., McGraw, P., and Schuler, R. S., *Human Resource Management in Australia*, 3rd edn (Melbourne: Addison Wesley Longman, 1997); Schuler, R. S., *Managing Human Resources*, 5th edn (Minneapolis, St Paul: West Publishing Company, 1995); Roan, A., Bramble, T., and Lafferty, G., 'Australian Workplace Agreements in practice: the "hard" and "soft" dimensions', *Journal of Industrial Relations* (2001), 43, 4, pp. 387–401.

12 Kochan, T. A., Katz, H. C., and McKersie, R. B., *The Transformation of American Industrial Relations* (New York: Basic Books, 1986; 2nd edn, New York: Cornell University Press, 1994). In the second edition, the authors argued that wide-scale change and concerted effort by business, labour, and government were more likely than they had been when they wrote the first edition.

13 Kochan, T. A., Katz, H. C., and McKersie, R. B., *The Transformation of American Industrial Relations*, 2nd edn (New York: Cornell University Press, 1994), p. 14.

14 Walton, R. E., 'From control to commitment in the workplace', *Harvard Business Review* (1985), 63, 2, pp. 77–84; Walton, R. E. 'Towards a Strategy of Eliciting Employee Commitment Based on Policies of Mutuality', in R. E. Walton and P. R. Lawrence (eds), *Human Resource Management—Trends and Challenges* (Boston: Harvard Business School Press, 1985), pp. 35–65.

15 Legge, K., 'Human Resource Management—A Critical Analysis', in J. Storey (ed.), *New Perspectives on Human Resource Management* (London: Routledge, 1989), pp. 19–40.

16 Storey, J., *Developments in the Management of Human Resources* (Oxford: Blackwell, 1992). Figure 2.2 in J. Storey (1992) was entitled 'Twenty-seven points of difference'. However, in J. Storey (1995) it was reproduced as table 1.1 'The twenty-five-item checklist'. We have adopted the later version.

17 Storey, J., *New Perspectives on Human Resource Management*, 2nd edn (London: Routledge, 1991); Storey, J., *Developments in the Management of Human Resources* (Oxford: Blackwell, 1992); Storey, J. (ed.), *Human Resource Management: A Critical Text* (London: Routledge, 1995).

18 Oliver, N. and Wilkinson, B., *The Japanization of British Industry* (Oxford: Blackwell, 1988); Oliver, N. and Wilkinson, B., *The Japanization of British Industry: New Developments in the 1990s* (Oxford: Blackwell, 1992).

19 Oliver, N. and Wilkinson, B., *The Japanization of British Industry: New Developments in the 1990s*, pp. 82–8; Ouchi, W., *Theory Z* (Reading, MA: Addison-Wesley, 1981).

20 Oliver, N. and Wilkinson, B., *The Japanization of British Industry: New Developments in the 1990s*, pp. 316–43; Pinder, C. C., 'Valence-Instrumentality-Expectancy Theory'; in V. H. Vroom, L. W. Porter, and E. E. Lawler III (eds), *Managerial Attitudes and Performance* (Homewood, IL: Irwin-Dorsey, 1968).

21 Oliver, N. and Wilkinson, B., *The Japanization of British Industry: New Developments in the 1990s*, pp. 323–5.

22 Womack, J. P., Jones, D. T., and Roos, D., *The Machine that Changed the World: The Triumph of Lean Production* (New York: Rawson, Macmillan, 1990).

23 Oliver, N. and Wilkinson, B., *The Japanization of British Industry: New Developments in the 1990s*, p. 18.

24 Wickens, P. D., *The Road to Nissan* (London: Macmillan, 1987).

25 Garrahan, P. and Stewart, P., *The Nissan Enigma: Flexibility at Work in a Local Economy* (London: Mansell, 1992); Whitehouse, G., Lafferty, G., and Boreham, P., 'From casual to permanent part-time? Non-standard employment in retail and hospitality', *Labour and Industry* (1997), 8, 2, pp. 33–48; Dabscheck, B. (1990) 'The BCA's plan to Americanise Australian Industrial Relations', *Journal of Australian Political Economy*, November, pp. 1–14.

26 Brewster, C. and Bournois, F., 'A European Perspective on Human Resource Management', *Personnel Review* (1991), 20, 6, pp. 4–13.

27 Brewster, C. and Hegewisch, A., *Policy and Practice in European Human Resource Management* (London: Routledge, 1994), p. 6; Guest, D. E., 'Human Resource Management and the American Dream', *Journal of Management Studies* (1990), 27, 4, pp. 378–97; Brewster, C., 'HRM: the European Dimension', in J. Storey (ed.), *Human Resource Management: A Critical Text* (London: Routledge, 1995), pp. 309–31; Leat, M., *Human Resource Issues of the European Union* (London: Financial Times, Pitman Publishing, 1998).

28 Brewster, C. and Hegewisch, A., *Policy and Practice in European Human Resource Management* (London: Routledge, 1994).

29 Brewster said his empirical survey found a Latin country cluster similar to that first reported by Filella (1991), p. 3 (full publication details provided in bibliography). (Brewster, C., 'HRM: The European Dimension', in J. Storey (ed.), *Human Resource Management: A Critical Text* (London: Routledge, 1995), pp. 309–31.)

30 Bournois, F., *La Gestion des Cadres en Europe (Personnel Management in Europe)* (Paris: Editions Eyrolles, 1991); Sparrow, P. R. and Hiltrop, J.-M., *European Human Resource Management Transition* (Hemel Hempstead: Prentice-Hall, 1994).

31 Storey, J. and Sisson, K., *Managing Human Resources and Industrial Relations* (Buckingham: Open University Press, 1993), p. 17.

32 Burrell, G. and Morgan, G., *Sociological Paradigms and Organizational Analysis* (London: Heinemann, 1979).

33 Legge, K., 'HRM: rhetoric, reality and hidden agendas', in J. Storey (ed.), *Human Resource Management: A Critical Text* (London: Routledge, 1995), pp. 33–59; Legge, K., *Human Resource Management: Rhetorics and Realities* (Basingstoke: Macmillan, 1995); Hope-Hailey, V., Gratton, L., McGovern, P., Stiles, P., and Truss, C., 'A Chameleon Function? HRM in the 90s', *Human Resource Management Journal* (1997), 7, 2, pp. 5–18.

34 Watson, T. J., *Management, Organization and Employment Strategy: New Directions in Theory and Practice* (London: Routledge & Kegan Paul, 1986), p. 176.

35 Keenoy, T., 'HRM: Rhetoric, Reality and Contradiction', *International Journal of Human Resource Management* (1990), 1, 3, pp. 363–84; Keenoy, T., 'HRM: A Case of the Wolf in Sheep's Clothing?', *Personnel Review* (1990), 19, 2, pp. 3–9; Keenoy, T. and Anthony, P., 'Human Resource Management: Metaphor, Meaning and Morality', in P. Blyton and P. Turnbull (eds), *Reassessing Human Resource Management* (London: Sage, 1992).

36 Legge, K., 'HRM: Rhetoric, Reality and Hidden Agendas', in J. Storey (ed.), *Human Resource Management: A Critical Text* (London: Routledge, 1995), pp. 33–59.

37 Guest, D. E., *People Management* (1998), 4, 24, 10th December, p. 14. '"The message is clear", said David Guest, professor of psychology at Birkbeck College, London, who has led research for the IPD [Institute of Personnel and Development] on the psychological contract. "We're beginning to get the kind of evidence that shows a link between investing in human resources management and improvement in the bottom line."'

2 The Environment of HRM

1 The term 'multinational corporation' (MNC) is also often used to refer to major corporations that operate across several countries. The use of 'MNC' suggests that these major corporations have multiple locations but no centre, whereas the use of 'TNC' implies that these corporations have a centre in their home country but have operations in other (host) countries. In this text, we adopt the term TNC, as used by the United Nations, since it allows us to interpret more adequately the degrees of 'transnationality' exhibited by different corporations—that is, the extent to which their investment and employment patterns are concentrated in their respective home or host countries, as summarised in tables 2.1 and 2.2. See United Nations, *World Investment Report 2001* (New York and Geneva: United Nations, 2001), pp. 89–124.

2 This is a composite index, synthesising foreign/total assets, foreign/total sales, and foreign/total employment.

3 Bryan, D., *The Chase Across the Globe: International Accumulation and the Contradictions for Nation States* (Boulder, Colorado: Westview Press, 1995); Quiggin, J., 'Globalisation, neoliberalism and inequality in Australia', *Economic and Labour Relations Review* (1999), 10, 2, pp. 240–59; Bryan, D., 'National competitiveness and the subordination of labour: an Australian policy study', *Labour and Industry* (2000), 11, 2, pp. 1–16; Gahan, P. and Harcourt, T., 'Australian labour market institutions, "deregulation" and the open economy', *Economic and Labour Relations Review* (1999), 10, 2, pp. 296–318; Bray, M. and Murray, G., 'Introduction: globalisation and labour deregulation', *Journal of Industrial Relations* (2000), 42, 2, pp. 167–72; Lansbury, R. D. and Westcott, M., 'Collective bargaining, employment and competitiveness: the case of Australia', *International Journal of Employment Studies* (2001), 9, 1, pp. 95–128.

4 Kriesler, P. and Neville, J., 'Symposium on the costs of unemployment', *Economic and Labour Relations Review* (2000), 11, 2, pp. 178–9; Watts, M. J. and Mitchell, W. F., 'The costs

of unemployment in Australia', *Economic and Labour Relations Review* (2000), 11, 2, pp. 180–97; McLelland, A., 'Effects of unemployment on the family', *Economic and Labour Relations Review* (2000), 11, 2, pp. 198–212; Hunter, B. H., 'The social costs of Indigenous unemployment', *Economic and Labour Relations Review* (2000), 11, 2, pp. 213–32; Encel, S., 'Mature age unemployment: a long-term cost to society', *Economic and Labour Relations Review* (2000), 11, 2, pp. 233–45; Burgess, J. and de Ruyter, A., 'Declining job quality in Australia: another hidden cost of unemployment', *Economic and Labour Relations Review* (2000), 11, 2, pp. 246–69; Dow, G., 'The legacy of orthodoxy: political causes of unemployment', *Economic and Labour Relations Review* (2001), vol. 12 supplement, pp. 83–98; Biddle, D. and Burgess, J., 'Youth unemployment in Australia: can mutual obligation and youth wages provide the solution?', *Economic and Labour Relations Review* (2001), vol. 12 supplement, pp. 183–99; Burgess, J., Mitchell, W., O'Brien, D., and Watts, M., 'Unemployment: promises, policies and progress', *Labour and Industry* (1998), 9, 2, pp. 103–22; Bell, S. (ed.), *The Unemployment Crisis in Australia—Which Way Out?* (Melbourne: Cambridge University Press, 2000).

5   Australian Bureau of Statistics (ABS), catalogue number 6202.0, *Labour Force Australia* (Canberra: AGPS, August 2001).

6   Department of Employment, Workplace Relations and Small Business, *Labour Market Review of Australia* (Canberra: AGPS, 2000), p. 11.

7   Australian Bureau of Statistics (ABS), catalogue number 6203.0, *Labour Force* (Canberra: AGPS, August 2001), p. 40.

8   Fordism is a term originally coined to describe Henry Ford's car factories in the 1920s, noted for their assembly-line mass production. Ford recognised the basic connection between production and consumption—if workers were paid more, they could afford to buy goods, including the vehicles that his company produced. During the period following World War II, Fordism as an overall approach to social and industrial organisation spread from North America to other developed economies, including Australia, to describe an era of regulated, full-time predominantly male employment and fairly steady economic growth that prevailed until the mid-1970s.

9   Boreham, P., Harley, B., and Lafferty, G., 'Machine gaming: a case study in service sector employment', *International Journal of Employment Studies* (1996) 4, 2, pp. 77–93; Burgess, J., 'Workforce casualisation in Australia', *International Employment Relations Review* (1996), 2, 1, pp. 35–54; Campbell, I., 'Casual employment, labour regulation and Australian trade unions', *Journal of Industrial Relations* (1996), 38, 4, pp. 571–99; Bailey, J. and Hocking, J., 'Part-time work for nurses: a case study', *International Employment Relations Review* (1997), 3, 1, pp. 1–20; Burgess, J., 'The flexible firm and the growth of non-standard employment', *Labour and Industry* (1997), 7, 3, pp. 85–102; Burgess, J., 'The flexible firm and the growth of non-standard employment', *Labour and Industry* (1997), 7, 3, pp. 85–102; Lafferty, G., Hall, R., Harley B., and Whitehouse G. (1997) 'Homeworking in Australia: an assessment of current trends', *Australian Bulletin of Labour* 23, 2, pp. 24–37; Still, L. V., 'Brave new world? Women and part-time employment: the impact on career prospects and employment relations', *International Journal of Employment Studies* (1997), 5, 1, pp. 45–66; Burgess, J. and Campbell, I., 'Casual employment in Australia: growth, characteristics, a bridge or a trap?', *Economic and Labour Relations Review* (1998), 9, 1, pp. 31–54; Hall, R., Harley, B., and Whitehouse, G., 'Contingent work and gender in Australia: evidence from the 1995 Australian Workplace Industrial Relations Survey', *Economic and Labour Relations Review* (1998), 9, 1, pp. 55–81; Mylett, T., 'Flexibility and labour market structures: the role of employers', *Economic and Labour Relations Review* (1998), 9, 2, pp. 285–309; Wooden, M. and Hawke, A., 'Factors associated with casual employment: evidence from the AWIRS', *Economic and Labour Relations Review* (1998), 9, 1, pp. 82–107; Allan, C., Brosnan, P., and Walsh, P., 'Workplaces employing homeworkers: an Australian and New Zealand comparison', *International Journal of Employment Studies* (2000), 8, 1, pp. 43–60; Campbell, I., 'The spreading net: age and gender in the process of casualisation in Australia', *Journal of Australian Political Economy* (2000), 45, pp. 68–99; Diamond, C. and Lafferty, G., 'Telework: issues for research, policy and regulation', *Labour and Industry* (2000), 11, 1, pp. 115–28; Lafferty, G. and Whitehouse, G., 'Telework in Australia: findings from a

national survey in selected industries', *Australian Bulletin of Labour* (2000), 26, 3, pp. 236–52; Buchanan, J. and Thornthwaite, L, 'Paid work and parenting: charting a new course for Australian families', ACIRRT working paper no. 71 (Sydney: ACIRRT, 2001); Campbell, I., 'Casual employees and the training deficit: exploring employer contributions and choices', *International Journal of Employment Studies* (2001), 9, 1, pp. 61–102; Lowry, D., 'The casual management of casual work: casual workers' perceptions of HRM practices in the highly casualised firm', *Asia Pacific Journal of Human Resources* (2001), 39, 1, pp. 42–62; Campbell, I. and Burgess, J., 'A new estimate of casual employment?', *Australian Bulletin of Labour* (2001), 27, 2, pp. 85–108; Murtough, G. and Waite, M., 'A new estimate of casual employment? Reply', *Australian Bulletin of Labour* (2001), 27, 2, pp. 109–17; Owens, R., 'The "long-term or permanent casual"—an oxymoron or "a well enough understood Australianism" in the law', *Australian Bulletin of Labour* (2001), 27, 2, pp. 118–36; Watts, R., 'The ACTU's response to the growth in long-term casual employment in Australia', *Australian Bulletin of Labour* (2001), 27, 2, pp. 137–49.

10 Cheal, D., *New Poverty: Families in Postmodern Society*, (Westport, Conn., and London: Greenwood Press, 1996); Lafferty, G., 'Responding to crisis: state withdrawal, postmodern fatalism, and the possibilities of radical economics', *Review of Radical Political Economics* (1999), 31, 1, pp. 148–61.

11 ABS, catalogue number 6203.0, *Labour Force, Australia* (Canberra: AGPS, August 2001), p. 6.

12 ABS, catalogue number 6202.0, *Labour Force, Australia* (Canberra: AGPS, August 2001).

13 Kane, R. L., 'HRM: changing concepts in a changing environment', *International Journal of Employment Studies* (1996), 4, 2, pp. 115–78; Fisher, R. and Dowling, P. J., 'Support for an HR approach in Australia: the perspective of senior HR managers', *Asia Pacific Journal of Human Resources* (1999), 37, 1, pp. 1–19.

14 Lansbury, R., Davis, E. M., and Simmons, D., 'Reforming the Australian workplace through employee participation', *Economic and Labour Relations Review* (1996), 7, 1, pp. 29–45; Warhurst, C. and Thompson, P. (1998), 'Hands, hearts and minds: changing work and workers at the end of the century', in P. Thompson and C. Warhurst (eds), *Workplaces of the Future* (London: Macmillan); Foster, D. and Hoggett, P., 'Changes in the Benefits Agency: empowering the exhausted worker?', *Work Employment & Society* (1999), 13, 1, pp. 19–39; Harley, B., 'The myth of empowerment: work organisation, hierarchy and employee autonomy in contemporary Australian workplaces', *Work Employment & Society* (1999), 13, 1, pp. 41–66; Benson, J., 'Employee voice in union and non-union Australian workplaces', *British Journal of Industrial Relations* (2000), 38, 3, pp. 453–60; Harley, B., Ramsay, H., and Scholarios, D., 'Employee direct participation in Britain and Australia: evidence from AWIRS95 and WERS98', *Asia Pacific Journal of Human Resources* (2000), 38, 2, pp. 42–54.

15 Morehead, A., Steele, M., Alexander, M., Stephen, K., and Duffin, L., *Changes at Work: the 1995 Australian Workplace Industrial Relations Survey* (Melbourne: Addison Wesley Longman, 1997), pp. 82–4.

16 Morehead, A. et al., pp. 87–8.

17 Morehead, A. et al., p. 104.

18 Fastenau, M. and Pullin, L., 'A comparative typology of employment relations, industrial relations, and human resource management', *International Employment Relations Review* (1998), 4, 1, pp. 1–22; Australian Centre for Industrial Relations Research and Training (ACIRRT), *Agreement Database and Monitor (ADAM) Report no. 22* (Sydney: ACIRRT, 1999); ACIRRT, *Trends in Queensland Workplace Agreements*, report produced for the Queensland Department of Training and Industrial Relations (Sydney: ACIRRT, 2000).

19 Pettigrew, A., *The Politics of Organisational Decision Making* (London: Tavistock, 1973); Mintzberg, H., 'Crafting strategy', *Harvard Business Review* (1987), July–August, pp. 65–75.

20 See Lewis, S. and Martin, C., 'Howard's $3bn for smarter nation', and Walker, T., 'After a long wait, it's time for bright ideas', *Australian Financial Review*, 30th January 2001.

21 Roan, A., 'The Australian National Training Reform Strategy and the promises for women employed in the service sector', *Policy, Organisation & Society* (1996), 12, pp. 47–63.

22 Boreham, P., Lafferty, G., Roan, A., and Whitehouse, G., 'Training, careers and numerical flexibility: equity implications in hospitality and retailing', *Journal of Industrial Relations*

(1996), 38, 1, pp. 3-21; Hunter, B., 'The determinants of Indigenous employment outcomes: the importance of education and training', *Australian Bulletin of Labour* (1997), 23, 3, pp. 177-92; Connell, J. and Burgess, J., 'Workforce and skill restructuring in Australia', *International Employment Relations Review* (1998), 4, 1, pp. 39-56; Ewer, P. 'Trade unions and Vocational Education Training: questions of strategy and identity', *Labour and Industry* (2000), 10, 3, pp. 37-56; Curtain, R., 'Flexible workers and access to training', *International Journal of Employment Studies* (2001), 9, 1, pp. 103-20; Lewer, J. and Gallimore, P., 'Are outsourcing and skill formation mutually exclusive? The experience of a heavy manufacturing firm', *International Journal of Employment Studies* (2001), 9, 1, pp. 141-62; Pickersgill, R., 'Skill formation in Australia beyond 2000: "flexibility" and Vocational Education and Training policy', *International Journal of Employment Studies* (2001), 9, 1, pp. 121-40; Whittard, J. and Reeves, K., 'Training and flexible labour: nurses in a New South Wales public hospital', *International Journal of Employment Studies* (2001), 9, 1, pp. 163-84.

23   Altman, J., 'Indigenous Work-for-the-Dole and mutual obligation: prospects for employment generation in remote Australia', *Australian Journal of Labour Economics* (2001) 5, 1, pp. 89-98.

24   Department of Employment, Workplace Relations and Small Business (2000) *Labour Market Review of Australia* (Canberra: AGPS), pp. 20-3.

25   ABS, catalogue number 6353.0, *Wage and Salary Earners* (Canberra: AGPS).

26   ABS, catalogue number 6353.0.

27   Fraser, L, *Impact of contracting out of female NESB workers: case study of the NSW Government Cleaning Service* (Sydney: Ethnic Communities Council of NSW, 1997); Benson, J., 'Outsourcing, organisational performance and employee commitment', *Economic and Labour Relations Review* (1999), 10, 1, pp. 1-21; Burgess, J., 'Outsourcing, employment and industrial relations in the public sector', *Economic and Labour Relations Review* (1999), 10, 1, pp. 36-55; Hall, R., 'Outsourcing, contracting-out and labour hire: implications for Human Resource Development in Australian organisations', *Asia Pacific Journal of Human Resources* (2000), 38, 2, pp. 23-41; Young, S. and Macneil, J., 'When performance fails to meet expectations: managers' objectives for outsourcing', *Economic and Labour Relations Review* (2000), 11, 1, pp. 136-68; Wooden, M., 'Outsourcing and the use of contractors: evidence from the AWIRS', *Economic and Labour Relations Review* (1999), 10, 1, pp. 22-35; Zappala, G., 'Outsourcing and Human Resource Management—a discussion starter', ACIRRT working paper no. 60 (Sydney: ACIRRT, 2000).

28   ABS, catalogue number 6248.0. *Wage and Salary Earners*, Australia (Canberra: AGPS, 1999)

29   Kane, R. L., 'Downsizing and HRM strategy: is there a relationship?', *International Journal of Employment Studies* (1998), 6, 2, pp. 43-72; Ryan, L. and Macky, K. A., 'Downsizing organisations: uses, outcomes and strategies', *Asia Pacific Journal of Human Resources* (1998), 36, 2, pp. 29-45; Kane, B., 'Downsizing, TQM, re-engineering, learning organisations and HRM strategy', *Asia Pacific Journal of Human Resources* (2000), 38, 1, pp. 26-49; Clarke, M. and Patrickson, M., 'Does downsized mean down and out?', *Asia Pacific Journal of Human Resources* (2001), 39, 1, pp. 63-78.

30   Pinnington, A. and Woolcock, P., 'How Far is IS/IT Outsourcing Enabling New Organizational Structure and Competences?', *International Journal of Information Management* (1995), 15, 5, pp. 353-65; Pinnington, A. and Woolcock, P., 'The Role of Vendor Companies in IS/IT Outsourcing?', *International Journal of Information Management* (1997), 17, 3, pp. 199-210.

31   Fraser, L., *Impact of Contracting Out on Female NESB Workers: Case Study of the NSW Government Cleaning Service* (Canberra: Department of Immigration and Multicultural Affairs, 1997).

32   Martin, G., Staines, H., and Pate, J., 'Linking Job Security and Career Development in a New Psychological Contract', *Human Resource Management Journal* (1998), 8, 3, pp. 20-40.

33   Graham, M. and Scarborough, H., 'Public Sector Outsourcing of Information Technology Services', *Australian Journal of Public Administration* (1996), 56, 3, pp. 30-9; Gratton, L., Hope-Hailey, V., Stiles, P., and Truss, C., *Strategic Human Resource Management* (Oxford: Oxford University Press, 1999); Lafferty, G. and Roan, A., 'Public sector outsourcing: implications for training', *Employee Relations* (2000), 22, 1, pp. 18-27; Young, S., 'Outsourcing: lessons from the literature', *Labour and Industry* (2000), 10, 3, pp. 97-118.

3 Australian Industrial Relations

1. ABS, catalogue number 6325.0, *Employee Earnings, Benefits and Trade Union Membership, Australia* (Canberra: AGPS, 2000).
2. Griffin, G. and Svensen, S., 'The decline of Australian union density—a survey of the literature', *Journal of Industrial Relations* (1996), 38, 4, pp. 505–47; Peetz, D., 'Unions, conflict and the dilemma of co-operation', *Journal of Industrial Relations* (1996), 38, 4, pp. 548–70; Peetz, D., *Unions in a Contrary World: the Future of the Australian Trade Union Movement* (Cambridge and Melbourne: Cambridge University Press, 1998); Peetz, D., 'Why join? Why stay? Instrumentality, beliefs, satisfaction and individual decisions on union membership', *Economic and Labour Relations Review* (1998), 9, 1, pp. 123–48; Holland, P., 'Organising works: meeting the challenge of trade union membership', *International Employment Relations Review* (1999), 5, 1, pp. 63–74.
3. Australian Council of Trade Unions, Trade Development Council (ACTU/TDC), *Australia Reconstructed: ACTU/TDC Mission to Western Europe: a Report by the Mission Members to the ACTU and the TDC* (Canberra: AGPS, 1987).
4. *Business Review Weekly*, November 1989.
5. Tilton, T., *The Political Theory of Swedish Social Democracy: Through the Welfare State to Socialism* (Oxford and New York: Clarendon Press and Oxford University Press, 1990).
6. Bodman, P. M., 'Trade union amalgamations, openness and the decline in Australian trade union membership', *Australian Bulletin of Labour* (1998), 24, 1, pp. 25–6; Pocock, B., 'Institutional sclerosis: prospects for trade union transformation', *Labour and Industry* (1998), 9, 1, pp. 17–36; Wooden, M., 'Union amalgamations and the decline in union density', *Journal of Industrial Relations* (1999), 41, 1, pp. 35–52; Davis, M., 'Is bigger better? Union size and expenditure on members', *Journal of Industrial Relations* (1999), 41, 1, pp. 3–34.
7. ABS, catalogue number 6310.0, *Employee Earnings, Benefits and Trade Union Membership, Australia* (Canberra: AGPS, 2000).
8. Gorz, A., *Reclaiming Work: Beyond the Wage-Based Society* (Oxford: Polity Press and Malden, Mass.: Blackwell, 1999), p. 17; Peetz, D., 'Nearly the year of living dangerously: in the emerging worlds of Australian industrial relations', *Asia Pacific Journal of Human Resources* (1999), 37, 2, pp. 3–23.
9. *Journal of Australian Political Economy* (1997), 39, special issue, Australia Reconstructed: Ten Years On, with articles by Bryan, D., Jones, E., Stilwell, F., Johnson, C., Beeson, M., Coates, N., Rafferty, M., Kriesler, P., Halevi, J., and Dow, G; Bramble, T., 'Australian union strategies since 1945', *Labour and Industry* (2001), 11, 3, pp. 1–26.
10. Harbridge, R., *Employment Contracts: New Zealand Experiences* (Wellington: Victoria University Press, 1993); Harbridge, R., Honebone, A., and Kiely, P., *Employment Contracts: Bargaining Trends and Employment Law Update 1993/4* (Wellington: VUW Industrial Relations Centre, 1994).
11. Fox, F. and Teicher, J., 'Victoria's Employee Relations Act: the way of the future?', in R. Callus and M. Schumacher (eds), *Current Research in Industrial Relations: Proceedings of the 8th AIRAANZ Conference* (Sydney: Australian Centre for Industrial Relations Research and Training, 1994), pp. 508–36; Hamberger, J., *Individual Contracts: Beyond Enterprise Bargaining?*, ACIRRT Working Paper number 39 (Sydney: Australian Centre for Industrial Relations Research and Training, 1995).
12. Merlo, O., 'Flexibility and stretching rights: the no disadvantage test in enterprise bargaining', *Australian Journal of Labour Law* (2000), 13, 3, pp. 207–35.
13. Green, R., 'The "death" of Comparative Wage Justice in Australia', *Economic and Labour Relations Review* (1996), 7, 2, pp. 224–53.
14. Hawke, A., 'A minimum wage: are we returning to Justice Higgins?', *Australian Bulletin of Labour* (1998), 24, 2, pp. 79–93.
15. ABS, catalogue number 6202.0, *Labour Force, Australia* (Canberra: AGPS, 2000).
16. Birmingham, A. and Fox, P., 'A guide to the Workplace Relations Act 1996', *Australian Bulletin of Labour* (1997), 23, 1, pp. 33–47; Hunter, B., 'An Indigenous worker's guide to the

Workplace Relations Act', *Journal of Industrial Relations* (1997), 39, 4, pp. 439-56; Bertone, S., 'Migrants, industry policy and decentralisation: from the Accord to the Workplace Relations Act 1996', *International Employment Relations Review* (1998), 4, 1, pp. 75-90; Lee, M., Bray, M., and Waring, P., 'The rhetoric and reality of bargaining structures under the Howard government', *Labour and Industry* (1998), 9, 2, pp. 61-80; Peetz, D., 'Trade unions and the Workplace Relations Act', *Labour and Industry* (1998), 9, 2, pp. 5-22; Thorpe, M. and McDonald, J., 'Freedom of association and union membership', *Labour and Industry* (1998), 9, 2, pp. 43-60; Timo, N., 'Precarious employment and individual contracts in an Australian mining company', *Labour and Industry* (1998), 9, 1, pp. 53-68; van Barneveld, K. and Arsovska, B., 'AWAs: changing the structure of wages?', *Labour and Industry* (2001), 12, 1, pp. 109-30; van Barneveld, K. and Arsovska, B., 'AWAs: changing the structure of wages?', ACIRRT working paper no. 67 (Sydney: ACIRRT, 2001); Grozier, D., 'Do individual and collective agreements make a difference?', ACIRRT working paper no. 65 (Sydney: ACIRRT, 2001).

17   Waring, P. and Lewer, J., 'The no disadvantage test: failing workers', *Labour and Industry* (2001), 12, 1, pp. 65-86.

18   Boxall, P. and Haynes, P., 'Unions and non-union bargaining agents under the Employment Contracts Act 1991: an assessment after 12 months', *New Zealand Journal of Industrial Relations* (1992), 17, pp. 223-32; Peetz, D., Quinn, D., Edwards, L., and Reidel, P., 'Workplace bargaining in New Zealand: radical change at work', in D. Peetz, A. Preston, and J. Docherty (eds), *Workplace Bargaining in the International Context*, Industrial Relations Research Monograph number 2 (Canberra: Department of Industrial Relations, 1992).

19   Dannin, E., 'We can't overcome? A case study of freedom of contract and labour law reform', *Berkeley Journal of Employment and Labour Law* (1995), 16, 1, pp. 1-168.

20   Wooden, M., 'Individual agreement-making in Australian workplaces: incidence, trends and features', *Journal of Industrial Relations* (1999), 42, 3, pp. 417-45.

21   Boreham, P., Hall, R., Harley, B., and Whitehouse, G., 'What does enterprise bargaining mean for gender equity? Some empirical evidence', *Labour and Industry* (1996), 7, 1, pp. 51-68; Lafferty, G., 'Decentralised industrial relations and internal labour markets: a case study in tourism employment', *International Employment Relations Review* (1998), 4, 2, pp. 19-32; Nelson, L., 'Enterprise bargaining and evolving Human Resource Management', *International Employment Relations Review* (1998), 4, 2, pp. 33-48; Allan, C., Brosnan, P., and Walsh, P., 'Labour regulation and adjustment in Australia and New Zealand', *International Employment Relations Review* (1999), 5, 1, pp. 1-14; Barry, M. and Waring, P., '"Shafted": Labour productivity and Australian coal miners', *Journal of Australian Political Economy* (1999), 44, pp. 89-112; Bowden, B., 'A collective catastrophe: productivity maximisation and workplace bargaining in the Australian coal industry', *Journal of Industrial Relations* (2000), 42, 3, pp. 364-82; Briggs, C., 'Australian exceptionalism: the role of trade unions in the emergence of enterprise bargaining', *Journal of Industrial Relations* (2001), 43, 1, pp. 27-43; Macdonald, D., Campbell, I., and Burgess, J., 'Ten years of enterprise bargaining in Australia: an introduction', *Labour and Industry* (2001), 12, 1, pp. 1-26; Buultjens, J. and Cairncross, G., 'Ten years of enterprise bargaining and the hospitality sector', *Labour and Industry* (2001), 12, 1, pp. 27-42.

22   Bramble, T., 'Union strategy and the 1998 waterfront dispute', *Queensland Review* (1998), 5, 2, pp. 76-91; Dabschek, B., 'The waterfront dispute: of vendettas and the Australian Way', *Economic and Labour Relations Review* (1998), 9, 2, pp. 155-87; Glasbeek, H. J., 'The MUA affair: the role of law vs. the rule of law', *Economic and Labour Relations Review* (1998), 9, 2, pp. 188-221; Harcourt, T., 'The economics of the Australian waterfront dispute', *Economic and Labour Relations Review* (1998), 9, 2, pp. 222-35; Sloan, J., 'An economic analysis of the 1998 Patrick dispute', *Economic and Labour Relations Review* (1998), 9, 2, pp. 236-45; McCallum, R. C., 'A priority of rights: freedom of association and the waterfront dispute', *Australian Bulletin of Labour* (1998), 24, 3, pp. 207-22; Orr, G., 'Conspiracy on the waterfront', *Australian Journal of Labour Law* (1998), 11, 3, pp. 159-85; Wiseman, J., 'Here to stay? The 1997-1998 Australian waterfront dispute and its implications', *Labour and Industry* (1998), 9, 1, pp. 1-16; Griffin, G. and Svensen, S., 'Industrial relations implications of the

Australian waterside dispute', *Australian Bulletin of Labour* (1998), 24, 3, pp. 194-206; McCallum, R., 'A priority of rights: freedom of association and the waterfront dispute', *Australian Bulletin of Labour* (1998), 24, 3, pp. 207-21; Evans, R., Cawthorne, P., and Wilson, S., 'On the waterfront', *Journal of Australian Political Economy* (1998), 41, pp. 1-6, 7-22, 23-37; Sheridan, S., 'The 1998 Australian waterfront dispute in its historical context', *International Employment Relations Review* (1999), 5, 2, pp. 1-16; Pocock, B., 'Success in defence: union strategy and the 1998 maritime dispute', *International Employment Relations Review* (1999), 5, 2, pp. 17-38; Baker, D., 'Avoiding "war on the wharves": is the non-confrontational policing of major industrial disputes "here to stay"?', *International Employment Relations Review* (1999), 5, 2, pp. 39-62; Griffin, G. and Svensen, S., 'Industrial relations and the 1998 waterfront dispute', *International Employment Relations Review* (1999), 5, 2, pp. 63-78; Stewart, A., 'The labour law implications of the 1998 waterfront dispute', *International Employment Relations Review* (1999), 5, 2, pp. 79-92; Hawke, A., 'Implications of the waterfront dispute on performance', *International Employment Relations Review* (1999), 5, 2, pp. 93-104; Treuren, G., 'The government, the state and industrial relations: the case of the Australian waterfront dispute of 1997/8', *International Employment Relations Review* (1999), 5, 2, pp. 107-24; Morris, R., 'From productivity crisis to industrial dispute: the 1998 waterfront troubles', *International Employment Relations Review* (2000), 6, 1, pp. 89-106; Dabschek, B., 'The Australian waterfront dispute and theories of the state', *Journal of Industrial Relations* (2000), 42, 4, pp. 497-516.

23 Hawke, A. and Wooden, M., 'Two steps forward, one step back: industrial relations developments in Australia in 1997', *Asia Pacific Journal of Human Resources* (1998), 36, 2, pp. 15-28.

24 Buchanan, J., Callus, R., and Biggs, C., 'What impact has the Howard Government had on wages and hours of work?', *Journal of Australian Political Economy* (1999), 43: 1-21; Australian Centre for Industrial Relations Research and Training (ACIRRT), *Agreement Database and Monitor (ADAM) Report no. 22* (Sydney: ACIRRT, 1999); ACIRRT, *Trends in Queensland Workplace Agreements*, report produced for the Queensland Department of Training and Industrial Relations (Sydney: ACIRRT, 2000); Roan, A., Bramble, T., and Lafferty, G., 'Australian Workplace Agreements in practice: the "hard" and "soft" dimensions', *Journal of Industrial Relations* (2001), 43, 4, pp. 387-401.

25 Australian Bureau of Statistics (ABS), *Australian Social Trends 2001* (Canberra: AGPS, 2001); Glezer, H. and Wolcott, I., 'Conflicting commitments: working mothers and fathers in Australia', in L. L. Haas, P. Hwang, and G. Russell (eds), *Organizational Change and Gender Equity: International Perspectives on Fathers and Mothers at the Workplace* (Thousand Oaks: Sage, 2001); Whitehouse, G and Zetlin, D., '"Family Friendly" Policies: Distribution and Implementation in Australian Workplaces', *Economic and Labour Relations Review* (2000), 10, 2, pp. 221-39; Probert, B., Ewer, P., and Whiting, K., 'Work versus life: union strategies reconsidered', *Labour and Industry* (2000), 11, 1, pp. 23-48.

26 Sappey, R. B., Maconachie, G., Sappey, J., and Teo, S., 'Work intensification and social relations: a study of enterprise agreements in the Queensland food processing industry', *International Journal of Employment Studies* (2000), 8, 1, pp. 105-24; Hayden, A., *Sharing the Work, Sparing the Planet: Work Time, Consumption and Ecology* (Sydney: Pluto Press, 2001); Watts, M. J. and Burgess, J., 'The polarisation of earnings and hours in Australia under a decentralised industrial relations system: the lessons for economic policy', *International Journal of Employment Studies* (2001), 9, 1, pp. 27-58.

27 Macdonald, D., 'Public sector industrial relations under the Howard government', *Labour and Industry* (1998), 9, 2, pp. 43-60; Quinlan, M., 'Labour market restructuring in industrialised societies: an overview', *Economic and Labour Relations Review* (1998), 9, 1, pp. 1-30; Sheehan, P., 'The changing nature of work: some implications', *Australian Bulletin of Labour* (1998), 24, 4, pp. 317-32; Rogers, M., 'Innovation in Australian workplaces: an empirical analysis', *Australian Bulletin of Labour* (1999), 25, 4, pp. 334-51; van Gramberg, B., Teicher, J., and Griffin, G., 'Industrial relations in 1999: workplace relations, legalism and individualisation', *Asia Pacific Journal of Human Resources* (2000), 39, 2, pp. 4-22; Bamber, G., Park, F. K., Lee, C. W., Ross, P., and Broadbent, K. (eds), *Employment Relations in the Asia-Pacific—Changing Approaches* (Sydney: Allen & Unwin, 2000); Dabschek, B., '"A felt

28 need for increased efficiency": industrial relations at the end of the millennium', *Asia Pacific Journal of Human Resources* (2001), 39, 2, pp. 4–30.
28 See the following text on which this section draws, for further information on negotiation and bargaining processes: Hudson, M. and Hawkins, L., *Negotiating Employment Relations* (Melbourne: Longman, 1995); Lewicki, R. J., Saunders, D. M., and Minton, J. W., *Essentials of Negotiation*, 2nd edn (Sydney, Irwin McGraw-Hill, 2001); Fells, R. and Skeffington, R., 'A critical examination of the strategic negotiations framework—the case of the Australian shearing industry', *International Employment Relations Review* (1998), 4, 1, pp. 23–38; Fells, R., 'A critical examination of the process of workplace negotiation', *Labour and Industry* (1998), 9, 1, pp. 37–52.

4 Labour Law

1 Naughton, R., review of Lord Wedderburn, *Labour Law and Freedom: Further Essays in Labour Law* (London: Lawrence & Wishart, 1995), in *Australian Journal of Labour Law* (1996), 9, 3, pp. 294–7; Chin, D., 'Exhuming the individual employment contract: a case of labour law exceptionalism', *Australian Journal of Labour Law* (1997), 10, 1, pp. 257–79; Sempill, J., 'Under the lens: electronic workplace surveillance', *Australian Journal of Labour Law* (2001), 14, 1, pp. 111–44.
2 Deery, S. and Walsh, J., 'Union decline in Australia: the role of Human Resource Management practices and the union-hostile workplace', *Australian Journal of Labour Law* (1999), 12, 1, pp. 21–31.
3 McIntyre, S. and Mitchell, R. (eds), *Foundations of Arbitration* (Melbourne: Oxford University Press, 1989).
4 Ford, W. J., 'Reconstructing Australian labour law: a Constitutional perspective', *Australian Journal of Labour Law* (1997), 10, 1, pp. 1–30; Kollmorgen, S., 'Towards a unitary national system of industrial relations? Commonwealth Powers (Industrial Relations) Act 1996 (Vic)'; 'Workplace Relations and Other Legislation Amendment Act (no. 2) 1996 (Cth)', *Australian Journal of Labour Law* (1997), 10, 1, pp. 158–69; Williams, G. and Simpson, A., 'The expanding frontiers of Commonwealth intervention in industrial relations', *Australian Journal of Labour Law* (1997), 10, 1, pp. 222–8; Wooden, M., *The Transformation of Australian Industrial Relations* (Sydney: Federation Press, 2000).
5 Stewart, A., 'Federal labour law and new uses for the corporations power', *Australian Journal of Labour Law* (2000), 13, 2, pp. 145–68.
6 Creighton, B. and Stewart, A., *Labour Law: an Introduction*, 3rd edn (Sydney: Federation Press, 2000), p. 84.
7 For a summary of the various responsibilities and composition of different panels, see Creighton, B. and Stewart, A., *Labour Law: an Introduction*, 3rd edn (Sydney: Federation Press, 2000), chapter 5.
8 Coulthard, A., 'Damages for unfair dismissal: the High Court's judgment in *Byrne and Frew vs Australian Airlines*', *Australian Journal of Labour Law* (1996), 9, 1, pp. 38–73; Chapman, A., 'Termination of employment under the Workplace Relations Act 1996 (Cth), *Australian Journal of Labour Law* (1997), 10, 1, pp. 89–111; Creighton, B., 'The Workplace Relations Act in international perspective', *Australian Journal of Labour Law* (1997), 10, 1, pp. 31–49; McCallum, R. C., 'Australian Workplace Agreements—an analysis', *Australian Journal of Labour Law* (1997), 10, 1, pp. 50–61; McCarry, G., 'Industrial action under the Workplace Relations Act 1996 (Cth), *Australian Journal of Labour Law* (1997), 10, 1, pp. 133–57; Naughton, R., 'Sailing into uncharted seas: the role of unions under the Workplace Relations Act 1996 (Cth)', *Australian Journal of Labour Law* (1997), 10, 1, pp. 112–32; Deery, S. and Mitchell, R. (eds), *Employment Relations, Individualism and Union Exclusion*, (Sydney: Federation Press, 2000); Meredith, F., 'Alternative dispute resolution in an industrial tribunal: conciliation of unfair dismissal disputes in South Australia', *Australian Journal of Labour Law* (2001), 14, 1, pp. 36–61.

9   Campo, R., 'The protection of employee entitlements in the event of employer insolvency: Australian initiatives in the light of international models', *Australian Journal of Labour Law* (2000), 13, 3, pp. 236-59.

10 Australian Industry Group and Office of the Employment Advocate, *Better Workplaces—the AWA Framework* (Canberra: AGPS, 1999), p. 3.

11 McCallum, R., 'Australian Workplace Agreements—an analysis', *Australian Journal of Labour Law* (1997), 10, 1, pp. 50-61; Barnevald, K. and Arsovska, B., 'AWAs: changing the structure of wages?', *Labour and Industry* (2001), 12, 1, pp. 87-108.

12 Creighton, B. and Stewart, A., *Labour Law: an Introduction*, 3rd edn (Sydney: Federation Press, 2000), pp. 57-9.

13 Crawley, M., 'Labour hire and the employment relationship', *Australian Journal of Labour Law* (2000), 13, 3, pp. 291-6; Lafferty, G. and Roan, A., 'Public sector outsourcing: implications for training and skills', *Employee Relations* (2000), 22, 1, pp. 18-27.

14 Lafferty, G., Whitehouse, G., Hall, R., and Harley, W., 'Homeworking in Australia: an assessment of current trends', *Australian Bulletin of Labour* (1996), 23, 2, pp. 24-37.

15 ABS cat. no. 6302.0, *Average Weekly Earnings, Australia, August 2000* (Canberra: AGPS, 2000).

16 Wright, S. J. and Sheridan, A., 'Making the rhetoric a reality: Sydney Water's experience with work and family policies', *Asia Pacific Journal of Human Resources* (1998), 36, 2, pp. 88-102; Burgess, J. and de Ruyter, A., 'Declining job quality in Australia: another hidden cost of unemployment', *The Economic and Labour Relations Review* (2000), 11, 2, pp. 246-69; Fastenau, M., 'Women's employment in Australia, 1986-1996: a period of glacial change', *International Employment Relations Review* (1997), 3, 1, pp. 61-90; Strachan, G. and Burgess, J., 'The incompatibility of decentralised bargaining and Equal Employment Opportunity in Australia', *British Journal of Industrial Relations* (2000), 38, 3, pp. 361-82; Whitehouse, G., 'Recent trends in pay equity: beyond the aggregate statistics', *Journal of Industrial Relations* (2001), 43, 1, pp. 66-78.

17 Andrades, C., 'Women, work and unfinished business: the Equal Opportunity for Women in the Workplace Act 1999 (Cth)', *Australian Journal of Labour Law* (2000), 13, 2, pp. 171-82; MacDermott, T. and Owens, R., 'Equality and flexibility for workers with family responsibilities: a troubled union?', *Australian Journal of Labour Law* (2000), 13, 3, pp. 278-90.

5 Employee Resourcing and Careers

1   Rothwell, S., 'Human Resource Planning', in J. Storey (ed.), *Human Resource Management: A Critical Text* (London: Routledge, 1995), pp. 167-202; Evenden, R., 'The strategic management of recruitment and selection', in R. Harrison (ed.), *Human Resource Management: Issues and Strategies* (Wokingham, England: Addison-Wesley, 1993); Miller, E., 'Strategic Staffing', in C. Fombrun, N. M. Tichy, and M. A. Devanna (eds), *Strategic Human Resource Management* (New York: John Wiley & Sons, 1984).

2   Beer, M., Spector, B., Lawrence, P. R., Quinn Mills, D., and Walton, R. E., *Managing Human Assets: The Groundbreaking Harvard Business School Program* (New York: Free Press, Macmillan, 1984), pp. 9, 66-112.

3   Walton, R. E., 'Toward a Strategy of Eliciting Employee Commitment Based on Policies of Mutuality', in R. E. Walton and P. R. Lawrence (eds), *Human Resource Management, Trends and Challenges* (Boston: Harvard Business School Press, 1985), pp. 35-65. 'The new HRM model is composed of policies that promote mutuality—mutual goals, mutual influence, mutual respect, mutual rewards, mutual responsibility. The theory is that policies of mutuality will elicit commitment which in turn will yield both better economic performance and greater human development.'

4   Hughes, E. C., 'Institutional Office and the Person', *American Journal of Sociology* (1937), 43, pp. 404-13.

5   Curnow, B. and McLean, F. J., *Third Age Careers* (London: Gower Press, 1994).

6   Kotter, J. P., *The General Managers* (New York: Free Press, 1982).

7. Handy, C. J., *Understanding Organizations*, 4th edn (London: Penguin, 1993).
8. Handy, *Understanding Organizations*.
9. Schein, E. H., *Career Dynamics: Matching Individual and Organisational Needs* (Reading, MA: Addison-Wesley, 1978); Schein, E. H., 'How "career anchors" hold executives to their career paths', in R. Katz (ed.), *Managing Professionals in Innovative Organizations* (Cambridge, MA: Ballinger Publishing Company, Harper & Row, 1988), pp. 487–97.
10. Herriot, P. and Pemberton, C., *New Deals: The Revolution in Managerial Careers* (Chichester: John Wiley & Sons, 1995).
11. Brooks, I. and Harfield, T., 'Breaking the psychological contract: the effects of changework on middle managers when implementing organizational change', *Asia Pacific Journal of Human Resources* (2000), 38, 3, pp. 91–103; Powell, M. J., Brock, D. M., and Hinings, C. R., 'The changing professional organization', in D. Brock, M. Powell, and C. R. Hinings (eds), *Restructuring the Professional Organization: Accounting, Health Care and Law* (London: Routledge, 1999), pp. 1–19; McGovern, P., *HRM, Technical Workers and the Multinational Corporation* (London: Routledge, 1998), pp. 136–45.
12. *Financial Times*, 15th and 16th December 1994, 1st May 1996.
13. Herriot, P., 'The Management of Careers', in S. Tyson (ed.), *Strategic Prospects for HRM* (London: Institute of Personnel and Development, 1995), pp. 184–205 (see p. 196); Hendry, C. and Jenkins, R., 'Psychological Contracts and New Deals', *Human Resource Management Journal* (1997), 7, 1, pp. 38–44.
14. For enterprise agreements and industrial awards, see: <www.osiris.gov.au>; *People Management* (1998) 4, 19, 1st October, p. 12.
15. Trompenaars, F., *Riding the Waves of Culture* (London: Economist Books, 1993).
16. Kamoche, K., 'Strategic Human Resource Management Within A Resource-Capability View of the Firm', *Journal of Management Studies* (1996), 33, 2, March, pp. 213–33 (see p. 213).
17. Prahalad, C. and Hamel, G., 'The Core Competence of the Corporation', *Harvard Business Review* (1990), May–June, pp. 79–91.
18. Guest, D. E., 'Beyond HRM: Commitment and the Contract Culture', in P. Sparrow and M. Marchington (eds), *Human Resource Management: The New Agenda* (London: Financial Times, Pitman Publishing, 1998), pp. 37–51.
19. Brewster, C., 'Flexible working in Europe: extent, growth and the challenge for HRM', in P. Sparrow and M. Marchington (eds), *Human Resource Management: The New Agenda*, pp. 245–58.
20. Hofstede, G., *Culture's Consequences: International Differences in Work Related Values* (Beverly Hills: Sage, 1980).
21. Wright, M. and Storey, J., 'Recruitment and selection', in I. Beardwell and L. Holden, *Human Resource Management: a Contemporary Perspective*, 2nd edn (London: Financial Times, Pitman Publishing, 1997), pp. 210–76.
22. Iles, P. and Salaman, G., 'Recruitment, Selection and Assessment', in J. Storey (ed.), *Human Resource Management: A Critical Text* (London: Routledge, 1995), pp. 203–33.
23. Townley, B., 'Selection and Appraisal: Reconstituting "Social Relations"?', in J. Storey (ed.), *New Perspectives on Human Resource Management*.
24. Boam, R. and Sparrow, P., *Designing and Achieving Competency: A Competency-Based Approach to Developing People and Organizations* (Maidenhead: McGraw-Hill, 1992).
25. Robertson, I. T., Iles, P. A., Gratton, L., and Sharpley, D., 'The Psychological Impact of Selection Procedures on Candidates', *Human Relations* (1991), 44, 9, pp. 963–82; Baron, H. and Janman, K., 'Fairness in the Assessment Centre', in C. L. Cooper and I. T. Robertson (eds), *International Review of Industrial and Organizational Psychology*, vol. II (Chichester: John Wiley, 1996), pp. 61–114.
26. Iles and Salaman, 'Recruitment, Selection and Assessment', p. 208.
27. Iles and Salaman, 'Recruitment, Selection and Assessment', p. 209.
28. Feltham, R., 'Using Competencies in Selection and Recruitment', in R. Boam and P. Sparrow, *Designing and Achieving Competency: A Competency-Based Approach to Developing People and Organizations* (Maidenhead: McGraw-Hill, 1992), pp. 89–103.

29 Feltham, R., 'Using Competencies in Selection and Recruitment', in R. Boam and P. Sparrow, *Designing and Achieving Competency: A Competency-Based Approach to Developing People and Organizations* (Maidenhead: McGraw-Hill, 1992), p. xxi.
30 Sparrow, P., 'New Organisational Forms, Processes, Jobs and Psychological Contracts: Resolving the HRM Issues', in P. Sparrow and M. Marchington (eds), *Human Resource Management: The New Agenda* (London: Financial Times, Pitman Publishing, 1998), pp. 117–41; Kandola, R. and Pearn, M., 'Identifying Competences', in R. Boam and P. Sparrow, *Designing and Achieving Competency*, p.XX.
31 Sparrow, P., 'New Organisational Forms, Processes, Jobs and Psychological Contracts', p. 120; Buchanan, D. A., 'Principles and practice in work design', in K. Sisson (ed.), *Personnel Management: A Comprehensive Guide to Theory and Practice in Britain*, 2nd edn (Oxford: Blackwell, 1994).
32 Parker, S. K. and Wall, T. D., 'Job Design and Modern Manufacturing', in P. Warr (ed.), *Psychology and Work*, 4th edn (London: Penguin, 1996).
33 West, M. A., Borrill, C. S., and Unsworth, K. L., 'Team effectiveness in organizations', in C. L. Cooper and I. T. Robertson (eds), *International Review of Industrial and Organizational Psychology*, vol. 13 (Chichester: John Wiley, 1998), pp. 1–48 (see p. 32). For more information on establishing everyday workplace teams, see: Mallon, M. and Kearney, T., 'Team development at Fisher and Paykell: the introduction of "Everyday Workplace Teams" ', *Asia Pacific Journal of Human Resources* (2001), 39, 1, pp. 93–106.
34 *People Management* (1999), 5, 1, 14th January, p. 15.
35 Hodgkinson, G. P. and Payne, R. L., 'Graduate Selection in Three European Countries', *Journal of Occupational Organizational Psychology* (1998), 71, pp. 359–65 (see p. 361); Shackleton, V. and Newell, S., 'European management selection methods: A comparison of five countries', *International Journal of Selection and Assessment* (1994), 2, pp. 91–102.
36 Hodgkinson, G. P., Daley, N., and Payne, R. L., 'Knowledge of, and attitudes towards, the demographic time-bomb: A survey of its impact on graduate recruitment in the UK', *International Journal of Manpower* (1995), 16, 8, pp. 59–76; Hodgkinson, G. P., Snell, S., Daley, N., and Payne, R. L., 'A Comparative Study of Knowledge of Changing Demographic Trends and the Importance of HRM Practices in Three European Countries', *International Journal of Selection and Assessment* (1996), 4, 4, October, pp. 184–94.
37 Fletcher, C., *People Management* (1998) 4, 23, 26th November, p. 40.
38 Hatch, M. J., *Organization Theory: Modern, Symbolic and Postmodern Perspectives* (Oxford: Oxford University Press, 1997), p. 228.
39 Fletcher, C. and Anderson, N., 'A superficial assessment', *People Management* (1998), 4, 10, 14th May, p. 44; *People Management* (2002), 8, 1, 10th January, p. 18
40 Beer, M., Spector, B., Lawrence, P. R., Quinn Mills, D., and Walton, R. E., *Managing Human Assets: The Groundbreaking Harvard Business School Program* (New York: Free Press, Macmillan, 1984), pp. 129–65; *People Management* (2001), 7, 2, 29th January, pp. 8–9.
41 Purcell, J. and Gray, A., 'Corporate personnel departments and the management of industrial relations: two case studies in ambiguity', *Journal of Management Studies* (1986), 23, 2, pp. 205–23.
42 <www.osiris.gov.au> Ford Australia Enterprise Agreement (2000); Flood, P. C., Turner, T., Ramamoorthy, N., and Pearson, J., 'Causes and consequences of psychological contracts among knowledge workers in the high technology and financial services industries', *International Journal of Human Resource Management* (2001), 12, 7, November, pp. 1152–65.
43 Dawkins, P., 'Chapter 1: Introduction', in P. Dawkins and C. R. Littler (eds), *Downsizing: Is it Working for Australia?* (Melbourne: Melbourne Institute for Applied Economic and Social Research, 2001), p. 2; Beer et al., *Managing Human Assets*, p. 93.
44 Dawkins, P., 'Chapter 1: Introduction', in Dawkins and Littler (eds), *Downsizing*, p. 2; Beer et al., *Managing Human Assets*, p. 93; Ference, T. P., Stoner, J. A. F., and Warren, K. E., 'Managing the career plateau', in R. Katz (ed.), *Managing Professionals in Innovative Organizations* (Cambridge, Mass.: Ballinger Publishing Company, Harper & Row, 1988).
45 Redman, T. and Keithley, D., 'Downsizing goes East? Employment re-structuring in post-Socialist Poland', *International Journal of Human Resource Management* (1998), 9, 2, April, pp. 274–95 (see p. 274).

46 Blyton, P. and Turnbull, P. (eds), *Reassessing Human Resource Management* (London: Sage, 1992).
47 Sparrow, P., 'New Organisational Forms, Processes, Jobs and Psychological Contracts' (n. 30 above), p. 129.
48 Kets de Vries, M. F. R. and Balazs, K., 'The Downside of Downsizing', *Human Relations* (1997), 50, 1, pp. 11–50.
49 Herriot, P., 'The Role of the HRM Function in Building a New Proposition for Staff', in P. Sparrow and M. Marchington (eds), *Human Resource Management: The New Agenda* (London: Financial Times, Pitman Publishing, 1998), pp. 106–16.
50 Feldman, D. C. and Kim, S., 'Acceptance of buyout offers in the face of downsizing: empirical evidence from the Korean electronics industry. Study of a major Korean electronics company', *International Journal of Human Resource Management* (1998), 9, 6, December, pp. 1008–25 (see p. 1008).
51 Westwood, R., Sparrow, P., and Leung, A., 'Challenges to the psychological contract in Hong Kong', *International Journal of Human Resource Management* (2001), 12, 4, June, pp. 621–51; Doherty, N., 'Downsizing', in S. Tyson (ed.), *The Practice of Human Resource Strategy* (London: Financial Times, Pitman Publishing, 1997), pp. 27–40.
52 Rothwell, S., 'Human Resource Planning' (n. 1 above).
53 Institute of Personnel Management, *Statement on Human Resource Planning* (London: IPM, 1992).
54 Storey, J. and Sisson, K., *Managing Human Resources and Industrial Relations* (Milton Keynes: Open University Press, 1993).
55 Armstrong, M., *A Handbook of Personnel Management Practice*, 6th edn (London: Kogan Page, 1996), p. 409.
56 *People Management* (1999), 5, 2, 28th January, p. 16; *HR Monthly*, October, 2001, p. 7; Whitehouse, G., Lafferty, G., and Boreham, P., 'From casual to permanent part-time? Non-standard employment in retail and hospitality', *Labour and Industry* (1997), 8, 2, pp. 33–48.
57 Bramham, J., *Human Resource Planning*, 2nd edn (London: Institute of Personnel and Development, 1994), p. 164.
58 Schuler and Jackson subdivide human resource planning into 5 phases: (1) identify the key business issues; (2) determine the human resource implications; (3) develop human resource objectives and goals; (4) design and implement human resource policies, programs, and practices; (5) evaluate, revise, and refocus. Schuler, R. S. and Jackson, S. E., *Human Resource Management: Positioning for the 21st century*, 6th edn (Minneapolis–St. Paul, MN: West Publishing Company, 1996), pp. 137–41.
59 Scullion, H., 'International HRM', in J. Storey (ed.), *Human Resource Management: a Critical Text* (London: Routledge, 1995), pp. 352–82 (see p. 377); Hofstede, G., *Culture's Consequences: International Differences in Work Related Values* (Beverly Hills: Sage, 1980).
60 Guirdham, M., *Interpersonal Skills at Work* (London: Prentice-Hall, 1990).
61 Cole, G. A., *Personnel Management*, 3rd edn (London: DP Publications, 1993), pp. 210–11.
62 Newell, S. and Rice, C., 'Assessment, Selection and Evaluation: Problems and Pitfalls', in J. Leopold, L. Harris, and T. Watson (eds), *Strategic Human Resourcing: Principles, Perspectives and Practices* (London: Financial Times, Pitman Publishing, 1999), pp. 129–65.
63 Athey, T. R. and Orth, M. S., 'Emerging Competency Methods for the Future', *Human Resource Management* (1999), 38, 3, pp. 215–26.
64 Briscoe, J. P. and Hall, D. T., 'Grooming and Picking Leaders Using Competency Frameworks: Do They Work? An Alternative Approach and New Guidelines for Practice', *Organizational Dynamics* (1999), 28, 2, pp. 37–51.

6 Motivating Employees

1 Maslow, A. H., 'A Theory of Human Motivation', *Psychological Review* (1943), 50, pp. 370–96.
2 Salancik, G. R. and Pfeffer, J., 'An Examination of Need Satisfaction Models of Job Attitudes', *Administrative Science Quarterly* (1977), 22, pp. 427–56.

3   Watson, T. J., *In Search of Management* (London: Routledge, 1994), p. 60; Vecchio, R. P., *Organizational Behaviour*, 3rd edn (Orlando, FL: Dryden Press, Harcourt Brace & Company, 1995), p. 190.
4   McClelland, D. C., *The Achieving Society* (Princeton, NJ: Van Nostrand, 1961).
5   *Harvard Business Review* (September–October, 1987), p. 117.
6   Vecchio defines organisational behaviour as follows: it 'is concerned with the scientific study of the behavioral processes that occur in work settings ... The content of this field is quite broad. It encompasses such topics as employee attitudes, motivation, and performance, to name a few. And it extends to larger organizational and environmental pressures, that influence an individual's behavior and attitudes ...' Vecchio, R. P., *Organizational Behaviour*, 3rd edn (Orlando, FL: Dryden Press, Harcourt Brace & Company, 1995), p. 4.
7   Hofstede, G., *Culture's Consequences: International Differences in Work Related Values* (Beverly Hills: Sage, 1980).
8   Wilson, F. M., *Organizational Behaviour and Gender* (Maidenhead: McGraw-Hill, 1995). Webb, J., 'The open door? Women and equal opportunity at ComCo (North)', in D. Gowler, K. Legge and C. Clegg (eds), *Case studies in Organizational Behaviour and Human Resource Management*, 2nd edn (London: Paul Chapman Publishing, 1993).
9   Latham, G. P. and Locke, E. A., 'Goal setting: a motivational technique that works', *Organizational Dynamics* (1979), 8, 2, pp. 68–80.
10 Vroom, V. H., *Work and Motivation* (New York: Wiley, 1964).
11 Porter, L. W. and Lawler III, E. E., *Managerial Attitudes and Performance* (Homewood, IL: Irwin-Dorsey, 1968).
12 Bandura, A., 'Self-efficacy: Toward a Unifying Theory of Behavioural Change', *Psychological Review* (1977), vol. 84, pp. 191–215; Bandura, A., *Social Learning Theory* (Englewood Cliffs, NJ: Prentice-Hall, 1977).
13 Estes, W. K., 'Reinforcement in human behavior', *American Scientist* (1972), 60, pp. 723–9.
14 Hackman and Oldman quoted in Vroom, V. H. and Deci, E. L. (eds), *Management and Motivation*, 2nd edn (Harmondsworth: Penguin Books, 1992) p. 260.
15 Hackman and Oldman quoted in Vroom, V. H. and Deci, E. L. (eds), *Management and Motivation*, 2nd edn (Harmondsworth: Penguin Books, 1992), p. 263; Hackman, J. R. and Oldham, G. R., *Work Redesign* (Reading, MA: Addison-Wesley, 1980); Hackman, J. R. and Oldham, G. R., 'Motivation through the design of work: test of a theory', *Organizational Behavior and Human Performance* (1976), 16, pp. 250–79.
16 *People Management* (2002), 8, 2, 24th January, p. 11; *People Management* (1998), 4, 24, 10th December, p. 14; Rogg, K. L., Schmidt, D. L., Skull, C., and Schmitt, N., 'Human resource practices, organisational climate, and customer satisfaction', *Journal of Management* (2001), 27, 4, pp. 431–49; Ogbonna, E. and Harris, L. C., 'The performance implications of the work-oriented cognitions of shopfloor workers: a study of British retailing', *International Journal of Human Resource Management* (2001), 12, 6, September, pp. 1005–28; Herron, M., 'The Job Satisfaction Study', in *Facing the Future: Gender, Employment and Best Practice Issues for Law Firms*, vol. 1 (Melbourne: Victoria Law Foundation, 1996); Woodger, A. and Beaton, G., 'Effective Practices Guide', in *Facing the Future: Gender, Employment and Best Practice Issues for Law Firms*, vol. 2 (Melbourne: Victoria Law Foundation, 1996).
17 Hofstede, *Culture's Consequences: International Differences in Work Related Values* (n. 7 above).
18 Alderfer simplified Maslow's hierarchy by subdividing it into three levels of need (existence, relatedness, and growth). Alderfer, C. P., *Existence, Relatedness and Growth* (New York: Free Press, 1972).
19 Salancik, G. R. and Pfeffer, J., 'An examination of need satisfaction models of job attitudes', *Administrative Science Quarterly* (1977), 22, pp. 427–56.
20 Salancik and Pfeffer, 'An examination of need satisfaction models of job attitudes'.
21 Robbins, S. P., *Organizational Behaviour: Concepts, Controversies, Applications* (Upper Saddle River, NJ: Prentice-Hall, 1998) p. 175; Wilson, F. M., *Organizational Behaviour and Gender* (n. 8 above), p. 139.
22 Adams, J. S., 'Toward an understanding of inequity', *Journal of Abnormal and Social Psychology* (1963), 67, pp. 422–36; Brown, M., 'Employee pay adjustment preferences: recent Australian evidence', *Asia Pacific Journal of Human Resources* (2001), 39, 3, pp. 1–22.

23 Adams, J. S., 'Inequity in social exchange', in L. Berkowitz (ed.), *Advances in Experimental Social Psychology*, vol. 2 (New York: Academic Press, 1965), pp. 267–99.
24 Jaques, E., *Equitable Payment* (New York: Wiley, 1961).
25 Armstrong, M., *Employee Reward* (London: Institute of Personnel and Development, 1996).
26 Torrington, D. and Chee Huat, T., *Human Resource Management for South-east Asia* (London: Prentice-Hall International (UK) Ltd, 1994).
27 Gomez-Mejia, L. R. and Balkin, D. B., *Compensation, Organisational Strategy, and Firm Performance* (Cincinnati: Southwestern Publishing, 1992).
28 Davis, J. H., Schoorman, F. D., and Donaldson, L., 'Toward a stewardship theory of management', *Academy of Management Review* (1997), 22, 1, pp. 20–47.
29 Donaldson, L. and Davis, J. H., 'CEO Governance and Shareholder Returns: Agency Theory or Stewardship Theory', Paper presented at the annual meeting of the Academy of Management, Washington, DC, 1989; Donaldson, L. and Davis, J. H., 'Stewardship Theory or Agency Theory: CEO Governance and Shareholder Returns', *Australian Journal of Management* (1991), 16, pp. 49–64.
30 Davis et al., 'Toward a stewardship theory of management'.
31 Vecchio, *Organizational Behaviour* (n. 6 above), p. 203.
32 Pettigrew, A., *The Politics of Organisational Decision Making* (London: Tavistock, 1973); Landy, F. J. and Becker, W. S., 'Motivation theory reconsidered', in L. L. Cummings and B. M. Staw (eds), *Research in Organizational Behaviour*, vol. 9 (Greenwich, CT: JAI Press, 1987).
33 *People Management* (1998), 4, 25, 24th December, p. 16; Yamine, E. '30 burned in firewalking mishap', *Daily Telegraph* (2002), 28th February, http://dailytelegraph.com.

7 Financial Rewards and Performance Management

1 Kessler, I., 'Reward Systems', in J. Storey (ed.), *Human Resource Management: A Critical Text* (London: Routledge, 1995), pp. 254–79 (see p. 256); Baron, A. and Armstrong, M., 'Out of the tick box', *People Management* 4, 15, 23rd July, 1998, p. 38.
2 Kessler, I., 'Reward Systems', p. 256.
3 Poole, M. and Jenkins, G., 'Developments in human resource management in manufacturing in modern Britain', *International Journal of Human Resource Management* (1997), 8, 6, December, pp. 841–56 (see p. 852).
4 For enterprise agreements and industrial awards, see: <www.osiris.gov.au>; Bratton, J. and Gold, J., *Human Resource Management: Theory and Practice*, 2nd edn (Basingstoke: Macmillan Business, 1999).
5 Cowling, A. and James, P., *The Essence of Personnel Management and Industrial Relations* (London: Prentice-Hall, 1994); Armstrong, M. and Murlis, H., *Reward Management*, 3rd edn (London: Kogan Page, 1994).
6 Armstrong, M., *Employee Reward* (London: Institute of Personnel and Development, 1996), pp. 271–9.
7 Kinnie, N. and Purcell, J., 'Teamworking', *People Management* (1998), 4, 9, 30th April, p. 35; Wiesner, R. and McDonald, J., 'Bleak house or bright prospect? Human resource management in Australian SMEs', *Asia Pacific Journal of Human Resources* (2001), 39, 3, pp. 31–53.
8 Swabe, A. I. R., 'Performance-related pay: a case study', *Employee Relations* (1989), 11, 2, pp. 17–23 (see p. 17).
9 Kinnie, N. and Lowe, D., 'Performance related pay on the shopfloor', *Personnel Management* (1990), November, pp. 45–9 (see p. 45), cited in I. Beardwell and L. Holden, *Human Resource Management: A Contemporary Perspective* (London: Pitman, 1997), p. 575.
10 Storey, J., *Developments in the Management of Human Resources* (Oxford: Blackwell, 1992).
11 Marsden, D. and Richardson, R., 'Performing for pay? The effects of "merit pay" on motivation in a public service', *British Journal of Industrial Relations* (1994), 32, 2, June, pp. 243–62, (see p. 251); *People Management* (1998), 4, 15, 23rd July, p. 11.
12 O'Donnell, M., 'Creating a performance culture? Performance-based pay in the Australian Public Service', *Australian Journal of Public Administration* (1998), 57, 3, pp. 28–40;

	Walsh, J., 'Human resource management in foreign-owned workplaces: evidence from Australia', *International Journal of Human Resource Management* (2001), 12, 3, May, pp. 425-44. Marchington, M. and Wilkinson, A., *Core Personnel and Development* (London: Institute of Personnel and Development, 1996); Kessler, I., 'Performance pay', in K. Sisson (ed.), *Personnel Management: A Comprehensive Guide to Theory and Practice in Britain*, 2nd edn (Oxford: Blackwell, 1994).
13	Cockerill, A., 'The kind of competence for rapid change', *Personnel Management* (1989), 21, 9, September, pp. 532-56; Cockerill, A., 'Managerial competence as a determinant of organizational performance', unpublished PhD thesis (London: University of London, London Business School, 1990); Schroder, H. M., *Managerial Competence: The Key to Excellence* (Iowa: Kendall-Hunt, 1989); Boyatzis, R., *The Competent Manager: A Model for Effective Managers* (New York: Wiley, 1982).
14	Woodruffe, C., 'What is meant by a competency?', in R. Boam and P. Sparrow (eds), *Designing and Achieving Competency: A Competency-Based Approach to Developing People and Organizations* (Maidenhead: McGraw-Hill, 1992), pp. 16-30 (see p. 29): '... competencies are dimensions of behaviour which are related to superior job performance'.
15	Armstrong, M., *Employee Reward* (n. 6 above), pp. 177-82.
16	*People Management* (1998) 4, 16, 13th August, p. 15.
17	Marchington, M. and Wilkinson, A., *Core Personnel and Development* (London: Institute of Personnel and Development, 1996), p. 334.
18	Long, R., 'The effects of employee ownership on organizational identification, employee job attitudes, and organizational performance: a tentative framework and empirical findings', *Human Relations* (1978), 31, 1, pp. 29-48; Baddon, L., Hunter, L., Hyman, J., Leopold, J., and Ramsay, H., *A Critical Analysis of Profit-sharing and Employee Share Ownership* (London: Routledge, 1989); Dunn, S., Richardson, R., and Dewe, P., 'The impact of employee share ownership on worker attitudes: a longitudinal case study', *Human Resource Management Journal* (1991), 1, 3, Spring, pp. 1-17.
19	Poole, M. and Jenkins, G., 'How employees respond to profit sharing', *Personnel Management* (1988), July, p. 33; Bakan, I., 'The effect of profit sharing and share option schemes on employee job attitudes', unpublished PhD thesis, Coventry University, June 1999.
20	Oliver, N., 'Work rewards, work values and organizational commitment in an employee owned firm: evidence from the UK', *Human Relations* (1990), 43, 6, pp. 513-26.
21	French, J. L., 'Employee perspectives on stock ownership: financial investment or mechanism of control?', *Academy of Management Review* (1987), 12, pp. 427-35.
22	Klein, K. J., 'Employee stock ownership and employee attitudes: a test of three models', *Journal of Applied Psychology Monograph* (1987), 72, 2, pp. 319-32.
23	Purcell (1993), unpublished, cited by Kessler, I., 'Reward Systems', in J. Storey (ed.), *Human Resource Management: A Critical Text* (London: Routledge, 1995), pp. 254-79 (see p. 256); Crystal, G. S., *In Search of Excess: the Overcompensation of American Executives* (New York: W. W. Norton, 1991).
24	For enterprise agreements and industrial awards, see: <www.osiris.gov.au>; *People Management* (1998), 4, 2, 22nd January, p. 16.
25	National Institute for Economic and Social Research (London: NIESR, 1994); Harding, A., Lloyd, R., and Greenwell, H., *Financial Disadvantage in Australia 1990-2000* (Canberra: National Centre for Social and Economic Modelling, 2001); Economic Policy Institute, *America's Well-Targeted Raise* (EPI: Washington, DC, 1997); Holland, P. J. and Dowling, P. J., 'CEO compensation in Australia: is there a relationship between principles, policies and practices?', *Asia Pacific Journal of Human Resources* (2001), 39, 3, pp. 41-58.
26	*HR Monthly* (2001), October, p. 10.
27	Pfeffer, J., *Competitive Advantage Through People* (Boston, MA: Harvard Business School Press, 1994); Huselid, M. A., 'The Impact of Human Resource Management Practices on Turnover, Productivity and Corporate Financial Performance', *Academy of Management Journal* (1995), 38, 3, pp. 635-72.
28	Guest, D., *Personnel Management* (1998), 4, 21, 29th October, pp. 64-5.
29	Guest, D. E., 'Human resource management: when research confronts theory', *International Journal of Human Resource Management* (2001), 12, 7, November, pp. 1092-106;

Wood, S. and Albanese, M., 'Can We Speak of a High Commitment Management on the Shop Floor?', *Journal of Management Studies* (1995), 32, 2, pp. 1–33; Gollan, P. J. and Davis, E. M., 'High involvement management and organisational change: beyond rhetoric', *Asia Pacific Journal of Human Resources* (1999), 37, 2, pp. 69–91.

30 Connock, S., *HR Vision: Managing a Quality Workforce* (London: Institute of Personnel Management, 1991).

31 For more information on AWIRS (1995) see: Morehead, A., Steele, M., Alexander, M., Stephen, K., and Duffin, L., *Changes at Work: The 1995 Australian Workplace Industrial Relations Survey* (Melbourne: Longman, 1997).

32 Cully, M. et al., 'Fourth Workplace Employee Relations Survey', *People Management* 4, 21, 29th October, 1998, p. 71; Marchington M. and Wilkinson A., *Core Personnel and Development* (see n. 12 above), pp. 136–7. For more information on Orica, its history and competence initiatives, consult: <www.orica.com.au>.

33 Anderson, G., 'Performance appraisal', in B. Towers (ed.), *The Handbook of Human Resource Management*, 2nd edn (Oxford: Blackwell, 1992), pp. 196–222 (see p. 198).

34 Harrison, R., *Human Resource Management: Issues and Strategies* (Wokingham: Addison-Wesley, 1993), p. 262.

35 Nankervis, A., Compton, R., and Baird, M., *Strategic Human Resource Management*, 4th edn (Melbourne: Nelson Thomson Learning, 2002), pp. 397–8; Unpublished internal review (1995) of the performance appraisal system of one part of the MoD conducted by a member of the British forces.

36 Stone, R. J., *Human Resource Management*, 4th edn (Brisbane: John Wiley & Sons, 2002), pp. 276. Peer appraisal tends to be popular among senior groups of professionals who resist appraisal by other non-professionals. The evidence from research on professional partnerships is that below partner level the main method of appraisal is superior-subordinate. Further reading on appraisal in professional firms: Morris, T. J. and Pinnington, A. H., 'Evaluating strategic fit in professional service firms', *Human Resource Management Journal* (1998), 8, 4, pp. 1–12.

37 Grint, K., 'What's wrong with performance appraisals? A critique and a suggestion', *Human Resource Management Journal* (1993), 3, 3, pp. 61–77.

38 Fraser, C. and Zarkada-Fraser, A., 'Perceptual polarization of managerial performance from a human resource management perspective', *International Journal of Human Resource Management* (2001), 12, 2, March, pp. 256–69; Dessler, G., Griffiths, J., Lloyd-Walker, B., and Williams A., *Human Resource Management* (Sydney: Prentice-Hall, 1999), p. 482; Fletcher, *People Management* (1998), 4, 19, 1st October, p. 46.

39 Bradley, L. M. and Ashkanasy, N. M., 'Formal performance appraisal interviews: can they really be objective, and are they useful anyway?' *Asia Pacific Journal of Human Resources* (2001), 39, 2, pp. 83–97.

40 Grint, K., 'What's wrong with performance appraisals?'

41 Entrekin, L. and Chung, Y. W., 'Attitudes towards different sources of executive appraisal: a comparison of Hong Kong Chinese and American managers in Hong Kong', *International Journal of Human Resource Management* (2001), 12, 6, September, pp. 965–87; Snape, E., Thompson, D., Yan, F. K., and Redman, T., 'Performance appraisal and culture: practice and attitudes in Hong Kong and Great Britain', *International Journal of Human Resource Management* (1998), 9, 5, October, pp. 841–61 (see p. 841).

42 Fletcher, C. and Williams, R., 'The route to performance management', *Personnel Management* (1992), October, pp. 42–7.

43 McGregor, D., *The Human Side of Enterprise* (New York: Harper & Row, 1960).

44 Williams, S., 'Strategy and objectives', in F. Neale (ed.), *The Handbook of Performance Management* (London: Institute of Personnel Management, 1992), pp. 7–24.

45 Sparrow, P. and Marchington, M., 'Re-engaging the HRM Function', in P. Sparrow and M. Marchington (eds), *Human Resource Management: The New Agenda* (London: Financial Times, Pitman Publishing, 1998), 296–313 (see p. 309).

46 Kaplan, R. S. and Norton, D. P., 'Begin by linking measurements to strategy', *Harvard Business Review* (1993), September–October, pp. 134–42.

47	Sparrow, P. and Marchington, M., 'Re-engaging the HRM Function' (n. 45 above), p. 309.
48	Guest, D. E., 'Human Resource Management and Performance: a Review and Research Agenda', *International Journal of Human Resource Management* (1997), 8, 3, June, pp. 263–76.
49	MacDuffie, J. P., 'Human Resource Bundles and Manufacturing Performance: Flexible Production Systems in the World Auto Industry', *Industrial Relations and Labor Review* (1995), 48, pp. 197–221.
50	Schuler, R. S. and Jackson, S. E., 'Linking Competitive Strategies with Human Resource Management Practices', *Academy of Management Executive* (1987), 1, 3, pp. 207–19; Lawler, E. E. III., 'The strategic design of reward systems', in C. Fombrun, N. M. Tichy, and M. A. Devanna (eds), *Strategic Human Resource Management* (New York: John Wiley & Sons, 1984).

8 Learning and Development

1	Finegold, D., 'The implications of training in Britain for the analysis of Britain's skill problem: how much do employers spend on training?', *Human Resource Management Journal* (1991), 2, 1, Autumn, pp. 110–15.
2	Deery, S., Walsh, J., and Knox, A., 'The non-union workplace in Australia: bleak house or human resource innovator?', *International Journal of Human Resource Management* (2001), 12, 4, June, pp. 669–83; For more on training and development in the UK, see: Finegold, D. and Soskice, D., 'The failure of training in Britain: analysis and prescription', *Oxford Review of Economic Policy* (1988), 4, 5, Autumn, pp. 41–53.
3	Kochan, T. A. and Osterman, P., *The Mutual Gains Enterprise: Forging a Winning Partnership Among Labor, Management, and Government* (Boston, MA: Harvard Business School Press, 1994).
4	Kochan and Osterman, *The Mutual Gains Enterprise*, pp. 5–6; Boydell, T. H., *A Guide to the Identification of Training Needs*, 4th impression (London: British Association for Commercial and Industrial Education, 1990); Boydell, T. H. and Leary, M., *Identifying Training Needs* (London: IPD, 1996).
5	Keep, E., 'Missing links', *People Management* (1999), 5, 2, 28th January, p. 35.
6	Hall, D. T., 'Human resource development and organizational effectiveness', in C. J. Fombrun, N. M. Tichy, and M. A. Devanna (eds), *Strategic Human Resource Management* (New York: John Wiley & Sons, 1984), pp. 159–81.
7	Starkey, K., *How Organizations Learn* (London: Thomson International Business Press, 1996), p. 1.
8	Harrison, R., *Employee Development* (London: Institute of Personnel and Development, 1992), p. 4.
9	Stiles, P., Gratton, L., Truss, C., Hope-Hailey, V., and McGovern, P., 'Performance management and the psychological contract', *Human Resource Management Journal* (1997), 7, 1, pp. 57–66 (see table 1, p. 59).
10	For enterprise agreements and industrial awards, see: <www.osiris.gov.au>.
11	Department of Employment, *Glossary of Training Terms*, 2nd edn (London: HMSO, 1978).
12	Department of Employment, *Glossary of Training Terms*.
13	Department of Employment, *Glossary of Training Terms*.
14	Storey, J., *Human Resource Management: A Critical Text* (London: Routledge, 1995), p. 26.
15	Storey, J. and Sisson, K., *Managing Human Resources and Industrial Relations* (Milton Keynes: Open University Press, 1993), p. 223.
16	Poole, M. and Jenkins, G., 'Developments in Human Resource Management in Manufacturing in Modern Britain', *International Journal of Human Resource Management* (1997), 8, 6, December, pp. 841–56 (see pp. 854–5); Campbell, I. and Burgess, J., 'National patterns of temporary employment: The distinctive case of casual employment in Australia', *NKCIR Working Paper no. 53* (Melbourne: National Key Centre for Industrial Relations, Monash University, 1997).
17	*People Management* (1998), 4, 16, 13th August, p. 11.

18	Storey, J., *Human Resource Management: A Critical Text*, p. 384.
19	Pedler, M., Burgoyne, J., and Boydell, T., *The Learning Company: A Strategy for Sustainable Development* (Maidenhead: McGraw-Hill, 1991), p. 1.
20	Pedler et al., *The Learning Company*, p. 1.
21	Pedler et al., *The Learning Company*, p. 19.
22	Pedler et al., *The Learning Company*, p. 13.
23	Pedler et al., *The Learning Company*, pp. 13–14.
24	The models that the systematic approach draws upon come from the following: Bloom, B. S. (ed.), *Taxonomy of Educational Objectives, the Classification of Educational Goals*, by a committee of college and university examiners (New York: David McKay & Co., 1956); Gagné, R. M., *Essentials of Learning for Instruction* (Illinois: Holt, Rinehart and Winston, 1975); Romiszowski, A. J., *Producing Instructional Systems* (London: Kogan Page, 1986).
25	Argyris, C., 'Skilled incompetence', in K. Starkey (ed.), *How Organizations Learn* (London: International Thomson Business Press, 1996), pp. 82–91; Argyris, C. and Schon, D. A., *Organizational Learning: A Theory of Action Perspective* (Reading, MA: Addison-Wesley, 1978); Schein, E., *Organizational Psychology* (Englewood Cliffs, NJ: Prentice-Hall, 1988).
26	Counselling: Summerfield, J. and van Oudtshoorn, L., *Counselling in the Workplace* (London: Institute of Personnel and Development, 1995); human relations: Mayo, E., *The Human Problems of an Industrial Civilization* (New York: Macmillan, 1933); gestalt psychology: Lewin, K., *Field Theory in Social Science* (New York: Harper, 1951); psychotherapy: Perls, F. S., Hefferline, R., and Goodman, P., *Gestalt Therapy: Excitement and Growth in the Human Personality* (Harmondsworth: Penguin Books (reprinted), 1977); transactional analysis: Berne, E., *Transactional Analysis in Psychotherapy* (New York: Grove Press, 1961); Berne, E., *Games People Play: the Psychology of Human Relationships* (New York: Grove Press, 1964); Rogers, C., *On Becoming a Person: a Therapist's View of Psychotherapy* (London: Constable, 1961); socio-technical systems theory: Trist, E. L. and Bamforth, K. W., 'Some social and psychological consequences of the longwall method of coal-getting', *Human Relations* (1951), 4, pp. 3–38; Trist, E. L., Higgin, C. W., Murray, H., and Pollock, A. M., *Organizational Choice* (London: Tavistock Institute, 1963).
27	Pettigrew, A. M., *The Awakening Giant* (Oxford: Blackwell, 1985).
28	Megginson, D. and Pedler, M., *Self-development: a Facilitator's Guide* (Maidenhead: McGraw-Hill, 1992).
29	Revans, R., *Action Learning* (London: Blond & Briggs, 1980); Revans, R., *The ABC of Action Learning* (London: Chartwell-Bratt, 1983).
30	Peters, T. J. and Waterman, Jr, R. H., *In Search of Excellence: Lessons from America's Best Run Companies* (New York: Harper & Row, 1982); Deal, T. E. and Kennedy, A., *Corporate Cultures* (Reading, MA: Addison-Wesley, 1982); Kanter, R. M., *The Change Masters: Corporate Entrepreneurs at Work* (London: Allen & Unwin, 1984).
31	Pedler et al., *The Learning Company* (n. 19 above), p. 15.
32	Legge, K., *Human Resource Management: Rhetorics and Realities* (Basingstoke: Macmillan, 1995), p. 80.
33	Pedler et al., *The Learning Company*, pp. 15–17.
34	Senge, P., *The Fifth Discipline: The Art and Practice of the Learning Organization* (New York: Doubleday/Currency, 1990); Senge, P., 'The Leader's New Work: Building Learning Organizations', in K. Starkey (ed.), *How Organizations Learn* (London: Thomson International Business Press, 1996), pp. 288–315.
35	Argyris, C. and Schon, D. A., *Organizational Learning* (1978) (n. 25 above).
36	Dixon, N. M., *The Organizational Learning Cycle: How We Can Learn Collectively* (Maidenhead: McGraw-Hill, 1994).
37	Kolb, D. A., *Individual Learning Styles and the Learning Process* (Massachusetts Institute of Technology Sloan School Working Paper no. 535-71, 1971); Kolb, D. A., Rubin, I. M., and McIntyre, J. M., *Organizational Psychology: An Experiential Approach* (Englewood Cliffs, NJ: Prentice-Hall, 1974).
38	Kolb, D. A., *Experiential Learning* (Englewood Cliffs, NJ: Prentice-Hall, 1984).
39	Kolb, D. A., 'Management and the learning process', in K. Starkey (ed.), *How Organizations Learn* (London: Thomson International Business Press, 1996), pp. 270–87.

40. Kolb, D. A., 'Management and the learning process'; Mumford, A., 'Individual and Organizational Learning: the Pursuit of Change', in C. Mabey and P. Iles (eds), *Managing Learning* (London: Routledge, in association with Open University Press, 1994), pp. 77–86.
41. Honey, P. and Mumford, A., *A Manual of Learning Styles*, 1st edn (Maidenhead: Peter Honey, 1981), pp. 25–9; Honey, P. and Mumford, A., *A Manual of Learning Styles*, 3rd edn (Maidenhead: Peter Honey, 1992); Mumford, A., Honey, P., and Robinson, G. *Directors' Development Guidebook* (London: Institute of Directors and Employment Department, 1991).
42. Verbal communication (1996) by UK-based manager in a major car company.
43. Dixon, N. M., *The Organizational Learning Cycle: How We can Learn Collectively* (Maidenhead: McGraw-Hill, 1994).
44. Pettigrew, A. M., *Awakening Giant* (1995) (n. 27 above).
45. Starkey, K. and McKinlay, A., *Strategy and the Human Resource* (Oxford: Blackwell, 1993); Starkey, K. and McKinlay, A., 'Product development in Ford of Europe: undoing the past/learning the future', in K. Starkey (ed.), *How Organizations Learn* (London: Thomson International Business Press, 1996), pp. 214–29; Department of Trade, *Australia's Trade: objectives and outcomes statement* (Commonwealth of Australia: Canberra, 2002), Appendix 2; ACTU, *Australian Manufacturing and Industry Development: Policies and Prospects for 1999 and into the 21st Century* (Melbourne, ACTU, 1999).
46. Guest, D. E., 'Human Resource Management and Performance: a Review and Research Agenda', *International Journal of Human Resource Management* (1997), 8, 3, June, pp. 263–76.
47. Galbraith, J. R., *Organization Design* (Reading, MA: Addison-Wesley, 1978); Galbraith, J. R., 'Designing the Innovating Organization', in K. Starkey (ed.), *How Organizations Learn* (London: Thomson International Business Press, 1996), pp. 151–81.
48. Peters, T. J. and Waterman, Jr, R. H., *In Search of Excellence* (1982) (n. 30 above), pp. 224–34.
49. See National Occupational Health and Safety Commission (NOHSC), *Data on OHS in Australia: the Overall Scene*, and *National Catalogue of State and Industry Based OHS Data* (Sydney: NOHSC, 2000).
50. NOHSC, *Data on OHS in Australia: the Overall Scene* (Sydney: NOHSC, 2000), pp. 3–13.
51. Leigh, J., Driscoll, T., and Hendrie, L., *Australian Mesothelioma Register Report* (Sydney: NOHSC, 2001).
52. Bohle, P. and Quinlan, M., *Managing Occupational Health and Safety: A Multidisciplinary Approach* (Melbourne: Macmillan, 2000); Gunningham, N., 'Towards innovative Occupational Health and Safety regulation', *Journal of Industrial Relations* (1998), 40, 2, pp. 204–31.
53. Spry, M., 'Workplace harassment: what is it, and what should the law do about it?', *Journal of Industrial Relations* (1998), 40, 2, pp. 232–46.
54. Purse, K., 'Workplace safety and microeconomic reform in Australia', *International Journal of Employment Studies* (1997), 5, 1, pp. 135–54.
55. See, for example, Hornberger, S., Knauth, P., Costa, G., and Folkard, S. (eds), *Shiftwork in the 21st Century: Challenges for Research and Practice* (Frankfurt am Main; New York: Peter Lang, 2000).
56. Organisation for Economic Cooperation and Development (OECD), *Employment Outlook 2001* (2001), p. 225; Wooden, M., Melbourne Institute of Applied Economic and Social Research, *HR Monthly* (2001), December, p. 8.
57. Purse, K., 'Workers' compensation, employment security and the return to work process', *Economic and Labour Relations Review* (1998), 9, 2, pp. 246–309; Purse, K., 'Workers' compensation policy in Australia: best practice or lowest common denominator?', *Journal of Industrial Relations* (1998), 40, 2, pp. 179–203.
58. Bottomley, B., *Occupational Health and Management Systems* (Sydney: NOHSC, 1999).
59. Marchington, M. and Wilkinson, A., *Core Personnel and Development* (London: Institute of Personnel and Development, 1996).
60. *Employee Development Bulletin* (1991), 14, p. 9, quoted in M. Marchington and A. Wilkinson, *Core Personnel and Development*.
61. Jones, P. J., 'Outdoor management development: a journey to the centre of the metaphor', in C. Oswick and D. Grant (eds), *Organization Development: Metaphorical Explorations* (London: Pitman Publishing, 1996), pp. 209–25.
62. Rowntree, D., *Exploring Open and Distance Learning* (London: Kogan Page, 1992); Pinnington, A. H., Using Video in Training and Education (Maidenhead: McGraw-Hill, 1991).

63 Pinnington, A. H., 'The formative evaluation of interactive video', unpublished PhD thesis (Henley Management College and Brunel University, Uxbridge, 1990).
64 Reynolds, A. and Iwinski, T., *Multimedia Training: Developing Technology-based Systems* (New York: McGraw-Hill, 1996); Browne, J., 'Unleashing the power of learning: an interview with British Petroleum's John Browne', *Harvard Business Review* (1997), reprint no. 97507, September–October, pp. 147-68.
65 Browne, J., 'Unleashing the Power of Learning: An Interview with BP's Chief Executive John Browne', *Harvard Business Review* (1997), September–October, p. 168.
66 Storey, J., *Developments in the Management of Human Resources* (Oxford: Blackwell, 1992).
67 Walsh, J., 'Human resource management in foreign-owned workplaces: evidence from Australia', *International Journal of Human Resource Management* (2001), 12, 3, May, pp. 425-44; Harley, B., Ramsay, H., and Scholarios, D., 'Employee direct participation in Britain and Australia: evidence from AWIRS95 and WERS98', *Asia Pacific Journal of Human Resources* (2000), 38, 2, pp. 42-54; Storey, J., *Human Resource Management* (1995) (n. 14 above); *People Management* (2002), 8, 2, 24th January, p. 8.
68 Morgan, G., *Riding the Waves of Change: Developing Managerial Competencies for a Turbulent World* (San Francisco, CA: Jossey-Bass Inc., 1988).
69 Sparrow, P. and Marchington, M., *Human Resource Management: The New Agenda* (London: Financial Times, Pitman Publishing, 1998), p. 6.
70 Storey, J. and Sisson, K., *Managing Human Resources and Industrial Relations* (1993) (n. 15 above), p. 163.
71 Some of these programs have awarded employees fixed sums of money to spend on internal training and education (for example, $600 equivalent each year). Some of the courses have not been directly related to their work tasks (for example, sheep husbandry), and some are similar to what has previously been offered solely through the WEA (Workers' Educational Association) and part-time adult further education (for example, foreign language skills for tourists).
72 Wharton Business School was established to provide business education in the 1880s, while comparable UK institutions such as Henley Management College and London Business School were both formed in the period after World War II and have been producing MBA graduates only since the late 1960s or early 1970s.
73 Storey, J. and Sisson, K., *Managing Human Resources and Industrial Relations* (1993), (n. 15 above), p. 171.
74 Constable, J. and McCormick, R., *The Making of British Managers* (London: British Institute of Management, 1987); Handy, C. B., *The Making of Managers* (London: Manpower Services Commission/National Economic Development Office/British Institute of Management, 1987); National Economic Development Office/Manpower Services Commission, *People: The Key to Success* (London: NEDO, 1987); Mangham, I. and Silver, M. S., *Management Training: Context and Practice* (London: Economic and Social Research Council, 1986).
75 Storey, J. and Sisson, K., *Managing Human Resources and Industrial Relations* (1993) (n. 15 above); Keep, E., 'Vocational education and training for the young', in K. Sisson (ed.), *Personnel Management: A Comprehensive Guide to Theory and Practice in Britain* (Oxford: Blackwell, 1994), pp. 299-333; Marchington, M. and Wilkinson, A., *Core Personnel and Development* (1996) (n. 59 above).
76 Ashton, D and Felstead, A., 'Training and development', in J. Storey, *Human Resource Management: A Critical Text* (London: Routledge, 1995), pp. 248-50.
77 Boyatzis, R., *The Competent Manager* (Chichester: John Wiley, 1982); Schroder, H. M., *Managerial Competence: the Key to Excellence* (Iowa: Kendall-Hunt, 1989).
78 Roan, A., 'The clever country: an examination of vocational education and training policy in Australia during the 1980s and 1990s', unpublished PhD dissertation (St Lucia: University of Queensland, 1998).
79 For more information on AIM and its courses, consult <www.aim.com.au> or <www.aimvic.com.au/coursedirectory/courses> ; Sparrow, P. and Marchington, M., *Human Resource Management* (1998) (n. 69 above), p. 127.
80 Dibella, A. J., Nevis, E. C., and Gould, J. M., 'Understanding organizational learning capability', *Journal of Management Studies* (1996), 33, 3, May, pp. 361-79 (see pp. 377-8);

Sparrow, P. and Hiltrop, J.-M., *European Human Resource Management in Transition* (Hemel Hempstead: Prentice-Hall, 1994).

81 Dixon, N. M., *The Organizational Learning Cycle* (1994) (n. 43 above).
82 Sparrow, P., 'New organisational forms, processes, jobs and psychological contracts: resolving the HRM issues', in P. Sparrow and M. Marchington (eds), *Human Resource Management: The New Agenda* (London, Financial Times, Pitman Publishing, 1998), pp. 117–41 (see p. 127).

9 Managing Change

1   Parry, C., overhead projector transparencies on 'UK experience of public sector change' (London (Whitehall): Public Information Services, Cabinet Office, 1998).
2   Chandler, A. D., *Strategy and Structure: Chapters in the History of the American Industrial Enterprise* (Cambridge, MA: MIT Press, 1962).
3   Pugh, D., 'The measurement of organisation structures: does context determine form?', *Organisational Dynamics* (1973), Spring, pp. 19–34.
4   Deming, W. E., *Quality, Productivity and Competitive Position* (Cambridge, MA: MIT Press, 1982); Juran, J. M., Sedler, L. A., and Gryna, Jr, F. M. (eds), *Quality Control Handbook*, 2nd edn (New York: McGraw-Hill, 1962).
5   Starkey, K. and McKinlay, A., *Strategy and the Human Resource: Ford and the Search for Competitive Advantage* (Oxford: Blackwell, 1993).
6   Greiner, L. E., 'Evolution and revolution as organisations grow', *Harvard Business Review* (1972), no. 72407, July–August, pp. 37–46.
7   Schein, E. H., *Organizational Culture and Leadership*, 2nd edn (San Francisco: Jossey-Bass, 1992), p. 12.
8   Deal and Kennedy, *Corporate Cultures—the Rites and Rituals of Corporate Life* (London: Penguin, 1982).
9   Deal, T. E. and Kennedy, A. A., *Corporate Cultures*, pp. 159–61.
10 Pettigrew, A. M., *The Awakening Giant: Continuity and Change in ICI* (Oxford: Blackwell, 1985).
11 Peters, T. J. and Waterman, R. H., *In Search of Excellence: Lessons from America's Best Run Companies* (New York: Harper & Row, 1982).
12 They were employed by organisations such as McKinsey and Harvard.
13 Wilson, D. C., *A Strategy of Change: Concepts and Controversies in the Management of Change* (London: Routledge, 1992), p. 75.
14 Guest, D. E., 'Right enough to be dangerously wrong: an analysis of the In Search of Excellence phenomenon', in G. Salaman, S. Cameron, H. Hamblin, P. Iles, C. Mabey, and K. Thompson (eds), *Human Resource Strategies* (London: Sage, 1992), pp. 5–19.
15 Based on Peters and Waterman, *In Search of Excellence*, pp. 14–16.
16 Legge, K., *Human Resource Management: Rhetorics and Realities* (London: Macmillan, 1995), pp. 79–80.
17 Video Arts (1985), *Excellent Companies*, video cassette tape. A more recent example of similar rhetoric emphasising the central role of people in organisations is Gary Hamel's remark during his address at the October 1998 Institute of Personnel and Development Conference (Harrogate): Hamel said, 'I look on HR as much more valuable compatriots in helping companies prepare for the future than financial or strategic planners.'
18 Derivatives of Lewin's ideas are often evident on OHP transparencies and Powerpoint slides.
19 Lewin, K., 'Frontiers in group dynamics', *Human Relations* (1947), 1, pp. 5–42; Lewin, K., *Field Theory in Social Science* (New York: Harper, 1951).
20 Pettigrew, A. M., *The Awakening Giant* (1985) (see n. 10 above); Pettigrew, A. and Whipp, R., *Managing Change for Competitive Success* (Oxford: Blackwell, 1991).
21 Lewin, K., 'Frontiers in group dynamics'; Lewin, K., *Field Theory in Social Science*.
22 Lewin, K., *A Dynamic Theory of Personality: Selected Papers* (New York: McGraw-Hill, 1935). Lewin was one of the well-known Gestalt psychologists who emigrated from Germany to the USA following Adolf Hitler's rise to power in 1933.

23   Handy, C., *Understanding Organizations*, 4th edn (New York: Penguin, 1993); Argyris, C., Review essay: 'First and Second-order Errors in Managing Strategic Change: the Role of Organizational Defensive Routines', in A. M. Pettigrew, *The Management of Strategic Change* (Oxford: Basil Blackwell, 1988).
24   Whittington, R., McNulty, T., and Whipp, R., 'Market-driven change in professional services: problems and processes', *Journal of Management Studies* (1994), 31, 6, November, pp. 829–45.
25   Morris, T. J. and Pinnington, A. H., 'Promotion to partner in professional firms', *Human Relations* (1998), 51, 1, pp. 3–24.
26   Handy, *Understanding Organizations* (1993).
27   Handy, *Understanding Organizations* (1993).
28   Handy, *Understanding Organizations* (1993).
29   Morehead, A., Steele., Alexander, M., Stephen, K., and Duffin, L., *Changes at Work: The 1995 Australian Workplace Industrial Relations Survey* (Melbourne: Longman, 1997), p. 566; ACTU Occupational Health and Safety Unit, *A Report on the 1997 ACTU National OHS Survey on Stress at Work* (Melbourne: ACTU, 1998), p. 7; Fang, Y., 'Turnover propensity and its causes among Singapore nurses: an empirical study', *International Journal of Human Resource Management* (2001), 12, 5, August, pp. 859–71; Cooper, C. and White, B., 'Organisational behaviour', in S. Tyson (ed.), *Strategic prospects for HRM* (London: Institute of Personnel and Development 1995), pp. 112–45 (see p. 120).
30   Reger, R. K., Gustafson, L. T., Demarie, S. M., and Mullane, J. V., 'Reframing the organisation: why implementing total quality is easier said than done', *Academy of Management Review* (1994), 19, 3, pp. 565–84.
31   Hill, S., 'Why quality circles failed but total quality management might succeed', *British Journal of Industrial Relations* (1991), December, vol. 29, pp. 541–68; Kerfoot, D. and Knights, D., 'Empowering the quality worker? The seduction and contradiction of the total quality phenomenon', in A. Wilkinson and H. Wilmott, *Making Quality Critical: New Perspectives on Organizational Change* (London: Routledge, 1995), pp. 219–39; Pinnington, A. H. and Hammersley, G. C., 'Quality circles under the new deal at Land Rover', *Employee Relations* (1997), 19, 5, pp. 415–29.
32   Burns, R., *Managing People in Changing Times: Coping with Change in the Workplace—a Practical Guide* (London: Allen & Unwin, 1993), p. iv.
33   Burns, *Managing People in Changing Times*, p. 56.
34   Tyson, S. (ed.), *The Practice of Human Resource Strategy* (London: Pitman, 1997); Nadler, D. A. and Tushman, M. L., 'Organisational frame bending: principles for managing reorientation', *The Academy of Management, Executive Magazine* (1989), 3, 3, pp. 194–204.
35   Jick, T., 'Implementing Change', Harvard Business School Teaching Case, no. 9 (1991), pp. 1–12.
36   Jick, 'Implementing Change', p. 10.
37   Jick, 'Implementing Change', p. 4.
38   Jick, 'Implementing Change', p. 8.
39   Welch, J. F., 'A matter of exchange rates', *Wall Street Journal* (1994), 21st June, p. 23; also quoted in R. S. Schuler and M. Huselid, 'HR strategy in the United States', in S. Tyson (ed.), *The Practice of Human Resource Strategy* (London: Pitman, 1997), pp. 174–202 (see p. 174).
40   Dawson, P., *Organizational Change: a Processual Approach* (London: Paul Chapman, 1994), pp. 180–2; Kotter, J. P., *A Force for Change: How Leadership Differs from Management* (New York: The Free Press, 1990).
41   Mueller, F., 'Societal Effect, Organisational Effect and Globalisation', *Organisation Studies* (1994), 15, 3, pp. 407–28; Mueller, F., 'Strategic Human Resource Management and the Resource-Based View of the Firm: Toward a Conceptual Integration', Aston University Business School Working Paper (1994); Mueller, F., 'Human Resources as Strategic Assets: An Evolutionary Resource-Based Theory', *Journal of Management Studies* (1996), 33, 6, November, pp. 757–86; Kamoche, K., 'The Integration–Differentiation Puzzle: A Resource-Capability Perspective in International HRM', *International Journal of Human Resource Management* (1996), 7, 1, pp. 230–44; Kamoche, K., 'Strategic Human Resource Management Within a Resource-Capability View of the Firm', *Journal of Management*

	Studies (1996), March, 33, 2, pp. 213-33; Kamoche, K., 'Knowledge Creation and Learning in International HRM', *International Journal of Human Resource Management* (1997), 8, 2, April, pp. 213-25.
42	Bae, J., Chen, S. J., and Lawler, J. J., 'Variations in human resource management in Asian countries: MNC home-country and host-country effects', *International Journal of Human Resource Management* (1998), 9, 4, August, pp. 653-70 (see pp. 667-8).
43	Webb, M. and Palmer, G., 'Evading surveillance and making time: an ethnographic view of the Japanese factory floor in Britain', *British Journal of Industrial Relations* (1998), 36, 4, December, pp. 611-27 (see p. 611); Delbridge, R., 'Surviving JIT: Control and Resistance in a Japanese Transplant', *Journal of Management Studies* (1995), 32, 6, November, pp. 803-17 (see p. 803); *People Management* (2001), 7, 25, 27th December, p. 11.
44	Tayeb, M., 'Transfer of HRM practices across cultures: an American company in Scotland', *International Journal of Human Resource Management* (1998), 9, 2, April, pp. 332-58 (see p. 353); *People Management* (2002), 8, 2, 24th January, p. 10.
45	Marchington and Wilkinson, in M. Marchington and A. Wilkinson, *Core Personnel and Development* (London: Institute of Personnel and Development 1996), call it 'personnel and development' rather than HRM. This different nomenclature acknowledges the role of the professional Institute of Personnel and Development and underlines their preference to remain open-minded to the potential for improved contribution by unions in joint regulation of the employment relationship.
46	Mayo, A., 'Economic Indicators of Human Resource Management', in S. Tyson (ed.), *Strategic Prospects for HRM* (London: Institute of Personnel and Development, 1995), pp. 229-65; Tyson, S. and Fell, A., *Evaluating the Personnel Function* (London: Hutchinson, 1986); *People Management* (2002), 8, 2, 24th January, p. 37; Campbell, D. J. and Campbell, K. M., 'Why individuals voluntarily leave: perceptions of human resource managers versus employees', *Asia Pacific Journal of Human Resources* (2001), 39, 1, pp. 23-41.
47	Watson, T. J., *The Personnel Managers: A Study in the Sociology of Work and Industry* (London: Routledge & Kegan Paul, 1977); Legge, K., *Power, Innovation and Problem-Solving in Personnel Management* (London: McGraw-Hill, 1978).
48	Tyson, S. and Fell, A., 'Looking Ahead', in S. Tyson (ed.), *Strategic Prospects for HRM* (London: Institute of Personnel and Development, 1995), pp. 266-89.
49	Cully, *People Management* (1998), 4, 21, 29th October, p. 71; Marchington, M., Wilkinson, A., Ackers, P., and Goodman, J., *New Developments in Employee Involvement*, Employment Department Research Paper, Series no. 2, 1992; see Alimo-Metcalfe, B., Alban-Metcalfe, J., and Pickard, J., 'The Great and the Good', article reporting on leadership research, *People Management* (2002), 8, 1, 10th January, p. 32.
50	Watson, T. J., *In Search of Management—Culture, Chaos and Control in Managerial Work* (London: Routledge, 1995); Hope, V. and Hendry, J., 'Corporate cultural change—is it relevant for the organisations of the 1990s?', *Human Resource Management* (1992), 5, 4, pp. 61-73.
51	The interested reader should obtain the *Excellent Companies* video distributed by Video Arts (previously a Melrose film) for more information on how these attributes work in practice. The video concentrates almost exclusively on the positive features and you will need to talk to people who have first-hand experience of the companies to get a balanced picture. Alternatively, if primary data collection is not feasible, you may wish to undertake research by consulting informative secondary materials (books, articles, newspapers, and magazines). The 'excellent companies' (said to have sound performance and possess the eight traits) were: Bechtel, Boeing, Caterpillar Tractor, Dana, Delta Airlines, Digital Equipment, Emerson Electric, Fluor, Hewlett-Packard, IBM, Johnson & Johnson, McDonald's, Procter & Gamble, and 3M.

10   Conclusion

1	Keenoy, T., Oswick, C., and Grant, D., 'Organizational Discourses: Text and Context', *Organization* (1997), 4, 1, pp. 147-57 (see p. 147)

2\tMartin, G. and Woldring, K., 'Ready for the mantle? Australian human resource managers as stewards of ethics', *International Journal of Human Resource Management* (2001), 12, 2, March, pp. 243–55.

3\tMarchington, M. and Wilkinson, A., *Core Personnel and Development* (London: Institute of Personnel and Development, 1996).

4\tLegge, K., *Power, Innovation and Problem Solving in Personnel Management* (London: McGraw-Hill, 1978).

5\tMarchington and Wilkinson, *Core Personnel and Development*, p. 411.

6\tHuselid, M. A., 'The Impact of Human Resource Management Practices on Turnover, Productivity, and Corporate Financial Performance', *Academy of Management Journal* (1995), 38, 3, pp. 635–72 (see p. 635).

7\tHall, R., 'Outsourcing, contracting-out and labour hire: implications for Human Resource Development in Australian organisations', *Asia Pacific Journal of Human Resources* (2000), 38, 2, pp. 23–41.

8\tHope-Hailey, V., 'Breaking the mould? Innovation as a strategy for corporate renewal', *International Journal of Human Resource Management* (2001), 12, 7, November, pp. 1126–40.

9\tZappala, G., 'Outsourcing and Human Resource Management: a discussion starter', Australian Centre for Industrial Relations Research and Training Working Paper no. 60 (Sydney: ACIRRT, 2000), pp. 7–8.

10\tStrauss, G., 'HRM in the USA: correcting some British impressions.' *International Journal of Human Resource Management* (2001), 12, 6, September, pp. 873–97.

11\tHarley, B., 'The Myth of Empowerment: Work Organisation, Hierarchy and Employee Autonomy in Contemporary Australian Workplaces', *Work, Employment and Society* (1999), 13, 1, March, pp. 41–66; *People Management* (2002), 8, 1, 8th January, p. 11; *People Management* (2002), 8, 2, 24th January, p. 10.

12\tBarney, J., 'Firm resources and sustained competitive advantage', *Journal of Management* (1991), 17, 1, March, pp. 99–120; Mueller, F., 'Human resources as strategic assets: an evolutionary resource-based theory', *Journal of Management Studies* (1996), 33, 6, pp. 757–85; Kamoche, K. and Mueller, F., 'Human resource management: an appropriation-learning perspective', *Human Relations* (1998), 51, 8, pp. 1033–60; Hamel, G., 'Strategy innovation and the quest for value', *Sloan Management Review* (1998), Winter, 39, 2, pp. 7–14. Hamel said, 'I look on HR as much more valuable compatriots in helping companies prepare for the future than financial or strategic planners.'; *Personnel Management* (1999), 4, 22, 12th November, p. 9.

13\tStorey, J., *Human Resource Management: A Critical Text* (London: Routledge, 1995), pp. 383–5.

14\tTony Abbott, interview with Laurie Oakes, the *Sunday* program, Channel 9, 2 December 2001. Even Simon Crean, newly elected ALP leader and former ACTU president, has indicated that he will seek a reduction in the influence that unions wield within the ALP.

15\tLowry, D., 'The casual management of casual work: casual workers' perceptions of HRM practices in the highly casualised firm', *Asia Pacific Journal of Human Resources* (2001), 39, 1, pp. 42–62.

16\tCockerill, A. P., 'Validation Study into the High Performance Managerial Competencies', occasional paper (London: University of London, Centre for Organisational Research, London Business School, 1993).

17\tAshkanasy, N. M., Hartel, C. E. J., and Zerbe, W. J., 'Managing emotions in the workplace—Introduction', in N. M. Ashkanasy, W. J. Zerbe, and C. E. J. Hartel (eds), *Managing Emotions in the Workplace* (New York: ME Sharpe, 2002).

18\tSome of the HRIS provider companies trading in Australia include: Aurion Corporation Pty Ltd; Favour Pty Ltd; Frontier Software Pty Ltd; Mantrack Australia Pty Ltd; Neller Software Pty Ltd; Oracle Corporation Australia Pty Ltd; PeopleSoft Australia Pty Ltd; Micropay Pty Ltd; and Rebus Australia Pty Ltd.

19\tLindorff, M., 'Home-based telework and telecommuting in Australia: more myth than modern work form', *Asia Pacific Journal of Human Resources* (2000), 38, 3, pp. 1–11.

20\tSchuler, R. S., 'Human resource issues and activities in international joint ventures', *International Journal of Human Resource Management* (2001), 12, 1, February, pp. 1–52. Note especially (Exhibit 3: p. 12) his four stage model of the IJV process and stage 4 involving learning from the partner and transferring new knowledge to parents and other locations; Wenger, E., McDermott, R., and Snyder, W. M., *Cultivating Communities of Practice* (Boston: Harvard Business School Press, 2002); Pfeffer, J. and Sutton, R. I., *The Knowing–Doing Gap: How Smart Companies Turn Knowledge Into Action* (Boston: Harvard Business School Press, 2000); *People Management*, 8, 4, 21st February, 2002, p. 9.

21. Tourish, D. and Pinnington, A., 'Transformational leadership, corporate cultism and the spirituality paradigm: An unholy trinity in the workplace?', *Human Relations* (2002), 55, 2, pp. 147–72.

22. Kerfoot, D. and Knights, D., 'Planning for Personnel?—Human Resource Management Reconsidered.' *Journal of Management Studies* (1992), 29, 5, July, pp. 651–68.

23. Benschop, Y., 'Pride, prejudice and performance: relations between HRM, diversity and performance', *International Journal of Human Resource Management* (2001), 12, 7, November, pp. 1166–81; Fujimoto, Y., Hartel, C. E. J., Hartel, G. F., and Baker, N. J., 'Openness to dissimilarity moderates the consequences of diversity in well-established groups', *Asia Pacific Journal of Human Resources* (2000), 38, 3, pp. 46–61.

24. Guest, D. E., 'Human Resource Management and the American Dream', *Journal of Management Studies* (1990), 27, 4, July, pp. 377–97.

25. Lansbury, R. D and Woo, S., 'Production systems, human resources and employment relations in Korea: the case of Kia Motors', *Asia Pacific Journal of Human Resources* (2001), 39, 2, pp. 54–65.

Bibliography

Adams, J. S., 'Toward an understanding of inequity', *Journal of Abnormal and Social Psychology* (1963), 67, pp. 422-36.
—— 'Inequity in social exchange', in L. Berkowitz (ed.), *Advances in Experimental Social Psychology*, vol. 2 (New York: Academic Press, 1965).
Alberga, T., Tyson, S., and Parsons, D., 'An Evaluation of the Investors in People Standard', *Human Resource Management Journal* (1997), 7, 2, pp. 47-60.
Alderfer, C. P., *Existence, Relatedness and Growth* (New York: Free Press, 1972).
Allan, C., Brosnan, P., and Walsh, P., 'Labour regulation and adjustment in Australia and New Zealand', *International Employment Relations Review* (1999), 5, 1, pp. 1-14.
—— 'Workplaces employing homeworkers: an Australian and New Zealand comparison', *International Journal of Employment Studies* (2000), 8, 1, pp. 43-60.
Altman, J., 'Indigenous Work-for-the-Dole and mutual obligation: prospects for employment generation in remote Australia', *Australian Journal of Labour Economics* (2001), 5, 1, pp. 89-98.
Anderman, S., 'Unfair Dismissal and Redundancy', in R. Lewis (ed.), *Labour Law in Britain* (Oxford: Blackwell, 1986).
Anderson, G., 'Performance appraisal', in B. Towers (ed.), *The Handbook of Human Resource Management*, 2nd edn (Oxford: Blackwell, 1992), pp. 196-222.
Andrades, C., 'Women, work and unfinished business: the Equal Opportunity for Women in the Workplace Act 1999 (Cth)', *Australian Journal of Labour Law* (2000), 13, 2, pp. 171-82.
Argyris, C., Review essay: 'First- and Second-order Errors in Managing Strategic Change: the Role of Organizational Defensive Routines', in A. M. Pettigrew (ed.), *The Management of Strategic Change* (Oxford: Basil Blackwell, 1988).
—— 'Skilled incompetence', in K. Starkey (ed.), *How Organizations Learn* (London: Thomson Business Press, 1996), pp. 82-91.
—— and Schon, D. A., *Organizational Learning: A Theory of Action Perspective* (Reading, MA: Addison Wesley, 1978).
Armstrong, M., *A Handbook of Personnel Management Practice*, 6th edn (London: Kogan Page, 1996).
—— *Employee Reward* (London: Institute of Personnel and Development, 1996).
—— *Employee Reward*, 2nd edn (London: Institute of Personnel and Development, 1999).
—— *Performance Management*, 2nd edn (London: Kogan Page, 2000).
—— *A Handbook of Human Resource Management Practice*, 8th edn (London: Kogan Page, 2001).
—— and Murlis, H., *Reward Management*, 3rd edn (London: Kogan Page, 1994).
Arulampalam, W., and Booth, A. L., 'Training and Labour Market Flexibility: Is there a Trade-off?', *British Journal of Industrial Relations* (1998), 36, 4, December, pp. 521-36.
Ashton, D. and Felstead, A., 'Training and development', in J. Storey (ed.), *Human Resource Management: A Critical Text* (London: Routledge, 1995), pp. 234-53.
Athey, T. R. and Orth, M. S., 'Emerging Competency Methods for the Future', *Human Resource Management* (1999), 38, 3, pp. 215-26.
Australian Bureau of Statistics (ABS), *Australian Social Trends 2001* (Canberra: ABS, 2001).
—— catalogue number 6202.0, *Labour Force Australia* (Canberra: AGPS, August 2001).
—— catalogue number 6203.0, *Labour Force Australia* (Canberra: AGPS, August 2001), pp. 6, 40.
—— catalogue number 6310.0, *Employee Earnings, Benefits and Trade Union Membership, Australia*, August 2000.
—— catalogue number 6325.0, *Labour Force Australia* (Canberra: AGPS, 2000).

—— catalogue number 6353.0, *Wage and Salary Earners* (Canberra: AGPS).
Australian Centre for Industrial Relations Research and Training (ACIRRT), *Agreement Database and Monitor (ADAM) Report no. 22* (Sydney: ACIRRT, 1999).
—— *Australia at Work: Just Managing?* (Sydney: Prentice-Hall, 1999).
—— *Trends in Queensland Workplace Agreements*, report produced for the Queensland Department of Training and Industrial Relations (Sydney: ACIRRT, 2000).
Australian Council of Trade Unions, Trade Development Council (ACTU/TDC), *Australia Reconstructed: ACTU/TDC Mission to Western Europe: A Report by the Mission Members to the ACTU and the TDC* (Canberra: AGPS, 1987).
—— Occupational Health and Safety Unit, *A Report on the 1997 ACTU National OHS Survey on Stress at Work* (Melbourne: ACTU, 1998).
—— *Australian Manufacturing and Industry Development: Policies and Prospects for 1999 and into the 21st Century* (Melbourne: ACTU, 1999).
Australian Industry Group and Office of the Employment Advocate, *Better Workplaces—the AWA Framework* (Canberra: AGPS, 1999).
Baddon, L., Hunter, L., Hyman, J., Leopold, J., and Ramsay, H., *A Critical Analysis of Profit-sharing and Employee Share Ownership* (London: Routledge, 1989).
Bae, J., Chen, S. J., and Lawler, J. J., 'Variations in human resource management in Asian countries: MNC home-country and host-country effects', *International Journal of Human Resource Management* (1997), 8, 2, April, pp. 213–25.
Bailey, J. and Hocking, J., 'Part-time work for nurses: a case study', *International Employment Relations Review* (1997), 3, 1, pp. 1–20.
Bakan, I., 'The effect of profit sharing and share option schemes on employee job attitudes', unpublished PhD thesis (Coventry University, June 1999).
Baker, D., 'Avoiding "war on the wharves": is the non-confrontational policing of major industrial disputes "here to stay"?', *International Employment Relations Review* (1999), 5, 2, pp. 39–62.
Bamber, G. J. and Lansbury, R. (eds), *International and Comparative Industrial Relations: A Study of Industrialised Market Economies* (St Leonards, NSW: Allen & Unwin, 1998).
Bamber, G. J., Park, F. K., Lee, C. W., Ross, P., and Broadbent, K. (eds), *Employment Relations in the Asia–Pacific—Changing Approaches* (Sydney: Allen & Unwin, 2000).
Bandura, A., *Social Learning Theory* (Englewood Cliffs, NJ: Prentice-Hall, 1977).
—— 'Self-efficacy: toward a unifying theory of behavioral change', *Psychological Review* (1977), 84, pp. 191–215.
Barnevald, K. and Arsovska, B., 'AWAs: changing the structure of wages?', *Labour and Industry* (2001), 12, 1, pp. 87–108.
Barney, J., 'Strategic Human Resource Management within a Resource-Capability View of the Firm', *Journal of Management* (1991), 17, 1, pp. 99–120.
Baron, A. and Armstrong, M., 'Out of the tick box', *People Management* (1998), 4, 15, 23rd July, p. 38.
—— and Janman, K., 'Fairness in the Assessment Centre', in C. L. Cooper and I. T. Robertson (eds), *International Review of Industrial and Organizational Psychology*, vol. II (Chichester: John Wiley, 1996), pp. 61–114.
Barry, M. and Waring, P., '"Shafted": Labour productivity and Australian coal miners', *Journal of Australian Political Economy* (1999), 44, pp. 89–112.
Bartlett, C. and Ghoshal, S., *Managing Across Borders* (London: Hutchinson, 1989).
Beardwell, I. and Holden, L., *Human Resource Management: A Contemporary Perspective*, 2nd edn (London: Financial Times, Pitman Publishing, 1997).
Beaumont, P., *Human Resource Management: Key Concepts and Skills* (London: Sage, 1993).
—— and Townley, B., 'Non-Union American Plants in Britain: Their Employment Practices', *Relationnes Industrielles* (1985), 40, 4, pp. 810–25.
—— Cressey, P. and Jakobsen, P., 'Key Industrial Relations: West German Subsidiaries in Britain', *Employee Relations* (1990), 12, 6, pp. 3–6.
Becker, B. and Gerhart, B., 'The Impact of Human Resource Management on Organizational Performance: Progress and Prospects', *Academy of Management Journal* (1996), 39, 4, pp. 779–801.
Beer, M. and Spector, B., 'Corporate wide transformations in human resource management', in R. E. Walton and P. R. Lawrence (eds), *Human Resource Management—Trends and Challenges* (Boston: Harvard Business School Press, 1985), pp. 219–53.

—— Lawrence, P. R., Quinn Mills, D., and Walton, R. E., *Managing Human Assets: The Groundbreaking Harvard Business School Program* (New York: Free Press, 1984).
Bell, S. (ed.), *The Unemployment Crisis in Australia—Which Way Out?* (Melbourne: Cambridge University Press, 2000).
Benschop, Y., 'Pride, prejudice and performance: relations between HRM, diversity and performance', *International Journal of Human Resource Management* (2001), 12, 7, November, pp. 1166–81.
Benson, J., 'Outsourcing, organisational performance and employee commitment', *Economic and Labour Relations Review* (1999), 10, 1, pp. 1–21.
—— 'Employee voice in union and non-union Australian workplaces', *British Journal of Industrial Relations* (2000), 38, 3, pp. 453–60.
Berne, E., *Transactional Analysis in Psychotherapy* (New York: Grove Press, 1961).
—— *Games People Play: The Psychology of Human Relationships* (New York: Grove Press, 1964).
Bertone, S., 'Migrants, industry policy and decentralisation: from the Accord to the Workplace Relations Act 1996', *International Employment Relations Review* (1998), 4, 1, pp. 75–90.
Biddle, D. and Burgess, J., 'Youth unemployment in Australia: can mutual obligation and youth wages provide the solution?', *Economic and Labour Relations Review* (2001), vol. 12 supplement, pp. 183–99.
Birmingham, A. and Fox, P., 'A guide to the Workplace Relations Act 1996', *Australian Bulletin of Labour* (1997), 23, 1, pp. 33–47.
Bloom, B. S. (ed.), *Taxonomy of Educational Objectives, the Classification of Educational Goals*, by a committee of college and university examiners (New York: David McKay Co., 1956).
Blyton, P., 'Working Hours', in K. Sisson (ed.), *Personnel Management: A Comprehensive Guide to Theory and Practice in Britain*, 2nd edn (Oxford: Blackwell Business, 1994).
—— and Turnbull, P. (eds), *Reassessing Human Resource Management* (London: Sage, 1992).
—— *The Dynamics of Employee Relations* (Basingstoke: Macmillan, 1998).
Boam, R. and Sparrow, P., *Designing and Achieving Competency: A Competency-Based Approach to Developing People and Organizations* (Maidenhead: McGraw-Hill, 1992).
Bodman, P. M., 'Trade union amalgamations, openness and the decline in Australian trade union membership', *Australian Bulletin of Labour* (1998), 24, 1, pp. 18–46.
—— Hall, R., Harley, B., and Whitehouse, G., 'What does enterprise bargaining mean for gender equity? Some empirical evidence', *Labour and Industry* (1996), 7, 1, pp. 51–68.
—— Harley, B., and Lafferty, G., 'Machine gaming: a case study in service sector employment', *International Journal of Employment Studies* (1996), 4, 2, pp. 77–93.
—— Lafferty, G., Roan, A., and Whitehouse, G., 'Training, careers and numerical flexibility: equity implications in hospitality and retailing', *Journal of Industrial Relations* (1996), 38, 1, pp. 3–21.
Bowden, B., 'A collective catastrophe: productivity maximisation and workplace bargaining in the Australian coal industry', *Journal of Industrial Relations* (2000), 42, 3, pp. 364–82.
Bournois, F., *La Gestion des Cadres en Europe (Personnel Management in Europe)* (Paris: Editions Eyrolles, 1991).
Boxall, P. and Haynes, P., 'Unions and non-union bargaining agents under the Employment Contracts Act 1991: an assessment after 12 months', *New Zealand Journal of Industrial Relations* (1992), 17, pp. 223–32.
Boyatzis, R., *The Competent Manager: A Model for Effective Managers* (New York: Wiley, 1982).
Boydell, T. H., *A Guide to the Identification of Training Needs* (London: British Association for Commercial and Industrial Education, 4th impression, 1990).
—— and Leary, M., *Identifying Training Needs* (London: IPD, 1996).
Bradley, L. M., and Ashkanasy, N. M., 'Formal performance appraisal interviews: can they really be objective, and are they useful anyway?', *Asia Pacific Journal of Human Resources* (2001), 39, 2, pp. 83–97.
Bramble, T., 'Union strategy and the 1998 waterfront dispute', *Queensland Review* (1998), 5, 2, pp. 76–91.
—— 'Australian union strategies since 1945', *Labour and Industry* (2001), 11, 3, pp. 1–26.
Bramham, J., *Human Resource Planning*, 2nd edn (London: Institute of Personnel and Development, 1994).
Bratton, J. and Gold, J., *Human Resource Management: Theory and Practice*, 1st edn (London: Macmillan, 1994), 2nd edn (London: Macmillan, 1999).

Bray, M. and Murray, G., 'Introduction: globalisation and labour deregulation', *Journal of Industrial Relations* (2000), 42, 2, pp. 167–72.
Brewster, C., 'Flexible working in Europe: extent, growth and the challenge for HRM', in P. Sparrow and M. Marchington (eds), *Human Resource Management: The New Agenda* (London: Financial Times, Pitman Publishing, 1998), pp. 245–58.
—— 'HRM: the European Dimension', in J. Storey (ed.), *Human Resource Management: A Critical Text* (London: Routledge, 1995), pp. 309–31.
—— 'National cultures and international management', in S. Tyson (ed.), *Strategic Prospects for HRM* (London: Institute of Personnel and Development, 1995).
—— and Bournois, F., 'A European Perspective on Human Resource Management', *Personnel Review* (1991), 20, 6, pp. 4–13.
—— and Hegewisch, A. (eds), *Policy and Practice in European Human Resource Management: The Price Waterhouse Cranfield Survey* (London: Routledge, 1994).
Briggs, C., 'Australian exceptionalism: the role of trade unions in the emergence of enterprise bargaining', *Journal of Industrial Relations* (2001), 43, 1, pp. 27–43.
Briscoe, J. P. and Hall, D. T., 'Grooming and Picking Leaders using Competency Frameworks: Do They Work? An Alternative Approach and New Guidelines for Practice', *Organizational Dynamics* (1999), 28, 2, pp. 37–51.
Brooks, I., and Harfield, T., 'Breaking the psychological contract: the effects of change-work on middle managers when implementing organizational change', *Asia Pacific Journal of Human Resources* (2000), 38, 3, pp. 91–103.
Brown, M., 'Employee pay adjustment preferences: recent Australian evidence', *Asia Pacific Journal of Human Resources* (2001), 39, 3, pp. 1–22.
Brown, W., Marginson, P., and Walsh, J., 'Management: Pay Determination and Collective Bargaining', in P. Edwards (ed.), *Industrial Relations: Theory and Practice in Britain* (Oxford: Blackwell, 1995), pp. 123–50.
Browne, J., 'Unleashing the power of learning: an interview with BP's Chief Executive John Browne', *Harvard Business Review* (1997), reprint number 97507, September–October, pp. 147–68.
Bryan, D., *The Chase Across the Globe: International Accumulation and the Contradictions for Nation States* (Boulder, Colorado: Westview Press, 1995).
—— 'National competitiveness and the subordination of labour: an Australian policy study', *Labour and Industry* (2000), 11, 2, pp. 1–16.
Buchanan, D. A., 'Principles and practice in work design', in K. Sisson (ed.), *Personnel Management: A Comprehensive Guide to Theory and Practice in Britain*, 2nd edn (Oxford: Blackwell, 1994), pp. 85–116.
Buchanan, J. and Allan, C., 'The growth of contracts in the construction industry: implications for tax revenue', *Economic and Labour Relations Review* (2000), 11, 1, pp. 136–68.
—— Callus, R., and Biggs, C., 'What impact has the Howard Government had on wages and hours of work?', *Journal of Australian Political Economy* (1999), 43, pp. 1–21.
—— and Thornthwaite, L, 'Paid work and parenting: charting a new course for Australian families', ACIRRT working paper no. 71 (Sydney: ACIRRT, 2001).
Buckley, P. and Enderwick, P., *The Industrial Relations Practices of Foreign-Owned Firms in Britain* (London: Macmillan, 1985).
Burgess, J., 'Workforce casualisation in Australia', *International Employment Relations Review* (1996), 2, 1, pp. 35–54.
—— 'The flexible firm and the growth of non-standard employment', *Labour and Industry* (1997), 7, 3, pp. 85–102.
—— 'Outsourcing, employment and industrial relations in the public sector', *Economic and Labour Relations Review* (1999), 10, 1, pp. 36–55.
—— and Campbell, I., 'Casual employment in Australia: growth, characteristics, a bridge or a trap?', *Economic and Labour Relations Review* (1998), 9, 1, pp. 31–54.
—— and de Ruyter, A., 'Declining job quality in Australia: another hidden cost of unemployment', *Economic and Labour Relations Review* (2000), 11, 2, pp. 246–69.
—— Mitchell, W., O'Brien, D., and Watts, M., 'Unemployment: promises, policies and progress', *Labour and Industry* (1998), 9, 2, pp. 103–22.

—— Strachan, G., and Watts, M. J., 'Labour market deregulation and gender equity in the Australian workforce: complementary or incompatible?', *Economic and Labour Relations Review* (2000), 11, supplement, pp. 187–214.

Burns, R., *Managing People in Changing Times: Coping with Change in the Workplace—a Practical Guide* (London: Allen & Unwin, 1993).

Burrell, G. and Morgan, G., *Sociological Paradigms and Organizational Analysis* (London: Heinemann, 1979).

Business Review Weekly, November, 1989.

Buultjens, J. and Cairncross, G., 'Ten years of enterprise bargaining and the hospitality sector', *Labour and Industry* (2001), 12, 1, pp. 27–42.

Campbell, D. J., and Campbell, K. M., 'Why individuals voluntarily leave: perceptions of human resource managers versus employees', *Asia Pacific Journal of Human Resources* (2001), 39, 1, pp. 23–41.

Campbell, I., 'Casual employment, labour regulation and Australian trade unions', *Journal of Industrial Relations* (1996), 38, 4, pp. 571–99.

—— 'The spreading net: age and gender in the process of casualisation in Australia', *Journal of Australian Political Economy* (2000), 45, pp. 68–99.

—— 'Casual employees and the training deficit: exploring employer contributions and choices', *International Journal of Employment Studies* (2001), 9, 1, pp. 61–102.

—— and Burgess, J., 'National patterns of temporary employment: The distinctive case of casual employment in Australia', *NKCIR Working Paper no. 53* (Melbourne: National Key Centre for Industrial Relations, Monash University, 1997).

—— 'A new estimate of casual employment?', *Australian Bulletin of Labour* (2001), 27, 2, pp. 85–108.

Campo, R., 'The protection of employee entitlements in the event of employer insolvency: Australian initiatives in the light of international models', *Australian Journal of Labour Law* (2000), 13, 3, pp. 236–59.

Capelli, P. and McElrath, R., 'The Transfer of Employment Practices through Multinationals', paper presented to Third Bargaining Group Conference (Berkeley: University of California, 1992).

Cawthorne, P., 'On the waterfront', *Journal of Australian Political Economy* (1998), 41, pp. 7–22.

Chandler, A. D., *Strategy and Structure: Chapters in the History of the American Industrial Enterprise* (Cambridge, MA: MIT Press, 1962).

Chapman, A., 'Termination of employment under the Workplace Relations Act 1996 (Cth)', *Australian Journal of Labour Law* (1997), 10, 1, pp. 89–111.

Cheal, D., *New Poverty: Families in Postmodern Society* (Westport, Conn. and London: Greenwood Press, 1996).

Chin, D., 'Exhuming the individual employment contract: a case of labour law exceptionalism', *Australian Journal of Labour Law* (1997), 10, 1, pp. 257–79.

Clark, I., 'Competitive Pressures and Engineering Process Plant Contracting', *Human Resource Management Journal* (1998), 8, 2, pp. 14–28.

—— and Winchester, D., 'Management and Trade Unions', in K. Sisson (ed.), *Personnel Management: A Comprehensive Guide to Theory and Practice in Britain* (1994), pp. 694–723.

Clark, J., 'Personnel Management, Human Resource Management and Technical Change', in J. Clark (ed.), *Human Resource Management and Technical Change* (London: Sage, 1993), pp. 1–19.

Clarke, M. and Patrickson, M., 'Does downsized mean down and out?', *Asia Pacific Journal of Human Resources* (2001), 39, 1, pp. 63–78.

Clegg, H., *The Changing System of Industrial Relations in Great Britain* (Oxford: Blackwell, 1979).

Cockerill, A., 'The kind of competence for rapid change', *Personnel Management* (1989), 21, 9, September, pp. 532–56.

—— 'Managerial competence as a determinant of organizational performance', unpublished PhD thesis (University of London, London Business School, 1990).

Cole, G. A., *Personnel Management*, 3rd edn (London: DP Publications, 1993).

Coller, X., 'Managing Flexibility in the Food Industry: A Cross-National Comparative Case Study of European Multinational Companies', *European Journal of Industrial Relations* (1996), 2, 2, pp. 153–72.

Colling, T. and Ferner, A., 'Privatization and Marketization', in P. Edwards (ed.), *Industrial Relations: Theory and Practice in Britain* (Oxford: Blackwell, 1995), pp. 491–514.

—— and Dickens, L., 'Selling the Case for Gender Equality: Deregulation and Equality Bargaining', *British Journal of Industrial Relations* (1998), 36, 3, pp. 389–411.

Commission on Public Policy and British Business, *Promoting Prosperity: A Business Agenda for Britain* (London: Vintage, 1997).
Connell, J. and Burgess, J., 'Workforce and skill restructuring in Australia', *International Employment Relations Review* (1998), 4, 1, pp. 39–56.
—— 'Skill, training and workforce restructuring in Australia: an overview', *International Journal of Employment Studies* (2001), 9, 1, pp. 61–102.
Connock, S., *HR Vision: Managing a Quality Workforce* (London: Institute of Personnel Management, 1991).
Constable, J. and McCormick, R., *The Making of British Managers* (London: British Institute of Management, 1987).
Cooper, C. and White, B., 'Organisational behaviour', in S. Tyson (ed.), *Strategic Prospects for HRM* (London: IPD, 1995), pp. 112–45.
Coulthard, A., 'Damages for unfair dismissal: the High Court's judgment in Byrne and Frew vs Australian Airlines', *Australian Journal of Labour Law* (1996), 9, 1, pp. 38–73.
Cowling, A. and James, P., *The Essence of Personnel Management and Industrial Relations* (London: Prentice-Hall, 1994).
Crawley, M., 'Labour hire and the employment relationship', *Australian Journal of Labour Law* (2000), 13, 3, pp. 291–6.
Creighton, B., 'The Workplace Relations Act in international perspective', *Australian Journal of Labour Law* (1997), 10, 1, pp. 31–49.
—— and Stewart, A., *Labour Law: an Introduction*, 3rd edn (Sydney: Federation Press, 2000).
Crystal, G. S., *In Search of Excess: The Overcompensation of American Executives* (New York: W. W. Norton, 1991).
Cully, M. et al., 'Fourth Workplace Employee Relations Survey', *People Management* (1998), 4, 21, 29th October, p. 71.
Curnow, B. and McLean F. J., *Third Age Careers* (London: Gower Press, 1994).
Curtain, R., 'Flexible workers and access to training', *International Journal of Employment Studies* (2001), 9, 1, pp. 103–20.
Dabscheck, B., 'The BCA's plan to Americanise Australian Industrial Relations', *Journal of Australian Political Economy* (1990), November, pp. 1–14.
—— 'The waterfront dispute: of vendettas and the Australian Way', *Economic and Labour Relations Review* (1998), 9, 2, pp. 155–87.
—— 'The Australian waterfront dispute and theories of the state', *Journal of Industrial Relations* (2000), 42, 4, pp. 497–516.
—— '"A felt need for increased efficiency": industrial relations at the end of the millennium', *Asia Pacific Journal of Human Resources* (2001), 39, 2, pp. 4–30.
Daniel, W. and Millward, N., *Workplace Industrial Relations in Britain* (London: Heinemann, 1983).
Daniels, K., Lamond, D., and Staden, P. (eds), *Managing Telework* (London: Business Press, 2000).
Dannin, E., 'We can't overcome? A case study of freedom of contract and labour law reform', *Berkeley Journal of Employment and Labour Law* (1995), 16, 1, pp. 1–168.
Davis, J. H., Schoorman, F. D., and Donaldson, L., 'Toward a stewardship theory of management', *Academy of Management Review* (1997), 22, 1, pp. 20–47.
Davis, M., 'Is bigger better? Union size and expenditure on members', *Journal of Industrial Relations* (1999), 41, 1, pp. 3–34.
Dawkins, P., 'Chapter 1: Introduction', in P. Dawkins and C. R. Littler (eds), *Downsizing: Is it Working for Australia?* (Melbourne: Melbourne Institute for Applied Economic and Social Research, 2001).
Dawson, P., *Organizational Change: A Processual Approach* (London: Paul Chapman, 1994).
Deakin, S. and Morris, D. S., *Labour Law* (London: Butterworths, 1998).
Deal, T. E. and Kennedy, A., *Corporate Cultures* (Reading, MA: Addison-Wesley, 1982).
—— *Corporate Cultures—The Rites and Rituals of Corporate Life* (London: Penguin Books, 1982).
De Cock, C. and Hipkin, I., 'TQM and BPR: Beyond the Myth', *Journal of Management Studies* (1997), 34, 5, September, pp. 659–75.
Dedoussis, V., 'Simply a Question of Cultural Barriers? The Search for New Perspectives in the Transfer of Japanese Management Practices', *Journal of Management Studies* (1995), 32, 6, pp. 731–45.

Deery, S. and Mitchell, R. (eds), *Employment Relations, Individualism and Union Exclusion* (Sydney: Federation Press, 2000).
—— Plowman, D., Walsh, J., and Brown, M., *Industrial Relations: A Contemporary Analysis* (Roseville, NSW: Irwin/McGraw-Hill, 2001).
—— and Walsh, J., 'Union decline in Australia: the role of Human Resource Management practices and the union-hostile workplace', *Australian Journal of Labour Law* (1999), 12, 1, pp. 21-31.
—— and Knox, A., 'The non-union workplace in Australia: bleak house or human resource innovator?', *International Journal of Human Resource Management* (2001), 12, 4, June, pp. 669-83.
Delbridge, R., 'Surviving JIT: Control and Resistance in a Japanese Transplant', *Journal of Management Studies* (1995), 32, 6th November, pp. 803-17.
Deming, W. E., *Quality, Productivity and Competitive Position* (Cambridge, MA: MIT Press, 1982).
Department of Employment (Australia), Workplace Relations and Small Business (2000), *Labour Market Review of Australia* (Canberra: AGPS, p. 11; 20-3).
Department of Employment (UK), *Glossary of Training Terms*, 2nd edn (London: HMSO, 1978).
—— 'Employment for the 1990s', Cm 540 (London: HMSO, 1989).
Department of Trade (Australia), *Australia's Trade: Objectives and Outcomes Statement* (Commonwealth of Australia: Canberra, 2002).
Devanna, M. A., Fombrun, C. J., and Tichy, N. M., 'A Framework for Strategic Human Resource Management', in C. J. Fombrun, N. M. Tichy, and M. A. Devanna, *Strategic Human Resource Management* (New York: John Wiley & Sons, 1984), pp. 33-51.
Diamond, C. and Lafferty, G., 'Telework: issues for research, policy and regulation', *Labour and Industry* (2000), 11, 1, pp. 115-28.
Dibella, A. J., Nevis, E. C., and Gould, J. M., 'Understanding organizational learning capability', *Journal of Management Studies* (1996), 33, 3, May, pp. 361-79.
Dickens, L., 'Anti-Discrimination Legislation: Exploring and Examining the Impact on Women's Employment', in W. McCarthy (ed.), *Legal Intervention in Industrial Relations: Gains and Losses* (Oxford: Blackwell, 1992).
—— 'Wasted Resources? Equal Opportunities in Employment', in K. Sisson (ed.), *Personnel Management: A Comprehensive Guide to Theory and Practice in Britain*, 2nd edn (Oxford: Blackwell, 1994), pp. 495-526.
—— 'Comparative Systems of Unjust Dismissal: The British Case', *Annals of the American Academy of Political and Social Sciences* (1994), November.
—— 'What HRM Means for Gender Equality', *Human Resource Management Journal* (1998), 8, 1, pp. 23-40.
—— and Hall, M., 'The State: Labour Law and Industrial Relations', in P. Edwards (ed.), *Industrial Relations: Theory and Practice in Britain* (Oxford: Blackwell, 1995), pp. 255-303.
—— Jones, M., Weekes, B., and Hart, M., *Dismissed: A Study of Unfair Dismissal and the Industrial Tribunal System* (Oxford: Blackwell, 1985).
Dickerson, A., Gibson, H., and Tsakalotos, E., *The Impact of Acquisitions on Company Performance: Evidence from a Large Panel of UK Firms* (Canterbury: University of Kent Press, 1995).
Dixon, N. M., *The Organizational Learning Cycle: How We Can Learn Collectively* (Maidenhead: McGraw-Hill, 1994).
Doherty, N., 'Downsizing', in S. Tyson (ed.), *The Practice of Human Resource Strategy* (London: Financial Times, Pitman Publishing, 1997).
Donaldson, L. and Davis, J. H., 'CEO Governance and Shareholder Returns: Agency Theory or Stewardship Theory', paper presented at the annual meeting of the Academy of Management (Washington, DC, 1989).
—— 'Stewardship Theory or Agency Theory: CEO Governance and Shareholder Returns', *Australian Journal of Management* (1991), 16, pp. 49-64.
Donovan Commission, *Royal Commission on Trade Unions and Employer Associations* (London: HMSO, 1968), p. 1.
Dow, G., 'The legacy of orthodoxy: political causes of unemployment', *Economic and Labour Relations Review* (2001), vol. 12 supplement, pp. 83-98.
—— and Parker, R. (eds), *Business, Work and Community: Into the New Millenium* (Melbourne: Oxford University Press, 2001).
Dowling, B. and Richardson, R., 'Evaluating Performance-Related Pay for Managers in the National Health Service', *International Journal of Human Resource Management* (1997), 8, 3, June, pp. 348-66.

DTI, *Annual Report* (London: DTI, 1997).
Dunn, S., Richardson, R., and Dewe, P., 'The impact of employee share ownership on worker attitudes: a longitudinal case study', *Human Resource Management Journal* (1991), 1, 3, Spring, pp. 1-17.
Ebadan, G. and Winstanley, D., 'Downsizing, Delayering and Careers—The Survivor's Perspective', *Human Resource Management Journal* (1997), 7, 1, pp. 79-91.
Eby, L. T. and Dobbins, G. H., 'Collectivist orientation in Teams: An Individual and Group-Level Analysis', *Journal of Organizational Behaviour* (1997), vol. 18, p. 227.
Economic Policy Institute, *America's Well-Targeted Raise* (EPI: Washington, DC, 1997).
Edwards, P., 'The Employment Relationship', in P. Edwards (ed.), *Industrial Relations: Theory and Practice in Britain* (Oxford: Blackwell, 1995).
Emmot, M. and Hutchinson, S., 'Employment Flexibility: Threat or Promise', in P. Sparrow and M. Marchington (eds), *Human Resource Management: The New Agenda* (London: Financial Times, Pitman Publishing, 1998), pp. 229-44.
Employment Gazette, various issues.
Encel, S., 'Mature age unemployment: a long-term cost to society', *Economic and Labour Relations Review* (2000), 11, 2, pp. 233-45.
Entrekin, L., and Chung, Y. W., 'Attitudes towards different sources of executive appraisal: a comparison of Hong Kong Chinese and American managers in Hong Kong', *International Journal of Human Resource Management* (2001), 12, 6, September, pp. 965-87.
Estes, W. K., 'Reinforcement in human behavior', *American Scientist* (1972), 60, pp. 723-9.
Evans, P., Doz, Y., and Laurent, A. (eds), *Human Resource Management in International Firms* (London: Macmillan, 1989).
Evans, R., 'On the waterfront', *Journal of Australian Political Economy* (1998), 41, pp. 1-6.
Evenden, R., 'The strategic management of recruitment and selection', in R. Harrison (ed.), *Human Resource Management: Issues and Strategies* (Wokingham, England: Addison-Wesley, 1993).
Ewer, P., 'Trade unions and Vocational Education Training: questions of strategy and identity', *Labour and Industry* (2000), 10, 3, pp. 37-56.
Fang, Y., 'Turnover propensity and its causes among Singapore nurses: an empirical study', *International Journal of Human Resource Management* (2001), 12, 5, August, pp. 859-71.
Fastenau, M., 'Women's employment in Australia, 1986-1996: a period of glacial change', *International Employment Relations Review* (1997), 3, 1, pp. 61-90.
—— and Pullin, L., 'A comparative typology of employment relations, industrial relations, and Human Resource Management', *International Employment Relations Review* (1998), 4, 1, pp. 1-22.
Feldman, D. C. and Kim, S., 'Acceptance of buyout offers in the face of downsizing: empirical evidence from the Korean electronics industry. Study of a major Korean electronics company', *International Journal of Human Resource Management* (1998), 9, 6, December, pp. 1008-25.
Fells, R., 'A critical examination of the process of workplace negotiation', *Labour and Industry* (1998), 9, 1, pp. 37-52.
—— and Skeffington, R., 'A critical examination of the strategic negotiations framework—the case of the Australian shearing industry', *International Employment Relations Review* (1998), 4, 1, pp. 23-38.
Feltham, R., 'Using Competencies in Selection and Recruitment', in R. Boam and P. Sparrow (eds), *Designing and Achieving Competency: A Competency-Based Approach to Developing People and Organizations* (Maidenhead: McGraw-Hill, 1992), pp. 89-103.
Ference, T. P., Stoner, J. A. F., and Warren, K. E., 'Managing the career plateau', in R. Katz (ed.), *Managing Professionals in Innovative Organizations* (Cambridge, MA: Ballinger Publishing Company, Harper & Row, 1988).
Ferner, A., 'Multinational Companies and Human Resource Management: An Overview of Research Issues', *Human Resource Management Journal* (1994), 4, 3, pp. 79-102.
—— 'Country of Origin Effects and HRM in Multinational Companies', *Human Resource Management Journal* (1997), 7, 1, pp. 19-37.
—— and Hyman, R. (eds), *Changing Industrial Relations in Europe* (Oxford: Blackwell, 1998).
Filella, J., 'Is there a Latin Model in the Management of Human Resources?', *Personnel Review* (1991), 20, 6, pp. 15-24.
Finegold, D., 'The implications of training in Britain for the analysis of Britain's skill problem: how much do employers spend on training?', *Human Resource Management Journal* (1991), 2, 1, Autumn, pp. 110-15.

—— and Sostice, D., 'The failure of training in Britain: analysis and prescription', *Oxford Review of Economic Policy* (1988), 4, 5, Autumn, pp. 41-53.

Fisher, R. and Dowling, P. J., 'Support for an HR approach in Australia: the perspective of senior HR managers', *Asia Pacific Journal of Human Resources* (1999), 37, 1, pp. 1-19.

Fletcher, C., *People Management* (1998), 4, 23, 26th November, p. 40.

—— and Anderson, N., 'A superficial assessment', *People Management* (1998), 4, 10, 14th May, p. 44.

—— and Williams, R., 'The route to performance management', *Personnel Management* (1992), October, pp. 42-7.

Flood, P. C., Turner, T., Ramamoorthy, N., and Pearson, J., 'Causes and consequences of psychological contracts among knowledge workers in the high technology and financial services industries', *International Journal of Human Resource Management* (2001), 12, 7, November, pp. 1152-65.

Fombrun, C. J., Tichy, N. M., and Devanna, M. A., *Strategic Human Resource Management* (New York: John Wiley & Sons, 1984).

Foot, M. and Hook, C., *Introducing Human Resource Management* (London: Longman Publishing, 1996).

Ford, W. J., 'Reconstructing Australian labour law: a Constitutional perspective', *Australian Journal of Labour Law* (1997), 10, 1, pp. 1-30.

Foster, D. and Hoggett, P., 'Changes in the Benefits Agency: empowering the exhausted worker?', *Work, Employment & Society* (1999), 13, 1, pp. 19-39.

Fox, F. and Teicher, J., 'Victoria's Employee Relations Act: the way of the future?', in R. Callus and M. Schumacher (eds), *Current Research in Industrial Relations: Proceedings of the 8th AIRAANZ Conference* (Sydney: Australian Centre for Industrial Relations Research and Training, 1994), pp. 508-36.

Frankel, B., *When the Boat Comes in: Transforming Australia in the Age of Globalisation* (Sydney: Pluto Press, 2001).

Franks, J. and Mayer, C., 'Do Hostile Take-overs Improve Performance?', *Business Strategy Review* (1996), 7, 4, pp. 1-6.

Fraser, C. and Zarkada-Fraser, A., 'Perceptual polarization of managerial performance from a human resource management perspective', *International Journal of Human Resource Management* (2001), 12, 2, March, pp. 256-69.

Fraser, L, *Impact of contracting out of female NESB workers: case study of the NSW Government Cleaning Service* (Sydney: Ethnic Communities Council of NSW, 1997).

—— *Impact of Contracting Out on Female NESB Workers: Case Study of the NSW Government Cleaning Service* (Canberra: Department of Immigration and Multicultural Affairs, 1997).

Freeman, R., 'The Limits to Wage Flexibility in Curing Unemployment', *Oxford Review of Economic Policy* (1995), 11, 1, pp. 63-72.

—— 'Does Globalisation Threaten Low-Skilled Western Workers?', in J. Philpott (ed.), *Working for Full Employment* (London: Routledge, 1997), pp. 132-50.

French, J. L., 'Employee perspectives on stock ownership: financial investment or mechanism of control?', *Academy of Management Review* (1987), 12, pp. 427-35.

Fujimoto, Y., Hartel, C. E. J., Hartel, G. F., and Baker, N. J., 'Openness to dissimilarity moderates the consequences of diversity in well-established groups', *Asia Pacific Journal of Human Resources* (2000), 38, 3, pp. 46-61.

Gagné, R. M., *Essentials of Learning for Instruction* (Illinois: Dryden Press; Holt, Rinehart & Winston, 1975).

Gahan, P. and Harcourt, T., 'Australian labour market institutions, "deregulation" and the open economy', *Economic and Labour Relations Review* (1999), 10, 2, pp. 296-318.

Galbraith, J. R., *Organization Design* (Reading, MA: Addison-Wesley, 1978).

—— 'Designing the innovating organization', in K. Starkey (ed.), *How Organizations Learn* (Thomson International Business Press, 1996), pp. 156-81.

—— and Nathanson, D., *Strategy Formulation: Analytical Concepts* (St Paul, MN: West Publishing Company, 1978).

Garrahan, P. and Stewart, P., *The Nissan Enigma: Flexibility at Work in a Local Economy* (London: Mansell, 1992).

Gilman, M., 'Performance Related Pay in Practice: Organization and Effect', unpublished PhD thesis (University of Warwick, 1998).

Glasbeek, H. J., 'The MUA affair: the role of law vs. the rule of law', *Economic and Labour Relations Review* (1998), 9, 2, pp. 188–221.
Glezer, H. and Wolcott, I., 'Conflicting commitments: working mothers and fathers in Australia', in L. L. Haas, P. Hwang, and G. Russell (eds), *Organizational Change and Gender Equity: International Perspectives on Fathers and Mothers at the Workplace* (Thousand Oaks: Sage, 2001).
Gomez-Mejia, L. R. and Balkin, D. B., *Compensation, Organizational Strategy, and Firm Performance* (Cincinnati: Southwestern Publishing, 1992).
—— and Cardy, R., *Managing Human Resources* (Englewood Cliffs, NJ: Prentice-Hall, 1995).
Goold, M. and Campbell, A., *Strategies and Styles: The Role of the Centre in Managing Diversified Corporations* (Oxford: Blackwell Business, 1987).
Gorz, A., *Reclaiming Work: Beyond the Wage-Based Society* (Oxford: Polity Press; and Malden, MA: Blackwell, 1999).
Gospel, H., 'The Revival of Apprenticeship Training in Britain?', *British Journal of Industrial Relations* (1998), 36, 3, September, pp. 435–57.
Gowler, D., Legge, K., and Clegg, C., *Case Studies in Organizational Behaviour and Human Resource Management*, 2nd edn (London: Paul Chapman Publishing, 1993).
Graham, M. and Scarborough, H., 'Public Sector Outsourcing of Information Technology Services', *Australian Journal of Public Administration* (1996), 56, 3, pp. 30–9.
Grant, D. and Oswick, C., 'Of believers, atheists and agnostics: practitioner views on HRM', *Industrial Relations Journal* (1998), 29, 3, pp. 178–93.
Gratton, L., Hope-Hailey, V., Stiles, P., and Truss, C., *Strategic Human Resource Management* (Oxford: Oxford University Press, 1999).
Green, R., 'The "death" of Comparative Wage Justice in Australia', *Economic and Labour Relations Review* (1996), 7, 2, pp. 224–53.
Greiner, L. E., 'Evolution and revolution as organisations grow', *Harvard Business Review* (1972), no. 72407, July–August, pp. 37–46.
Grewal, H., *A Guide to the Sex Discrimination Act* (London: Macdonald, 1990).
Griffin, G. and Svensen, S., 'The decline of Australian union density—a survey of the literature', *Journal of Industrial Relations* (1996), 38, 4, pp. 505–47.
—— 'Industrial relations implications of the Australian waterside dispute', *Australian Bulletin of Labour* (1998), 24, 3, pp. 194–206.
—— 'Industrial relations and the 1998 waterfront dispute', *International Employment Relations Review* (1999), 5, 2, pp. 63–78.
Grint, K., 'What's wrong with performance appraisals? A critique and a suggestion', *Human Resource Management Journal* (1993), 3, 3, pp. 61–77.
Grozier, D., 'Do individual and collective agreements make a difference?', ACIRRT working paper no. 65 (Sydney: ACIRRT, 2001).
Guest, D. E., 'Human Resource Management and Industrial Relations', *Journal of Management Studies* (1987), 24, 5, pp. 503–21.
—— 'Personnel and HRM: Can You Tell the Difference?', *Personnel Management* (1987).
—— 'Human Resource Management and the American Dream', *Journal of Management Studies* (1990), 27, 4, pp. 378–97.
—— 'Right enough to be dangerously wrong: an analysis of the In Search of Excellence phenomenon', in G. Salaman et al., *Human Resource Strategies* (London: Sage, 1992), pp. 5–19.
—— 'Human Resource Management, Trade Unions and Industrial Relations', in J. Storey (ed.), *Human Resource Management: A Critical Text* (London: Routledge, 1995), pp. 110–41.
—— 'Human Resource Management and Performance: a Review and Research Agenda', *International Journal of Human Resource Management* (1997), 8, 3, June, pp. 263–76.
—— 'Beyond HRM: Commitment and the Contract Culture', in P. Sparrow and M. Marchington (eds), *Human Resource Management: The New Agenda* (London: Financial Times, Pitman Publishing, 1998), pp. 37–51.
—— *People Management* (1998), 4, 21, 29th October, pp. 64–5.
—— *People Management* (1998), 4, 24, 10th December, p. 14.
—— 'Human resource management: when research confronts theory', *International Journal of Human Resource Management* (2001), 12, 7, November, pp. 1092–106;

Guirdham, M., *Interpersonal Skills at Work* (London: Prentice-Hall, 1990).
Gunningham, N., 'Towards innovative Occupational Health and Safety regulation', *Journal of Industrial Relations* (1998), 40, 2, pp. 204-31.
Hackman, J. R. and Oldham, G. R., 'Motivation through the design of work: test of a theory', *Organizational Behavior and Human Performance* (1976), 16, pp. 250-79.
—— *Work Redesign* (Reading, MA: Addison-Wesley, 1980).
Haggar, A. J., 'Employment statistics and the growth of part-time work', *Australian Journal of Labour Economics* (1998), 2, 2, pp. 135-56.
Hall, D. T., 'Human resource development and organizational effectiveness', in C. J. Fombrun, N. M. Tichy, and M. A. Devanna (eds), *Strategic Human Resource Management* (New York: John Wiley & Sons, 1984), pp. 159-81.
Hall, L. and Torrington, D., 'Letting Go or Holding On—The Devolution of Operational Personnel Activities', *Human Resource Management Journal* (1998), 8, 1, pp. 41-55.
Hall, M. and Sisson, K., *Coming to Terms with the EU Working Time Directive* (London: IRS, 1997).
Hall, R., 'Outsourcing, contracting-out and labour hire: implications for human resource development in Australian organisations', *Asia Pacific Journal of Human Resources* (2000), 38, 2, pp. 23-41.
—— Harley, B., and Whitehouse, G., 'Contingent work and gender in Australia: evidence from the 1995 Australian Workplace Industrial Relations Survey', *Economic and Labour Relations Review* (1998), 9, 1, pp. 55-81.
Hamberger, J., *Individual Contracts: Beyond Enterprise Bargaining?*, ACIRRT Working Paper no. 39 (Sydney: Australian Centre for Industrial Relations Research and Training, 1995).
Hampson, I., 'The Accord: a post-mortem', *Labour and Industry* (1996), 11, 2, pp. 1-16.
Handy, C. B., *The Making of Managers* (London: MSC/NEDO/BIM, 1987).
Handy, C. J., *Understanding Organizations*, 4th edn (London: Penguin Books, 1993).
Hanson, C. and Mather, G., *Striking Out Strikes* (London: IEA, 1988).
Harbridge, R., *Employment Contracts: New Zealand Experiences* (Wellington: Victoria University Press, 1993).
—— Honebone, A., and Kiely, P., *Employment Contracts: Bargaining Trends and Employment Law Update 1993/4* (Wellington: VUW Industrial Relations Centre, 1994).
Harcourt, T., 'The economics of the Australian waterfront dispute', *Economic and Labour Relations Review* (1998), 9, 2, pp. 222-35.
Harding, A., Lloyd, R., and Greenwell, H., *Financial Disadvantage in Australia 1990-2000* (Canberra: National Centre for Social and Economic Modelling, 2001).
Hargadon, A. B., and Sutton, R. I., 'Technology Brokering and Innovation in a Product Development Firm', *Administrative Science Quarterly* (1997), 42: 716-49.
Harley, B., 'The myth of empowerment: work organisation, hierarchy and employee autonomy in contemporary Australian workplaces', *Work, Employment & Society* (1999), 13, 1, pp. 41-66.
—— Ramsay, H. and Scholarios, D., 'Employee direct participation in Britain and Australia: evidence from AWIRS95 and WERS98', *Asia Pacific Journal of Human Resources* (2000), 38, 2, pp. 42-54.
Harrison, R., *Employee Development* (London: IPD, 1992).
—— *Human Resource Management: Issues and Strategies* (Wokingham: Addison-Wesley, 1993).
Hatch, M. J., *Organization Theory: Modern, Symbolic and Postmodern Perspectives* (Oxford: Oxford University Press, 1997).
Hawke, A., 'A minimum wage: are we returning to Justice Higgins?', *Australian Bulletin of Labour* (1998), 24, 2, pp. 79-93.
—— 'Implications of the waterfront dispute on performance', *International Employment Relations Review* (1999), 5, 2, pp. 93-104.
—— and Wooden, M., 'Two steps forward, one step back: industrial relations developments in Australia in 1997', *Asia Pacific Journal of Human Resources* (1998), 36, 2, pp. 15-28.
Hayden, A., *Sharing the Work, Sparing the Planet: Work Time, Consumption and Ecology* (Sydney: Pluto Press, 2001).
Hendry, C. and Jenkins, R., 'Psychological Contracts and New Deals', *Human Resource Management Journal* (1997), 7, 1, pp. 38-44.
Hepple, R., 'The Rise and Fall of Unfair Dismissal', in W. McCarthy (ed.), *Legal Intervention in Industrial Relations: Gains and Losses* (Oxford: Blackwell, 1992).
Herriot, P., 'The Management of Careers', in S. Tyson (ed.), *Strategic Prospects for HRM* (London: Institute of Personnel and Development, 1995), pp. 184-205.

—— 'The Role of the HRM Function in Building a New Proposition for Staff', in P. Sparrow and M. Marchington (eds), *Human Resource Management: The New Agenda* (London: Financial Times, Pitman Publishing, 1998), pp. 106–16.
—— and Pemberton, C., *New Deals: The Revolution in Managerial Careers* (Chichester: John Wiley & Sons, 1995).
Herron, M., 'The Job Satisfaction Study', in Victoria Law Foundation, *Facing the Future: Gender, Employment and Best Practice Issues for Law Firms*, vol. 1 (Melbourne: Victoria Law Foundation, 1996).
Herzberg, F., 'One more time: how do you motivate employees?', *Harvard Business Review* (1968), 46, 1, pp. 53–62.
Hill, C. W. L. and Jones, T. M., 'Stakeholder-Agency Theory', *Journal of Management Studies* (1992), 29, 2, March, pp. 131–54.
Hill, S., 'Why quality circles failed but total quality management might succeed', *British Journal of Industrial Relations* (1991), 29, December, pp. 541–68.
Hodgkinson, G. P. and Payne, R. L., Short research note: 'Graduate Selection in Three European Countries', *Journal of Occupational Organizational Psychology* (1998), 71, pp. 359–65.
—— Daley, N., and Payne, R. L., *International Journal of Manpower* (1995), 16, 8, pp. 59–76.
—— Snell, S., Daley, N., and Payne, R. L., 'A Comparative Study of Knowledge of Changing Demographic Trends and the Importance of HRM Practices in Three European Countries', *International Journal of Selection and Assessment* (1996), 4, 4, October, pp. 184–94.
Hofstede, G., *Culture's Consequences: International Differences in Work Related Values* (Beverly Hills: Sage, 1980).
—— 'Motivation, Leadership and Organization: Do American Theories Apply Abroad?', *Organizational Dynamics* (1980), Summer, p. 48.
—— *Cultures and Organisations: Software of the Mind* (London: McGraw-Hill, 1991).
Holland, P. J., 'Organising works: meeting the challenge of trade union membership', *International Employment Relations Review* (1999), 5, 1, pp. 63–74.
—— and Dowling, P. J., 'CEO compensation in Australia: is there a relationship between principles, policies and practices?', *Asia Pacific Journal of Human Resources* (2001), 39, 3, pp. 41–58.
Honey, P. and Mumford, A., *The Manual of Learning Styles*, 1st edn (Maidenhead: Peter Honey, 1981), 2nd edn (1992).
Hoogvelt, A., *Globalization and the Postcolonial world: The New Political Economy of Development* (Baltimore: Johns Hopkins University Press, 1997).
Hope, V. and Hendry, J., 'Corporate cultural change—is it relevant for the organisations of the 1990s?', *Human Resource Management Journal* (1992), 5, 4, pp. 61–73.
Hope-Hailey, V., 'Breaking the mould? Innovation as a strategy for corporate renewal', *International Journal of Human Resource Management* (2001), 12, 7, November, pp. 1126–40.
—— Gratton, L., McGovern, P., Stiles, P., and Truss, C., 'A Chameleon Function? HRM in the 90s', *Human Resource Management Journal* (1997), 7, 2, pp. 5–18.
Hornberger, S., Knauth, P., Costa, G., and Folkard, S. (eds), *Shiftwork in the 21st Century: Challenges for Research and Practice* (Frankfurt am Main and New York: Peter Lang, 2000).
Hu, Y., 'Global or Stateless Corporations are National Firms with International Operations', *California Management Review* (1992), 34, 2, pp. 107–26.
Hudson, M. and Hawkins, L., *Negotiating Employment Relations* (Melbourne: Longman, 1995).
Hughes, E. C., 'Institutional Office and the Person', *American Journal of Sociology* (1937), 43, pp. 404–13.
Humphrey, J., 'The Adoption of Japanese Management Techniques in Brazilian Industry', *Journal of Management Studies* (1985), 32, 6, pp. 767–88.
Hunter, B. H., 'The determinants of Indigenous employment outcomes: the importance of education and training', *Australian Bulletin of Labour* (1997), 23, 3, pp. 177–92.
—— 'An Indigenous worker's guide to the Workplace Relations Act', *Journal of Industrial Relations* (1997), 39, 4, pp. 439–56.
—— 'The social costs of Indigenous unemployment', *Economic and Labour Relations Review* (2000), 11, 2, pp. 213–32.
—— and Hawke, A. E., 'A comparative analysis of the industrial relations experience of Indigenous and other Australian workers', *Journal of Industrial Relations* (2001), 43, 1, pp. 66–78.
Huselid, M. A., 'The Impact of Human Resource Management Practices on Turnover, Productivity, and Corporate Financial Performance', *Academy of Management Journal* (1995), 38, 3, pp. 635–72.

Hutton, W., *The State We're In* (London: Jonathan Cape, 1996).
Hyman, R., 'The Historical Evolution of British Industrial Relations', in P. Edwards (ed.), *Industrial Relations: Theory and Practice in Britain* (Oxford: Blackwell, 1995), pp. 27–49.
Iles, P. and Salaman, G., 'Recruitment, Selection and Assessment', in J. Storey (ed.), *Human Resource Management* (London: Routledge, 1995), pp. 203-33.
Industrial Relations Review and Report, 'Recruitment and Training Abroad. The Labour Market in France', no. 500, November 1991.
Inns, D., 'Organization Development as a journey', in C. Oswick and D. Grant (eds), *Organization Development: Metaphorical Explorations* (London: Pitman, 1996), pp. 20-34.
Institute of Personnel Management, *Statement on Human Resource Planning* (London: IPM, 1992).
Jaques, E., *Equitable Payment* (New York: Wiley, 1961).
Jarvis, V. and Prais, S., 'Two Nations of Shopkeepers: Training for Retailing in Britain and France', *National Institute Economic Review* (1989), May, pp. 58-74.
Jenkins, A., 'The French Experience of Flexibility: Lessons for British HRM', in P. Sparrow and M. Marchington (eds), *Human Resource Management* (London: Financial Times, Pitman Publishing, 1998), pp. 259-71.
Jick, T., 'Implementing change', Harvard Business School: Teaching Case no. 9 (1991), pp. 491-514.
Jones, P. J., 'Outdoor management development: a journey to the centre of the metaphor', in C. Oswick and D. Grant (eds), *Organization Development: Metaphorical Explorations* (London: Pitman, 1996), pp. 209-25.
Journal of Australian Political Economy (1997), 39, special issue, 'Australia Reconstructed: Ten Years On', with articles by: Bryan, D., Jones, E., Stilwell, F., Johnson, C., Beeson, M., Coates, N., Rafferty, M., Kriesler, P., Halevi, J., and Dow, G.
Juran, J. M., Sedler, L. A., and Gryna, F. M. Jr (eds), *Quality Control Handbook*, 2nd edn (New York: McGraw-Hill, 1962).
Kamoche, K., 'The Integration-Differentiation Puzzle: A Resource-Capability Perspective in International HRM', *International Journal of Human Resource Management* (1996), 7, 1, pp. 230-44.
—— 'Strategic Human Resource Management Within A Resource-Capability View of the Firm', *Journal of Management Studies* (1996), March, 33, 2, pp. 213-33.
—— 'Knowledge Creation and Learning in International HRM', *International Journal of Human Resource Management* (1997), 8, 2, April, pp. 213-25.
—— and Mueller, F., 'Human Resource Management and the Appropriation-Learning Perspective', *Human Relations* (1998), 51, 8, pp. 1033-60.
Kandola, R. and Pearn, M., 'Identifying Competences', in R. Boam and P. Sparrow (eds), *Designing and Achieving Competency: A Competency-Based Approach to Developing People and Organizations* (Maidenhead: McGraw-Hill, 1992), pp. 31-49.
Kane, B., 'Downsizing, TQM, re-engineering, learning organisations and HRM strategy', *Asia Pacific Journal of Human Resources* (2000), 38, 1, pp. 26-49.
Kane, R. L., 'HRM: changing concepts in a changing environment', *International Journal of Employment Studies* (1996), 4, 2, pp. 115-78.
—— 'Downsizing and HRM strategy: is there a relationship?', *International Journal of Employment Studies* (1998), 6, 2, pp. 43-72.
Kanter, R. M., *The Change Masters: Corporate Entrepreneurs at Work* (London: Allen & Unwin, 1984).
Kaplan, R. S. and Norton, D. P., 'Begin by linking measurements to strategy', *Harvard Business Review* (1993), September-October, pp. 134-42.
Keenoy, T., 'HRM: Rhetoric, Reality and Contradiction', *International Journal of Human Resource Management* (1990), 1, 3, pp. 363-84.
—— 'HRM: a Case of the Wolf in Sheep's Clothing?', *Personnel Review* (1990), 19, 2, pp. 3-9.
—— and Anthony, P., 'Human Resource Management: Metaphor, Meaning and Morality', in P. Blyton and P. Turnbull (eds), *Reassessing Human Resource Management* (London: Sage, 1992), pp. 233-55.
—— Oswick, C., and Grant, D., 'Organizational Discourses: Text and Context', *Organization* (1997), 4, 1, pp. 147-57.
Keep, E., 'Performance pay', in K. Sisson (ed.), *Personnel Management: A Comprehensive Guide to Theory and Practice in Britain*, 2nd edn (Oxford: Blackwell, 1994).
—— 'Vocational education and training for the young', in K. Sisson (ed.), *Personnel Management: A Comprehensive Guide to Theory and Practice in Britain* (Oxford: Blackwell, 1994), pp. 299-333.

—— 'Missing links', *People Management* (1999), 5, 2, 28th January, p. 35.
—— and Mayhew, K., 'Training Policy for Competitiveness', in H. Metcalf (ed.), *Future Skill Demand and Supply* (London: PSI, 1995).
—— and Rainbird, H., 'Training', in P. Edwards (ed.), *Industrial Relations: Theory and Practice in Britain* (Oxford: Blackwell, 1995).
Kerfoot, D. and Knights, D., 'Empowering the quality worker? The seduction and contradiction of the total quality phenomenon', in A. Wilkinson and H. Wilmott (eds), *Making Quality Critical: New Perspectives on Organizational Change* (London: Routledge, 1995) pp. 219-39.
Kessler, I., 'Reward Systems', in J. Storey (ed.), *Human Resource Management: A Critical Text* (London: Routledge, 1995), pp. 254-79.
Kets de Vries, M. F. R. and Balazs, K., 'The Downside of Downsizing', *Human Relations* (1997), 50, 1, pp. 11-50.
Kinnie, N. and Lowe, D., 'Performance related pay on the shopfloor', *Personnel Management* (1990), November, pp. 45-9.
—— and Purcell, J., 'Teamworking', *People Management* (1998), 4, 9, 30th April, p. 35.
Klein, K. J., 'Employee stock ownership and employee attitudes: a test of three models', *Journal of Applied Psychology Monograph* (1987), 72, 2, pp. 319-32.
Knights, D. and McCabe, D., 'How Would You Measure Something Like That?: Quality in a Retail Bank', *Journal of Management Studies* (1997), 34, 3, May, pp. 371-88.
—— 'The Times they are a Changin'? Transformative Organizational Innovations in Financial Services in the UK', *International Journal of Human Resource Management* (1998), 9, 1, February, pp. 168-84.
Kochan, T. A., Katz, H. C., and McKersie, R. B., *The Transformation of American Industrial Relations*, 1st edn (New York: Basic Books, 1986).
—— *The Transformation of American Industrial Relations*, 2nd edn (New York: Cornell University Press, 1994).
—— and Osterman, P., *The Mutual Gains Enterprise: Forging a Winning Partnership among Labor, Management and Government* (Boston, MA: Harvard Business School Press, 1994).
Kolb, D. A., *Individual Learning Styles and the Learning Process* (MIT Sloan School Working Paper no. 535-71, 1971).
—— *Experiential Learning* (Englewood Cliffs, NJ: Prentice-Hall, 1984).
—— 'Management and the learning process', in K. Starkey (eds), *How Organizations Learn* (London: Thomson International Business Press, 1996), pp. 270-87.
—— Rubin, I. M., and McIntyre, J. M., *Organizational Psychology: An Experiential Approach* (Englewood Cliffs, NJ: Prentice-Hall, 1974).
Kollmorgen, S., 'Towards a unitary national system of industrial relations? Commonwealth Powers (Industrial Relations) Act 1996 (Vic.)', *Australian Journal of Labour Law* (1997), 10, 1, pp. 158-69.
Kotter, J. P., *The General Managers* (New York: Free Press, 1982).
—— *A Force for Change: How Leadership Differs from Management* (New York: Free Press, 1990).
—— *Leading Change* (Boston, MA: Harvard Business School Press, 1996).
Kramar, R., McGraw, P., and Schuler, R. S., *Human Resource Management in Australia*, 3rd edn (Melbourne: Addison Wesley Longman, 1997).
Kriesler, P. and Neville, J., 'Symposium on the costs of unemployment', *Economic and Labour Relations Review* (2000), 11, 2, pp. 178-9.
Lafferty, G., 'Decentralised industrial relations and internal labour markets: a case study in tourism employment', *International Employment Relations Review* (1998), 4, 2, pp. 19-32.
—— 'Responding to crisis: state withdrawal, postmodern fatalism, and the possibilities of radical economics', *Review of Radical Political Economics* (1999), 31, 1, pp. 148-61.
—— Hall, R., Harley, B., and Whitehouse, G., 'Homeworking in Australia: an assessment of current trends', *Australian Bulletin of Labour* (1997), 23, 2, pp. 24-37.
—— and Roan, A., 'Public sector outsourcing: implications for training', *Employee Relations* (2000), 22, 1, pp. 18-27.
—— Whitehouse, G., Hall, R., and Harley, W., 'Homeworking in Australia: an assessment of current trends', *Australian Bulletin of Labour* (1996), 23, 2, pp. 24-37.
Landy, F. J. and Becker, W. S., 'Motivation theory reconsidered', in L. L. Cummings and B. M. Staw (eds), *Research in Organizational Behaviour*, vol. 9 (Greenwich, CT: JAI Press, 1987).

—— 'Industrial Order and the Transformation of Industrial Relations: Britain, Germany and France Compared', in R. Hyman and A. Ferner (eds), *New Frontiers in European Industrial Relations* (Oxford: Blackwell, 1994).

Lansbury, R. D., Davis, E. M., and Simmons, D., 'Reforming the Australian workplace through employee participation', *Economic and Labour Relations Review* (1996), 7, 1, pp. 29-45.

—— and Westcott, M., 'Collective bargaining, employment and competitiveness: the case of Australia', *International Journal of Employment Studies* (2001), 9, 1, pp. 95-128.

—— and Woo, S., 'Production systems, human resources and employment relations in Korea: the case of Kia Motors', *Asia Pacific Journal of Human Resources* (2001), 39, 2, pp. 54-65.

Latham, G. P. and Locke, E. A., 'Goal setting: a motivational technique that works', *Organizational Dynamics* (1979), 8, 2, pp. 68-80.

Lawler, E. E. III, 'The strategic design of reward systems', in C. Fombrun, N. M. Tichy, and M. A. Devanna (eds), *Strategic Human Resource Management* (New York: John Wiley & Sons, 1984), pp. 127-47.

Leat, M., *Human Resource Issues of the European Union* (London: Financial Times, Pitman Publishing, 1998).

Lee, M., Bray, M., and Waring, P., 'The rhetoric and reality of bargaining structures under the Howard government', *Labour and Industry* (1998), 9, 2, pp. 61-80.

—— and Peetz, D., 'Trade unions and the Workplace Relations Act', *Labour and Industry* (1998), 9, 2, pp. 5-22.

Legge, K., *Power, Innovation and Problem Solving in Personnel Management* (London: McGraw-Hill, 1978).

—— 'Human Resource Management—A Critical Analysis', in J. Storey (ed.), *New Perspectives on Human Resource Management* (London: Routledge, 1989), pp. 19-40.

—— *Human Resource Management: Rhetorics and Realities* (Basingstoke: Macmillan, 1995).

—— 'HRM: Rhetoric, Reality and Hidden Agendas', in J. Storey (ed.), *Human Resource Management: A Critical Text* (London: Routledge, 1995), pp. 33-59.

Lewer, J. and Gallimore, P., 'Are outsourcing and skill formation mutually exclusive? The experience of a heavy manufacturing firm', *International Journal of Employment Studies* (2001), 9, 1, pp. 141-62.

Lewicki, R. J., Saunders, D. M., and Minton, J. W., *Essentials of Negotiation*, 2nd edn (Sydney, Irwin/McGraw-Hill, 2001).

Lewin, K., *A Dynamic Theory of Personality: Selected Papers* (New York: McGraw-Hill, 1935).

—— 'Frontiers in group dynamics', *Human Relations* (1947), 1, pp. 5-42.

—— *Field Theory in Social Science* (New York: Harper, 1951).

Lewis, P., 'Managing Performance-Related Pay based on Evidence from the Financial Services Sector', *Human Resource Management Journal* (1998), 8, 2, pp. 66-77.

Lewis, S. and Martin, C., 'Howard's $3bn for smarter nation', *Australian Financial Review*, 30 January 2001.

Lindorff, M., 'Home-based telework and telecommuting in Australia: more myth than modern work form', *Asia Pacific Journal of Human Resources* (2000), 38, 3, pp. 1-11.

Long, R., 'The effects of employee ownership on organizational identification, employee job attitudes, and organizational performance: a tentative framework and empirical findings', *Human Relations* (1978), 31, 1, pp. 29-48.

Lorenz, C., 'Learning to Live with a Cultural Mix', *Financial Times*, 23 April 1993.

Loveridge, R. and Mok, A., *Theories of Labour Market Segmentation: A Critique* (The Hague: Martinus Nijhoff, 1979).

Lowry, D., 'The casual management of casual work: casual workers' perceptions of HRM practices in the highly casualised firm', *Asia Pacific Journal of Human Resources* (2001), 39, 1, pp. 42-62.

Lyon, P., Hallier, J., and Glover, I., 'Divestment or Investment? The Contradiction of HRM in Relation to Older Employees', *Human Resource Management Journal* (1998), 8, 1, pp. 56-66.

Lyons, M., 'The study of gender in the employment relationship: some evidence from the Australian child-care industry', *International Journal of Employment Studies* (1998), 6, 2, pp. 175-200.

MacDermott, T. and Owens, R., 'Equality and flexibility for workers with family responsibilities: a troubled union?', *Australian Journal of Labour Law* (2000), 13, 3, pp. 278-90.

Macdonald, D., 'Public sector industrial relations under the Howard government', *Labour and Industry* (1998), 9, 2, pp. 43-60.

—— Campbell, I., and Burgess, J., 'Ten years of enterprise bargaining in Australia: an introduction', *Labour and Industry* (2001), 12, 1, pp. 1-26.

MacDuffie, J. P., 'Human Resource Bundles and Manufacturing Performance: Flexible Productions in the World Auto Industry', *Industrial Relations and Labor Review* (1995), 48, pp. 97–221.
Mallon, M., and Kearney, T., 'Team development at Fisher and Paykell: the introduction of "Everyday Workplace Teams"', *Asia Pacific Journal of Human Resources* (2001), 39, 1, pp. 93–106.
Management Charter Initiative (MCI), Management standards information pack (1997), MCI, Russell Square House, 10-12 Russell Square, London WC1B 5BZ.
Mangham, I. and Silver, M. S., *Management Training: Context and Practice* (London: ESRC, 1986).
Marchington, M. and Wilkinson, A., *Core Personnel and Development* (London: IPD, 1996).
—— Ackers, P., and Goodman, J., *New Developments in Employee Involvement*, Employment Department Research Paper, Series no. 2, 1992.
Marginson, P. et al., *Beyond the Workplace: Managing Industrial Relations in the Multi-Establishment Enterprise* (Oxford: Blackwell, 1988).
—— Armstrong, P., Edwards, P., Purcell, J. with Hubbard, N., *Warwick Papers in Industrial Relations*, no. 45, December, 1993.
—— and Sisson, K., 'The Structure of Transnational Capital in Europe: The Emerging Euro-Company and its Implications for Industrial Relations', in R. Hyman and A. Ferner (eds), *New Frontiers in European Industrial Relations* (Oxford: Blackwell, 1994), pp. 15–51.
Marsden, D. and Richardson, R., 'Performing for pay? The effects of "merit pay" on motivation in a public service', *British Journal of Industrial Relations* (1994), 32, 2, June, pp. 243-62.
Marshall, V., and Wood, R. E., 'The dynamics of effective performance appraisal: an integrated model', *Asia Pacific Journal of Human Resources* (2000), 38, 3, pp. 62–90.
Martin, G. and Woldring, K., 'Ready for the mantle? Australian human resource managers as stewards of ethics', *International Journal of Human Resource Management* (2001), 12, 2, March, pp. 243-55.
—— Staines, H., and Pate, J., 'Linking Job Security and Career Development in a New Psychological Contract', *Human Resource Management Journal* (1998), 8, 3, pp. 20–40.
Maslow, A. H., 'A Theory of Human Motivation', *Psychological Review* (1943), 50, pp. 370–96.
Mayo, A., 'Economic Indicators of Human Resource Management', in S. Tyson (ed.), *Strategic Prospects for HRM* (London: Institute of Personnel and Development, 1995), pp. 229-65.
Mayo, E., *The Human Problems of an Industrial Civilisation* (New York: Macmillan, 1933).
McCallum, R. C., 'Australian Workplace Agreements—an analysis', *Australian Journal of Labour Law* (1997), 10, 1, pp. 50–61.
—— 'A priority of rights: freedom of association and the waterfront dispute', *Australian Bulletin of Labour* (1998), 24, 3, pp. 207–22.
McCarry, G., 'Industrial action under the Workplace Relations Act 1996 (Cth), *Australian Journal of Labour Law* (1997), 10, 1, pp. 133–57.
McClelland, D. C., *The Achieving Society* (Princeton, NJ: Van Nostrand, 1961).
McGovern, P., *HRM, Technical Workers and the Multinational Corporation* (London: Routledge, 1998).
—— Gratton, L., Hope-Hailey, V., and Stiles, P., 'Human Resource Management on the Line?', *Human Resource Management Journal* (1997), 7, 4, pp. 12–29.
McGregor, D., *The Human Side of Enterprise* (New York: Harper & Row, 1960).
McIntyre, S. and Mitchell, R. (eds), *Foundations of Arbitration* (Melbourne: Oxford University Press, 1989).
McKenna, E. and Beech, N., *The Essence of Human Resource Management* (London: Prentice-Hall, 1995).
McLelland, A., 'Effects of unemployment on the family', *Economic and Labour Relations Review* (2000), 11, 2, pp. 198–212.
Megginson, D. and Pedler, M., *Self-development: A Facilitator's Guide* (Maidenhead: McGraw-Hill, 1992).
Meredith, F., 'Alternative dispute resolution in an industrial tribunal: conciliation of unfair dismissal disputes in South Australia', *Australian Journal of Labour Law* (2001), 14, 1, pp. 36–61.
Merlo, O., 'Flexibility and stretching rights: the no disadvantage test in enterprise bargaining', *Australian Journal of Labour Law* (2000), 13, 3, pp. 207–35.
Miller, E., 'Strategic staffing', in C. Fombrun, N. M. Tichy, and M. A. Devanna (eds), *Strategic Human Resource Management* (New York: John Wiley & Sons, 1984).
Millward, N., *The New Industrial Relations?* (London: PSI, 1994).
—— Stevens, M., Smart, D., and Hawes, W., *Workplace Industrial Relations in Transition* (Aldershot: Dartmouth, 1992).

Mintzberg, H., 'Crafting Strategy', *Harvard Business Review* (1987), July–August, pp. 65–75.
Morehead, A., Steele, M., Alexander, M., Stephen, K., and Duffin, L., *Changes at Work: The 1995 Australian Workplace Industrial Relations Survey* (Melbourne: Addison Wesley Longman, 1997), pp. 82–4.
Morgan, G., *Riding the Waves of Change: Developing Managerial Competencies for a Turbulent World* (San Francisco, CA: Jossey-Bass Inc., 1988).
Morris, J. and Wilkinson, B., 'The Transfer of Japanese Management to Alien Institutional Environments', *Journal of Management Studies* (1995), 32, 6, pp. 719–30.
Morris, R., 'From productivity crisis to industrial dispute: the 1998 waterfront troubles', *International Employment Relations Review* (2000), 6, 1, pp. 89–106.
—— Mortimer, D., and Leece, P. (eds), *Workplace Reform and Enterprise Bargaining*, 2nd edn (Sydney: Harcourt Brace, 1999).
Morris, T. J. and Pinnington, A. H., 'Promotion to partner in professional firms', *Human Relations* (1998), 51, 1, pp. 3–24.
—— and Pinnington, A. H., 'Evaluating strategic fit in professional service firms', *Human Resource Management Journal* (1998), 8, 4, pp. 1–12.
Mueller, F., 'Societal effect, organisational effect and globalisation', *Organisation Studies* (1994), 15, 3, pp. 407–28.
—— 'Strategic Human Resource Management and the Resource-Based View of the Firm: Toward a Conceptual Integration', Aston University Business School Working Paper (1994).
—— 'Human Resources As Strategic Assets: An Evolutionary Resource-Based Theory', *Journal of Management Studies* (1996), 33, 6, November, pp. 757–86.
Mumford, A., 'Individual and Organizational Learning: the Pursuit of Change', in C. Mabey and P. Iles (eds), *Managing Learning* (London: Routledge, in association with Open University Press, 1994), pp. 77–86
—— Honey, P. and Robinson, G., *Director's Development Guidebook* (London: Institute of Directors and Employment Department, 1991).
Murakami, T., 'The formation of teams: a British and German comparison', *International Journal of Human Resource Management* (1998), 9, 5, October, pp. 800–17.
Murtough, G. and Waite, M., 'A new estimate of casual employment? Reply', *Australian Bulletin of Labour* (2001), 27, 2, pp. 109–17.
Mylett, T., 'Flexibility and labour market structures: the role of employers', *Economic and Labour Relations Review* (1998), 9, 2, pp. 285–309.
Nadler, D. A. and Tushman, M. L., 'Organisational frame bending: principles for managing reorientation', *Academy of Management Executive Magazine* (1989), 3, 3, pp. 194–204.
Nankervis, A., Compton, R., and Baird, M., Strategic Human Resource Management, 4th edn (Melbourne: Nelson Thomson Learning, 2002).
Naughton, R., 'Review of Lord Wedderburn, *Labour Law and Freedom: Further Essays in Labour Law* (London: Lawrence and Wishart, 1995)', in *Australian Journal of Labour Law* (1996), 9, 3, pp. 294–7.
—— 'Sailing into uncharted seas: the role of unions under the Workplace Relations Act 1996 (Cth)', *Australian Journal of Labour Law* (1997), 10, 1, pp. 112–32.
Nelson, L., 'Enterprise bargaining and evolving Human Resource Management', *International Employment Relations Review* (1998), 4, 2, pp. 33–48.
Newell, S., and Rice, C., 'Assessment, Selection and Evaluation: Problems and Pitfalls', in J. Leopold, L. Harris, and T. Watson (eds), *Strategic Human Resourcing: Principles, Perspectives and Practices* (London: Financial Times, Pitman Publishing, 1999), pp. 129–65.
O'Donnell, M., 'Creating a performance culture? Performance-based pay in the Australian Public Service', *Australian Journal of Public Administration* (1998), 57, 3, pp. 28–40.
Office for National Statistics, *Labour Market Trends* (London: ONS, 1998).
Ogbonna, E. and Harris, L. C., 'The performance implications of the work-oriented cognitions of shopfloor workers: a study of British retailing', *International Journal of Human Resource Management* (2001), 12, 6, September, pp. 1005–28.
Ohmae, K., *The Borderless World* (London: Collins, 1990).
Oliver, N., 'Work rewards, work values and organizational commitment in an employee owned firm: evidence from the UK', *Human Relations* (1990), 43, 6, pp. 513–26.
—— and Wilkinson, B., *The Japanization of British Industry* (Oxford: Blackwell, 1988).

—— *The Japanization of British Industry: New Developments in the 1990s* (Oxford: Blackwell, 1992).
Orr, G., 'Conspiracy on the waterfront', *Australian Journal of Labour Law* (1998), 11, 3, pp. 159–85.
Ouchi, W., *Theory Z* (Reading, MA: Addison-Wesley, 1981).
Owens, R., 'The "long-term or permanent casual"—an oxymoron or "a well enough understood Australianism" in the law', *Australian Bulletin of Labour* (2001), 27, 2, pp. 118–36.
Pancharatnam, K., '"Contestability" in competitive tendering and contracting: a critique', *Economic and Labour Relations Review* (1999), 10, 1, pp. 56–72.
Parker, S. K. and Wall, T. D., 'Job Design and Modern Manufacturing', in P. Warr (ed.), *Psychology and Work*, 4th edn (London: Penguin Books, 1996).
Parry, C., 'Overhead projector transparencies on UK experience of public sector change' (Whitehall, London: Public Information Services, Cabinet Office, 1998).
Pedler, M., Burgoyne, J., and Boydell, T., *The Learning Company: A Strategy for Sustainable Development* (Maidenhead: McGraw-Hill, 1991).
Peetz, D., 'Unions, conflict and the dilemma of co-operation', *Journal of Industrial Relations* (1996), 38, 4, pp. 548–70.
—— *Unions in a Contrary World: the Future of the Australian Trade Union Movement* (Cambridge and Melbourne: Cambridge University Press, 1998).
—— 'Why join? Why Stay? Instrumentality, beliefs, satisfaction and individual decisions on union membership', *Economic and Labour Relations Review* (1998), 9, 1, pp. 123–48.
—— 'Nearly the year of living dangerously: in the emerging worlds of Australian industrial relations', *Asia Pacific Journal of Human Resources* (1999), 37, 2, pp. 3–23.
—— Quinn, D., Edwards, L., and Reidel, P., 'Workplace bargaining in New Zealand: radical change at work', in D. Peetz, A. Preston and J. Docherty (eds), *Workplace Bargaining in the International Context*, Industrial Relations Research Monograph number 2 (Canberra: Department of Industrial Relations, 1992).
People Management, 4, 15, 23rd July, 1998.
—— 4, 16, 13th August, 1998.
—— 4, 19, 1st October, 1998.
—— 4, 24, 10th December, 1998.
—— 4, 25, 24th December, 1998.
—— 5, 1, 14th January, 1999.
—— 5, 2, 28th January, 1999.
—— 7, 2, 29th January, 2001.
—— 7, 25, 27th December, 2001.
—— 8, 1, 10th January, 2002.
—— 8, 2, 24th January, 2002.
—— 8, 4, 28th February, 2002.
Perls, F. S., Hefferline, R., and Goodman, P., *Gestalt Therapy: Excitement and Growth in the Human Personality* (Harmondsworth: Penguin Books (reprinted), 1977).
Peters, T. J. and Waterman, R. H. Jr., *In Search of Excellence: Lessons from America's Best Run Companies* (New York: Harper & Row, 1982).
Pettigrew, A. M., *The Politics of Organisational Decision Making* (London: Tavistock, 1973).
—— *The Awakening Giant: Continuity and Change in ICI* (Oxford: Blackwell, 1985).
—— and Whipp, R., *Managing Change for Competitive Success* (Oxford: Blackwell, 1991).
Pfeffer, J., *Competitive Advantage Through People* (Boston, MA: Harvard Business School Press, 1994).
—— and Sutton, R. I., *The Knowing–doing Gap: How Smart Companies Turn Knowledge Into Action* (Boston: Harvard Business School Press, 2000).
Pickersgill, R., 'Skill formation in Australia beyond 2000: "flexibility" and Vocational Education and Training policy', *International Journal of Employment Studies* (2001), 9, 1, pp. 121–40.
Pinder, C. C., 'Valence-Instrumentality-Expectancy Theory', in V. H. Vroom and E. L. Deci (eds), *Management and Motivation*, 2nd edn (Harmondsworth: Penguin Books, 1992).
Pinnington, A. H., 'The formative evaluation of interactive video', unpublished PhD thesis (Henley Management College and Brunel University, Uxbridge, 1990).
Pinnington, A. H., *Using Video in Training and Education* (Maidenhead: McGraw-Hill, 1991).
—— and Hammersley, G. C., 'Quality circles under the new deal at Land Rover', *Employee Relations* (1997), 19, 5, pp. 415–29.

—— and Woolcock, P., 'How Far is IS/IT Outsourcing Enabling New Organizational Structure and Competences?', *International Journal of Information Management* (1995), 15, 5, pp. 353-65.
—— 'The Role of Vendor Companies in IS/IT Outsourcing', *International Journal of Information Management* (1997), 17, 3, pp. 199-210.
Pitt, G., *Employment Law* (London: Sweet & Maxwell, 1995).
Pocock, B., 'Success in defence: union strategy and the 1998 maritime dispute', *International Employment Relations Review* (1999), 5, 2, pp. 17-38.
—— 'Institutional sclerosis: prospects for trade union transformation', *Labour and Industry* (1998), 9, 1, pp. 17-36.
Poole, M. and Jenkins, G., 'How employees respond to profit sharing', *Personnel Management* (1988), July, p. 33.
—— 'Developments in Human Resource Management in Manufacturing in Modern Britain', *International Journal of Human Resource Management* (1997), 8, 6, December, pp. 841-56.
Porter, L. W. and Lawler III, E. E., *Managerial Attitudes and Performance* (Homewood, IL: Irwin-Dorsey, 1968).
Porter, M., *Competitive Advantage: Creating and Sustaining Superior Performance* (New York: Macmillan, Free Press, 1985).
—— *The Competitive Advantage of Nations* (New York: Free Press, 1990).
Prahalad, C. and Hamel, G., 'The core competence of the corporation', *Harvard Business Review* (1990), May-June, pp. 79-91.
Probert, B., Ewer, P., and Whiting, K., 'Work versus life: union strategies reconsidered', *Labour and Industry* (2000), 11, 1, pp. 23-48.
Pugh, D. S., 'The Measurement of Organisation Structures: Does Context Determine Form?', *Organisational Dynamics* (1973), Spring, pp. 19-34; also in D. S. Pugh (ed.), *Organization Theory: Selected Readings*, 3rd edn (London: Penguin Books, 1990) pp. 44-63.
Purcell, J. and Gray, A., 'Corporate personnel departments and the management of industrial relations: two cases in ambiguity', *Journal of Management Studies* (1986), 23, 2, pp. 205-23.
Purse, K., 'Workplace safety and microeconomic reform in Australia', *International Journal of Employment Studies* (1997), 5, 1, pp. 135-54.
—— 'Workers' compensation, employment security and the return to work process', *Economic and Labour Relations Review* (1998), 9, 2, pp. 246-309.
—— 'Workers compensation policy in Australia: best practice or lowest common denominator?', *Journal of Industrial Relations* (1998), 40, 2, pp. 179-203.
Quiggin, J., 'Globalisation, neoliberalism and inequality in Australia', *Economic and Labour Relations Review* (1999), 10, 2, pp. 240-59.
Quinlan, M., 'Labour market restructuring in industrialised societies: an overview', *Economic and Labour Relations Review* (1998), 9, 1, pp. 1-30.
Redman, T. and Keithley, D., 'Downsizing goes East? Employment re-structuring in post-Socialist Poland', *International Journal of Human Resource Management* (1998), 9, 2, April, pp. 274-95.
Reger, R. K., Gustafson, L. T., Demarie, S. M., and Mullane, J. V., 'Reframing the organisation: why implementing total quality is easier said than done', *Academy of Management Review* (1994), 19, 3, pp. 565-84.
Reich, R., 'Who Is Us?', *Harvard Business Review* (1990), January-February, pp. 53-64.
Revans, R., *Action Learning* (London: Blond & Briggs, 1980).
—— *The ABC of Action Learning* (London: Chartwell-Bratt, 1983).
Reynolds, A. and Iwinski, T., *Multimedia Training: Developing Technology-based Systems* (New York: McGraw-Hill, 1996).
Roan, A., 'The Australian National Training Reform Strategy and the promises for women employed in the service sector', *Policy, Organisation & Society* (1996), 12, pp. 47-63.
—— 'The clever country: an examination of vocational education and training policy in Australia during the 1980s and 1990s', unpublished PhD dissertation (St Lucia: University of Queensland, 1998).
—— Bramble, T., and Lafferty, G., 'Australian Workplace Agreements in practice: the "hard" and "soft" dimensions', *Journal of Industrial Relations* (2001), 43, 4, pp. 387-401.
Robbins, S. P., *Organizational Behaviour: Concepts, Controversies, Applications* (Upper Saddle River, NJ: Prentice-Hall, 1998).

Robertson, I. T., Iles, P. A., Gratton, L., and Sharpley, D., 'The Psychological Impact of Selection Procedures on Candidates', *Human Relations* (1991), 44, 9, pp. 963–82.
Rogers, C., *On Becoming a Person: A Therapist's View of Psychotherapy* (London: Constable, 1961).
Rogers, M., 'Innovation in Australian workplaces: an empirical analysis', *Australian Bulletin of Labour* (1999), 25, 4, pp. 334–51.
Rogg, K. L., Schmidt, D. L., Skull, C., and Schmitt, N., 'Human resource practices, organisational climate, and customer satisfaction', *Journal of Management* (2001), 27, 4, pp. 431–49.
Romiszowski, A. J., *Producing Instructional Systems* (London: Kogan Page, 1986).
Rosenzweig, P. and Nohria, N., 'Influences on Human Resource Management Practices in Multinational Corporations', *Journal of International Business Studies* (1994), 25, 2, pp. 229–51.
Rothwell, S., 'Human Resource Planning', in J. Storey (ed.), *Human Resource Management: A Critical Text* (London: Routledge, 1995), pp. 167–202.
Rowntree, D., *Exploring Open and Distance Learning* (London: Kogan Page, 1992).
Royal Commission on Trade Unions and Employers' Associations Report (Donovan Commission) (HMSO: London, 1968).
Ruigrok, W. and Van Tulder, R., *The Logic of International Restructuring* (London: Routledge, 1996).
Ryan, L. and Macky, K. A., 'Downsizing organisations: uses, outcomes and strategies', *Asia Pacific Journal of Human Resources* (1998), 36, 2, pp. 29–45.
Salancik, G. R., and Pfeffer, J., 'An Examination of Need Satisfaction Models of Job Attitudes', *Administrative Science Quarterly* (1977), 22, pp. 427–56.
Sandberg, J., 'Understanding Human Competence at Work: An Interpretive Approach', *Academy of Management Journal* (2000), 43, 1, pp. 9–25.
Sappey, R. B., Maconachie, G., Sappey, J., and Teo, S., 'Work intensification and social relations: a study of enterprise agreements in the Queensland food processing industry', *International Journal of Employment Studies* (2000), 8, 1, pp. 105–24.
Schein, E. H., *Career Dynamics: Matching Individual and Organisational Needs* (Reading, MA: Addison-Wesley, 1978).
—— 'How "career anchors" hold executives to their career paths', in R. Katz (ed.), *Managing Professionals in Innovative Organizations* (Cambridge, MA: Ballinger Publishing Company, Harper & Row, 1988), pp. 487–97.
—— *Organizational Culture and Leadership*, 2nd edn (San Francisco: Jossey-Bass, 1992).
Schoenberger, R., *World Class Manufacturing* (New York: Free Press, 1986).
Schroder, H. M., *Managerial Competence: The Key to Excellence* (Iowa: Kendall Hunt, 1989).
Schuler, R. S., *Managing Human Resources*, 5th edn (Minneapolis, St Paul: West Publishing Company, 1995).
—— 'Human resource issues and activities in international joint ventures', *International Journal of Human Resource Management* (2001), 12, 1, February, pp. 1–52.
—— and Huselid, M., 'HR strategy in the United States', in S. Tyson (ed.), *The Practice of Human Resource Strategy* (London: Pitman, 1997).
—— and Jackson, S. E., *Human Resource Management: Positioning for the 21st Century*, 6th edn (Minneapolis, St Paul: West Publishing Company, 1996), pp. 137–41.
—— 'Linking Competitive Strategies with Human Resource Management Practices', *Academy of Management Executive* (1987), 1, 3, pp. 207–19.
Scullion, H., 'International HRM', in J. Storey (ed.), *Human Resource Management: A Critical Text* (London: Routledge, 1995), pp. 352–82.
Sempill, J., 'Under the lens: electronic workplace surveillance', *Australian Journal of Labour Law* (2001), 14, 1, pp. 111–44.
Senge, P., *The Fifth Discipline: The Art and Practice of the Learning Organization* (New York: Doubleday/Currency, 1990).
—— 'The Leader's New Work: Building Learning Organizations', in K. Starkey (ed.), *How Organizations Learn* (London: International Thomson Business Press, 1996), pp. 288–315.
Shackleton, V. and Newell, S., 'European management selection methods: A comparison of five countries', *International Journal of Selection and Assessment* (1994), 2, pp. 91–102.
Shapira, Z., 'Expectancy Determinants of Intrinsically Motivated Behavior', abridged from the *Journal of Personality and Social Psychology* (1976), vol. 34, pp. 235–44; also in V. H. Vroom and E. L. Deci (eds), *Management and Motivation*, 2nd edn (London: Penguin Books, 1992).

Sheehan, P., 'The changing nature of work: some implications', *Australian Bulletin of Labour* (1998), 24, 4, pp. 317-32.
Sheridan, S., 'The 1998 Australian waterfront dispute in its historical context', *International Employment Relations Review* (1999), 5, 2, pp. 1-16.
Sisson, K., *The Management of Collective Bargaining: An International Comparison* (Oxford: Blackwell, 1987).
—— 'In Search of HRM', *British Journal of Industrial Relations* (1993), 31, 2, pp. 201-10.
—— (ed.), *Personnel Management: A Comprehensive Guide to Theory and Practice in Britain*, 2nd edn (Oxford: Blackwell Business, 1994).
—— and Marginson, P., 'Management: Systems, Structures and Strategy', in P. Edwards (ed.), *Industrial Relations: Theory and Practice in Britain* (Oxford: Blackwell, 1995), pp. 89-122.
Sloan, J., 'An economic analysis of the 1928 Patrick dispute', *Economic and Labour Relations Review* (1998), 9, 2, pp. 236-45.
Snape, E., Thompson, D., Yan, F. K., and Redman, T., 'Performance appraisal and culture: practice and attitudes in Hong Kong and Great Britain', *International Journal of Human Resource Management* (1998), 9, 5, October, pp. 841-61.
Sparrow, P., 'New Organisational Forms, Processes, Jobs and Psychological Contracts: Resolving the HRM Issues', in P. Sparrow and M. Marchington (eds), *Human Resource Management: The New Agenda* (London: Financial Times, Pitman Publishing, 1998), pp. 117-41.
—— and Hiltrop, J.-M., *European Human Resource Management in Transition* (Hemel Hempstead: Prentice-Hall, 1994).
—— and Marchington, M., 'Re-engaging the HRM Function', in P. Sparrow and M. Marchington (eds), *Human Resource Management: The New Agenda* (London: Financial Times, Pitman Publishing, 1998), pp. 296-313.
—— (eds), *Human Resource Management: The New Agenda* (London: Financial Times, Pitman Publishing, 1998).
Starkey, K. (ed.), *How Organizations Learn* (London: International Thomson Business Press, 1996).
—— and McKinlay, A., *Strategy and the Human Resource: Ford and the Search for Competitive Advantage* (Oxford: Blackwell, 1993).
—— 'Product Development in Ford of Europe: Undoing the Past/Learning the Future', in K. Starkey (ed.), *How Organizations Learn* (London: International Thomson Business Press, 1996), pp. 214-29.
Spry, M., 'Workplace harassment: what it is, and what should the law do about it?', *Journal of Industrial Relations* (1998), 40, 2, pp. 232-46.
Steedman, H. and Wagner, K., 'Productivity, Machinery and Skills: Clothing Manufacture in Britain and Germany', *National Institute Economic Review* (1989), 128, May, pp. 40-57.
Stewart, A., 'The labour law implications of the 1998 waterfront dispute', *International Employment Relations Review* (1999), 5, 2, pp. 79-92.
—— 'Federal labour law and new uses for the corporations power', *Australian Journal of Labour Law* (2000), 13, 2, pp. 145-68.
Stiles, P., Gratton, L., Truss, C., Hope-Hailey, V., and McGovern, P., 'Performance Management and the Psychological Contract', *Human Resource Management Journal* (1997), 7, 1, pp. 57-66.
Still, L. V., 'Brave new world? Women and part-time employment: the impact on career prospects and employment relations', *International Journal of Employment Studies* (1997), 5, 1, pp. 45-66.
Storey, J., 'Developments in the management of human resources: an interim report', *Warwick Papers in International Relations* (University of Warwick, November, 1987).
—— *Developments in the Management of Human Resources* (Oxford: Blackwell, 1992).
—— *New Perspectives on Human Resource Management*, 2nd edn (London: Routledge, 1991).
—— (ed.), *Human Resource Management: A Critical Text* (London: Routledge, 1995).
—— and Bacon, N., with J. Edmonds and P. Wyatt, 'The "New Agenda" and Human Resources Management: A Roundtable Discussion with John Edmonds', *Human Resource Management Journal* (1993), 4, 1, pp. 63-70.
—— and Sisson, K., *Managing Human Resources and Industrial Relations* (Milton Keynes: Open University Press, 1993).
Strachan, G. and Burgess, J., 'The incompatibility of decentralised bargaining and equal employment opportunity in Australia', *British Journal of Industrial Relations* (2000), 38, 3, pp. 361-82.
Strauss, G., 'HRM in the USA: correcting some British impressions', *International Journal of Human Resource Management* (2001), 12, 6, September, pp. 873-97.

Streeck, W., 'Skills and the Limits of neo-Liberalism', *Work, Employment and Society* (1989), 3, 2, pp. 89–104.
Summerfield, J. and van Oudtshoorn, L., *Counselling in the Workplace* (London: IPD, 1995).
Swabe, A. I. R., 'Performance-related pay: a case study', *Employee Relations* (1989), 11, 2, pp. 17–23.
Tayeb, M., 'Transfer of HRM practices across cultures: An American company in Scotland', *International Journal of Human Resource Management* (1998), 9, 2, April, pp. 332–58.
Taylor, P. and Walker, A., 'Policies and Practices Towards Older Workers: A Framework For Comparative Research', *Human Resource Management Journal* (1998), 8, 3, pp. 61–76.
Terry, M., 'Trade Unions: Shop Stewards and the Workplace', in P. Edwards (ed.), *Industrial Relations: Theory and Practice in Britain* (Oxford: Blackwell, 1995).
Thorpe, M. and McDonald, J., 'Freedom of association and union membership', *Labour and Industry* (1998), 9, 2, pp. 43–60.
Tilton, T., *The Political Theory of Swedish Social Democracy: Through the Welfare State to Socialism* (Oxford and New York: Clarendon Press and Oxford University Press, 1990).
Timo, N., 'Precarious employment and individual contracts in an Australian mining company', *Labour and Industry* (1998), 9, 1, pp. 53–68.
Torrington, D. and Chee Huat, T., *Human Resource Management for South-east Asia* (London: Prentice-Hall International (UK) Ltd, 1994).
—— and Hall, L., *Personnel Management: HRM in Action*, 3rd edn (Hemel Hempstead: Prentice-Hall, 1995).
Tourish, D. and Pinnington, A., 'Transformational leadership, corporate cultism and the spirituality paradigm: An unholy trinity in the workplace?', *Human Relations* (2002), 55, 2, pp. 147–72.
Towers, B., *The Handbook of Human Resource Management*, 2nd edn (Oxford: Blackwell, 1992).
Townley, B., 'Selection and Appraisal: Reconstituting "Social Relations"?', in J. Storey (ed.), *New Perspectives on Human Resource Management* (London: Routledge, 1991), pp. 92–108.
—— *Reframing Resource Management: Power, Ethics, and the Subject at Work* (London: Sage, 1994).
Treuren, G., 'The government, the state and industrial relations: the case of the Australian waterfront dispute of 1997/8', *International Employment Relations Review* (1999), 5, 2, pp. 107–24.
Trist, E. L. and Bamforth, K. W., 'Some social and psychological consequences of the longwall method of coal-getting', *Human Relations* (1951), 4, pp. 3–38.
—— Higgin, C. W., Murray, H., and Pollock, A. M., *Organizational Choice* (London: Tavistock Institute, 1963).
Trompenaars, F., *Riding the Waves of Culture* (London: Economist Books, 1993).
Truss, C., Gratton, L., Hope-Hailey, V., McGovern, P., and Stiles, P., 'Soft and Hard Models of Human Resource Management: A Reappraisal', *Journal of Management Studies* (1997), 34, 1, January, pp. 53–73.
Tyson, S. (ed.), *The Practice of Human Resource Strategy* (London: Financial Times, Pitman Publishing, 1997).
—— and Fell, A., *Evaluating the Personnel Function* (London: Hutchinson, 1986).
—— 'Looking Ahead', in S. Tyson (ed.), *Strategic Prospects for HRM* (London, Institute of Personnel and Development, 1995), pp. 266–89.
United Nations, *World Investment Report 1998* (New York: United Nations, 1998).
—— *World Investment Report 2001* (New York and Geneva: United Nations, 2001), pp. 89–124.
van Barneveld, K. and Arsovska, B., 'AWAs: changing the structure of wages?', ACIRRT working paper no. 67 (Sydney: ACIRRT, 2001).
—— 'AWAs: changing the structure of wages?', *Labour and Industry* (2001), 12, 1, pp. 109–30.
van Gramberg, B., Teicher, J., and Griffin, G., 'Industrial relations in 1999: workplace relations, legalism and individualisation', *Asia Pacific Journal of Human Resources* (2000), 39, 2, pp. 4–22.
Vecchio, R. P., *Organisational Behavior*, 3rd edn (Orlando, FL: Dryden Press, 1995).
Vroom, V. H., *Work and Motivation* (New York: Wiley, 1964).
—— and Deci, E. L. (eds), *Management and Motivation*, 2nd edn (Harmondsworth: Penguin Books, 1992).
Waddington, J. and Whitston, C., 'Trade Unions: Growth, Structure and Policy', in P. Edwards (ed.), *Industrial Relations: Theory and Practice in Britain* (Oxford: Blackwell, 1995).
Walker, T., 'After a long wait, it's time for bright ideas', *Australian Financial Review*, 30th January 2001.
Walsh, J., 'Human resource management in foreign-owned workplaces: evidence from Australia', *International Journal of Human Resource Management* (2001), 12, 3, May, pp. 425–44.
Walton, R. E., 'Toward a Strategy of Eliciting Employee Commitment Based on Policies of Mutuality', in R. E. Walton and P. R. Lawrence (eds), *Human Resource Management—Trends and Challenges* (Boston: Harvard Business School Press, 1985), pp. 35–65.

—— 'From control to commitment in the workplace', *Harvard Business Review* (1985), 63, 2, pp. 77-84.
Warhurst, C. and Thompson, P., 'Hands, hearts and minds: changing work and workers at the end of the century', in P. Thompson and C. Warhurst (eds), *Workplaces of the Future* (London: Macmillan, 1998).
Waring, P. and Lewer, J., 'The no disadvantage test: failing workers', *Labour and Industry* (2001), 12, 1, pp. 65-86.
Watson, T. J., *The Personnel Managers: A Study in the Sociology of Work and Industry* (London: Routledge and Kegan Paul, 1977).
—— *Management, Organization and Employment Strategy: New Directions in Theory and Practice* (London: Routledge and Kegan Paul, 1986).
—— *In Search of Management—Culture, Chaos and Control in Managerial Work* (London: Routledge, 1994).
Watts, M. J. and Burgess, J., 'The polarisation of earnings and hours in Australia under a decentralised industrial relations system: the lessons for economic policy', *International Journal of Employment Studies* (2001), 9, 1, pp. 27-58.
—— and Mitchell, W. F., 'The costs of unemployment in Australia', *Economic and Labour Relations Review* (2000), 11, 2, pp. 180-97.
Watts, R., 'The ACTU's response to the growth in long-term casual employment in Australia', *Australian Bulletin of Labour* (2001), 27, 2, pp. 137-49.
Webb, J., 'The open door? Women and equal opportunity at ComCo (North)', in D. Gowler, K. Legge and C. Clegg (eds), *Case Studies in Organizational Behaviour and Human Resource Management*, 2nd edn (London: Paul Chapman Publishing, 1993), pp. 92-105.
—— and Palmer, G., 'Evading surveillance and making time: an ethnographic view of the factory floor in Britain', *British Journal of Industrial Relations* (1998), 36, 4, December, pp. 611-27.
Welch, J. F., 'A matter of exchange rates', *Wall Street Journal* (1994), 21 June, p. 23.
Wenger, E., McDermott, R., and Snyder, W. M., *Cultivating Communities of Practice* (Boston: Harvard Business School Press, 2002).
West, M. A., Borril, C. S., and Unsworth, K. L., 'Team effectiveness in organizations', in C. L. Cooper and I. T. Robertson (eds), *International Review of Industrial and Organizational Psychology*, vol. 13 (Chichester, John Wiley, 1998), pp. 1-48.
Westwood, R., Sparrow, P., and Leung, A., 'Challenges to the psychological contract in Hong Kong', *International Journal of Human Resource Management* (2001), 12, 4, June, pp. 621-51.
Wheelwright, K., *Labour Law* (Sydney: Butterworths, 1999).
Whitehouse, G., 'Recent trends in pay equity: beyond the aggregate statistics', *Journal of Industrial Relations* (2001), 43, 1, pp. 66-78.
—— and Earnshaw, J., 'Prosecuting pay equity: evolving strategies in Britain and Australia', *Gender, Work and Organisation* (2001), 8, 4, pp. 365-86.
—— Lafferty, G., and Boreham, P., 'From casual to permanent part-time? Non-standard employment in retail and hospitality', *Labour and Industry* (1997), 8, 2, pp. 33-48.
—— and Zetlin, D., '"Family Friendly" Policies: Distribution and Implementation in Australian Workplaces', *Economic and Labour Relations Review* (2000), 10, 2, pp. 221-39.
Whitley, R. (ed.), *European Business Systems: Firms and Markets in their National Contexts* (London: Sage, 1992).
Whittard, J. and Reeves, K., 'Training and flexible labour: nurses in a New South Wales public hospital', *International Journal of Employment Studies* (2001), 9, 1, pp. 163-84.
Whittington, R., *What is Strategy—and Does it Matter?* (London: Routledge, 1993).
—— McNulty, T., and Whipp, R., 'Market-driven change in professional services: problems and processes', *Journal of Management Studies* (1994), 31, 6, November, pp. 829-45.
Wickens, P. D., *The Road to Nissan* (London: Macmillan, 1987).
Wiesner, R., and McDonald, J., 'Bleak house or bright prospect? Human resource management in Australian SMEs', *Asia Pacific Journal of Human Resources* (2001), 39, 3, pp. 31-53.
Wilkinson, B., Morris, J., and Munday, M., 'Japan in Wales: a New IR', *Industrial Relations Journal* (1993), 24, 4, pp. 273-83.
Williams, G. and Simpson, A., 'The expanding frontiers of Commonwealth intervention in industrial relations', *Australian Journal of Labour Law* (1997), 10, 1, pp. 222-8.
Williams, S., 'Strategy and objectives', in F. Neale (ed.), *The Handbook of Performance Management* (London: Institute of Personnel Management, 1992), pp. 7-24.

Williamson, D. E., *Markets and Hierarchies: Analysis and Anti-trust Implications* (New York: Free Press, 1975).
Wilson, D. C., *A Strategy of Change: Concepts and Controversies in the Management of Change* (London: Routledge, 1992).
Wilson, F. M., *Organizational Behaviour and Gender* (Maidenhead: McGraw-Hill, 1995).
Wilson, S., 'On the waterfront', *Journal of Australian Political Economy* (1998), 41, pp. 23–37.
Wiseman, J., 'Here to stay? The 1997–1998 Australian waterfront dispute and its implications', *Labour and Industry* (1998), 9, 1, pp. 1–16.
Womack, J. P., Jones, D. T., and Roos, D., *The Machine that Changed the World: The Triumph of Lean Production* (New York: Rawson, Macmillan, 1990).
Wood, S. and Albanese, M., 'Can We Speak of a High Commitment Management on the Shop Floor?', *Journal of Management Studies* (1995), 32, 2, pp. 1–33.
Wooden, M., 'Individual agreement-making in Australian workplaces: incidence, trends and features', *Journal of Industrial Relations* (1999), 42, 3, pp. 417–45.
—— 'Outsourcing and the use of contractors: evidence from the AWIRS', *Economic and Labour Relations Review* (1999), 10, 1, pp. 22–35.
—— 'Union amalgamations and the decline in union density', *Journal of Industrial Relations* (1999), 41, 1, pp. 35–52.
—— *The Transformation of Australian Industrial Relations* (Sydney: Federation Press, 2000).
—— and Hawke, A., 'Factors associated with casual employment: evidence from the AWIRS', *Economic and Labour Relations Review* (1998), 9, 1, pp. 82–107.
Woodger, A. and Beaton, G., 'Effective Practices Guide', in Victoria Law Foundation, *Facing the Future: Gender, Employment and Best Practice Issues for Law Firms*, vol. 2 (Melbourne: Victoria Law Foundation, 1996).
Woodruffe, C., 'What is meant by a competency', in R. Boam, and P. Sparrow (eds), *Designing and Achieving Competency: A Competency-Based Approach to Developing People and Organizations* (Maidenhead: McGraw-Hill, 1992), pp. 16–30.
Wright, M., and Storey, J., 'Recruitment and Selection', in I. Beardwell and L. Holden (eds), *Human Resource Management: A Contemporary Perspective*, 2nd edn (London: Financial Times, Pitman Publishing, 1997), pp. 210–76.
Wright, S. J. and Sheridan, A., 'Making the rhetoric a reality: Sydney Water's experience with work and family policies', *Asia Pacific Journal of Human Resources* (1998), 36, 2, pp. 88–102.
Young, S., 'Outsourcing: lessons from the literature', *Labour and Industry* (2000), 10, 3, pp. 97–118.
—— and Macneil, J., 'When performance fails to meet expectations: managers' objectives for outsourcing', *Economic and Labour Relations Review* (2000), 11, 1, pp. 136–68.
Zappala, G., 'Outsourcing and Human Resource Management—a discussion starter', ACIRRT working paper no. 60 (Sydney: ACIRRT, 2000).

Index

Entries in **bold** refer to glossary.

Abbott, Tony 64
absenteeism 159, 160
Academy of Management (Nadler and Tushman) 220-1
Accord 24, 54-8, 64
accountabilities 160
achievement 122-3
action learning 178, 179, 180, 202
activist learners 184-5
Adams, J.S. 133
adaptation 220, 221
adaptive learning 180,
affiliation 122-3
affirmative action 85-6, **243**
Affirmative Action (Equal Opportunity for Women) Act 85
age based pay rates 149
agency **243**
agency theory 135, 136-7, 138, **243**
agency workers 45
Alderfer, C.P. 132
allowable matters 79-80, **243**
alternative working arrangements 35, 81-2, 237
Amalgamated Engineering and Electrical Union (AEEU) 223
ambit claims 76, **243**
annualised hours 22, 115
anti-discrimination 81, 83, **243**
arbitration **244**
appraisal 13
Argyris, C. 183
Armstrong, Michael 134, 142
Asia Pacific Economic Cooperation 30
Asian economic crisis 179
Asian economic growth 31
Aston school 209
Atari 211
attracting employees 14
Australia
    employee learning 172-3 *see also* training
    HRM and internationalisation 37-9, 235-6, 241
    Japanese management practices and 19

Australia Reconstructed 56, 201
Australian Chamber of Commerce and Industry (ACCI) 78, **244**
Australian Council of Trade Unions (ACTU) 55-9, 64, 77, 78, 201, **244**
Australian Customer Service Association 106
Australian Industrial Relations Commission (AIRC) 76, **244**
Australian Labor Party (ALP) 54-8, 73, **244**
Australian National Training Authority (ANTA) 40, 152
Australian Workplace Agreements (AWAs) 61, 63, 64, 74-5, 80-1, 156-7, 237, **244**
Australian Workplace Industrial Relations Survey (AWIRS) 38, 160, 188, 197, 216
autonomy 130
awards 51, 61, 74-5, 78, **257**
    simplication 79-80
balanced scorecard 163-4
Balazs, K. 113
Balkin, D.B. 135
Bandura, Albert 128-9
basic needs 122-3, 239
Becker, Brian 234
Beer, Michael 5-8, 95, 111-12
benchmarking 39
best practice models 233
BHP Coal Pty Ltd Enterprise Agreement 148
BHS Ltd 153
Bilby City Council case study 117-19
bodysnatching 77
Boral Window Systems' 154
Bournois, François 20-2, 23, 103
Boyatzis, Richard E. 238
Bramham, John 116
Brewster, Chris 20-2, 23, 103, 104
Brisbane City Council 106
British Aerospace 112
British Gas 99
British industry, Japanisation 19, 223
British models 8-10, 112, 223
    CEO pay 157-8
    competence, training and pay 152

broad banding   143, 145–6
Brown & Root   164
Brown, Cedric   99
Browne, John   196
Bundaberg Brewed Drinks Pty Ltd   156
Burger King   157
Burns, R.   218–19
business process re-engineering   106, 177, 233

Cable and Wireless   234
Cadbury Report   157
cafeteria benefit systems   153–4
capability   176
car industry   187, 223
case study   166–70
careers   96–101
casualisation   35, 36, 37, 81, 82, 176, 237, **244–5**
Caterpillar Tractor   209, 211
Cattell's 16PF   110
Central Provident Fund   135
centralisation   60, **245**
certified agreements   60, **245**
CEO rewards   157–8
Chandler, A.D.   209
change acceptance   217–18
change management   9, 208–29, 240
   creating major change   229
   frameworks   213–20, 225
   HR function and   222–4, 225
   implementing   220–2
   organisational culture and   210–13, 240
   organisational structure and culture   208–10
   processual approach   228
Chee Huat, T.   134–5
clever country   40
client focused learning   125
Cole, Gerald A.   111
collective bargaining   54–9, 73, 134, **244**
commitment   5, 6, 8, 98, 158, 159, 165, 176, 214
Commonwealth Employment Service   41
Community and Public Sector Union (CPSU)   88–9
company values   193
comparative wage justice   52, 61, 242, **246**
competence   6, 97, 117, 197, 199, 203, 238
   development   143
   based pay   152–3
   recruitment and   106
competition   30–3, 53, 56
competitive advantage   173, 241
Compulsory Competitive Tendering (CCT)   225–7
conciliation and arbitration system   51–2, 53, 74–6, **246**

Confederation of British Industry (CBI)   152, 216
congruence   6
Connock, S.   160
Constitution and industrial relations powers   74–6
consultation   159
content theories   121–5, 132–3, 137–8, **246**
   limitations of   132–3
contract work   82
contracting out   42–3, 44–5
control   113
coping behaviours   128–9, 216, 218
core competences   102–3, 197, 203, 238
core processes   177
corporations, multidivisional structures   12
corporations power   75, **247**
corporatisation   43
cost-effectiveness   6
CRA   60
crony effect   162
cultural leave   80

Daimaru   179
Davis, J.H.   135
Dawson, Patrick   228
Deal, Terence A.   209, 210, 212–13
decentralisation   41, 242, **247**
Deery, Stephen   172
delayering   112
Demarie, S.M.   217
demergers   160
Deming, W. Edwards   209
deregulation   41–2, 58–64, 236, **247**
Devanna, M.A.   10
development strategies   115, 238
Digby's case study   65–9
discrimination   111
dismissal   111–12
Disneyland Paris   176
dispute resolution   81
distributive justice   134, **247**
diversity   241
Dixon, N.M.   183, 184, 185
Donaldson, L.   135
downsizing   97, 113, 153, 198
DuPont   209

early retirement   111, 112–13
economic restructuring   32, 55–8, 191, 208, 235–6, 241–2
education   175
effort-to-performance expectancy   126, 127
Eiffel Tower culture   101
employees   **248**
   attracting, retaining and motivating   14

change management and   214-22, 240
development   13, 174-7, 188-206
HR and change management   222-4
influence of   5-6
involvement   235
learning   172-3
resources   94, 102
share options   155
empowerment   38, 179
Enron   223
enterprise bargaining   60, 62, 73, **248**
enterprise culture   24
enterprise flexibility agreements   60
entitlements   79-80, 88-9
equal opportunity   22, 84-6, **248**
Equal Opportunity for Women in the Workplace Act   85
Equal Opportunity for Women in the Workplace Agency (EOWWA)   86
equal pay   83-5
equity theory   133-7
ethical responsibility   136, 233
European environment of HRM   20-3, 237
European Union   30
excellence cultures   210-13
expatriate managers   116
expectancy motivation theory   126-8, 130, 132, 136, 216
extrinsic rewards   6, 126, **249**

family culture   101
felt fair principle   134
financial rewards   142-58
Fletcher, C.   163
flexibility strategies   115, 236
flexibility   8, 22, 32-3, 63-4, 81, 100, 165, 235, **249**
flexible benefit systems   153-4
Fombrun, C.J.   10
force field analysis   213-17, 215
Ford Motor Company   106, 112, 187-8
foreign direct investment   31
France   63-4
freedom of association   63, 73, **249**
fringe benefits   123
Fujitsu   193

gainsharing   154
Galbraith, J.R.   189
General Electric   209
General Motors Holden Enterprise Agreement   175
generative learning   180, 182
Gerhart, Barry   234
Germany, learning in   198
goal directed motivation theory   125-6

Gold Coast Skill Centre Enterprise Agreement   153, 203
Gomez-Mejia, L.R.   135
Greenbury Report   157
greenfield sites   20
Grint, K.   162
group bonuses and incentives   151
group motivation theories   133-40
GTE   103
Guest, David   8-10, 23, 104, 158, 159, 165, 242
guided missile culture   101
Gustafson, L.T.   217

Hackman, J.R.   130-2, 133, 138
Halliburton   164
halo effect   162
Hamel, G.   102-3, 117
Handy, Charles   97
hard human resources management   4, 10-13, 23, **250**
change management and   222-4
mixed with soft   13-15
motivation theories and 137-8
Harrison, R.   161, 175
Harvard Business Review   102
Harvard Business School   210
Harvard model   5-8
Harvester Judgment   51, 52, 84
Harvey-Jones, John   210
Hawke, Bob   39, 241
hazards   190
Hegewisch, A.   21
Herriot, Peter   98, 99, 100, 113
Herzberg, Frederick   123-5, 132
Hewlett Packard   112, 210
Hewson, John   60
hierarchy of needs   121-2, 132
Higgins, Justice   51, 52, 84
Hofstede, Geert   104, 105
home based learning   195
home-based work   82
Honey, Peter   184-5
Hong Kong managers   163
horn effect   162
Hughes, Everett   96
human resource cycle   12, 13
human resource flow policies   6, 94-105, **95**
careers and   100
managing   105-14
national culture and   104
human resource management   7
Australia   37-9
best practice models   233
credibility   224, 234
European   20-2, 23
industrial relations and   15-18, 236

INDEX | 315

internal fit   234
internationalisation and   30-3, 45-6, 241
Japanese management and   18-20, 23
learning and   176-7
legitimacy of   233-5
outsourcing of   223-4, 234
personnel management and   16-18, 24-5, 224
practices and outcomes   165-6
radical   24
territory of   8
human resource planning   114-16
human resource system diagram   7
Huselid, Mark   158, 234
hygiene factors   123-5, 239, **250**

IBM   112, 153, 209
ICI   160, 178, 210
identity   96, 217
immigration and skills   172
In Search of Excellence (Peters & Waterman)   211-12
incentives   125
incubator   101, 102
individual bonuses   151
individual contracts   60, 73
individual grievances   176
individual learning styles   184-5
individualism-collectivism   104
individuals   **250-1**
   motivating   121-33
   needs   95, 96-101, 113-14, 116, 137-8
industrial disputes   53, 73, 77
industrial relations
   decentralisation   41, 85, 236, 242
   HRM and   15-18
   labour law and   72-91
   pressure and change in the Australian system   32-3, 50-69, 236
   USA   15-16, 23
Industrial Relations Reform Act   60, 75, 79
Industry Lead Bodies   152
Industry Training Assistance Boards   152
Industry Training Boards   177
inflation   58
inflow management   105-11, 237
informal agreements   78
informal learning   199
information flows   9, 185, 239-40
innovation   179-80, 189, 202, 233, 239
   occupational health and safety and   190-3
integration, of development programs   194
internal fit of HRM   234
International Labour Organisation (ILO)   81
internationalisation   30-3, 45, 56, 241
   labour standards and   81-2

interviews   108-11
intrinsic rewards   6, 126, **251**
irregular employment   35, 81, 104, 236, 237, **251**
Iwinski, T.   196

Jacques, E.   134
Japan, economic growth in   31, 209
Japanese management practices   18-20, 108, 209, 223
   selection procedures   108
   training and learning   179, 180, 182, 187-8, 198
Jick, Todd   221-2, 240
job design   9, 107, 123-5, 130-2
job families   146
job feedback   131
job insecurity   37, 46, 81, 83, 237
Job Network   41
job satisfaction   155
job security   112
job-sharing   35, 36
Johnson & Johnson   210
Jones, P.J.   194
Jones, Stephen   89
Juran, Joseph M.   209
just-in-time (JIT) production processes   19, 106, **252**

Kaplan, R.S.   163-4
Karmel Report   201
Katz, H.C.   15
Keating government   202
Keating, Paul   60, 241
Kelty, Bill   56
Kennedy, Allan A.   209, 210, 212-13
Kennett, Jeff   74
Kernot, Cheryl   60
Kets de Vries, M.F.   113
key performance indicators   118
Kirby Report   201
Knox, A.   172
Kochan, Thomas   15-16, 20, 23, 25, 173-4
Kolb, D.A.   183, 184, 203
Kotter, John   96, 229
Kraft Jacob Suchard   234
Kramar, R.   14

labour force   **252**
   participation rate   36-7
labour law   72-**91**, 236
   increasing complexities of   81-3
   trade unions and   72-4, 79-81, 236
labour markets **248, 251, 252**
   internationalisation and flexibility   32, 241

restructuring and union decline   55–64, 79
  segmentation   83–5
Latham, G.P   125–6
Lawler, E.E.   126–8
leadership   208, 209, 240
learning   175
  companies   180–3
  cycle   183–4
  styles   184–5
learning organisations   172, 174, 202, 240
  creating   177–88
leave entitlements   79–80
Legge, Karen   18, 24, 233
Lewin, Kurt   213–17
Liberal-National Party Coalition   59–63
lifelong employment   112
living wage   52, 64, 84, 242, **252**
Locke, E.A.   125–6
London School of Economics   152
loyalty   98, 101
Lucas Industries   106
Luxor Grand Hotel case study   46–7

McBer Consultancy   238
McClelland, David   122–3, 136
McDonalds   157, 211
McGraw, P.   14
McGregor, D.   163, 242
McKersie, R.B.   15
McKinlay, A.   187
McKinsey   210
major change   229
Management Charter Initiative   197, 199–201
management
  development   197–202
  hierarchy   148, 198
  motivation theories   135–7
  pay   157–8
  strategy and performance measurement   163–4
managerial competence   97, 117
managerialism   43, **253**
Managing Human Assets (Beer et al)   5–8
manpower flow   9
manpower planning   115
Marchington, M.   159, 194, 216, 223, 233
Marconi Instruments   112
Maritime Union of Australia (MUA)   62–3, 64
masculinity   104
Maslow, Abraham   121–2, 132, 136
Massachusetts Institute of Technology   209
matrix management   **253**
Mazda   187–8
MBA degrees   198, 239
measured day work   150
mentoring   179

Michigan model   10, 25
Mincom   196
minority groups   83
Modern Apprenticeship and Traineeship
   System (MAATS)   41
Morgan, Gareth   197
motivation   14, 121–40, 238–9, **253**
  content theories   121–5, 132–3
  groups   133–40
  individuals   121–33
  process theories   125–33
Mullane, J.V.   217
multi-appraisal methods   162
Mumford, A.   184–5
Murrays case study   138–40
mutual obligation   **253**
Myers-Briggs Type Indicators   110

Nadler, D.A.   220–1
National Competency Training Schedules   152
National Council for Vocational Qualifications   152
national culture   22, 103–5, 209, 223, **245**, **251**
National Institute for Economic and Social
   Research   157
National Training Reform Agenda   40, 143, 201
national wage cases   78
needs   96–101, 121–3, 239, **253–4**
NEC   103
negotiations, unions and   66–9, 76–7
new deal   99
New Right   32, 55, 64
Nissan   108
no disadvantage test   62, **254**
non-financial rewards   142
non-standard employment   35, 81, 104, 236, **252**
North American Free Trade Agreement
   (NAFTA)   30
Norton, D.P.   163–4

O'Keefe Centre case study   225–7
occupational health and safety   190–3
Office of the Employment Advocate (OEA)
   61–2, 80–1, **254**
old deal   98
Oldham, G.R.   130–2, 133, 138
Oliver, N.   19–20, 23
One Nation Statement   202
One.Tel   88–9
open learning   194–6, 203
Open University   196
Optical Fibres   148
Organisation for Economic Cooperation and
   Development (OECD)   35, 39
organisational behaviour   **255**

organisational cultures   45, 101–3, 116, 179, 208–10, 238, **254**
  change management and   208–13, 224–5, 240
  learning and   187
  strong and excellent   210–13
organisational design   9
organisational development   178, 202, **255**
organisational effectiveness   7
organisational learning   186–8
organisational memory   45, 113
organisational performance
  HRM and   165–6
  rewards and   154–8
organisational requirements   95
  careers and   100
organisational restructuring   45, 99, 107, 112–14, 147, 208–29, 235, 241–2
organisational transformation   180
Orica   178
Osterman, P.   173–4
outdoor development   193–4
outflow management   111–14, 237
outsourcing   42–3, 44–5, 177, 223, **255**
outworkers   82

Parker, S.K.   107
part-time work   35, 36, 81, 100, 114, **255**
Patrick Stevedores   62–3, 64, 77
pay curves   146–7
pay gap   157–8, 236
pay spines   147, 148
pay structures   144–9, 165, 239
pay systems   22, 52, 143, 149–58, 165, 236, 239
Pedler, M.   177, 178, 179, 180, 203
peer appraisal   161–2
Pemberton, C.   98, 99, 100
performance
  accomplishments   129
  appraisal   160–70
  management   38, 142, 158–66
performance-related pay   151–2, 156–7
performance-to-reward expectancy   126, 127
personal change   218–19
personnel management   16–18, 24–5, 224
  learning and   176–7
Peters, Tom J.   210–12
Pettigrew, A.   178, 210
Pfeffer, J.   132, 158
Philip Morris Corporation   234
physiological states   129
piecework   149
policy formulation   9
political unionism   56–7, 58
Porter, L.W.   126–8
power   122–3

power distance   104, **255–6**
pragmatists   184–5
Prahalad, C.   102–3, 117
preference clauses   73
Price Waterhouse   195, 209
prices and incomes policy   58
privatisation   43–4, 97
process theories   125–32, 138, **256**
  limitations of   132–3
processual approach to change   229
Procter & Gamble   210
product focused learning   125
productivity   10, 53, 173–4
profit sharing   154–5
Prudential Financial   234
psychological contract   112, **249**
psychological well-being   218
psychometric testing   108, 110–11
public sector employment   43, 113
public sector, cutbacks in   43–4, 46, 113
Purcell, J.   156

Qantas   194, 195
quality management   179, 180
quality of work life movement   125
quality   165

rational planning   115
re-creation   220, 221
reactive change   220–1
recruitment   105–11
redundancy   79–80, 101, 113
reflector learners   184–5
reframing organisations   217
Reger, R.K.   217–18
rehabilitation   192–3
Reith, Peter   60, 63, 75
reorientation   220, 221
research and development   39–42
resistance and change   214–17
retail industry
  industrial relations in   65
  motivation case study   138–40
retention strategies   14, 115, 238
return on investment   163
Revans, Reg   179
reward systems   6, 13, 126–7, 142–4, 143
Reynolds, A.   196
Riding the Waves of Change (Morgan)   197
Robbins, Stephen   **255**
Robens Model   192
Rockwater   164
Rowntree, Derek   195

safety net   61, **257**
Sainsbury's   131

Salancik, G.R.   132
salary packaging   115
satisficing behaviour   197
save-as-you-earn   155–6
Saville & Holdsworth's OPQ   110
Schein, Ed   97, 98, 99, 209
Schon, D.A   183
Schoorman, F.D.   135
Schroder, Harry   238
Schuler, R.S.   13–15, 239–40
selection   9, 105-11, 238
self-development   178, 179, 180
self-efficacy theory   128–9
self-employment   82
self-management   219
Senge, Peter   180, 182, 183, 203
Shell Canada   197
short termism   223
sick leave   80
Singapore   135
Single European Market   30
Sisson, K.   115, 176
skills   130
    development   40, 176, 236
    immigration   172
    reward systems   143, 152–3
small and medium sized enterprises (SMEs)   173
Smarna Gora Holdings case study   203–6
SMART objectives   160
social learning   129, **257**
social partnerships   242
social wage   55, 57
socialisation   9
socio-economic development and HRM systems   21
soft human resources management   4, 23, **257**
    change management and   222–4
    motivation theories and   121–6, 132–3, 137–8
    Guest (UK) model   8–10
    Harvard model   5–8
    human resource flow   94, 96
    mixed with hard   13–15
South Korea   114, 242
Sparrow, Paul   106
spot rate   147
stability index   115–16
stakeholders   6
Standard Chartered Bank   223
Starkey, Ken   187
state, role of   43, 46
stewardship theory   135–7, 138
Storey, John   16–18, 24, 115, 156, 176, 197, 208, 224
    twenty-five-item checklist   17
strategic change   220

strategic management and environmental pressures   11, 38–9, 235
strategic unionism   56–7, 58, 236
Strauss, George   235
stress   190-2, 216, 218–19
strong culture companies   209–13
structural efficiency principle   60
superannuation   80
survival rate   116
Swedish model   56
systematic training   202

task identity   130
task significance   130
taxation and profit sharing   155
team building   137, 193
team incentives   150–1
team selection   108
team working   38, 108, 176, 184, 198
technological change   235
    and training   189, 203
technology-based learning   194–6, 203
ten commandments of change implementation   221–2
termination of employment   79
theorist learners   184–5
third way   57
3M   189, 209, 211
Three Steps framework   214
Tichy, N.M.   10
time rates   149
Torrington, D.   134–5
total quality control and management   **257–8**
Toyota   108
Toys 'R' Us   20
trade unions
    Australia   24, 50, 53–64, 236
    avoidance   20, 23
    employer attitudes to in Australia   50
    Great Britain   9, 223
    labour law and   72–89
    political role   53–8
    soft and hard HRM and   13
Training Guarantee Levy   40
training   40, 46, 80, 105, 143, 172–4, 175, 236, 237
    HRM and   189
    innovations in   177–80, 239
    SMEs and   173
Transformation of American Industrial Relations (Kochan et al)   15
transition curve   219
transnational companies   30–3, 116, **258**
    outsourcing   223
    training and   178, 197, 239–40
transparency   157–8
Triple A project   160

Trompenaars, Fons   101, 102, 117
trust   98, 176
tuning   220, 221
turnover index   115
Tushman, M.L.   220-1

UK Institute of Personnel and Development   114-15
uncertainty avoidance   104
unemployment and underemployment   3-6, 46
Unisys   153
unitarist approaches   15, 23, 37, 60, 72, 137, 237, 242, **258**
upward appraisal   161
US management, union avoidance by   20
US models   111, 112, 173, 223, 235

Veblen effect   162
verbal persuasion   129
vicarious experience   129
Victorian government   59, 74
vocational education and training   201, 202
Vroom, Victor   126, 127

wages   52, 53, 61, 78, 242
Wall, T.D.   107

Walsh, J.   172
Walt Disney   211
Walton, Richard   5, 18
Water Wheel Flour Mills   154
waterfront dispute   62-3, 64
Waterman, R.H.   210-12
West, M.A.   107
Wilkinson, A   216, 223, 233
Wilkinson, B.   19-20, 23
William Mercer   152
Williams, R.   163
women, work and wages   83-5, 235
Wood, Stephen   158
Work for the Dole   41
work intensification   191
work practices   6, 32, 191
worker participation   159, 235, 238
workers' compensation   192-3
working hours   22, 63-4, 115, 191
work-measured schemes   150
Workplace Employee Relations Survey   160, 224
Workplace Relations Act 1996   59-64, 73, 74, 75, 77, 78-81, 236, 237

Zeneca   160, 178
zero-based budgeting   177